W9-CUJ-713

CHILTON'S REPAIR & TUNE-UP GUIDE
VOLKSWAGEN 1970 to 1981

**Beetle, Super Beetle 1970-80 • Karmann Ghia 1970-74
Transporter 1970-79 • Vanagon 1980-81 • Fastback, Squareback
1970-74 • 411 1971-72 • 412 1973-74**

Vice President and General Manager JOHN P. KUSHNERICK
Managing Editor KERRY A. FREEMAN, S.A.E.
Senior Editor RICHARD J. RIVELE, S.A.E.
Editor LANCE EALEY

CHILTON BOOK COMPANY
Radnor, Pennsylvania
19089

TL
215
V6
C53
1981

SAFETY NOTICE

Proper service and repair procedures are vital to the safe, reliable operation of all motor vehicles, as well as the personal safety of those performing repairs. This book outlines procedures for servicing and repairing vehicles using safe, effective methods. The procedures contain many NOTES, CAUTIONS and WARNINGS which should be followed along with standard safety procedures to eliminate the possibility of personal injury or improper service which could damage the vehicle or compromise its safety.

It is important to note that repair procedures and techniques, tools and parts for servicing motor vehicles, as well as the skill and experience of the individual performing the work vary widely. It is not possible to anticipate all of the conceivable ways or conditions under which vehicles may be serviced, or to provide cautions as to all of the possible hazards that may result. Standard and accepted safety precautions and equipment should be used when handling toxic or flammable fluids, and safety goggles or other protection should be used during cutting, grinding, chiseling, prying, or any other process that can cause material removal or projectiles.

Some procedures require the use of tools specially designed for a specific purpose. Before substituting another tool or procedure, you must be completely satisfied that neither your personal safety, nor the performance of the vehicle will be endangered.

Although information in this guide is based on industry sources and is as complete as possible at the time of publication, the possibility exists that the manufacturer made later changes which could not be included here. While striving for total accuracy, Chilton Book Company cannot assume responsibility for any errors, changes, or omissions that may occur in the compilation of this data.

PART NUMBERS

Part numbers listed in this reference are not recommendations by Chilton for any product by brand name. They are references that can be used with interchange manuals and aftermarket supplier catalogs to locate each brand supplier's discrete part number.

ACKNOWLEDGMENTS

Chilton Book Company expresses appreciation to Volkswagenwerk AG Wolfsburg, the Arnolt Corporation, and the Ford Motor Company for technical information and illustrations.

The editor wishes to give special thanks to CVW Enterprises, Exton, Pa., Devon Motors, Inc., Devon, Pa., Group Seven Imports, Phoenixville, Pa., Arrington and Ritter VW Service, Avondale, Pa., Foreign Car Service of Willow Grove, Willow Grove, Pa., and Volks Tool Supply, Houston, Texas, for their contributions to the technical accuracy and clarity of the information herein.

Manufactured in the United States of America
7890   0987654

Chilton's Repair & Tune-Up Guide: Volkswagen 1970–81
ISBN 0-8019-6837-2 pbk.
Library of Congress Catalog Card No. 80-70339

CONTENTS

Quick Reference Specifications For Your Vehicle

Fill in this chart with the most commonly used specifications for your vehicle. Specifications can be found in Chapters 1 through 3 or on the tune-up decal under the hood of the vehicle.

 Tune-Up

Firing Order_____

Spark Plugs:

   Type_____

   Gap (in.)_____

Point Gap (in.)_____

Dwell Angle (°)_____

Ignition Timing (°)_____

   Vacuum (Connected/Disconnected)_____

Valve Clearance (in.)

   Intake_____   Exhaust_____

Capacities

Engine Oil (qts)

   With Filter Change_____

   Without Filter Change_____

Cooling System (qts)_____

Manual Transmission (pts)_____

   Type_____

Automatic Transmission (pts)_____

   Type_____

Front Differential (pts)_____

   Type_____

Rear Differential (pts)_____

   Type_____

Transfer Case (pts)_____

   Type_____

FREQUENTLY REPLACED PARTS

Use these spaces to record the part numbers of frequently replaced parts.

PCV VALVE	OIL FILTER	AIR FILTER
Manufacturer_____	Manufacturer_____	Manufacturer_____
Part No._____	Part No._____	Part No._____

General Information and Maintenance

HOW TO USE THIS BOOK

This book will aid you in performing basic maintenance, tune-ups and repairs on your Volkswagen. The depth to which you proceed in your mechanical endeavors depends upon the levels of confidence and ambition you have concerning the upkeep of your car. If you don't know a micrometer from a thermostat, the best place to start off is with chapters one and two, as they cover basic maintenance and tune-up procedures. If you're having a specific problem with your VW, turn to Chapter 10, Troubleshooting, for step by step diagnosis. There is also a handy full-color section of tune-up tips which includes spark plug troubleshooting illustrations and many other tricks of the automotive trade.

As your knowledge of your VW broadens, you can proceed to larger, more complex operations such as replacing brake shoes or overhauling your engine.

For the experienced back yard mechanic, this manual makes plain the mechanical aspects of the Volkswagen with step by step procedures and illustrations.

Two basic rules of automobile mechanics deserve mentioning here. Whenever the left-side of the car is referred to, it is meant to specify the driver's side. Likewise, the right-side of the car means the passenger's side. Also, most screws, nuts, and bolts are removed by turning counterclockwise and tightened by turning clockwise.

Before performing any repairs, read the entire section of the book that deals with that job. In many places a description of the system is provided. By reading this first, and then reading the entire repair procedure, you will understand the function of the system you will be working on and what will be involved in the repair operation, prior to starting the job. This will enable you to avoid problems and also to help you learn about your car while you are working on it.

While every effort was made to make the book as simple, yet as detailed as possible, there is no substitute for personal experience. You can gain the confidence and feel for mechanical things needed to make auto repairs only by doing them yourself. If you take your time and concentrate on what you are doing, you will be amazed at how fast you can learn.

TOOLS AND EQUIPMENT

Now that you have purchased this book and commited yourself to maintaining your car, a small set of basic tools and equipment will

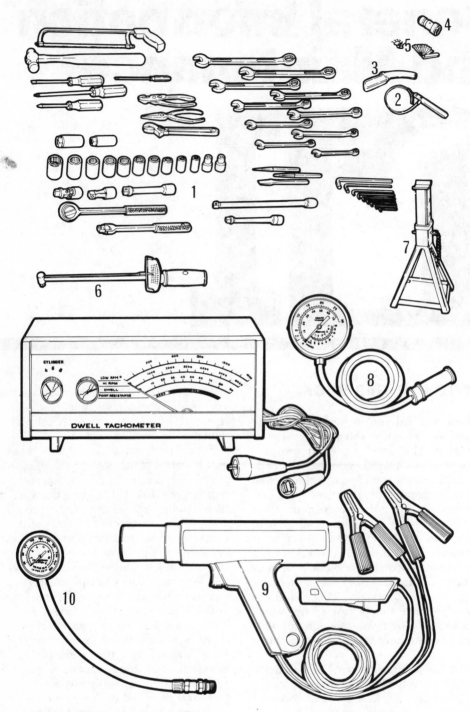

1. Basic assortment of tools
2. Oil filter strap
3. Oil filler spout
4. Battery terminal cleaner
5. Feeler gauge and spark plug wire gauge
6. Torque wrench
7. Jack stand
8. Vacuum gauge
9. DC timing light
10. Compression gauge

Typical tool assortment

prove handy. The first group of items should be adequate for most maintenance and light repair procedures:
* Sliding T-bar handle or ratchet wrench
* ⅜ in. drive socket wrench set (with breaker bar) (metric) (including a 36 mm socket)
  * Universal adapter for socket wrench set
  * Flat blade and phillips head screwdrivers
  * Pliers
  * Adjustable wrench
  * Locking pliers
  * Open-end wrench set (metric)
  * Feeler gauge set
  * Oil filter strap wrench
  * Brake adjusting spoon
  * Drift pin
  * Torque wrench (0–150 ft. lb. type with half-length adaptor)
  * Hammer

Along with the above mentioned tools, the following equipment should be on hand:
* Scissors jack or hydraulic jack of sufficient capacity
  * Jackstands of sufficient capacity
  * Wheel blocks
  * Grease gun (hand-operated type)
  * Drip pan (low and wide)
  * Drop light
  * Tire pressure gauge
  * Penetrating oil (spray lubricant)
  * Waterless hand cleaner

Special Tools

The following special tools are not absolutely necessary to perform basic maintenance or tune-up and repair operations, but they can take a lot of the guess work out of maintaining your car:
* 12 volt test light
* Compression gauge—the screw-in type is slower to use but eliminates the possibility of a faulty reading due to escaping air pressure
  * Manifold vacuum gauge
* Induction meter for determining whether or not there is current in a wire (these are handy for use if a wire is broken somewhere in a wiring harness)
* Timing light, preferably a DC battery hook-up type
* A dwell-tachometer which can be set for four cylinder engines
* A Uni-syn® gauge for balancing twin carburetor Type 2 models

Throughout this book references are made

to special VW tools. These tools can be purchased from Zelenda Tool and Machine Co., 66–12 Austin Street, Forest Hills, NY 11374.

SERVICING YOUR CAR SAFELY

It is virtually impossible to anticipate all of the hazards involved with automotive maintenance and service, but care and common sense will prevent most accidents.

The rules of safety for mechanics range from "don't smoke around gasoline," to "use the proper tool for the job." The trick to avoiding injuries is to develop safe work habits and take every possible precaution.

Dos

* Do keep a fire extinguisher and first aid kit within easy reach.
* Do wear safety glasses or goggles when cutting, drilling, grinding or prying, even if you have 20-20 vision. If you wear glasses for the sake of vision, they should be made of hardened glass that can serve also as safety glasses, or wear safety goggles over your regular glasses.
* Do shield your eyes whenever you work around the battery. Batteries contain sulphuric acid. In case of contact with the eyes or skin, flush the area with water or a mixture of water and baking soda and get medical attention immediately.
* Do use safety stands for any undercar service. Jacks are for raising vehicles; safety stands are for making sure the vehicle stays raised until you want it to come down. Whenever the car is raised, block the wheels remaining on the ground and set the parking brake.
* Do use adequate ventilation when working with any chemicals or hazardous materials. Like carbon monoxide, the asbestos dust resulting from brake lining wear can be poisonous in sufficient quantities.
* Do disconnect the negative battery cable when working on the electrical system. The secondary ignition system can contain up to 40,000 volts.
* Do follow manufacturer's directions whenever working with potentially hazardous materials. Both brake fluid and antifreeze are poisonous if taken internally.
* Do properly maintain your tools. Loose hammerheads, mushroomed punches and chisels, frayed or poorly grounded electrical

cords, excessively worn screwdrivers, spread wrenches (open end), cracked sockets, slipping ratchets, or faulty droplight sockets can cause accidents.

• Do use the proper size and type of tool for the job being done.

• Do when possible, pull on a wrench handle rather than push on it, and adjust your stance to prevent a fall.

• Do be sure that adjustable wrenches are tightly closed on the nut or bolt and pulled so that the face is on the side of the fixed jaw.

• Do select a wrench or socket that fits the nut or bolt. The wrench or socket should sit straight, not cocked.

• Do strike squarely with a hammer; avoid glancing blows.

• Do set the parking brake and block the drive wheels if the work requires the engine running.

Don'ts

• Don't run the engine in a garage or anywhere else without proper ventilation— EVER! Carbon monoxide is poisonous; it takes a long time to leave the human body and you can build up a deadly supply of it in your system by simply breathing in a little every day. You may not realize you are slowly poisoning yourself. Always use power vents, windows, fans or open the garage doors.

• Don't work around moving parts while wearing a necktie or other loose clothing. Short sleeves are much safer than long, loose sleeves; hard-toed shoes with neoprene soles protect your toes and give a better grip on slippery surfaces. Jewelry such as watches, fancy belt buckles, beads or body adornment of any kind is not safe working around a car. Long hair should be hidden under a hat or cap.

• Don't use pockets for toolboxes. A fall or bump can drive a screwdriver deep into your body. Even a wiping cloth hanging from the back pocket can wrap around a spinning shaft or fan.

• Don't smoke when working around gasoline, cleaning solvent or other flammable material.

• Don't smoke when working around the battery. When the battery is being charged, it gives off explosive hydrogen gas.

• Don't use gasoline to wash your hands; there are excellent soaps available. Gasoline may contain lead, and lead can enter the body through a cut, accumulating in the body until you are very ill. Gasoline also removes all the natural oils from the skin so that bone dry hands will suck up oil and grease.

• Don't service the air conditioning system unless you are equipped with the necessary tools and training. The refrigerant, R-12, is extremely cold when compressed, and when released into the air will instantly freeze any surface it contacts, including your eyes. Although the refrigerant is normally non-toxic, R-12 becomes a deadly poisonous gas in the presence of an open flame. One good whiff of the vapors from burning refrigerant can be fatal.

HISTORY

In 1932, Ferdinand Porsche produced prototypes for the NSU company of Germany which eventually led to the design of the Volkswagen. The prototypes had a rear mounted, air-cooled engine, torsion bar suspension, and the spare tire mounted at an angle in the front luggage compartment. In 1936, Porsche produced three Volkswagen prototypes, one of which was a 995 cc, horizontally opposed, four cylinder automobile. Passenger car development was sidetracked during World War II, when all attention was on military vehicles. In 1945, Volkswagen production began and 1,785 Beetles were built. The Volkswagen convertible was introduced in 1949, the same year that only two Volkswagens were sold in the United States. 1950 marked the beginning of the sunroof models and the transporter series. The Karmann Ghia was introduced in 1956, and remained in the same basic styling format until its demise in 1974. The 1500 Squareback was introduced in the United States in 1966 to start the Type 3 series. The Type 4 was imported into the U.S.A. beginning with the 1971 model. 1977 marked the last year for the Beetle. The Beetle convertible was available through 1980 and the new VW bus, the Vanagon, was introduced in 1980.

Type numbers are the way Volkswagen designates its various groups of models. The type 1 group contains the Beetle, Super Beetle, and the Karmann Ghia. Type 2 vehicles are the Delivery Van, the Micro Bus, The Vanagon, the Kombi and the Campmobile. The Type 3 designation is for the Fastback and Squareback sedans. The Type 4 is for the 411 and 412 sedans and wagon. These type

Type 2 Van (Model 21)

Type 2 Bus (Model 22)

Type 2 (1980–81 Vanagon)

Type 3 Fastback (Model 31)

Type 3 Squareback (Model 36)

Type 4 411 Station Wagon (1971–72 Model 46)

Type 4 411 4-door Sedan (1971–72 Model 41)

Type 4 412 4-door Sedan (1973–74 Model 41)

Type 4 412 Station Wagon (1973–74 Model 46)

numbers will be used throughout the book when it is necessary to refer to models.

An explanation of the terms suitcase engine and upright fan engine is, perhaps, necessary. The upright fan engine refers to the engine used in the Type 1 and 2 (1970–71) vehicles. This engine has the engine cooling fan mounted on the top of the engine and is driven by the generator. The fan is mounted vertically in contrast to a horizontally mounted fan as found on the Chevrolet Corvair engine. The suitcase engine is a comparatively compact unit to fit in the Type 3, 4 and 1972 and later Type 2 engine compartments. On this engine, the cooling fan is mounted on the crankshaft giving the engine a rectangular shape similar to that of a suitcase.

SERIAL NUMBER IDENTIFICATION

Vehicle (Chassis) Number

The chassis number consists of ten digits. The first two numbers indicate the model type, and the third number gives the model year. For example, a 2 as the third digit means that the car was produced during the 1972 model year run.

The chassis number is stamped on a metal plate. On Type 1, 3, and 4 models, the plate is located in the luggage compartment, on the frame tunnel under the back seat, and on the driver's side of the instrument panel (visible through the windshield). On Type 2 models, the plate is located behind the front passenger's seat, on the left-hand engine

Chassis number location on dashboard (Type 1 Karmann Ghia shown, others similar)

Chassis number location under rear seat (Type 1 Karmann Ghia shown; Types 3 and 4 similar)

Chassis number location behind front passenger seat—Type 2 through 1979

Chassis number location on left hand engine cover plate—most Type 2 models

Chassis number location in luggage compartment—Type 1 Super Beetle shown; Types 3 and 4 similar

cover plate, and on top of the driver's side of the instrument panel.

Vehicle Certification Label

The vehicle certification label is a decal affixed to the left door jamb. It indicates that the vehicle meets all U.S. federal safety standards as of the date of manufacture. The label also gives the chassis number of the car. Beginning with the 1973 model year, the label lists the gross vehicle weight rating and the gross axle weight rating. The gross vehicle weight rating is useful in determining the load carrying capacity of your car. Merely substract the curb weight from the posted gross weight and what is left over is about how much you can haul around. The gross axle weight rating is a good guide to the weight distribution of your car.

```
MANUFACTURED BY VOLKSWAGENWERK AG        0 8/71
THIS VEHICLE CONFORMS TO ALL APPLICABLE FEDERAL MOTOR
VEHICLE SAFETY STANDARDS IN EFFECT ON THE DATE OF MANU-
FACTURE SHOWN ABOVE.    1                    2
```

Vehicle certification label—1970–72 (Type 1 shown)

```
 MANUFACTURED BY VOLKSWAGENWERK AG        (month/year)
                 WEST GERMANY
*  INCOMPLETE VEHICLE MANUFACTURED        (month/year)
   GVWR LB (     )
   GAWR LB FRONT (     )/REAR(     )
   THIS VEHICLE CONFORMS TO ALL APPLICABLE FEDERAL MOTOR VEHICLE
   SAFETY STANDARDS IN EFFECT
                          (vehicle identification number)

  IN    (month/year)    TYPE MULTIPURPOSE PASSENGER VEHICLE
```

Vehicle certification label. Type 2 (1980–81 Vanagon) shown. All 1973–81 labels similar. The line beside the asterisk refers to Campmobile only

The vehicle certification label is conshructed of special material to guard against its alteration. If it is tampered with or removed, it will be destroyed or the word "VOID" will appear.

Engine Number

The engine can be identified by a letter or pair of letters preceding the serial number. Engine specifications are listed according to the letter code and model ysar.

On all Type 1 models, and on 1970–71 Type 2/1600 models using the upright fan engine, the engine number is stamped into the crankcase flange for the generator support. The number can readily be seen by looking through the center of the fan belt.

On all Type 3 and 4 models, and on 1972–79 Type 2/1700, Type 2/1800, and

Engine number location—Type 1 and 2/1600 (1970–71)

Engine number location Types 2, 3, 4 through 1979 with suitcase engine. Type 2/2000 shown

Type 2/2000 models using the "suitcase" engine, the engine number is stamped into the crankcase along the crankcase joint near the oil breather. On the 1980–81 Type 2 (Vanagon) the engine number is located on the right side of the engine compartment, directly in front of the fan housing.

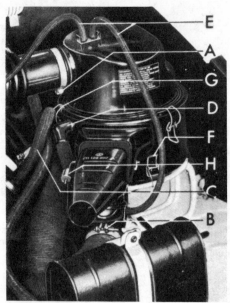

A. Hose clamp
B. Hose clamp
C. Hose
D. Hose
E. Intake air preheating vacuum control hoses
F. Mounting spring clips
G. Retaining spring clips
H. Intake air preheating weighted flap

Oil bath air cleaner—1973–74 Type 1 Karmann

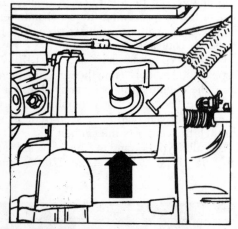

1980–81 Type 2 engine number location

Transmission Identification

Transmission identification marks are stamped either into the bellhousing or on the final drive housing.

Oil bath oil cleaner—1972 Type 2

ROUTINE MAINTENANCE

Air Cleaner Service

OIL BATH TYPE

This type cleaner should be cleaned at 6,000 mile intervals, or when the oil is changed.

Type 1 and 2 (1970–73)

1. To clean the air cleaner, remove the hoses attached to the air cleaner.
   CAUTION: *Be careful to note the places where the hoses are attached. Interchanging the hoses will affect the operation of the engine.*
2. Next, loosen the air cleaner support bracket screw and the air cleaner clamp screw.
3. On 1970 models, disconnect the warm air flap cable. Lift the air cleaner off the engine. Keep the carburetor hole down to prevent spilling the oil out of the air cleaner.

4. Loosen the spring clips which secure the top of the air cleaner to the bottom and then separate the halves. Do not invert the upper half.
5. Put the upper half of the air cleaner down with the filter element facing downward. Thoroughly clean the bottom half.
6. Fill the air cleaner with 0.9 pints of SAE 30 (SAE 10W in sub-freezing climates) oil or, if present, to the oil level mark stamped into the side of the air cleaner.

Chassis Number Chart

Model Year	Vehicle	Model No.	Chassis Number					
			From			To		
1970	Beetle	113	110	2000	001	110	3096	945
	Karmann Ghia	14	140	2000	001	140	3100	000
	Beetle Convertible	15	150	2000	001	150	3100	000
	Van	21	210	2000	001	210	2300	000
	Bus	22	220	2000	001	220	2300	000
	Camper, Kombi	23	230	·2000	001	230	2300	000
	Type 3 Fastback	31	310	2000	001	310	2500	000
	Type 3 Squareback	36	360	2000	001	360	2500	000
1971	Beetle/Super Beetle	111/113	111	2000	001	111	3143	118
	Karmann Ghia	14	141	2000	001	141	3200	000
	Beetle Convertible	15	151	2000	001	151	3200	000
	Van	21	211	2000	001	211	2300	000
	Bus	22	221	2000	001	221	2300	000
	Camper, Kombi	23	231	2000	001	231	2300	000
	Type 3 Fastback	31	311	2000	001	311	2500	000
	Type 3 Squareback	36	361	2000	001	361	2500	000
	411 2 Door	41	411	2000	001	411	2100	000
	411 4 Door	42	421	2000	001	421	2100	000
	411 Wagon	46	461	2000	001	461	2100	000
1972	Beetle/Super Beetle	111/113	112	2000	001	112	2961	362
	Karmann Ghia	14	142	2000	001	142	3200	000
	Beetle Convertible	15	152	2000	001	152	3200	000
	Van	21	212	2000	001	212	2300	000
	Bus	22	222	2000	001	222	2300	000
	Camper, Kombi	23	232	2000	001	232	2300	000

Chassis Number Chart (cont.)

Model Year	Vehicle	Model No.	Chassis Number From			Chassis Number To		
1972	Type 3 Fastback	31	312	2000	001	312	2500	000
	Type 3 Squareback	36	362	2000	001	362	2500	000
	411 2 Door	41	412	2000	001	412	2100	000
	411 4 Door	42	422	2000	001	422	2100	000
	411 Wagon	46	462	2000	001	462	2100	000
1973	Beetle	111	113	2000	001	113	3021	954
	Super Beetle	113	133	2000	001	133	3021	860
	Karmann Ghia	14	143	2000	001	143	3200	000
	Beetle Convertible	15	153	2000	001	153	3200	000
	Van	21	213	2000	001	213	2300	000
	Bus	22	223	2000	001	223	2300	000
	Camper, Kombi	23	233	2000	001	233	2300	000
	Type 3 Fastback	31	313	2000	001	313	2500	000
	Type 3 Squareback	36	363	2000	001	363	2500	000
	412 2 Door	41	413	2000	001	413	2100	000
	412 4 Door	42	423	2000	001	423	2100	000
	412 Wagon	46	463	2000	001	463	2100	000
1974	Beetle	111	114	2000	001	114	2818	456
	Super Beetle	113	134	2000	001	134	2798	165
	Karmann Ghia	14	144	2000	001	144	3200	000
	Beetle Convertible	15	154	2000	001	154	3200	000
	Van	21	214	2000	001	214	2300	000
	Bus	22	224	2000	001	224	2300	000
	Camper, Kombi	23	234	2000	001	234	2300	000
	412 2 Door	41	414	2000	001	414	2100	000

Chassis Number Chart (cont.)

Model Year	Vehicle	Model No.	Chassis Number From			Chassis Number To		
1974	412 4 Door	42	424	2000	001	424	2100	000
	412 Wagon	46	464	2000	001	464	2100	000
1975	Beetle	111	115	2000	001	115	3200	000
	Super Beetle (La Grande Bug)	113	135	2000	001	135	3200	000
	Beetle Convertible	15	155	2000	001	155	3200	000
	Van	21	215	2000	001	215	2300	000
	Bus	22	225	2000	001	225	2300	000
	Camper, Kombi	23	235	2000	001	235	2300	000
1976	Beetle	111	116	2000	001	116	3200	000
	Beetle Convertible	15	156	2000	001	156	2000	001
	Bus	22	226	2000	001	226	2300	000
	Camper, Kombi	23	236	2000	001	236	2300	001
1977	Beetle	111	117	2000	001	—		
	Beetle Convertible	15	157	2000	001	—		
	Bus	22	227	2000	001	—		
	Camper, Kombi	23	237	2000	001	—		
1978	Beetle Convertible	15	158	2000	001	—		
	Bus	22	228	2000	001	—		
	Camper	23	238	2000	001	—		
1979–80	Beetle Convertible	15	159	2000	001	—		
	Bus	22	229	2000	001	—		
	Camper	23	239	2000	001	—		
1980–81	Vanagon	24	24A	0000	001	—		

Engine Identification Chart

Engine Code Letter	Type Vehicle	First Production Year	Last Production Year ①	Engine Type	Common Designation
B	1, 2	1967	1970	Upright Fan	1600
AE	1, 2	1971	1972	Upright Fan	1600
AH (Calif)	1	1972	1974	Upright Fan	1600
AK	1	1973	1974	Upright Fan	1600
AJ	1	1975	1979	Upright Fan	1600
CB	2	1972	1973	Suitcase	1700
CD	2	1973	1973	Suitcase	1700
AW	2	1974	1974	Suitcase	1800
ED	2	1975	1975	Suitcase	1800
GD, GE, CV	2	1976	In Production	Suitcase	2000
U	3	1968	1973	Suitcase	1600
X	3	1972	1973	Suitcase	1600
W	4	1971	1971	Suitcase	1700
EA	4	1972	1974	Suitcase	1700
EB (Calif)	4	1973	1973	Suitcase	1700
EC	4	1974	1974	Suitcase	1800

① In production as of the publication of this book

7. Reassemble the air cleaner and install it on the engine.

All Type 3, Type 4 (1971–72)

1. Disconnect the activated charcoal filter hose, the rubber elbow, and the crankcase ventilation hose. Remove the wing nut in the center of the air cleaner and lift the air cleaner assembly off of the engine.

2. Release the spring clips which keep the air cleaner halves together and take the cleaner apart. Do not invert the upper half.

3. Clean the lower half and refill it with 0.085 pints of SAE 30 oil (SAE 10W in subfreezing climates) to the level mark. When reassembling the air cleaner, align the marks for the upper and lower halves.

4. Reinstall the air cleaner on the engine. Make sure it is properly seated.

PAPER ELEMENT TYPE

Type 1 (1973–74), and Type 4 (1973–74)

1. Label and disconnect the hoses from the air cleaner.

CAUTION: *Do not interchange the position of the hoses.*

2. Loosen the air cleaner clamp and re-

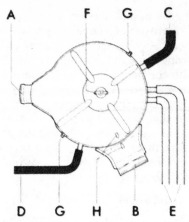

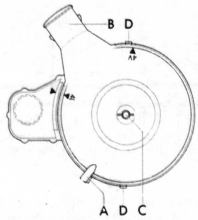

A. Hose clamp
B. Retaining clip
C. Hose
D. Hose
E. Hoses
F. Wing nut
G. Retaining spring clips
H. Alignment marks for upper and low halves

Oil bath air cleaner—1973 Type 3

A. Hose to air intake pipe
B. Hose to intake air distributor
C. Wing nut
D. Retaining spring clips
4L. Alignment mark for 2 and 4-door sedans
(match arrow on lower half)
4V. Alignment mark for station wagons
(match arrow on lower half)

Paper element air cleaner—1973–74 Type 4

move the air cleaner from the engine. Release spring clamps which keep the halves of the cleaner together and separate the halves.

3. Clean the inside of the air cleaner housing.

4. The paper element should be replaced every 18,000 miles under normal service. It should be replaced more often under severe operating conditions. A paper element may be cleaned by blowing through the element

Capacities Chart

Year	Type and Model	Engine Displacement (cc)	Engine Crankcase (qts) With Filter	Without	Transaxle (pts) Manual	Automatic Conv	Final Drive	Gasoline Tank (gals)
1970–79	1, 111, 114	1600	—	2.5	6.3	7.6	6.3 ①	10.6
1970–80	1, 113, 15	1600	—	2.5	6.3	7.6	6.3 ①	11.1
1970–71	2, All	1600	—	2.5	7.4	12.6 ②	3.0	15.8
1972–81	2, All	1700, 1800, 2000	3.7	3.2	7.4	12.6 ②	3.0	15.8 ③
1970–73	3, All	1600	—	2.5	6.3	12.6 ②	2.1	10.6
1971–74	4, All	1700, 1800	3.7	3.2	5.3	12.6 ②	2.1	13.2

Conv—Torque Converter
① 5.3 when changed
② 6.3 when changed
③ 1980–81—15.9 gals

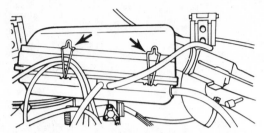

1973–74 Type 1 Beetle and Super Beetle air cleaner—undo snaps (arrows) to remove air filter

from the inside with compressed air. Never use a liquid solvent to clean a paper element.

5. Install the air cleaner element in the air cleaner housing and install the spring clips, making sure the halves are properly aligned. Install the cleaner on the engine.

Type 1 (1975–80)

1. Release the four clips at the top, side and bottom of the air cleaner housing and pull the front cover off the housing just enough to slide off the cardboard vent pipe at the bottom of the housing.

2. Take the filter out and clean it by striking it against a hard surface or blowing through it with compressed air. The filter should be replaced every 18,000 miles under normal conditions and more frequently under severe conditions.

3. When installing filter, make sure it is seated properly and that the bottom hose is connected.

Type 2/1700 Engine (1972–73), Type 2/1800 Engine (1974)

The air filter is removed through the hatch in the interior of the bus above the engine on some models. Remove the rear mat to gain access.

1. Label and disconnect the hoses from the air cleaner.

CAUTION: *Do not interchange the position of the hoses.*

2. Release the two clamps which secure the air cleaner to the carburetors. Release the clips which secure the air ducts to each carburetor.

3. Remove the air ducts separately. Remove the air cleaner housing.

4. Release the four spring clips which secure the cleaner halves together and then separate the halves.

5. Clean the inside of the housing. The paper element should be replaced every 18,000

miles under normal service. It should be replaced more often under severe operating conditions. A paper element may be cleaned by blowing through the element from the inside with compressed air. Never use a liquid solvent.

6. Assemble the air cleaner halves, making sure that they are properly aligned. Install the air cleaner by reversing the above. Make sure that the rubber sleeves on the air ducts and the rubber seals on the carburetors are seated properly.

Type 2 (1975–79)

1. Disconnect the upper part of hose A from the heater air blower. Open the clamp at the lower part of hose A and remove the hose.

2. Open clamps B on the air cleaner housing (2 at both the front and rear). Open the cover on the left side and remove the air filter cartridge. The element may be cleaned by striking it against a hard surface face first and then by blowing compressed air through it from the opposite direction of air flow then the filter is installed.

To remove the right section of the air cleaner housing to either clean it or remove the battery, proceed as follows:

3. Open clamp C.

4. Lift the right section of the air cleaner housing up and pull it out of the engine compartment.

Clean the insides of the housing with a cloth. Reverse the procedure to install both the housing and filter. Observe the following:

When inserting the right section of the housing, insert the locating projection into the side grommet first, then pull the housing

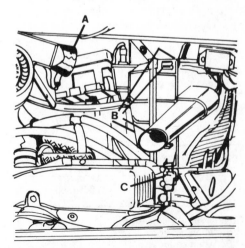

Fuel injected Type 2 air cleaner

toward the rear as you insert the lower locating projection in its seat. The paper element should be replaced every 18,000 miles under normal operating conditions, more often if the vehicle is used in severe climates or conditions.

Type 2 (1980–81)

1. Open the hatch inside the luggage compartment at the rear of the vehicle.
2. The air cleaner is located off to the side of the engine. Unfasten the five clips holding the top cover to the air cleaner housing and remove the top cover.
3. Pull the filter out and shake it to remove dust, or replace it as necessary.
4. When replacing, install the filter in the lower housing and install the top cover, securing it first with the top clamps.
5. Secure the remaining clamps. The air filter must be replaced every 18,000 miles, more often if the vehicle is used in severe conditions.

Crankcase Ventilation Service

Type 1/1600, 2/1600, 2/1700, 2/1800 (Carbureted)

The crankcase is vented by a hose running from the crankcase breather to the air cleaner. In some cases the hose is attached to the air inlet for the air cleaner. No PCV valve is used. No regular service is required.

Type 2/1800, 3/1600, 4/1700, 4/1800 (Fuel Injected)

Air is drawn in from the air cleaner to the cylinder head covers and pushrod tubes where it passes into the crankcase. From there, blow-by fumes then pass into the crankcase breather where they are drawn into the intake air distributor. On some models a PCV valve is used to control the flow of crankcase fumes. These systems usually need no maintenance other than keeping the hoses clear and all connections tight.

NOTE: *Many VW engines do not use a conventional PCV valve because engine design limits crankcase pressure pulsing and allows almost no oil vapor to go into the PCV system.*

Fuel Evaporation Control System Service

This system consists of an expansion chamber, an activated charcoal filter, and a hose which connects the parts into a closed system.

When fuel in the gas tank expands due to heat, the fuel travels to the expansion chamber. Any fumes generated either in the gas tank or the expansion chamber are trapped in

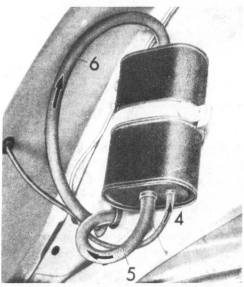

Evaporative control canister location—Type 1 Beetle; Super Beetle

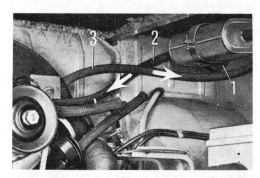

Evaporative control canister locations—1970–71 Type 2/1600

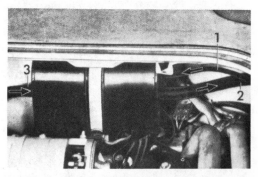

Evaporative control canister location—Type 3

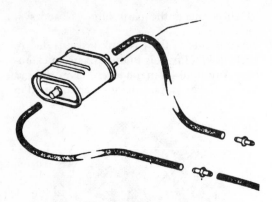

Evaporative control canister—Type 4

the activated charcoal filter found in a line connecting the tank and chamber. The fumes are purged from the filter when the engine is started. Air from the engine cooling fan is forced through the filter when the engine is started. From the filter, this air/fuel vapor mixture is routed to the inside of the air cleaner where it is sent to the engine to be burned.

1976 and later Type 2 models have an Evaporative Emission Control (EEC) cutoff valve which prevents fuel fumes from entering the air cleaner when the engine is stopped or idling. The cutoff is located in the air cleaner body. To test the valve, turn off the engine and disconnect the charcoal filter to air cleaner hose from the charcoal filter (this hose is usually transparent). Blow into the hose. The valve should be closed and no air should be going into the air cleaner. If the cutoff valve is open and air is getting through, the valve must be replaced.

The only maintenance required on the system is checking the tightness of all hose connections, and replacement of the charcoal filter element at 48,000 miles or 2 year intervals (whichever occurs first).

The filter canister is located under the right rear fender on Beetles and Super Beetles, at the lower right hand side of the engine compartment on Karmann Ghias, at the upper right hand side of the engine compartment on Type 3 models, beneath the floor near the forward end of the transaxle on Type 4 models and in the engine compartment on Type 2 models.

Battery

The battery is located in the engine compartment on all 1970–79 Type 2 models and on

Type 1 Karmann Ghias. On 1980–81 Type 2 models the battery is located under the front passenger seat. On Type 1 models except the Karmann Ghia and on Type 3 models, the battery is located under the back seat. On Type 4 models it is located under the driver's seat. On fuel injected Type 2 models through 1979, the air cleaner housing must be removed to gain access to the battery: see the air filter removal and installation procedure, above for instructions.

To properly clean dirty battery posts, the cables must be removed from the posts and the contact surfaces on both the posts and the cables must be cleaned to a shiny finish. You can purchase a handy tool just for this purpose at your local automotive store, or use a wire brush.

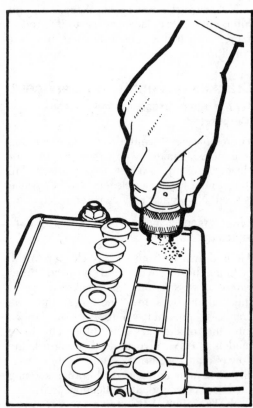

Clean the battery posts with a wire terminal cleaner. Rotate the tool until the post shines

Routinely check the battery electrolyte level and specific gravity. A few minutes occasionally spent monitoring battery condition is worth saving hours of frustration when your car won't start due to a dead battery. Only distilled water should be used to top up the battery, as tap water, in many areas, contains harmful minerals. Two tools which will

Clean the terminal end of the cable with the pointed end of the cleaning tool

facilitate battery maintenance are a hydrometer and a squeeze bulb filler. These are inexpensive and widely available at automotive parts stores, hardware stores, etc. The specific gravity of the electrolyte should be between 1.285 and 1.25. Keep the top of the battery clean, as a film of dirt can sometimes completely discharge a battery. A solution of baking soda and water may be used to clean the top surface, but be careful to flush this off with clear water and that none of the solution enters the filler holes. Lightly coat the posts and clamps with petroleum jelly or chassis grease after cleaning them.

Regular battery maintenance is important on all cars, but especially on those Volkswagens in which the battery is located under the seat, as the battery pan is also the floor pan and is subjected not only to the corrosive action of spilled battery acid but also to road water and salt underneath the car. A good precaution against battery pan rust-through is to remove the battery every now and then and clean off the pan. Investing in a rubber battery seat will also help.

V-Belts

GENERATOR/ALTERNATOR DRIVE BELT ADJUSTMENT

Improper fan belt adjustment can lead to either overheating of the engine or to loss in generating power, or both. In the Type 1, Type 2 or Type 4 a loose fan belt can cause both, while the slipping of the generator or alternator belt of the Type 3 engine will cause loss of generator efficiency only. In any case, it is important that the fan belt adjustment be checked and, if necessary, corrected at periodic intervals. When adjusted prop-

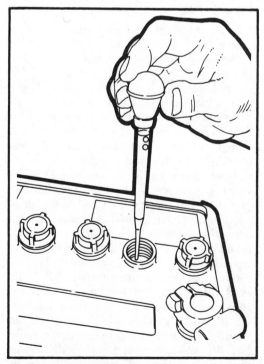

An inexpensive hydrometer will quickly check the state of charge of the battery

Checking drive belt (V-belt) tension (a.¼ to ½ in.)

erly, the belt of any Volkswagen engine should deflect approximately ½ in. when pressed firmly in the center with the thumb. Check the tension at 6,000 mile intervals.

Type 1/1600, Type 2/1600

Adjustment of the Type 1/1600 and Type 2/1600 fan belt is made as follows: loosen the fan pulley by unscrewing the nut while at the same time holding the pulley from rotating by using a screwdriver inserted into the slot cut into the inner half of the generator pulley and supported against the upper generator bolt to cause a counter-torque. Remove the nut from the generator shaft pulley and remove the outer half of the pulley. The spacer washers must then be arranged so as to make the fan belt tension either greater or less. The greater the number of washers between the pulley halves, the smaller the effective diameter of the pulley, and the less the fan belt tension will be. Conversely, the subtraction of washers from between the pulley halves will lead to a larger effective diameter and to a greater degree of fan belt tension. If it is impossible to achieve proper adjustment with all the washers removed, then the fan belt is excessively stretched, and must be replaced. If it is impossible to adjust a new belt properly by using some combination of the available washers, the belt is the wrong size and must not be used. After the correct number of washers has been applied between the pulley halves, install the outer pulley half and place all surplus washers between the outer pulley half and the pulley nut so that

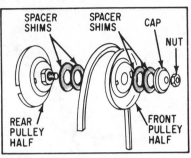

Adjust belt tension by adding or subtracting shims between the pulley halves—Type 1/1600, Type 2/1600, Type 3/1600

they will be available if needed in a subsequent adjustment. Tighten the pulley nut and recheck the adjustment. If incorrect, add or subtract washers between the pulley halves until the proper amount of deflection is achieved. If the belt is too tight, the generator bearings will be subjected to undue stress and to very early failure. On the other hand, if the belt is too loose, it will slip and cause overheating. Cracked or frayed belts should be replaced. There is no comparison between the cost of a fan belt and that of repairing a badly overheated engine. If it is necessary to replace the belt, remove the three sheet metal screws and the crankshaft pulley cover plate to gain access to the pulley.

Type 3/1600

Adjustment of the fan belt on the Type 3 engine is much the same as that of the smaller Volkswagen engines. On the Type 3 engine, the fan belt is subject to a great deal less stress because it has no fan to turn. Therefore, a loose adjustment is not quite so critical as on the Beetle models. However, the ½ in. deflection should nevertheless be maintained, because a loose fan belt could possibly climb over the pulley and foul the fan. In addition, loose fan belts have a shorter service life. In adjusting the Type 3 fan belt, the first step is to remove the cover of the air intake housing. Next, hold the generator pulley with a suitable wrench, and unscrew the retaining nut. (Note: a 27 mm and a 21 mm wrench will come in handy here. Also, be careful that no adjusting washers fall off the shaft into the air intake housing, for they could be quite difficult to remove.) Loosen the generator strap and push the generator slightly forward. Remove the outer pulley half, sleeve and washers included. Arrange the spacer washers as was described in the

Use a screwdriver to keep generator/alternator from turning while loosening/tightening pulley nut—Type 1/1600, 2/1600 and 3/1600

Type 1/1600, 2/1600 belt adjustment; i.e., more washers between halves mean a looser belt, and fewer washers mean a tighter belt. Install outer half of pulley. Install unused washers on outside of outer pulley half so that the total number of washers on the shaft will remain the same. Fit the nut into place and tighten down the generator strap after pulling the generator back to the rear. Tighten the retaining nut and make sure that the generator belt is parallel to the air intake housing and at least 4 mm away from it at all points. Install housing cover.

Type 2/1700, 2/1800, 2/2000 and Type 4

To adjust the alternator/cooling belt tension on these models, first remove the plastic insert in the cover plate over the alternator. Then, loosen the 12 point allen head adjusting bolt and the hex-head mounting bolt. Adjust the tension so that light thumb pressure applied midway in the belts longest run causes a deflection of approximately ½ in. Tighten the bolts.

When installing a new belt, move the alternator fully to the left and slip off the old belt. Install a new belt and tighten by moving the alternator to the right.

Adjust belt tension at the 12 point allen head bolt—Type 2/1700, 2/1800, 2/2000 and Type 4

AIR INJECTION AIR PUMP DRIVE BELT ADJUSTMENT

1973–74 Type 2

To provide proper air pump output for the emission control system on 1973–74 Type 2 models, the belt tension must be checked at 6,000 mile intervals. Deflection is correct when light thumb pressure applied midway in the longest run of the belt deflects about ¼ in. To adjust, loosen the adjusting and

Type 2 air pump adjusting nut locations

mounting bolts (black arrows). Hold the air pump in position while tightening the bolts.

Air Conditioning

Many VWs are equipped with either aftermarket or factory installed air conditioning

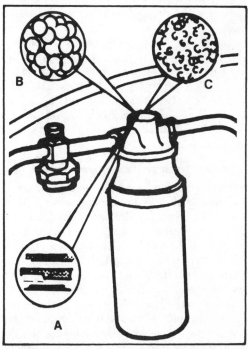

Oil streaks (A), constant bubbles (B) or foam (C) indicate there is not enough refrigerant in the system. Occasional bubbles during initial operation is normal. A clear sight glass indicates a proper charge of refrigerant or no refrigerant at all, which can be determined by the presence of cold air at the outlets in the car. If the glass is clouded with a milky white substance, have the receiver/drier checked professionally systems. Since the compressed refrigerant inside the system is at very high pressure and will have a temperature of −21.7°F or lower when released into the atmosphere, a temperature low enough to freeze your skin or eyes, it is recommended that any repairs, including the removal and installation of refrigerant hoses, be left to a qualified technician.

To check the system for proper refrigerant charge, follow the directions in the illustration.

NOTE: *Some systems may not have the indicated sight glass. In this case, consult the manufacturer of the system for instruction.*

Windshield Wipers

BLADE AND ARM REPLACEMENT

See Chapter 5 "Chassis Electrical" for wiper blade and arm replacement.

Fluid Level Checks

ENGINE OIL

To check the engine oil level, park the car on level ground and wait 5 minutes to allow all the oil in the engine to drain into the crankcase.

Check the oil level by withdrawing the dipstick and wiping it clean. Insert the dipstick into its hole and note the position of the oil level on the bottom of the stick. The level should be between the two marks on the bottom of the stick, preferably closer to the top mark. The distance between the two marks represents one quart of oil.

On upright fan engines, the dipstick is located directly beneath the generator or alternator; oil is added through the capped opening beside the generator/alternator support post. On Type 2 suitcase engines through 1979, the dipstick is located next to the alternator with the oil filler right beside it. On the 1980–81 Type 2 the dipstick is accessible by pulling down the hinged license plate holder: the filler cap is below it. On the Type 3 the dipstick and filler are located in the lower door jamb of the rear compartment lid. On Type 4 two door and four door models, the dipstick is located at the center of the engine next to the oil filler cap: on wagon models, it is under the rear door jamb.

TRANSMISSION

Manual Transmission

The oil level is checked by removing the 17 mm socket head plug located on the driver's

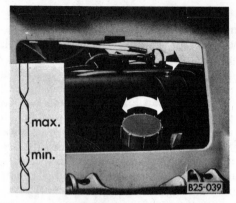

Filler cap and dipstick are accessible through license plate hole—Vanagon

side of the transaxle. The oil level should be even with the hole when the vehicle is level. Check it with your finger.

CAUTION: *Do not fill the transaxle too quickly because it may overflow from the filler hole and give the impression that the unit has been filled when it has not.*

Top up as necessary with SAE 90 gear oil.

Automatic Stick Shift Transmission—Type 1

The automatic Stick Shift transmission is checked by means of a dipstick. The oil level should be between two marks at the bottom of the stick. The engine should be warm when the transmission oil level is checked. Top up as necessary with DEXRON®.

NOTE: *The engine must be turned off when checking the transmission oil level.*

Type 1 Automatic stick shift dipstick location

Automatic Transmission—Types 2, 3, and 4

Automatic transmissions are checked in the same manner as Automatic Stick Shift transmissions, except that the engine should be running at an idle, transmission in neutral, and parking brake firmly applied. Top up as necessary with DEXRON® through the transmission dipstick tube located above the distributor (Type 2) or above the air manifold pipes (Types 3 and 4). The difference between the two marks on the dipstick is less than one pint. On all Type 2 and 4 models and on Squareback Type 3 models the dipstick is accessible through the hatch in the luggage compartment. On Fastback Type 3 models the dipstick is reached through the rear engine lid.

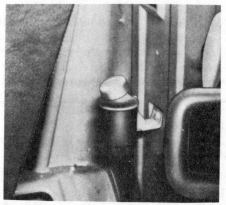

1971–72 Type 2 master cylinder reservoir locations

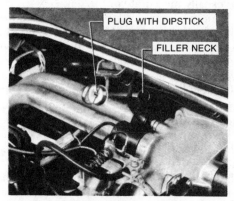

Type 3 and Type 4 Automatic transmission dipstick location; Type 2 dipstick similar

1973–79 Type 2 master cylinder reservoir location showing minimum fill line visible through access window

BRAKE FLUID RESERVOIR

The brake fluid reservoir is located above the clutch pedal on 1970 Type 2 models, behind the drivers seat on 1971–72 Type 2 models, under the driver's seat on 1973–79 Type 2s

Luggage compartment-mounted master cylinder reservoir maximum fill (arrow)—Type 1, 3, and 4

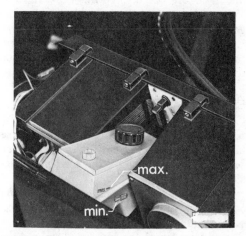

1980–81 Type 2 master cylinder location

and under the instrument cluster on 1980–81 Vanagons. It is located in the front luggage compartment on all other models. The fluid level in all vehicles should be above the upper seam of the reservoir. On 1973–79 Type 2 models, the fluid level is visible through a cutout beneath the seat. Fill the reservoir only with the new, clean heavy-duty brake fluid. If the vehicle is equipped with disc brakes make sure the fluid is marked for use with disc brakes. All fluid used should meet DOT 3, DOT 4, or SAE J1703 specifications.

DIFFERENTIAL HOUSING

Automatic Transmission Only—All Types

The filler hole is in basically the same position as on the manual transmission. Make sure the oil level is even with the bottom of the hole when the vehicle is level. Fill the differential housing with 90W hypoid oil.

NOTE: *The differential gears are lubricated by the transmission oil on manual transmission models.*

STEERING GEAR (EXCEPT RACK AND PINION TYPE)

NOTE: *The rack and pinion steering systems used on the 1975 and later Type 1 Super Beetle and Convertible and the 1980–81 Type 2 Vanagon are sealed systems which do not need regular maintenance.*

Types 1 and 3 except the 1971–74 Super Beetle and 1971–74 Beetle Convertible, are filled with 5.4 ozs of gear oil which is added to a plug at the top of the gearbox. The 1971–74 Super Beetle and 1971–74 Convertible hold 5.9 ozs of steering gear oil. The Type 2 holds 9.4 ozs of gear oil in the steering gear box. Type 4 holds 9 ozs.

Unless the steering gear box has been rebuilt or is leaking severely, there is no reason to add or change gear box oil.

BATTERY

Check the electrolyte level frequently. Use only distilled water to top up the battery, as tap water contains minerals that will shorten battery life by corroding the lead plates inside the battery.

NOTE: *See battery section above, under "Routine Maintenance" for battery location and maintenance.*

Keep the top of the battery clean and dry to prevent current leakage which can completely discharge the battery.

When checking the electrolyte level of the battery never smoke or use an open flame for light: the battery generates hydrogen gas which is explosive. Never let battery acid (electrolyte) come in contact with skin, eyes, fabric or painted surfaces. Do not attempt to drive the car with the battery disconnected or you may damage the electrical system.

Tires

Check the air pressure in your tires every few weeks. Make sure that the tires are cool, as you will get a false reading when the tires are heated because air pressure increases with temperature. A decal tells you the proper tire pressure for the standard equipment tires. Naturally, when you replace tires you will want to get the correct tire pressures for the new ones from the dealer or manufacturer. It pays to buy a tire pressure gauge to keep in the car, since those at service stations are usually inaccurate or broken.

While you are checking the tire pressure, take a look at the tread. The tread should be wearing evenly across the tire. Excessive wear in the center of the tread could indicate overinflation. Excessive wear on the outer edges could indicate underinflation. An irregular wear pattern is usually a sign of incorrect front wheel alignment or wheel balance. A front end that is out of alignment will usually pull the car to one side of a flat road when the steering wheel is released. Incorrect wheel balance will produce vibration in the steering wheel, while unbalanced rear wheels will result in floor or trunk vibration.

Rotating the tires every 6,000 miles or so will result in increased tread life. Use the correct pattern for your tire switching. Most automotive experts agree that radial tires are better all around performers, giving longer wear and better handling. An added benefit which you should consider when purchasing tires is that radials have less rolling resistance and can give up to a 10% increase in fuel economy over a bias-ply tire.

Tires of different construction should never be mixed. Always replace tires in sets of four or five when switching tire types and never substitute a belted tire for a bias-ply, a radial for a belted tire, etc. An occasional pressure check and periodic rotation could make your tires last much longer than a neglected set and maintain the safety margin which was designed into them.

Recommended tire pressures are usually found on a sticker located on the door jamb or on the inside of the glove compartment lid.

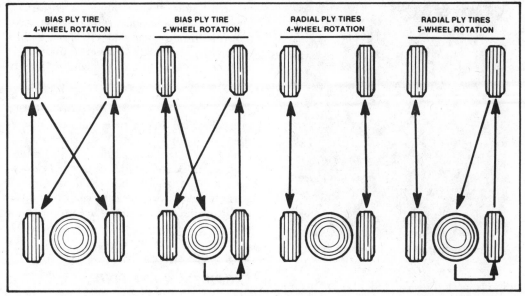

| BIAS PLY TIRE 4-WHEEL ROTATION | BIAS PLY TIRE 5-WHEEL ROTATION | RADIAL PLY TIRES 4-WHEEL ROTATION | RADIAL PLY TIRES 5-WHEEL ROTATION |

Tire rotation

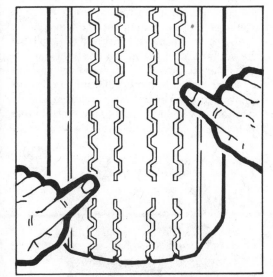

Since 1968, tread wear indicators have been built into the tire tread and appear as ½ in. wide bands when 1/16 in. of tread remains

Fuel Filter Service

On carbureted models, the fuel filter is located in the mechanical fuel pump. There are three types of fuel pumps. Two types have a single screw holding a cover on the top of the pump. To remove the filter screen, undo the screw and carefully lift the cover off the pump. Remove the cover gasket and filter screen taking careful note of the position of the screen. Blow the screen out with air and replace the screen and cover using a new gasket if necessary.

The third type of fuel pump has four screws securing the top cover to the pump. This type of pump has a large plug with a hexagonal head. Remove this plug and washer (gasket) to gain access to the cylindrical filter screen located beneath the plug. Blow the screen out with air and replace it in its bore with the open end facing into the pump. Install the washer and plug. Do not overtighten the plug.

Fuel injected engines have an electric fuel pump located near the front axle on all models except the Type 2, in which the fuel

Fuel filter location—Types 3 and 4

Fuel filter direction of flow—Types 3 and 4

pump is located near the fuel tank. This type of engine has an in-line fuel filter located atop the fuel pump in the suction line for the fuel pump. The suction line is the line running from the gas tank to the "S" connection at the fuel pump. To change the fuel filter, clamp the lines shut, then release the retaining pin and bracket, disconnect the gas lines from either end of the filter and insert a new filter. Filter should be installed with arrow (if any) pointing in the direction of fuel flow. This type of filter cannot be cleaned. VW recommends replacement at 12,000 mile intervals. A small speck of dirt entering a fuel injector may completely block the flow of fuel, necessitating disassembly of the injection system.

LUBRICATION

Oil and Fuel Recommendations

Only oils which are high detergent and are graded MS or SE should be used in the engine. Oils should be selected for the SAE viscosity which will perform satisfactorily in the temperature expected before the next oil change.

Factory recommendations for fuel are regular gasoline with an octane rating of 91 RON or higher for Types 1, 2, 3, 1972–73 Type 4 and 1974 Type 4 equipped with automatic transmission. The 1971 Type 4 and 1974 Type 4 equipped with manual transmission require premium gasoline with an octane rating of 98 RON or better.

All 1975 and later models sold in California and all 1977 and later models sold in the

other 49 states use catalytic converters to lower exhaust emissions, requiring the use of only lead-free regular (91 RON) fuel. Failure to do so will render the converter ineffective.

If the vehicle is used for towing, it may be necessary to buy a higher grade of gasoline. The extra load caused by the trailer may be sufficient to cause elevated engine knock or ping. This condition, when allowed to continue over a period of time, will cause extreme damage to the engine. Furthermore, ping or knock has several causes besides low octane. An engine in need of a tune-up will ping. If there is an excessive carbon build-up and lead deposits in the combustion chamber, ping will also result.

Fluid Changes

ENGINE OIL AND FILTER

The engine oil should be changed only after the engine has been warmed up to operating temperatures. In this way, the oil holds in suspension many of the contaminants that would otherwise remain in the engine. As the oil drains, it carries dirt and sludge from the engine. After the initial oil change at 600 miles the oil should be changed regularly at a period not to exceed 3,000 miles or three months. If the car is being operated mainly for short low speed trips, it may be advisable to change the oil at 2,000 mile intervals.

Oil strainer and related parts—1979 convertible

Types 1, 2/1600, 3

When changing the oil in Type 1, 2/1600, and 3 vehicles, first unscrew the drain plug in the crankcase (1970–72 models) or strainer cover cap nuts (1973–80 models); and allow dirty

Oil Viscosity Selection Chart

	Anticipated Temperature Range	SAE Viscosity
Multigrade	Above 32° F	10W–40
		10W–50
		20W–40
		20W–50
		10W–30
	May be used as low as −10° F	10W–30
		10W–40
	Consistently below 10° F	5W–20
		5W–30
Single-grade	Above 32° F	30
	Between 0°–32° F	20
	Temperature below 0° F	10W

Adaptor extension used to remove Type 2/1700/1800/2000 engine oil filter

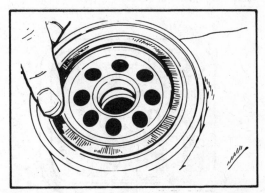

When installing new filter, lubricate the rubber seal with clean oil

oil to drain. The oil strainer should also be cleaned. This wire mesh strainer is held in place by six cap nuts, and should be cleaned thoroughly with solvent. The strainer plate should also be cleaned. The lower part of the crankcase collects a great deal of sludge in the course of 3,000 miles. Replace the assembly using a new paper gasket and copper washers. Refill the crankcase with 2.5 quarts of oil. Tighten the cap nuts to no more than 5 ft lbs. The drain plug (1970–72 models) is tightened to 9 ft. lbs.

Types 2/1700, 2/1800, 2/2000 and Type 4

Types 2/1700, 2/1800, 2/2000 and 4 require a different oil changing procedure. The crankcase drain plug is to one side of the oil strainer. The oil should be drained before removing the strainer. The strainer is located in the center of the crankcase and is held in position by a single plug. Remove the plug and remove the strainer assembly from the crankcase. Clean the strainer in solvent and reinstall it in the crankcase with a new paper gasket and copper washers. Tighten the drain plug and strainer nut to 9 ft. lbs.

The Type 2/1700, 2/1800, 2/2000 and Type 4 also have a spin-on oil filter located near the engine cooling fan. This filter is removed by unscrewing it from its fitting using a special adaptor extension. When reinstalling the new filter, lubricate the filter gasket with oil. Refill the crankcase and start the engine. Run the engine until it picks up oil pressure and

then stop the engine. Recheck the engine oil level. The filter should be changed every 6,000 miles (carbureted engine) or 15,000 miles (fuel injected engines).

TRANSMISSION

Automatic Transmission—Types 2, 3 and 4

The automatic transmission fluid (ATF) should be changed every 30,000 miles, or every 18,000 miles under heavy duty operating conditions. Heavy operating conditions include: continued stop and go driving; extended mountain driving; extremely high outside temperatures.

Automatic Transmission and Final Drive Drain Plug Location—Types 2, 3 and 4

Drain the ATF by removing the drain plug (E) from the pan. Remove the pan and clean the ATF strainer. Install the pan using a new gasket and tighten the pan screws in a criss-cross pattern to 7 ft. lbs. Retighten the

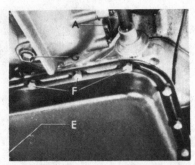

A. Final drive filler plug
E. Automatic transmission drain plug
F. Automatic transmission fluid pan retaining
   bolts
G. Final drive drain plug

Automatic transmission and final drive drain plug location—Types 2, 3 and 4

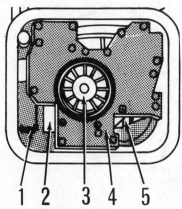

1. Manual valve
2. Kickdown solenoid
3. ATF strainer
4. Transfer plate
5. Valve body

Automatic transmission strainer location—Types 2, 3 and 4

screws two or three times at five minute intervals to compensate for settling of the gasket. Refill the transmission with the proper type transmission fluid using a funnel with a 20 in. long neck. Use Type A or Dexron®.

Manual Transmission

The manual transmission is drained by removing the 17 mm plug in the bottom of the transmission case. It is refilled through another 17 mm plug in the side of the transmission case. The plug in the side of the case also functions as the fluid level hole.

NOTE: *When refilling the transmission, do not fill it too fast because it may overflow*

from the filler hole and give the impression that the unit has been filled when it has not.

After the transmission oil is changed at 600 miles, it is generally not necessary to change the oil. However, the factory does recommend the fluid level be checked every 6,000 miles and topped up if necessary. Refill the transmission with SAE 90 hypoid gear oil.

Automatic Stick Shift—Type 1

The Automatic Stick Shift transmission uses hypoid gear oil in the final drive section of the transmission, see below for draining procedures. The front section of the transmission uses ATF, however it does not have to be changed. The level should be checked every 6,000 miles.

NOTE: *The engine should be off when the level is checked.*

Use Type A or Dexron®.

FINAL DRIVE HOUSING

Automatic Transmission Only—All Models

The automatic transmission unit has a separate housing for final drive gears which uses 90 weight hypoid gear oil. The unit is drained in much the same manner as the manual transmission.

Chassis Greasing

There are four grease fittings on Type 1 and 3 models. They are located at the end of each front torsion bar housing. There is a fifth fitting at the center of the front torsion bar housing for the steering linkage on Type 2 vehicles through 1979. Wipe off each fitting before greasing. Super Beetles, 1971–80 Super Beetle Convertibles, and Type 4 models require no greasing. The vehicle should be greased every 6,000 miles (1970–72 Types 1 and 3 and 1970 Type 2) or 18,000 miles (1973–80 Type 1, 1973 Type 3, 1971–79 Type 2). The 1980–81 Type 2 does not need chassis lubrication.

PUSHING AND TOWING

A vehicle equipped with an automatic or Automatic Stick Shift cannot be pushed or tow started. To push start a vehicle with a manual transmission, switch on the ignition, select the highest forward gear, and keep the clutch

Type 3 front end grease fitting locations

Rear **Front**

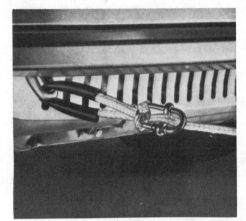 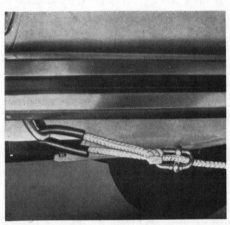

Typical towing sling location—1971–72 Type 4 shown

pedal depressed until suitable speed has been provided by pushing the vehicle. When the vehicle is going about 15 mph, slowly release the clutch to start the engine.

There are two towing eyes on all models except the 1973–74 Type 4. The front eye is located on the lower right front and the rear eye is located under the right rear bumper bracket. Tow the vehicle with the transmission in Neutral and the brakes off. Tow the 1973–74 Type 4 by its bumper bracket.

When towing an automatic transmission vehicle, it is always wise to tow with the drive wheels in a towing cradle or off the ground to avoid damage to the transmission.

JACKING AND HOISTING

Jacking points are provided at the sides of all models for the standard equipment jack. The

jack supplied with the car should never be used for any service operation other than tire changing. NEVER get under the car while it is supported by just a jack. If the jack should slip or tip over, as jacks often do, it would be exceedingly difficult to raise the car again while pinned underneath. Always block the wheels when changing tires.

The service operations in this book often require that one end or the other, or both, of the car be raised and supported safely. The best arrangement is a grease pit or a vehicle hoist. A hydraulic floor jack is also referred to. It is realized that these items are not often found in the home garage, but there are reasonable and safe substitutes. Small hydraulic, screw, or scissors jacks are satisfactory for raising the car. Heavy wooden blocks or adjustable jackstands should be used to support the car while it is being worked on.

Drive-on trestles, or ramps, are a handy

JUMP STARTING A DEAD BATTERY

The chemical reaction in a battery produces explosive hydrogen gas. This is the safe way to jump start a dead battery, reducing the chances of an accidental spark that could cause an explosion.

Jump Starting Precautions

1. Be sure both batteries are of the same voltage.
2. Be sure both batteries are of the same polarity (have the same grounded terminal).
3. Be sure the vehicles are not touching.
4. Be sure the vent cap holes are not obstructed.
5. Do not smoke or allow sparks around the battery.
6. In cold weather, check for frozen electrolyte in the battery.
7. Do not allow electrolyte on your skin or clothing.
8. Be sure the electrolyte is not frozen.

Jump Starting Procedure

1. Determine voltages of the two batteries; they must be the same.
2. Bring the starting vehicle close (they must not touch) so that the batteries can be reached easily.
3. Turn off all accessories and both engines. Put both cars in Neutral or Park and set the handbrake.
4. Cover the cell caps with a rag—do not cover terminals.
5. If the terminals on the run-down battery are heavily corroded, clean them.
6. Identify the positive and negative posts on both batteries and connect the cables in the order shown.
7. Start the engine of the starting vehicle and run it at fast idle. Try to start the car with the dead battery. Crank it for no more than 10 seconds at a time and let it cool off for 20 seconds in between tries.
8. If it doesn't start in 3 tries, there is something else wrong.
9. Disconnect the cables in the reverse order.
10. Replace the cell covers and dispose of the rags.

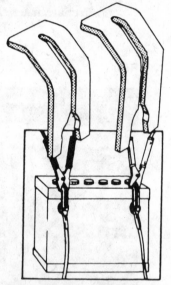

Side terminal batteries occasionally pose a problem when connecting jumper cables. There frequently isn't enough room to clamp the cables without touching sheet metal. Side terminal adaptors are available to alleviate this problem and should be removed after use.

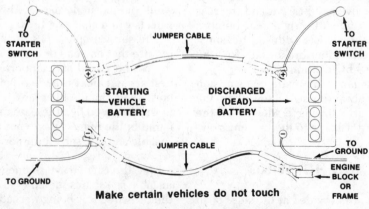

Make certain vehicles do not touch

This hook-up for negative ground cars only

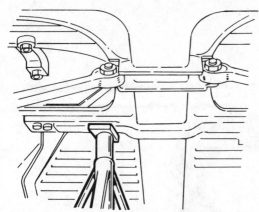

Front of vehicle supported with jackstand under crossmember—Type 1 Super Beetle and Type 4

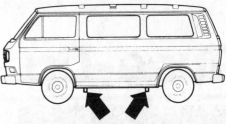

Vanagon jacking points—other Type 2s similar. For fixing flats only

Type 1 jacking point for flat tire repair

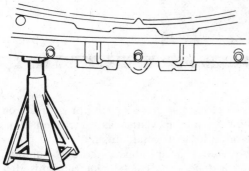

Front of vehicle supported with jackstands under front axle—Type 1 Beetle, Karmann Ghia, all type 2 through 1979, type 3

and safe way to raise the car. These can be bought or constructed from suitable heavy boards or steel.

When raising the car with a floor, screw or scissors jack, or when supporting the car with jack stands, care should be taken in the placement of this equipment. The front of the car may be supported beneath the axle tube on Type 1 Beetles, 1970 Beetle convertibles, all Karmann Ghias, Type 2 models through 1979, and all Type 3 models. The front of all Super Beetles, 1971–77 Beetle convertibles, and all Type 4 models may be supported at the reinforced member to the rear of the lower control arms. 1980–81 Type 2 models should be supported at the frame crossmembers.

In any case, it is always best to spend a little extra time to make sure that the car is lifted and supported safely.

NOTE: *Concrete blocks are not recommended. They may break if the load is not evenly distributed.*

Tune-Up

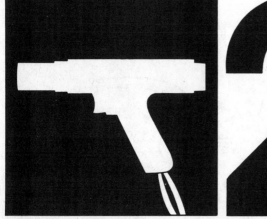

TUNE-UP PROCEDURES

The tune-up is a routine maintenance operation which is essential for the efficient and economical operation, as well as the long life of your car's engine. The interval between tune-ups is a variable factor which depends upon the way you drive your car, the conditions under which you drive it (weather, road type, etc.), and the type of engine installed in your car. It is generally correct to say that no car should be driven more than 12,000 miles between tune-ups, especially in this age of emissions controls and fuel shortages. If you plan to drive your car extremely hard or under severe weather conditions, the tune-ups should be performed at closer intervals. High-performance engines require more frequent tuning than other engines, regardless of weather or driving conditions.

The replaceable parts involved in a tune-up include the spark plugs, breaker points, condenser, distributor cap, rotor, spark plug wires and the ignition coil high-tension (secondary) wire. In addition to these parts and the adjustments involved in properly adapting them to your engine, there are several adjustments of other parts involved in completing the job. These include carburetor idle speed and air/fuel mixture, ignition timing, and dwell angle.

This section gives specific procedures on how to tune-up your Volkswagen and is intended to be as complete and basic as possible. Later in this book, there is another, more generalized section for tune-ups that includes troubleshooting diagnosis for the more experienced weekend mechanic.

CAUTION: *When working with a running engine, make sure that there is proper ventilation. Also make sure that the transmission is in Neutral (unless otherwise specified) and the parking brake is fully applied. Always keep hands, long hair, clothing, neckties and tools well clear of the engine. On a warm engine, keep clear of the hot exhaust manifold(s) and exhaust pipe. When the ignition is turned on and the engine running, do not grasp the ignition wires, distributor cap, or coil wire, as a shock in excess of 20,000 volts may result. Whenever working around the distributor, even if the engine is not running, make sure that the ignition is switched off.*

Spark Plugs

Before attempting any work on the cylinder head, it is very important to note that the cylinder head is cast aluminum alloy. This means that it is extremely easy to damage threads in the cylinder head. Care must be

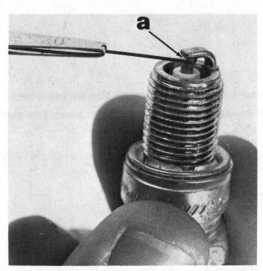

Checking plug gap

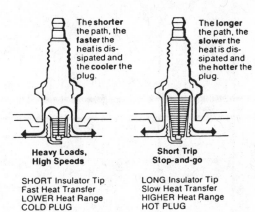

The **shorter** the path, the **faster** the heat is dissipated and the **cooler** the plug.

The **longer** the path, the **slower** the heat is dissipated and the **hotter** the plug.

Heavy Loads, High Speeds

Short Trip Stop-and-go

SHORT Insulator Tip
Fast Heat Transfer
LOWER Heat Range
COLD PLUG

LONG Insulator Tip
Slow Heat Transfer
HIGHER Heat Range
HOT PLUG

Spark plug heat range

taken not to cross-thread the spark plugs or any bolts or studs. Never overtighten the spark plugs, bolts, or studs.

CAUTION: *To prevent seizure, always lubricate the spark plug threads with liquid silicon or Never-Seez®.*

To avoid cross-threading the spark plugs, always start the plugs in their threads with your fingers. Never force the plugs into the cylinder head. Do not use a wrench until you are certain that the plug is correctly threaded.

VW spark plugs should be cleaned and re-gapped every 6,000 miles and replaced every 12,000 miles.

SPARK PLUG HEAT RANGE

While spark plug heat range has always seemed to be somewhat of a mystical subject for many people, in reality the entire subject is quite simple. Basically, it boils down to this; the amount of heat the plug absorbs is determined by the length of the lower insulator. The longer the insulator (or the farther it extends into the engine), the hotter the plug will operate; the shorter the insulator the cooler it will operate. A plug that absorbs little heat and remains too cool will quickly accumulate deposits of oil and carbon since it is not hot enough to burn them off. This leads to plug fouling and consequently to misfiring. A plug that absorbs too much heat will have no deposits, but, due to the excessive heat, the electrodes will burn away quickly and in some instances, preignition may result. Preignition takes place when plug tips get so hot that they glow sufficiently to ignite the

fuel/air mixture before the actual spark occurs. This early ignition will usually cause a pinging during low speeds and heavy loads. In severe cases, the heat may become high enough to start the fuel/air mixture burning throughout the combustion chamber rather than just to the front of the plug as in normal operation. At this time, the piston is rising in the cylinder making its compression stroke. The burning mass is compressed and an explosion results, forcing the piston back down in the cylinder while it is still trying to go up. Obviously, something must go, and it does— pistons are often damaged.

The general rule of thumb for choosing the correct heat range when picking a spark plug is: if most of your driving is long distance, high speed travel, use a colder plug; if most of your driving is stop and go, use a hotter plug. Factory-installed plugs are, of course, compromise plugs, since the factory has no way of knowing what sort of driving you do. It should be noted that most people never have occasion to change their plugs from the factory-recommended heat range.

REMOVAL AND INSTALLATION

To remove the spark plugs, remove the spark plug wire from the plug. Grasp the plug connector and, while removing, do not pull on the wire. Using a $^{13}/_{16}$ in. spark plug socket, remove the old spark plugs. Check the plugs against the spark plugs in the full color "Tune-Up Tips" Section. Examine the threads of the old plugs; if one or more of the plugs have aluminum clogged threads, it will be necessary to rethread the spark plug hole. See the following section for the necessary information.

Obtain the proper heat range and type of new plug. Set the gap by bending the side

Tune-Up Specifications

Year	Engine Code	Type	Factory Recommended Spark Plugs Type	Gap (in.)	Distributor Point Dwell (deg)	Point Gap (in.)	Ignition Timing (deg) MT	AT	Fuel Pump Pressure (psi) @ 4000 rpm	Compression Pressure (psi)	Idle Speed (rpm) MT	AT	Valve Clearance (in.) Cold In	Ex
1970	B	1, 2	Bosch W145T1 Champion L88A	.024	44–50	.016	TDC②	TDC②	3.5	114–142	800–900	900–1000	.006	.006
	U	3	Bosch W145T1 Champion L88A	.024	44–50	.016	TDC②	TDC②	28	114–142	800–900	900–1000	.006	.006
1971	AE	1, 2	Bosch W145T1 Champion L88A	.024	44–50	.016	5ATDC①	5ATDC①	3.5	114–142	800–900	900–1000	.006	.006
	U	3	Bosch W145T1 Champion L88A	.024	44–50	.016	TDC②	TDC②	28	114–142	800–900	900–1000	.006	.006
	W	4	Bosch W175T2	.024	44–50	.016	27BTDC③	27BTDC③	28	128–156	800–900	900–1000	.006	.006
1972	AE	1	Bosch W145T1 Champion L88A	.024	44–50	.016	5ATDC①	5ATDC①	3.5	107–135	800–900	900–1000	.006	.006
	AH (Calif only)	1	Bosch W145T1 Champion L88A	.024	44–50	.016	5ATDC①	5ATDC①	3.5	107–135	800–900	900–1000	.006	.006
	CB	2	Bosch W145T2 Champion N88	.024	44–50	.016	5ATDC①	—	5.0	100–135	800–900	—	.006	.006
	U, X	3	Bosch W145T1 Champion L88A	.024	44–50	.016	5BTDC②	5BTDC②	28	107–135	800–900	900–1000	.006	.006
	EA	4	Bosch W175T2	.024	44–50	.016	27BTDC③	27BTDC③	28	128–156	800–900	900–1000	.006	.006

Year	Model	No.												
1973	AK	1	1600	Bosch W145T1 Champion L88A	.024	44–50	.016	5ATDC ①④	5ATDC ①④	3.5	107–135	800–900	900–1000	.006	.006
	AH (Calif only)	1	1600	Bosch W145T1 Champion L88A	.024	44–50	.016	5ATDC ①	5ATDC ①	3.5	107–135	800–900	900–1000	.006	.006
	CB	2	1700	Bosch W145T2 Champion N88	.024	44–50	.016	10ATDC ①	—	5.0	100–135	800–900	—	.006	.008
	CD	2	1700	Bosch W145T2 Champion N88	.024	44–50	.016	—	5ATDC ①	5.0	100–135	—	900–1000	.006	.008
	U, X	3	1600	Bosch W145T1 Champion L88A	.024	44–50	.016	5BTDC ②	5BTDC ②	28	107–135	800–900	900–1000	.006	.006
	EA	4	1700	Bosch W145T2 Champion N88	.024	44–50	.016	27BTDC ③	27BTDC ③	28	128–156	800–900	900–1000	.006	.006
	EB (Calif only)	4	1700	Bosch W175T2 Champion N88	.024	44–50	.016	27BTDC ③	27BTDC ③	28	107–135	800–900	900–1000	.006	.006
1974	AK	1	1600	Bosch W145T1 Champion L88A	.024	44–50	.016	7½BTDC ②	7½BTDC ②	3.5	107–135	800–900	900–1000	.006	.006
	AH (Calif only)	1	1600	Bosch W145T1 Champion L88A	.024	44–50	.016	5ATDC ①	5ATDC ①	3.5	107–135	800–900	900–1000	.006	.006
	AW	2	1800	Bosch W175T2 Champion N88	.024	44–50	.016	10ATDC ①	5ATDC ①	5.0	85–135	800–900	900–1000	.006	.008
	EA	4	1700	Bosch W175T2 Champion N88	.024	44–50	.016	27BTDC ③	—	28	128–156	800–900	—	.006	.006
	EC	4	1800	Bosch W175T2 Champion N88	.024	44–50	.016	—	7½BTDC ②	28	85–135	—	900–1000	.006	.006

Tune-Up Specifications (cont.)

Year	Engine Code	Type	Factory Recommended Spark Plugs — Type	Gap (in.)	Distributor — Point Dwell (deg)	Distributor — Point Gap (in.)	Ignition Timing (deg) — MT	Ignition Timing (deg) — AT	Fuel Pump Pressure (psi) @ 4000 rpm	Compression Pressure (psi)	Idle Speed (rpm) — MT	Idle Speed (rpm) — AT	Valve Clearance (in.) Cold — In	Valve Clearance (in.) Cold — Ex
1975	AJ	1	Bosch W145M1 Champion L288	.024	44–50	.016	5ATDC ⑤	TDC ⑤	28	85–135	875	875	.006	.006
	ED	2	Bosch W145M2 Champion N288	.024	44–50	.016	5ATDC ⑤	5ATDC ⑤	28	85–135	900	900	.006	.006
1976–77	AJ	1	Bosch W145M1 Champion L288	.024 ⑥	44–50	.016	5ATDC ⑤	TDC ⑤	28	85–135	875	925	.006	.006
	GD	2	Bosch W145M2 Champion N288	.028	44–50	.016	7½BTDC ⑤	7½BTDC ⑤	28	85–135	900	950	.006	.006
1978	AJ	1	Bosch W145M1 Champion L288	.028 .028	44–50	.016	5ATDC	5ATDC	28	85–135	800–950	800–950	.006	.006

Year	Engine	No. Cyl.	Displacement (cc)	Spark Plugs Type	Gap (in.)	Dwell (deg)	Point Gap (in.)	Ignition Timing MT	Ignition Timing AT	(deg)	Compression (psi)	Idle Speed MT	Idle Speed AT	Valve Clearance Intake	Valve Clearance Exhaust
	GE	2	2000	Bosch W145M2 / Champion N288	.028 / .028	44–50	.016	7½BTDC	7½BTDC	28	85–135	800–950	900–1000	Hydraulic	Hydraulic / .006
1979–80	AJ	1	1600	Bosch W145M1 / Champion L288	.028 / .028	44–50	.016	5ATDC	5ATDC	28	85–135	800–950	800–950	Hydraulic	.006
1979–81	GE, CV (49 states)	2	2000	Bosch W145M2	.028	44–50	.016	7½BTDC ⑧	7½BTDC ⑧	28	85–135	850–950	850–1000	Hydraulic	Hydraulic
	GE, CV (California)	2	2000	Bosch W145M2	.028	Electronic		5ATDC ⑨⑩	5ATDC ⑨⑩	28	85–135	850–950	850–950	Hydraulic	Hydraulic

① At idle, throttle valve closed (Types 1 & 2), vacuum hose(s) on
② At idle, throttle valve closed (Types 1 & 2), vacuum hose(s) off
③ At 3,500 rpm, vacuum hose(s) off
④ From March 1973, vehicles with single diaphragm distributor (one vacuum hose); adjust timing to 7½° BTDC with hose disconnected and plugged. The starting serial numbers for those type 1 vehicles using the single diaphragm distributors are # 113 2674 897 (manual trans) and 113 2690 032 (auto stick shift)
⑤ Carbon canister hose at air cleaner disconnected; at idle; vacuum hose(s) on
MT Manual Transmission
AT Automatic Transmission
BTDC Before Top Dead Center

ATDC After Top Dead Center
⑥ 1977—.028
⑦ 5ATDC—California
⑧ Vacuum hose(s) off
⑨ Vacuum hose(s) on
⑩ Idle Stabilizer bypassed

Part numbers in this chart are not recommendations by Chilton for any product by brand name. They are references that can be used with interchange manuals and aftermarket supplier catalogs to locate each brand supplier's discrete part number.

electrode only. Do not bend the center electrode to adjust the gap. The proper gap is listed in the "Tune-Up Specifications" chart. Lubricate the plug threads.

Start each new plug in its hole using your fingers. Tighten the plug several turns by hand to assure that the plug is not cross-threaded. Using a wrench, tighten the plug just enough to compress the gasket. Do not overtighten the plug. Consult the torque specifications chart.

RETHREADING SPARK PLUG HOLE

It is possible to repair light damage to spark plug hole threads by using a spark plug hole tap of the proper diameter and thread. Plenty of grease should be used on the tap to catch any metal chips. Exercise caution when using the tap as it is possible to cut a second set of threads instead of straightening the old ones.

If the old threads are beyond repair, then the hole must be drilled and tapped to accept a steel bushing or Heli-Coil®. It is not always necessary to remove the cylinder head to rethread the spark plug holes. Bushing kits, Heli-Coil® kits, and spark plug hole taps are available at most auto parts stores. Heli-Coil® information is contained in the "Engine Rebuilding" section of this book.

CHECKING AND REPLACING SPARK PLUG CABLES

Visually inspect the spark plug cables for burns, cuts, or breaks in the insulation. Check the spark plug boots and the nipples on the distributor cap and coil. Replace any damaged wiring. If no physical damage is obvious, the wires can be checked with an ohmmeter for excessive resistance. Remove the distributor cap and leave the wires connected to the cap. Connect one lead of the ohmmeter to the corresponding electrode inside the cap and the other lead to the spark plug terminal (remove it from the spark plug for the test). Remove the static suppressor boot from the end of the cable by un-screwing it before testing cable. Replace any wire which shows over 50,000 ohms. Generally speaking, however, resistance should not run over 35,000 ohms and 50,000 ohms should be considered the outer limits of acceptability. Test the coil wire by connecting the ohmmeter between the center contact in the cap and either of the primary terminals at the coil. If the total resistance of the coil and cable is more than 25,000 ohms, remove the cable

from the coil and check the resistance of the cable alone. If the resistance is higher than 15,000 ohms, replace the cable. It should be remembered that wire resistance is a function of length, and that the longer the cable, the greater the resistance. Thus, if the cables on your car are longer than the factory originals, resistance will be higher and quite possibly outside of these limits. Test the static suppressor boots separately—resistance should not exceed 5000–10,000 ohms.

When installing a new set of spark plug cables, replace the cables one at a time so there will be no mixup. Start by replacing the longest cable first. Install the boot firmly over the spark plug. Route the wire exactly the same as the original. Insert the nipple firmly into the tower on the distributor cap. Repeat the process for each cable.

Breaker Points and Condenser
REMOVAL AND INSTALLATION

1. Release the spring clips which secure the distributor cap and lift the cap from the distributor. Pull the rotor from the distributor shaft.

2. Disconnect the points wire from the condenser snap connection (1) inside the distributor.

3. Remove the locking screw (2) from the stationary breaker point.

4. To remove the condenser which is located on the outside of the distributor, remove the screw which secures the condenser bracket and condenser connection to the distributor.

5. Disconnect the condenser wire from the coil.

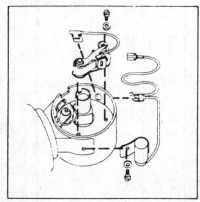

Typical breaker points and condenser location on distributor

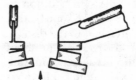

CORRECT LATERAL MISALIGNMENT BY BENDING FIXED CONTACT SUPPORT. **NEVER BEND BREAKER LEVER**

Make sure point surfaces are aligned

Breaker point removal is accomplished by disconnecting snap connection and removing attaching screw

6. With a clean rag, wipe the excess oil from the breaker plate.

NOTE: *Make sure that the new point contacts are clean and oil free.*

7. Installation of the point set and condenser is the reverse of the above; however, it will be necessary to adjust the point gap, also known as the dwell, and check the timing. Lubricate the point cam with a small amount of lithium or white grease. Set the dwell, or gap, before the ignition timing.

POINT GAP ADJUSTMENT

1. Remove the distributor cap and rotor.
2. Turn the engine by hand until the fiber rubbing block on the movable breaker point rests on a high point of the cam lobe. The point gap is the maximum distance between the points and must be set at the top of a cam lobe.

Adjust the points using a screwdriver and feeler gauge

3. Using a screwdriver, slightly loosen the locking screw. Make sure that the feeler gauge is clean. After tightening the screw, recheck the gap.

4. Move the stationary point plate so that the gap is set as specified and then tighten the screw. Make sure that the feeler gauge is clean. After tightening the screw, recheck the gap.

5. It is important to set the point gap before setting the timing.

Dwell Angle

Setting the dwell angle with a dwell meter achieves the same effect as setting the point gap but offers better accuracy.

NOTE: *The dwell must be set before setting the timing. Setting the dwell will alter the timing, but when the timing is set, the dwell will not change.*

Attach the positive lead of the dwell meter to that coil terminal which has a wire leading to the distributor. The negative lead should be attached to a good ground.

Remove the distributor cap and rotor. Turn the ignition ON and turn the engine over using the starter or a remote starter switch. Read the dwell from the meter and open or close the points to adjust the dwell.

NOTE: *Increasing the gap decreases the dwell and decreasing the gap increases the dwell.*

Dwell specifications are listed in the "Tune-Up Specifications" chart.

Reinstall the cap and rotor and start the engine. Check the dwell and reset it if necessary.

Electronic Ignition System

1979–81 Type 2s destined for California are equipped with a Hall Effect electronic ignition system which does away with the convention breaker points and condenser used on all other models in this book.

Located in the distributor, in addition to the normal rotor cap, is a round, four bladed rotor unit. This unit is attached to the distributor shaft below the rotor cap and in about the same position as the breaker points cam on conventional ignition systems. Mounted on the distributor base, in about the same position as the breaker points on conventional ignition systems, is a pickup coil unit.

The basic operating principle of the Hall Effect ignition is this: the rotor unit revolves with the top rotor cap and, as each of its four blades passes between the stationary pick-up coils, a magnetic shift occurs which signals the control unit to break primary ignition current in the coil and thus generate the spark. The control unit is used in conjunction with an idle stabilizer unit which controls idle speed according to engine load by adjusting the ignition timing. The idle stabilizer must be by-passed to adjust the idle speed and timing.

To bypass the idle stabilizer, remove its two leads and connect them together as shown. Ignition control unit is to right of stabilizer—electronic ignition models

ELECTRONIC IGNITION PRECAUTION

To avoid damaging the electronic ignition system, always observe the following:
• Do not disconnect and connect ignition system wires with the ignition switch in the ON position (whether the engine is running or not);
• Do not install any ignition coil except the factory recommended one (part No. 211 905 115 C);
• To disable the engine to prevent it from starting while performing any of the several tests in this book (compression test, etc.), disconnect the high tension wire from the

center of the distributor cap and connect it to ground;
• Never attempt to connect a condenser to terminal 1 (−) of the ignition coil;
• Do not connect a quick charger to the battery for longer than one minute when attempting to boost start the engine;
• Do not disconnect the battery with the engine running;
• Do not wash the engine while it is running;
• Do not electric weld the vehicle with the battery connected;
• Disconnect the plug at the ignition control unit when towing a car with a damaged ignition system;
• Do not connect test instruments with a 12V supply on terminal 15 of ignition coil.

ELECTRONIC IGNITION MAINTENANCE

Periodic maintenance is not required on the Hall Effect ignition system, as it has no points and condenser. It would be wise to check the distributor cap and rotor cap for cracks and wear occasionally.

TROUBLESHOOTING THE ELECTRONIC IGNITION

All troubleshooting should be left to a qualified technician as for the most part, substitution of components is the usual method. The ignition coil can be checked using an ohmmeter, but the reading for primary resistance is so low (0.65 ohm) that the standard ohmmeter normally cannot measure it. The best method for checking the coil (if you're on good terms with your dealer) is to substitute another coil with the same part number and see if it works.

Ignition Timing

Dwell or point gap must be set before the timing is set. Also, the idle speed must be set to specifications.

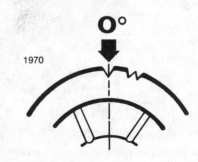

Type 1—1970 engines

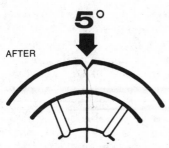

Type 1—carburetor cars from August 1970 to spring 1973 and fuel injected cars with manual transmissions

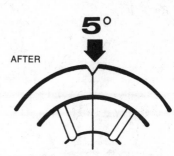

Type 2—1971 engines

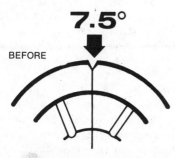

Type 1—carbureted cars with a single vacuum hose to the distributor, starting spring 1973

Type 2—1972 all engines, 1972–74 models equipped with automatic transmissions, and 1975 all models

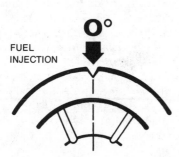

Type 1—fuel injected cars equipped with the Automatic Stick Shift

Type 2—1973–74 carbureted models with manual transmissions

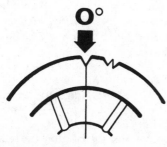

Type 2—1970 engines

Type 2—1976–81 fuel injected models—except 1979–81 California

5°ATDC CALIF.

Type 2—1979–81 California

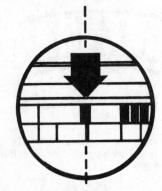

Type 3—1970–71 engines

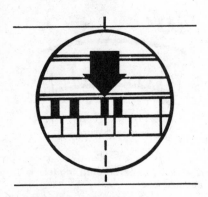

Type 3—1972–73 engines

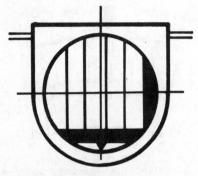

Type 4—1971–74 engines

NOTE: *the engine must be warmed up before the timing is set (oil temperature of 122°F–158°F.).*

1. Connect timing light. On most VWs, you won't be able to hook the timing light power leads to the battery, therefore, connect the positive lead from the timing light to terminal #15 on the ignition coil, and hook the negative lead from the test light to ground (intake manifold, etc.). This procedure is for DC lights only and cannot be used on Hall electronic ignition systems.

After hooking up the timing light according to manufacturer's instructions, disconnect the vacuum hose if so advised by the "Tune-up Specifications" chart and re-adjust the idle speed if necessary.

NOTE: *On Hall electronic ignition systems, the idle stabilizer must be bypassed before the idle can be adjusted. See the illustration.*

2. Start the engine and run it at the specified rpm. Aim the timing light at the crankshaft pulley on upright fan engines and at the engine cooling fan on the suitcase engines. The rubber plug in the fan housing will have to be removed before the timing marks on Type 3 and Type 4 engines can be seen.

3. Read the timing and rotate the distributor accordingly.

NOTE: *Rotate the distributor in the opposite direction of normal rotor rotation to advance the timing. Retard the timing by turning the distributor in the normal direction of rotor rotation.*

4. It is necessary to loosen the clamp at the base of the distributor before the distributor can be rotated. It may also be necessary to put a small amount of white paint or chalk on the timing marks to make them more visible.

Valve Lash Adjustment

NOTE: *1978–81 Type 2 models have hydraulic lifters that require no adjustment.*

Preference should be given to the valve clearance specified on the engine fan housing sticker, if they differ from those in the "Tune-Up Specifications" chart.

NOTE: *The engine must be as cool as possible before adjusting the valves.*

NOTE: *If the spark plugs are removed, rotating the crankshaft from position to position will be much easier.*

1. Remove the distributor cap and turn the engine until the rotor points to the No.

one spark plug wire post in the distributor cap. To bring the piston to exactly top dead center (TDC) on the compression stroke, align the crankshaft timing marks on TDC.

2. Remove the rocker arm covers. At TDC, the pushrods should be down and there should be clearance between the rocker arms and valve stems of both valves of the subject cylinder.

3. With the proper feeler gauge, check the clearance between the adjusting screw and the valve stem of both valves for the No. 1 cylinder (see cylinder numbering diagram). If the feeler gauge slides in snugly without being forced, the clearance is correct. It is better that the clearance is a little loose than a little tight, as a tight adjustment may result in burned exhaust valves. While a little looseness is somewhat desirable, too much looseness will cause the tappets to rap loudly as the engine reaches operating temperature. This is because the cylinder barrels and the heads on the engine expand or "grow" when hot, whereas the valve pushrods do not. This

Checking valve clearance with feeler gauge

growing action increases the valve lash slightly.

4. If the clearance is incorrect, the locknut must be loosened and the adjustment screw turned until the proper clearance is obtained. After tightening down the locknut, it

No. 1 piston at Top Dead Center—Types 1, 2/1600

No. 1 piston at Top Dead Center—Type 3

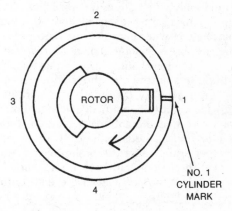

DISTRIBUTOR FIRING ORDER
1-4-3-2

ROTOR

NO. 1
CYLINDER
MARK

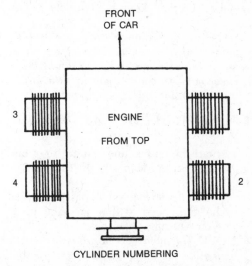

FRONT
OF CAR

ENGINE

FROM TOP

CYLINDER NUMBERING

Cylinder numbering and firing order diagram

is then advisable to recheck the clearance. It is possible to accidently alter the adjustment when tightening the locknut.

5. The valves are adjusted in a 1-2-3-4 (exact opposite of firing [1-4-3-2] order) sequence. To adjust cylinders 2 through 4, the distributor rotor must be pointed at the appropriate distributor cap post 90° apart from each other. In addition, the crankshaft must be rotated counterclockwise (opposite normal rotation) in 180° degree increments to adjust valves 2, 3 and 4.

NOTE: *There should be a red paint mark on the crankshaft 180° opposite of the TDC mark for adjusting valves 2 and 4.*

NOTE: *Always use new valve cover gaskets.*

Fuel System Adjustments

CARBURETOR IDLE SPEED AND MIXTURE

A carburetor adjustment should be performed only after all other variables in a tune-up have been checked and adjusted. This includes checking valve clearance, spark plug gap, breaker point gap and/or dwell angle, and ignition timing. Prior to making any carburetor adjustments, the engine should be brought to operating temperature (122–158°F oil temperature) and you should make sure that the automatic choke is fully open and off of the fast idle cam. Once you have performed all of the preliminary steps, shut off the engine and hook up a tachometer. Connect the hot lead to the distributor side of the ignition coil and the ground wire to an engine bolt or other good metal to metal connection. Keep the wire clear of the fan.

NOTE: *An improper carburetor adjustment may have an adverse effect on exhaust emission levels. If any doubt exists, check your state laws regarding the adjusting of emission control equipment.*

Solex 30 PICT-3 (1970 Type 1 and Type 2 Models)

1. Start the engine and bring it to operating temperature. Make sure the car is in neutral.

2. Using the idle speed (bypass) screw, adjust the idle speed to that specified in the "Tune-Up Specifications" chart.

NOTE: *The bypass screw adjustment is the only adjustment that should be made to 30 PICT-3 carburetor. Do not attempt to ad-*

just the mixture or idle speed by turning the throttle valve adjustment screw, as increased exhaust emissions or poor driveability would result. The bypass screw is the larger adjustment screw.*

Solex PICT-3 (1971–74 Type 1 Models, 1971 Type 2 Models) and Solex 34 PICT-4 (1973–74 Type 1 California Models)

1. Start the engine and bring it to operating temperature. Make sure the car is in neutral.

2. Shut off the engine. On 1971 models, turn out the throttle valve adjustment screw until it clears the fast idle cam. Then turn in the screw until it makes contact with the fast idle cam. Finally, turn the throttle valve adjusting screw in another one-quarter turn.

3. Slowly turn in the idle mixture (volume control) screw until it bottoms. Then, carefully counting the complete revolutions of the screwdriver, turn it out 2½ to 3 turns.

4. With a tachometer connected to the engine as previously described, start the engine.

5. Using the idle speed (bypass) screw, adjust the idle speed to specifications. Then, using the idle mixture (volume control) screw, adjust until the fastest idle is obtained. Observing the tachometer, turn the volume control screw until the engine speed drops by 20–30 rpm.

6. Finally, using the bypass screw, adjust the idle to specifications.

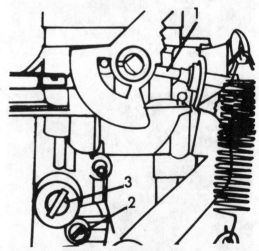

1. Throttle valve adjustment
2. Volume control (mixture) screw
3. By-pass (idle speed) screw

Solex 34 PICT-3 and 34 PICT-4 idle adjustments (30 PICT-3 similar)

Solex 34 PDST-2/3 Twin Carb (1972–74 Type 2 Models

PERIODIC ADJUSTMENT

1. Start the engine and bring it to operating temperature (122–158°F oil temperature). Make sure the car is in neutral and the parking brake firmly applied.

2. Using the central idle speed adjusting screw (4) on the left carburetor, adjust the idle speed to that listed in the "Tune-Up Specifications" chart.

3a. If a CO meter/exhaust analyzer is available, adjust the carbon monoxide (CO) level to 1–3% CO using the central mixture control screw (5) also on the left carburetor.

3b. If a CO meter is not available, the following procedure is used: First, slowly turn the central mixture control screw (5) in (clockwise) until the engine speed drops noticeably, then turn the screw out (counterclockwise) until maximum idle speed is attained. Next, turn the screw in once again until rpm drops to 20–50 rpm. Finally, turn the screw out ¼ turn.

4. Recheck the idle speed, and adjust as necessary using the central idle speed adjusting screw (4) on the left carburetor.

5. If a satisfactory idle cannot be obtained using this procedure, proceed to "Basic Adjustment."

BASIC ADJUSTMENT

Whenever a carburetor has been removed for service, or if a new or rebuilt carburetor has been installed, a basic carburetor adjustment should be performed.

NOTE: *The throttle valve setting (distance "a") must be 0.004 in.*

NOTE: *An exhaust analyzer/CO meter and tachometer is required for this adjustment.*

1. Check the synchronization of the carburetors as outlined under "Balancing Multiple Carburetor Installations."

2. Disconnect the throttle linkage rod from the right carburetor.

3. Disconnect the vacuum retard hose from the distributor.

4. Disconnect the cut-off valve wire at the central idling system. Disconnect and plug the left side air pump hose (1973–74 models).

5. Turn the idle volume control screws (6) in on both carburetors until they contact their seats.

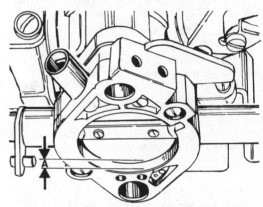

34 PDSIT-2/3 carburetors, the throttle valve closing gap (distance "a") must be 0.004 in.

Terminal connection for central idling system electromagnetic cut-off valve—34 PDSIT-2

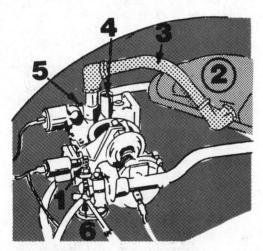

1. Synchronizing screw
2. Central idling system left end piece
3. Central idling system left end connecting hose
4. Central idling (idle speed) adjusting screw
5. Central mixture control screw
6. Volume control screw

Type 2 twin carb adjustments—34 PICT-2 (left carburetor shown)

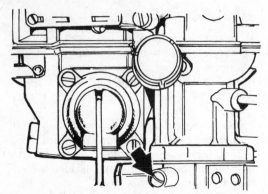

Arrow indicates volume control screw in throttle bodies of 34 PDSIT-2, 34 PDSIT-3 (right) carburetors

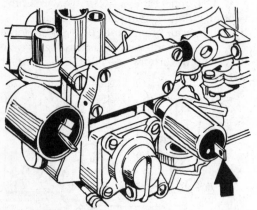

Terminal connection for idling cut-off valve of both right and left carburetors

CAUTION: *Do not force the screws or the tips may become distorted.*

Then, turn both screws out exactly 2½ turns.

6. Start the engine and bring it to operating temperature (122–158°F oil temperature). Set the idle speed to 500–700 rpm by equally adjusting both volume control screws (6).

7. Disconnect the wire from the electromagnetic idling cut-off valve (smaller of the two valves) at the left carburetor and note the decrease in idle speed. Then, repeat this operation for the right carburetor. The idle speed drop should be equal for both sides. If not, readjust the volume control screws accordingly.

8. Connect the wire for the cut-off valve at the central idling system. Unplug, and connect the left air pump hose. Connect the vacuum retard hose.

9. Take the engine through the upper rpm range for a few quick bursts. Then, adjust the

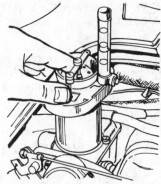

Airflow meter installed on left carburetor

idle speed to specifications as outlined under steps 2–5 of "Periodic Adjustment."

BALANCING MULTIPLE CARBURETOR INSTALLATIONS

Synchronizing 1972–74 Type 2 Twin Carb

If a carburetor has been removed or disassembled, or if any part of the linkage has been repaired, the carburetors must be synchronized prior to performing any idle adjustments. To synchronize the carburetors, a special instrument is used to measure air flow, such as the UniSyn® or Auto-Syn®. This commonly available device measures the vacuum created inside the carburetors and provides an index for adjusting the carburetors equally. In order to use the air flow gauge on the 34 PDSIT carburetors, a special diameter adaptor (or a small frozen juice can with both ends removed) must be used.

1. Disconnect the linkage connecting rod from the lower socket of the right carburetor. Without moving the throttle from its closed position, you should be able to snap the linkage connecting rod back onto the socket for the right carburetor. If the ball and socket at the right carburetor do not align perfectly, for 1972 models, adjust with the synchronizing screw (1) at the left carburetor; on 1973–74 models, adjust the length of the connecting rod on the right carburetor until the rod can be snapped onto the socket without disturbing the throttle from its fully closed position. Connect the linkage and hook up a tachometer.

2. Remove the air cleaner ducts from the tops of both carburetors, taking care to leave the central idle system connecting hose (3) and left end piece (2) connected.

3. Start the engine and bring it to operating temperature (122–158°F oil tempera-

ture). Make sure the choke flaps are fully open. Using the air flow meter, balance the carburetors using the synchronizing screw (1) on the left carburetor on 1972 models or the connecting rod on the right carburetor on 1973–74 models. Balance the carburetors with the engine running at 2000–3000 rpm.

4. Adjust the idle speed to specifications.

FUEL INJECTION IDLE SPEED

All Type 3 and Type 4, 1975 and Later Type 1 and Type 2

NOTE: *The idle stabilizer on "Hall Effect" electronic ignitions must be bypassed before the idle is set. See electronic ignition section, above, for procedures.*

The idle speed is adjusted by a screw located on the left side of the intake air distributor. To adjust the idle speed, loosen the

locknut (Type 3 only) and turn the screw with a screwdriver until the idle speed is adjusted to specification. Turning the screw clockwise decreases idle speed, counterclockwise increases idle speed.

On automatic transmission Type 4 and 1975–76 Type 2 models, the idle speed regulator should also be adjusted. With the vehicle idling at 900–1,000 RPM in Park or Neutral, measure "a" in the illustration. It should be 0.020–0.040 in. If not, adjust at arrow. See Chapter 4 for a test for the idle speed regulator.

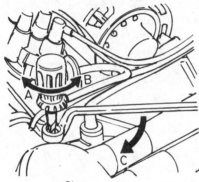

a. Slower
b. Faster
c. Tighten locknut

Fuel injection idle speed adjustment—Type 3

Fuel injection idle speed adjustment (by-pass screw)—1975–81 Type 2

Fuel injection idle speed adjustment—Type 4

Fuel injection idle speed (by-pass screw) Adjustment—1975–80 Type 1

Idling speed regulator dashpot adjustment—type 4 and 1975–76 type 2 automatic transmission models (distance "A" is 0.020–0.040 in.)

If turning the screw either in or out does not noticeably affect idle speed, check for the following:

a. Air leaks in the intake manifold system.

b. Air leaks into the crankcase (make sure the oil cap is on correctly).

c. Faulty EGR components (See Chapter 4).

d. If the bypass screw must be turned fully in to lower the idle speed, or if the idle speed is fast prior to adjustment, check the auxiliary air regulator as covered in Chapter 4. If the auxiliary air regulator is OK, check the pressure regulator and deceleration valve as described in Chapter 4.

If, after checking these systems, the bypass screw still makes little change in the idle speed, it is possible that someone has fiddled with the throttle valve adjustment screw. Refer this operation to a competent mechanic.

FUEL INJECTION IDLE MIXTURE

The idle mixture must be adjusted using an exhaust gas analyzer, a tool not usually owned by amateur mechanics; therefore idle mixture adjustment procedures are not given here. The idle mixture does not have to be adjusted unless exhaust emissions are above specified levels, the intake air sensor is replaced or after an engine overhaul.

Engine and Engine Rebuilding

ENGINE ELECTRICAL

Understanding the Engine Electrical System

The engine electrical system can be broken down into three separate and distinct systems: (1) the starting system; (2) the charging system; (3) the ignition system.

BATTERY AND STARTING SYSTEM

The battery is the first link in the chain of mechanisms which work together to provide cranking of the automobile engine. In most modern cars, the battery is a lead-acid electrochemical device consisting of six two-volt (2 V) subsections connected in series so the unit is capable of producing approximately 12 V of electrical pressure. Each subsection, or cell, consists of a series of positive and negative plates held a short distance apart in a solution of sulfuric acid and water. The two types of plates are of dissimilar metals. This causes a chemical reaction to be set up, and it is this reaction which produces current flow from the battery when its positive and negative terminals are connected to an electrical appliance such as a lamp or motor. The continued transfer of electrons would eventually convert the sulfuric acid in the electrolyte to water, and make the two plates identical in chemical composition. As electrical energy is removed from the battery, its voltage output tends to drop. Thus, measuring battery voltage and battery electrolyte composition are two ways of checking the ability of the unit to supply power. During the starting of the engine, electrical energy is removed from the battery. However, if the charging circuit is in good condition and the operating conditions are normal, the power removed from the battery will be replaced by the generator (or alternator) which will force electrons back through the battery, reversing the normal flow, and restoring the battery to its original chemical state.

The battery and starting motor are linked by very heavy electrical cables designed to minimize resistance to the flow of current. Generally, the major power supply cable that leaves the battery goes directly to the starter, while other electrical system needs are supplied by a smaller cable. During starter operation, power flows from the battery to the starter and is grounded through the car's frame and the battery's negative ground strap.

The starting motor is a specially designed, direct current electric motor capable of producing a very great amount of power for its size. One thing that allows the motor to produce a great deal of power is its tremendous rotating speed. It drives the engine through a tiny pinion gear (attached to the starter's armature), which drives the very large flywheel ring gear at a greatly reduced speed. Another factor allowing it to produce so much power is that only intermittent operation is required of it. Thus, little allowance for air circulation is required, and the windings can be built into a very small space.

The starter solenoid is a magnetic device which employs the small current supplied by the starting switch circuit of the ignition switch. This magnetic action moves a plunger which mechanically engages the starter and electrically closes the heavy switch which connects it to the battery. The starting switch circuit consists of the starting switch contained within the ignition switch, a transmission neutral safety switch or clutch pedal switch, and the wiring necessary to connect these in series with the starter solenoid or relay.

A pinion, which is a small gear, is mounted to a one-way drive clutch. This clutch is splined to the starter armature shaft. When the ignition switch is moved to the "start" position, the solenoid plunger slides the pinion toward the flywheel ring gear via a collar and spring. If the teeth on the pinion and flywheel match properly, the pinion will engage the flywheel immediately. If the gear teeth butt one another, the spring will be compressed and will force the gears to mesh as soon as the starter turns far enough to allow them to do so. As the solenoid plunger reaches the end of its travel, it closes the contacts that connect the battery and starter and then the engine is cranked.

As soon as the engine starts, the flywheel ring gear begins turning fast enough to drive the pinion at an extremely high rate of speed. At this point, the one-way clutch begins allowing the pinion to spin faster than the starter shaft so that the starter will not operate at excessive speed. When the ignition switch is released from the starter position, the solenoid is de-energized, and a spring contained within the solenoid assembly pulls the gear out of mesh and interrupts the current flow to the starter.

Some starters employ a separate relay, mounted away from the starter, to switch the motor and solenoid current on and off. The relay thus replaces the solenoid electrical switch, but does not eliminate the need for a solenoid mounted on the starter used to mechanically engage the starter drive gears. The relay is used to reduce the amount of current the starting switch must carry.

THE CHARGING SYSTEM

The automobile charging system provides electrical power for operation of the vehicle's ignition and starting systems and all the electrical accessories. The battery serves as an electrical surge or storage tank, storing (in chemical form) the energy originally produced by the engine-driven generator. The system also provides a means of regulating generator output to protect the battery from being overcharged and to avoid excessive voltage to the accessories.

The storage battery is a chemical device incorporating parallel lead plates in a tank containing a sulfuric acid-water solution. Adjacent plates are slightly dissimilar, and the chemical reaction of the two dissimilar plates produces electrical energy when the battery is connected to a load such as the starter motor. The chemical reaction is reversible, so that when the generator is producing a voltage (electrical pressure) greater than that produced by the battery, electricity is forced into the battery, and the battery is returned to its fully charged state.

The vehicle's generator is driven mechanically, through V belts, by the engine crankshaft. It consists of two coils of fine wire, one stationary (the "stator"), and one movable (the "rotor"). The rotor may also be known as the "armature," and consists of fine wire wrapped around an iron core which is mounted on a shaft. The electricity which flows through the two coils of wire (provided initially by the battery in some cases) creates an intense magnetic field around both rotor and stator, and the interaction between the two fields creates voltage, allowing the generator to power the accessories and charge the battery.

There are two types of generators; the earlier is the direct current (DC) type. The current produced by the DC generator is generated in the armature and carried off the spinning armature by stationary brushes contacting the commutator. The commutator is a series of smooth metal contact plates on the end of the armature. The commutator plates, which are separated from one another by a very short gap, are connected to the armature circuits so that current will flow in one direction only in the wires carrying the generator output. The generator stator consists of two stationary coils of wire which draw some of the output current of the generator to form a powerful magnetic field and create the interaction of fields which generates the voltage. The generator field is wired in series with the regulator.

Newer automobiles use alternating current generators or "alternators," because they are more efficient, can be rotated at higher speeds, and have fewer brush problems. In an alternator, the field rotates while all the current produced passes only through the stator windings. The brushes bear against continuous slip rings rather than a commutator. This causes the current produced to periodically reverse the direction of its flow. Diodes (electrical one-way switches) block the flow of current from traveling in the wrong direction. A series of diodes is wired together to permit the alternating flow of the stator to be converted to a pulsating, but unidirectional flow at the alternator output. The alternator's field is wired in series with the voltage regulator.

The regulator consists of several circuits. Each circuit has a core, or magnetic coil of wire, which operates a switch. Each switch is connected to ground through one or more resistors. The coil of wire responds directly to system voltage. When the voltage reaches the required level, the magnetic field created by the winding of wire closes the switch and inserts a resistance into the generator field circuit, thus reducing the output. The contacts of the switch cycle open and close many times each second to precisely control voltage.

While alternators are self-limiting as far as maximum current is concerned, DC generators employ a current regulating circuit which responds directly to the total amount of current flowing through the generator circuit rather than to the output voltage. The current regulator is similar to the voltage regulator except that all system current must flow through the energizing coil on its way to the various accessories.

Safety Precautions

Observing these precautions will ensure safe handling of the electrical system components, and will avoid damage to the vehicle's electrical system.

A. Be *absolutely* sure of the polarity of a booster battery before making connections. Connect the cables positive to positive, and negative to negative. Connect positive cables first and then make the last connection to a ground on the body of the booster vehicle so that arcing cannot ignite hydrogen gas that may have accumulated near the battery. Even momentary connection of a booster battery with the polarity reserved will damage alternator diodes.

B. Disconnect both vehicle battery cables before attempting to charge a battery.

C. Never ground the alternator or generator output or battery terminal. Be cautious when using metal tools around a battery to avoid creating a short circuit between the terminals.

D. Never ground the field circuit between the alternator and regulator.

E. Never run an alternator or generator without load unless the field circuit is disconnected.

F. Never attempt to polarize an alternator.

G. Keep the regulator cover in place when taking voltage and current limiter readings.

H. Use insulated tools when adjusting the regulator.

I. Whenever DC generator-to-regulator wires have been disconnected, the generator *must* be repolarized. To do this with an externally grounded, light duty generator, momentarily place a jumper wire between the battery terminal and the generator terminal of the regulator. With an internally grounded heavy duty unit, disconnect the wire to the regulator field terminal and touch the regulator battery terminal with it.

POINT-TYPE IGNITION SYSTEMS

NOTE: *See Chapter 2 for electronic ignition information.*

There are two basic functions the automotive ignition system must perform: (1) it must control the spark and the timing of the firing to match varying engine requirements; (2) it must increase battery voltage to a point where it will overcome the resistance offered by the spark plug gap and fire the plug.

To accomplish this, an automotive ignition system is divided into two electrical circuits. One circuit, called the primary circuit, is the low voltage circuit. This circuit operates only on battery current and is controlled by the breaker points and the ignition switch. The second circuit is the high voltage circuit, and is called the secondary circuit. This circuit consists of the secondary windings in the coil, the high tension lead between the distributor and the coil (commonly called the coil wire), the distributor cap and rotor, the spark plug leads and the spark plugs.

The coil is the heart of the ignition system. Essentially, a coil is nothing more than a transformer which takes the relatively low voltage available from the battery and increases it to a point where it will fire the spark plug. This increase is quite large, since modern coils produce on the order of about 40,000 volts. The term "coil" is perhaps a misnomer since a coil consists of *two* coils of wire wound about an iron core. These coils are insulated from each other and the whole assembly is enclosed in an oil-filled case. The primary coil is connected to the two primary terminals located on top of the coil and consists of relatively few turns of heavy wire. The secondary coil consists of many turns of fine wire and is connected to the high tension connection on top of the coil. This secondary connection is simply the tower into which the coil wire from the distributor is plugged.

Energizing the coil primary with battery voltage produces current flow through the primary windings. This in turn produces a very large, intense magnetic field. Interrupting the flow of primary current causes the field to collapse. Just as current moving through a wire produces a magnetic field, moving a field across a wire will produce a current. As the magnetic field collapses, its lines of force cross the secondary windings, inducing a current in them. The force of the induced current is concentrated because of the relative shortness of the secondary coil of wire.

The distributor is the controlling element of the system, switching the primary current on and off and distributing the current to the proper spark plug each time a spark is produced. It is basically a stationary housing surrounding a rotating shaft. The shaft is driven at one-half engine speed by the engine's camshaft through the distributor drive gears. A cam which is situated near the top of the shaft has one lobe for each cylinder of the engine. The cam operates the ignition contact points, which are mounted on a plate located on bearings within the distributor housing. A rotor is attached to the top of the distributor shaft. When the bakelite distributor cap is in place, on top of the unit's metal housing, a spring-loaded contact connects the portion of the rotor directly above the center of the shaft to the center connection on top of the distributor. The outer end of the rotor passes

very close to the contacts connected to the four, six, or eight high-tension connections around the outside of the distributor cap.

Under normal operating conditions, power from the battery is fed through a resistor or resistance wire to the primary circuit of the coil and is then grounded through the ignition points in the distributor. During cranking, the full voltage of the battery is supplied through an auxiliary circuit routed through the solenoid switch. In an eight-cylinder engine, the distributor cam will allow the points to close about 60 crankshaft degrees before the firing of the spark plug. Current will begin flowing through the primary wiring to the positive connection on the coil, through the primary winding of the coil, through the ground wire between the negative connection on the coil and the distributor, and to ground through the contact points. Shortly after the engine is ready to fire, the current flow through the coil primary will have reached a near maximum value, and an intense magnetic field will have formed around the primary windings. The distributor cam will separate the contact points at the proper time for ignition and the primary field will collapse, causing current to flow in the secondary circuit. A capacitor, known as the "condenser," is installed in the circuit in parallel with the contact points in order to absorb some of the force of the electrical surge that occurs during collapse of the magnetic field. The condenser consists of several layers of aluminum foil separated by insulation. These layers of foil, upon an increase in voltage, are capable of storing electricity, making the condenser a sort of electrical surge tank. Voltages just after the points open may reach 250 V because of the vast amount of energy stored in the primary windings and their magnetic field. A condenser which is defective or improperly grounded will not absorb the shock from the fast-moving stream of electrons when the points open and these electrons will force their way across the point gap, causing burning and pitting.

The very high voltage induced in the secondary windings will cause a surge of current to flow from the coil tower to the center of the distributor, where it will travel along the connecting strip along the top of the rotor. The surge will arc its way across the short gap between the contact on the outer end of the rotor and the connection in the cap for the high-tension lead of the cylinder to be fired. After passing along the high-tension lead, it will travel down the center electrode of the spark plug, which is surrounded by ceramic insulation, and arc its way over to the side electrode, which is grounded through threads which hold the plug in the cylinder head. The heat generated by the passage of the spark will ignite the contents of the cylinder.

Most distributors employ both centrifugal and vacuum advance mechanisms to advance the point at which ignition occurs for optimum performance and economy. Spark generally occurs a few degrees before the piston reaches top dead center (TDC) in order that very high pressures will exist in the cylinder as soon as the piston is capable of using the energy—just a few degrees after TDC. Centrifugal advance mechanisms employ hinged flyweights working in opposition to springs to turn the top portion of the distributor shaft, including the cam and rotor, ahead of the lower shaft. This advances the point at which the cam causes the points to open. A more advanced spark is required at higher engine speeds because the speed of combustion does not increase in direct proportion to increases in engine speed, but tends to lag behind at high revolutions. If peak cylinder pressures are to exist at the same point, advance must be used to start combustion earlier.

Vacuum advance is used to accomplish the same thing when part-throttle operation reduces the speed of combustion because of less turbulence and compression, and poorer scavenging of exhaust gases. Carburetor vacuum below the throttle plate is channeled to a vacuum diaphragm mounted on the distributor. The higher the manifold vacuum, the greater the motion of the diaphragm against spring pressure. A rod between the diaphragm and the plate on which the contact points are mounted rotates the plate on its bearings causing the cam to open the points earlier in relation to the position of the crankshaft.

Ignition Coil
PRIMARY RESISTANCE CHECK (NON-ELECTRONIC IGNITION)

1. Disconnect all wires from the ignition coil.
2. Connect ohmmeter leads to terminals 15 (positive) and 1 (negative) on the top of the coil.
3. The ohmmeter should read between

1.7 and 2.1 ohms. If much higher, replace the coil.

SECONDARY RESISTANCE CHECK (NON-ELECTRONIC IGNITION)

1. Disconnect all wires from the ignition coil.
2. Connect ohmmeter leads to terminals 1 (negative) and 4 (large, center plug-in terminal).
3. The ohmmeter should read between 7,000 and 12,000 ohms. If much higher, replace the coil.

ELECTRONIC IGNITION COIL

The coil can be checked, but the primary resistance reading is too low to be read on a standard ohmmeter. The best way to check the coil is to substitute another of the same part number and see if it works. See Chapter 2 under Electronic Ignition for more information on electronic ignition.

Distributor
REMOVAL AND INSTALLATION

1. Take off the vacuum hoses at the distributor.
2. Disconnect the coil wire and remove the distributor cap.
3. Disconnect the condenser wire.
4. Bring No. 1 cylinder to top dead center

Type 4 timing mark and distributor rotor alignment

(TDC) on the compression stroke by rotating the engine so that the rotor points to the No. 1 spark plug wire tower on the distributor cap and the timing marks are aligned at 0°. Mark the rotor-to-distributor relationship. Also match mark the distributor housing-to-crankcase relationship.

5. Unscrew the distributor retaining screw on the crankcase and lift the distributor out.

6. If the engine has been rotated since the distributor was removed, bring the No. 1 cylinder to TDC on the compression stroke and align the timing marks on 0°. Align the match marks and insert the distributor into the crankcase. If the match marks are gone, have the rotor pointing to the No. 1 spark plug wire tower upon insertion.

7. Replace the distributor retaining screw and reconnect the condenser and coil wires. Reinstall the distributor cap.

8. Retime the engine.

DISTRIBUTOR DRIVESHAFT REMOVAL AND INSTALLATION

1. On carbureted engines remove the fuel pump.

2. Bring the engine to TDC on the compression stroke of No. 1 cylinder. Align the timing marks at 0°.

3. Remove the distributor.

4. Remove the spacer spring from the driveshaft.

5. Grasp the shaft and turn it slowly to the left while withdrawing it from its bore.

6. Remove the washer found under the shaft.

CAUTION: *Make sure that this washer does not fall down into the engine.*

7. To install, make sure that the engine is at TDC on the compression stroke for No. 1 cylinder with the timing marks aligned at 0°.

8. Replace the washer and insert the shaft into its bore.

NOTE: *Due to the slant of the teeth on the drive gears, the shaft must be rotated slightly to the left when it is inserted into the crankcase.*

9. When the shaft is properly inserted, the offset slot in the drive shaft of Type 1 and 2/1600 engines will be perpendicular to the

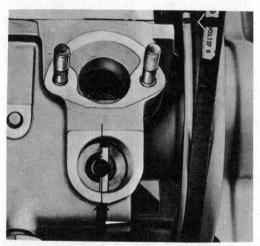

Type 1 and 2/1600 distributor driveshaft alignment

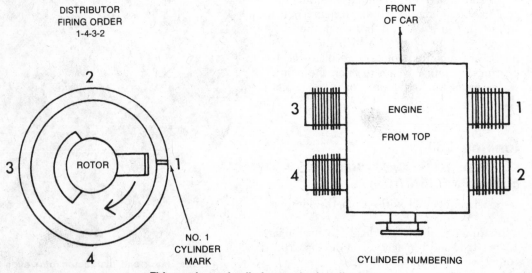

Firing order and cylinder numbering diagram

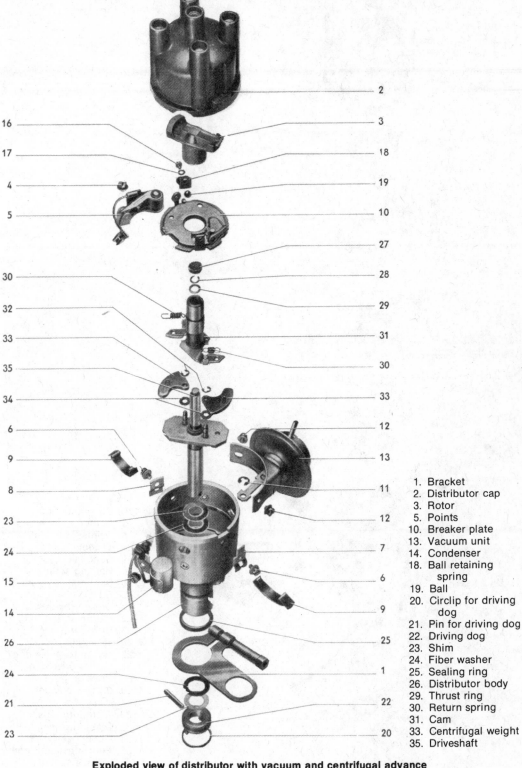

1. Bracket
2. Distributor cap
3. Rotor
5. Points
10. Breaker plate
13. Vacuum unit
14. Condenser
18. Ball retaining
    spring
19. Ball
20. Circlip for driving
    dog
21. Pin for driving dog
22. Driving dog
23. Shim
24. Fiber washer
25. Sealing ring
26. Distributor body
29. Thrust ring
30. Return spring
31. Cam
33. Centrifugal weight
35. Driveshaft

Exploded view of distributor with vacuum and centrifugal advance

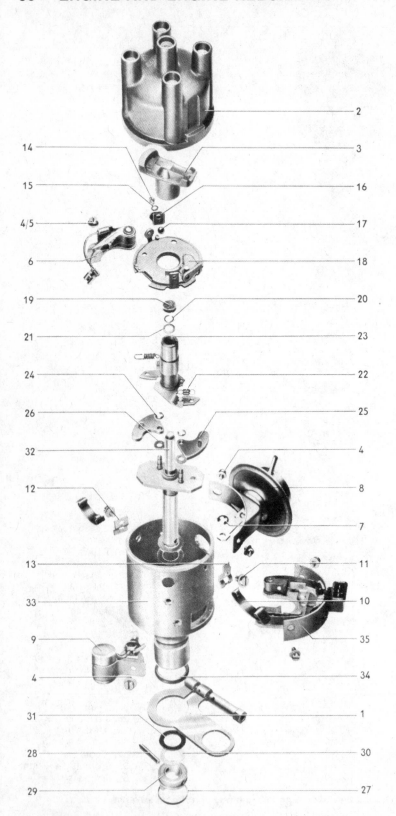

2. Distributor cap
3. Rotor
6. Points
8. Vacuum unit
9. Condenser
10. Holding spring
16. Ball retaining spring
17. Ball
18. Breaker plate
22. Return spring
23. Distributor cam
25. Flyweight
27. Circlip for drive dog
28. Pin for drive dog
29. Drive dog
30. 0.1 mm compensating washer
32. Distributor shaft
33. Distributor housing
34. Rubber sealing ring
35. Fuel injection trigger contacts

Exploded view of Type 3 and Type 4 distributor (except 1974 Type 4 with automatic transmission and airflow controlled fuel injection

Type 3 distributor driveshaft alignment

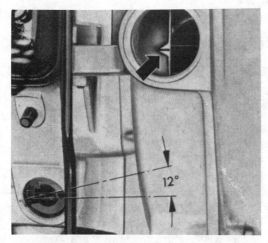

Type 4, Type 2/1700, 2/1800, 2/3000 distributor driveshaft alignment

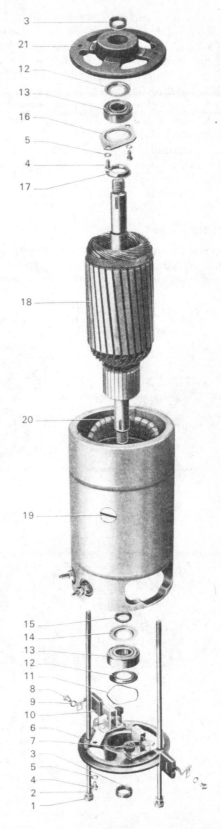

1. Through-bolt
2. Lockwasher
3. Spacer ring
4. Fillister head screw
5. Lockwasher
6. Commutator end plate
7. Brush spring
8. Fillister head screw
9. Lockwasher
10. Carbon brush
11. Lockwasher

12. Dished washer
13. Ball bearing
14. Splash shield
15. Thrust washer
16. Retaining plate
17. Splash shield
18. Armature
19. Pole shoe screw
20. Field coil
21. Fan end plate

Exploded view of Type 1 and 2/1600 generator

crankcase joint and the slot offset will be facing the crankshaft pulley. On Type 3, the slot will form a 60° angle with the crankcase joint and the slot offset will be facing the oil cooler. On Type 4 engines, and Type 2/1700, 2/1800 and 2/2000 engines, the slot should be about 12° out of parallel with the center line of the engine and the slot offset should be facing outside the engine.

10. Reinstall the spacer spring.

11. Reinstall the distributor and fuel pump, if removed.

12. Retime the engine.)

Firing Order

A general firing order diagram is shown because distributor positioning varies from model to model. All VW distributors have a scribed notch on the housing which locates the No. 1 rotor position.

The firing order of all VW engines is 1-4-3-2. Correct rewiring of the distributor cap would then begin at the No. 1 notch and proceed clockwise in the firing order.

NOTE: *To avoid confusion, replace spark plug cables one at a time.*

Generator and Alternator
ALTERNATOR PRECAUTIONS

1. Battery polarity should be checked before any connections, such as jumper cables or battery charger leads, are made. Reversing the battery connections will damage the diodes in the alternator. It is recommended that the battery cables be disconnected before connecting a battery charger.

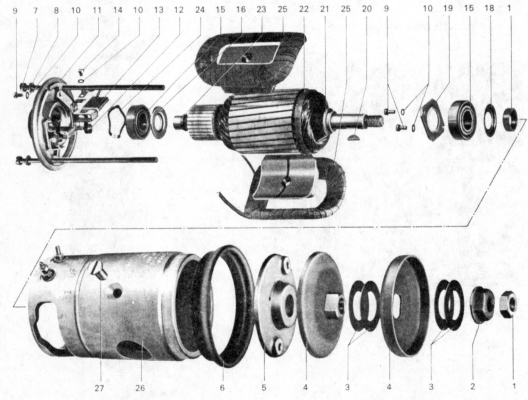

1. Nut for pulley	10. Washer	20. Woodruff key
2. Special washer	11. End plate with carbon brushes	21. Splash shield
3. Shim	12. Spring	22. Armature
4. Pulley	13. Carbon brushes	23. Armature flange
5. End plate	14. Screw	24. Gasket
6. End ring	15. Ball bearing	25. Field coil
7. Through-bolt	16. Splash shield	26. Housing
8. Washer	18. Splash shield	27. Field screw
9. Screw	19. Retaining plate	

Exploded view of Type 3 generator

2. The battery must never be disconnected while the alternator is running.

3. Always disconnect the battery ground lead before working on the charging system, especially when replacing an alternator.

4. Do not short across or ground any alternator or regulator terminals.

5. If electric arc welding has to be done to the car, first disconnect the battery and alternator cables. Never start the car with the welding unit attached.

BELTS

See Chapter One.

GENERATOR/ALTERNATOR REMOVAL AND INSTALLATION

Types 1 and 2/1600

The generator (alternator) can be removed without removing the engine on these models by loosening the fan housing and lifting it up enough to remove the four generator (alternator) to fan housing bolts.

1. Disconnect the battery.

2. Disconnect the leads from the generator (alternator) and mark them for reassembly.

3. Remove the air cleaner housing and the carburetor or air flow sensor (fuel injected models). See Chapter 4 for details.

4. Slide the accelerator cable out through the fan housing and remove the cable's guide tube.

5. Separate the generator (alternator) pulley halves, noting the number and position of the pulley shims, and remove the belt from the pulley.

Removing generator with fan cover—Type 1, 2/1600

6. Remove the retaining strap from the generator (alternator).

7. Remove the cooling air thermostat. See end of this section of Chapter 3 for details.

8. Remove the hot air hoses from the fan housing.

9. Remove any wires and hoses which may hinder lifting the fan housing up.

10. On 1971 Type 2s and on all Type 1s except the 1970 model, use a 10 mm wrench to remove the bolt that holds the oil cooler cover to the front (flywheel side) of the engine and the bolt that holds the fan housing to the oil cooler flange. Remove the oil cooler cover and flange.

11. Remove the screws at both sides of the fan housing and on 1971 Type 2s and all Type 1s except 1970 models, pry off the clip and disconnect the fan housing flap linkage from the left control flap.

12. Lift up the fan housing enough to remove the four 10 mm head bolts that hold the generator (alternator) to the fan housing and remove the generator (alternator) from the vehicle.

13. Remove the fan from the generator (alternator) by unscrewing the special nut and pulling the fan off the keyed generator (alternator) shaft. Note the position of any shims found on Type 2 generators, from chassis number 219000001, as these shims are used to maintain a gap of 0.047 in. between the fan and the fan cover. The Type 1 gap is 0.08 in.

14. Reverse the above steps to install. When installing the generator (alternator) the cooling air intake slot in the fan cover must face downward and the generator (alternator) pulley must align with the crankshaft pulley.

Type 2/1800, 2/2000 (Fuel Injected)

1. Disconnect the negative battery cable.

2. Disconnect the alternator wiring harness at the voltage regulator and starter.

3. Pull out the dipstick and remove the oil filler neck. Disconnect the heater blower from the front of the alternator on 1980–81 Type 2.

4. Loosen the alternator adjusting bolt and remove the drive belt.

5. Remove the right rear engine cover plate and the alternator cover plate.

6. Disconnect the warm air duct at the right side, and remove the heat exchanger

bracket and connecting pipe from the blower.

7. Disconnect the cool air intake elbow at the alternator. Remove the attaching bolt and lift out the alternator from above.

8. Reverse the above procedure to install, taking care to ensure that the rubber grommet on the intake cover for the wiring harness is installed correctly. After installation, adjust the drive belt so that the moderate thumb pressure midway on the belt depresses the belt about ½ in.

Type 3

1. Remove the cooling air intake cover and disconnect the battery.

2. Loosen the fan belt adjustment and remove the fan belt. Removal of the belt is accomplished by removing the nut in the center of the generator pulley and removing the outer pulley half.

3. Remove the two nuts which hold the generator securing strap in place and then remove the strap.

4. Disconnect the generator wiring.

5. Remove the generator.

6. Installation is the reverse of the above. Install the generator so that the mark on the generator housing is in line with the notch on the clamping strap. The generator pulley must be aligned with the crankshaft pulley. Make sure that the boot which seals the generator to the air intake housing is properly placed.

Type 4, Type 2/1700, 2/1800, 2/2000

The factory procedure recommends removing the engine to remove the alternator. However, it is possible to reach the alternator by first removing the right heater box which will provide access to the alternator.

Type 3 generator alignment

1. Disconnect the battery.

2. The following is the alternator removal and installation procedure after removing the engine; however, all bolts and connections listed below must be removed, except the engine cooling fan, if the right heater box is removed to gain access to the alternator.

3. Remove the engine.

4. Remove the dipstick, if necessary and the rear engine cover plate.

5. Remove the fan belt.

6. Remove the lower alternator bolt and the alternator cover plate.

7. Disconnect the wiring harness from the alternator.

8. Remove the allen head screws which attach the engine cooling fan, then remove the fan.

9. Remove the rubber elbow from the fan housing.

NOTE: *This elbow must be in position upon installation because it provides cooling air for the alternator.*

10. Remove the alternator adjusting bracket.

1. Motorola alternator	19. Brush holder
2. Bosch alternator	20. Carbon brush holder plate
3. Housing	21. End plate
4. Claw-pole rotor	22. O-ring
5. Claw-pole rotor	23. Retaining plate
6. End plate ball bearing	24. Fan cover bolt
7. Ball bearing	25. Diode carrier screw
8. Fan end spacer ring	26. Retaining plate screw
9. Drive end spacer ring	27. Brush holder cover screw
10. Rotor locating plate	28. End plate screw
11. Stator winding	29. Voltage regulator
12. Stator winding	30. Voltage regulator
13. Diode carrier	31. Boot
14. Diode carrier	32. Terminal sleeve housing
15. Diode carrier retainer	33. Terminal pin housing
16. B+ terminal nut	34. Spring washer
17. B+ terminal insulating washer	35. Screw
18. B+ terminal insulating bushing	

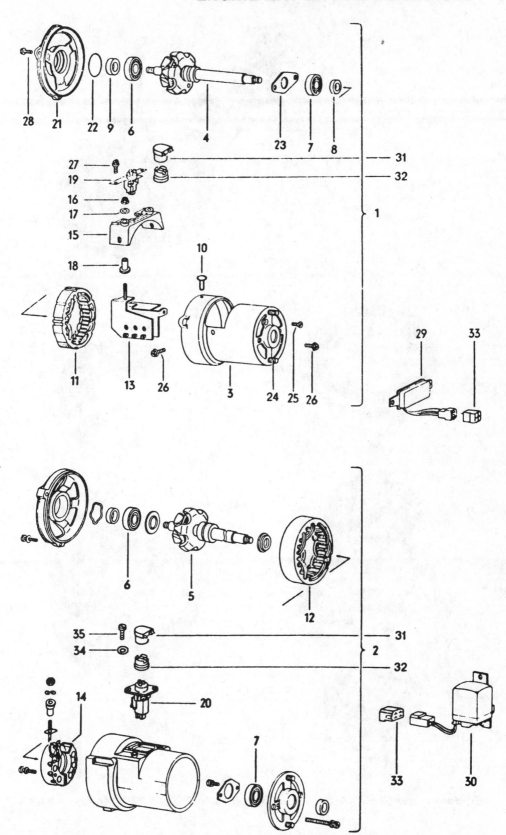

Exploded view of 50 AMP alternator used on 1973–80 Type 1 models

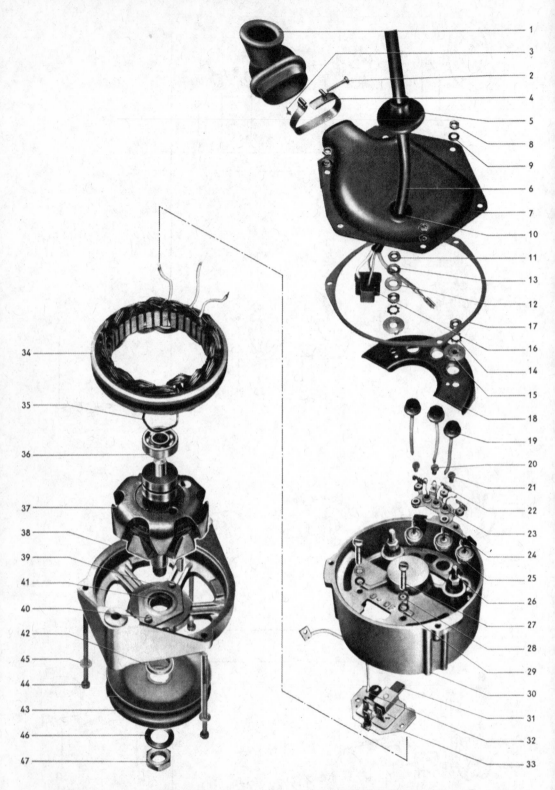

1
3
2
4
5
8
9
6
7
10
11
13
12
17
16
14
15
18
19
20
21
22
23
24
25
26
27
28
29
30
31
32
33

34
35
36
37
38
39
41
40
42
45
44
43
46
47

Exploded view of 55 amp alternator used in Type 2/1700, 2/1800, 2/2000, and Type 4 models

1. Elbow
2. Screw for hose clip
3. Threaded portion for hose clip
4. Cable hose clamp
5. Rubber grommet
6. Alternator wiring harness
7. Intake cover for alternator
8. Hex nut
9. Lockwasher
10. Rubber grommet for intake cover
11. B+ connection hex nut
12. Washer
13. Washer
14. Star washer
15. Contact disc
16. Three pin plug
17. Intake cover gasket
18. Positive diode carrier
19. Positive diodes
20. Screw
21. Stator winding connection screw
22. Exciter diode carrier
23. Exciter diodes
24. Seal
25. Negative diodes
26. Positive diode carrier pin
27. Brush holder screw
28. Washer
29. Spring washer
30. Alternator housing
31. Carbon brush
32. Brush retaining spring
33. Brush holder
34. Stator
35. Spring washer
36. Slip ring ball bearings
37. Claw pole rotor
38. End plate
39. Bearing end plate
40. Screw
41. Drive end ball bearing
42. Intermediate ring
43. Pulley
44. Housing bolt
45. Washer
46. Washer
47. Nut

11. Remove the alternator.
12. Installation is the reverse of the above. Make sure that the belt is properly adjusted.

Voltage Regulator

Many 1974 and all later Type 1 VWs with alternators are equipped with integral circuit regulators mounted on the alternators. On all other models, the regulator is mounted separately. Some early model regulators do not have a ground wire; all replacement regulators do. When installing a replacement regulator on an early model vehicle without a ground wire, be sure to attach the ground wire that comes with the replacement regulator.

REMOVAL AND INSTALLATION

CAUTION: *Interchanging the connections on the regulator will destroy the regulator and generator.*

Type 1 and 3

The regulator is located under the rear seat on the left side. It is secured to the frame by two screws. Take careful note of the wiring connections before removing the wiring from the regulator. Disconnect the battery before removing the regulator.

Type 2 and Model 14 (Karmann Ghia)

Disconnect the battery. The regulator is located in the engine compartment and is secured in place by two screws. Take careful note of the wiring connections before removing the wiring from the regulator.

D+ to generator D+
DF to generator DF (protected by cap on 1972 and later models)
B+/51 to negative battery terminal and terminal 30 of electrical system
61 to generator charging warning light

Voltage regulator details—Type 1 Beetle, Super Beetle, Type 3 similar

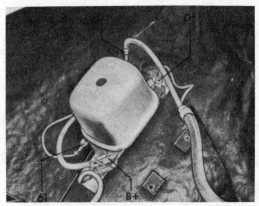

Voltage regulator details—Type 1 Karmann Ghia; Type 2 and Type 4 similar

Alternator, Generator, and Regulator Specifications

Year	Type	Generator Maximum Output (Amps)	Alternator			Regulator	
			Maximum Output (Amps)	Stator Winding Resistance (Ohms)	Exciter Winding Resistance (Ohms)	Load Current (Amps)	Regulating Voltage Under Load (Volts)
1970–73	1	30	—	—	—	25 ①	12.5–14.5
1973–80	1	—	50	0.13 ± 0.013	4.0 ± 0.4	25–30	13.8–14.9 ②
1970–71	2/1600	38	—	—	—	25 ①	12.5–14.5
1972–73	2/1700	—	55	0.13 ± 0.013	4.0 ± 0.4	25–30	13.8–14.9 ②
1974–81	2/1800, 2/2000	—	55	0.13 ± 0.013	4.0 ± 0.4	25–30	13.8–14.9 ②
1970–73	3	30	—	—	—	25 ①	12.5–14.5
1971–74	4	—	55	0.13 ± 0.013	4.0 ± 0.4	25–30	13.8–14.9 ②

① @2000–2500 generator rpm
② @2000 engine rpm
—Not Applicable

Type 4

Disconnect the battery and do not disconnect any other wiring until the engine is turned off. Make careful note of the wiring connections. The regulator is located near the air cleaner and is mounted either on the air cleaner or on the firewall. It is secured by two screws.

VOLTAGE ADJUSTMENT

Volkswagen voltage regulators are sealed and cannot be adjusted. A malfunctioning regulator must be replaced as a unit.

Starter

The starter motor of the Volkswagen is of the sliding gear type and is rated at about 0.6, 0.7, or 0.8 horsepower. The motor used in the starter is a series wound type and draws a heavy current in order to provide the high torque needed to crank the engine during starting. The starter cannot be switched on accidently while the engine is still running— the device responsible for this safeguard is a nonrepeat switch in the ignition switch. If the engine should stall for any reason, the ignition key must be turned to the "off" posi-

tion before it is possible to re-start the engine.

The starter is flange-mounted on the right-hand side of the transmission housing. Attached to the starter motor housing is a solenoid which engages the pinion and connects the starting motor to the battery when the ignition key is turned on. When the engine starts, and the key is released from the start position, the solenoid circuit is opened and the pinion is returned to its original position by the return spring. However, if for any reason the starter is not switched off immediately after the engine starts, a pinion free-wheeling device stops the armature from being driven so that the starter will not be damaged.

STARTER/SEAT BELT INTERLOCK

All 1974 and some 1975 models are equipped with a seat belt/starter interlock system. This system prevents operation of the starter motor until both front seat occupants buckle up their seat belts. For details, see Chapter 5.

STARTER REMOVAL AND INSTALLATION

1. Disconnect the battery.
2. Disconnect the wiring from the starter.

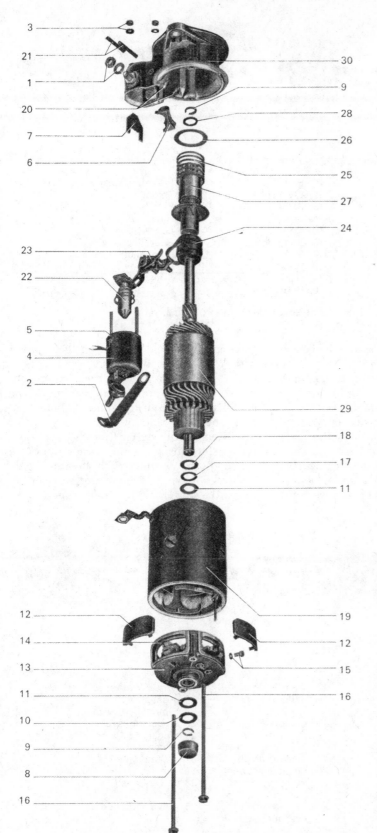

1. Nut and lockwasher
2. Connecting strip
3. Nut and lockwasher
4. Solenoid
5. Insulating disc
6. Seal
7. Insulating plate
8. Cap
9. Circlip
10. Steel washer
11. Bronze washer
12. Brush inspection cover
13. Commutator end plate
14. Brush holder
15. Screw and lockwasher
16. Housing screws
17. Dished washer
18. Steel washer
19. Housing and field windings
20. Spring clip
21. Pin
22. Solenoid core
23. Linkage
24. Bushing
25. Spring
26. Washer
27. Drive pinion
28. Dished washer
29. Armature
30. Mounting bracket

Exploded view of VW No. 111 911 023A starter

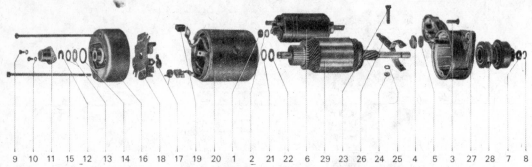

1. Nut	11. End cap	21. Insulating washer
2. Lockwasher	12. C-washer	22. Thrust washer
3. Screw	13. Shim	23. Pin
4. Rubber seal	14. Sealing ring	24. Nut
5. Disc	15. Housing screw	25. Lockwasher
6. Solenoid switch	16. End plate	26. Operating lever
7. Stop-ring	17. Spring	27. Drive end plate
8. Circlip	18. Brush holder	28. Drive pinion
9. Screw	19. Rubber grommet	29. Armature
10. Washer	20. Housing	

Exploded view of Bosch No. 311 911 023B starter

It will probably be easier if the right-hand rear wheel is removed.

NOTE: *On fuel injection models, take special note of the terminals from which the various wires are dis-attached (terminal 30, 50, etc.). If the cold start valve wire, which should be connected to terminal 50, is connected to terminal 30 by mistake, the cold start valve will run constantly, causing poor gas mileage, rough idle and flooding.*

3. The starter is held in place by two bolts. Have a helper hold the nut on the top bolt with a wrench in the engine compartment while you remove the bolt from underneath the vehicle. This top bolt is also one of the four main engine to transmission bolts. Remove the lower bolt.

4. Remove the starter from the car.

5. Before installing the starter, lubricate the outboard bushing with grease. Apply sealing compound to the mating surfaces between the starter and the transmission.

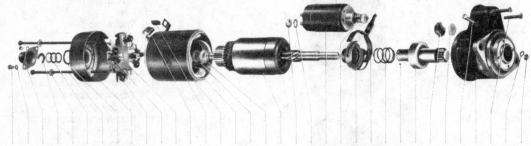

1. Nut	13. Shim	25. Thrust washer
2. Lockwasher	14. Screws	26. Armature
3. Screw	15. Washer	27. Operating sleeve
4. Molded rubber	16. End plate	28. Engaging lever
5. Disc	17. Brush holder	29. Engaging spring
6. Solenoid	18. Negative brush	30. Detent balls
7. Spring	19. Positive brush	31. Drive pinion
8. Screw	20. Retaining spring	32. Pin
9. Washer	21. Rubber grommet	33. Lockwasher
10. End cap	22. Housing	34. Nut
11. Seal	23. Field winding	35. Drive end plate
12. C-ring	24. Insulating washer	

Exploded view of Bosch No. 003 911 023A starter

Starter Specifications

| Starter Number | Lock Test | | No-Load Test | | | Brush Spring Tension (oz) |
	Amps	Volts	Amps	Volts	rpm	
111 911 023A	270–290	6	25–40	12	6700–7800	42
311 911 023B	250–300	6	35–45	12	7400–8100	42
003 911 023A	250–300	6	35–50	12	6400–7900	42

6. Place the long starter bolt in its hole in the starter and locate the starter on the transmission housing. Install the other bolt.

7. Connect the starter wiring and battery cables.

SOLENOID REPLACEMENT

1. Remove the starter.

2. Remove the nut which secures the connector strip at the end of the solenoid.

3. Take out the two retaining screws on the mounting bracket and withdraw the solenoid after it has been unhooked from its actuating lever.

4. When replacing a defective solenoid with a new one, care should be taken to see that the distance (a) in the accompanying diagram is 19 mm when the magnet is drawn inside the solenoid.

5. Installation is the reverse of removal. In order to facilitate engagement of the actuating rod, the pinion should be pulled out as far as possible when inserting the solenoid.

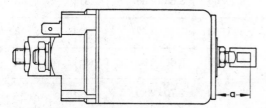

Solenoid adjustment (distance "a" is 19 mm)

When installing the solenoid make sure that the eye hooks on the actuating lever

Battery

The electrical system of the Volkswagen is a negative grounded type. All models except the 1975 and later Type 2 use a 45 amp battery. The 1975 and later Type 2 uses a 54 amp battery. On Type 1 and Type 3 VW models, the battery is located under the right-hand side of the rear seat. On Karmann Ghias and Type 2 models through 1979, the battery is located in the engine compartment. On 1980–81 Type 2s (Vanagon), it is located under the passenger's seat. On Type 4 models, the battery is beneath the driver's seat. On Type 2 Campmobiles equipped with a refrigerator, an additional 45 amp battery is available.

REMOVAL AND INSTALLATION

1. Disconnect the battery cables. Note the position of the battery cables for installation. The small diameter battery post is the negative terminal. The negative battery cable is usually black.

2. Undo the battery holddown strap and lift the battery out of its holder.

CAUTION: *Do not tilt the battery as acid will spill out.*

3. Install the battery in its holder and replace the clamp. Reconnect the battery cables.

ENGINE MECHANICAL

The Volkswagen engine is a flat four cylinder design. This four cycle, overhead valve en-

General Engine Specifications

Year	Engine Code	Displacement (cc)	Horsepower @rpm	Torque @rpm (ft lbs)	Bore x Stroke (in.)	Compression Ratio	Oil Pressure @rpm (psi)
1970	B	1584	57/4400	82/3000	3.37 x 2.72	7.5:1 ②	42
1971–72	AE	1584	46/4000	72/2000	3.37 x 2.72	7.3:1	42
1971–74	AK	1584	46/40000	72/2000	3.37 x 2.72	7.3:1	42
1972–74	AH ①, AM	1584	46/4000	72/2000	3.37 x 2.72	7.5:1	42
1972–73	CB	1679	63/4800	81/3200	3.54 x 2.60	7.3:1	42
1973	CD	1679	59/4200	82/3200	3.54 x 2.60	7.3:1	42
1970–73	U	1584	65/4600	87/2800	3.37 x 2.72	7.7:1	42
1972–73	X	1584	52/4000	77/2200	3.37 x 2.72	7.3:1	42
1971	W	1679	85/5000	99.5/3500	3.54 x 2.60	8.2:1	42
1972–74	EA	1679	76/4900	95/2700	3.54 x 2.60	8.2:1	42
1973	EB ①	1679	69/5000	87/2700	3.54 x 2.60	7.3:1	42
1974	EC	1795	72/4800	91/3400	3.66 x 2.60	7.3:1	42
1974	AW	1795	65/4200	92/3000	3.66 x 2.60	7.3:1	42
1975–80	AJ	1584	48/4200	73.1/2800	3.37 x 2.72	7.3:1	42
1975	ED	1795	67/4400	90/2400	3.66 x 2.60	7.3:1	42
1976–81	GD, GE, CV	1970	67/4200	101/3000	3.70 x 2.80	7.3:1	42

① California only
② Type 2—7.7:1

gine has two pairs of horizontally opposed cylinders. All rear engined VW models are air cooled.

The Type 1 and 2/1600 engine is known as an upright fan engine, that is, the engine cooling fan is mounted vertically on top of the engine and is driven by the generator shaft. The Type 2/1700, Type 2/1800, Type 2/2000, Type 3 and 4 engine, although of the same basic design, i.e. flat four, has the cooling fan driven by the crankshaft and is therefore mounted on the front of the engine. This type of engine is known as the suitcase engine.

Because it is air cooled, the VW engine is slightly noisier than a water cooled engine. This is due to the lack of water jacketing around the cylinders which provides sound deadening on water cooled engines. In addition, air cooled engines tend to run at somewhat higher temperatures, necessitating larger operating clearances to allow more room for the expansion of the parts. These larger operating clearances cause an increase in noise level over a water cooled engine.

The crankshaft of all Volkswagen engines is mounted in a two piece crankcase. The halves are machined to very close tolerances

Valve Specifications

Year	Vehicle Type Displacement	Seat Angle (deg) Intake	Exhaust	Face Angle (deg) Intake	Exhaust	Valve Seat Width (in.) Intake	Exhaust	Spring Test Pressure (lbs @in.))	Valve Guide Inside Dia (in.) Intake	Exhaust	Stem to Guide Clearance (in.) Intake	Exhaust	Stem Diameter (in.) Intake	Exhaust
1970–80	1, 2, 3 1600	45	45	44	45	0.05–0.10	0.05–0.10	117.7–134.8 @1.22	0.3150–0.3157	0.3150–② 0.3157	0.009–0.010	0.009–0.010	0.3125–0.3129	0.3113–① 0.3117
1971–81	2, 4 1700, 1800, 2000	30	45	30	45	0.07–0.08	0.078–0.098	168–186 @1.14	0.3150–0.3157	0.3534–0.3538	0.018	0.014	0.3125–0.3129	0.3507–0.3511

① On 1975 Type 1 models, exhaust valve stem diameter is 0.350–0.351 in.
② On 1975 Type 1 models, exhaust valve guide inside diameter is 0.353–0.354 in.

Crankshaft and Connecting Rod Specifications
(All measurements are given in inches)

Year	Type Engine	Crankshaft Main Bearing Journal Dia No. 1, 2, 3	No. 4	Main Bearing Oil Clearance No. 1, 3	No. 2	No. 4	Crankshaft End-Play	Thrust on No.	Connecting Rods Journal Dia	Oil Clearance	End-Play
1970–80	1, 2, 3 1600	2.1640–2.1648	1.5379–1.5748	0.0016–0.0004	0.001–0.0003	0.002–0.0004	0.0027–0.0005	1 at flywheel	2.1644–2.1653	0.0008–0.0027	0.004–0.016
1971–81	2, 4 1700, 1800, 2000	2.3609–2.3617	1.5739–1.5748	0.002–0.004	0.0012–0.0035	0.002–0.004	0.0027–0.005	1 at flywheel	2.1644–2.1653 ①	0.0008–0.0027	0.004–0.016

① On 1976 Type 2/2000 models, connecting rod journal diameter is 1.968 in. (50 mm)

Piston and Ring Specifications
(All measurements in inches)

Year	Type Engine Displacement	Piston Clearance	Ring Gap			Ring Side Clearance		
			Top Compression	Bottom Compression	Oil Control	Top Compression	Bottom Compression	Oil Control
1970–80	1, 2, 3 1600	0.0016–0.0023	0.012–0.018	0.012–0.018	0.010–0.016	0.0027–0.0039	0.002–0.0027	0.0011–0.0019
1971–81	2, 4 1700, 1800, 2000	0.0016–0.0023	0.014–0.021	0.012–0.022	0.010–0.016	0.0023–0.0035	0.0016–0.0027	0.0008–0.0019

Torque Specifications
(All readings in ft. lbs.)

Year	Type Vehicle	Cylinder Head Nuts	Rod Bearing Bolts	Generator Pulley	Crankshaft Pulley Bolt	Flywheel to Crankshaft Bolts	Fan to Hub	Hub to Crankshaft	Crankcase Half Nuts		Drive Plate to Crankshaft	Spark Plugs	Oil Strainer Cover
									Sealing Nuts	Non-Sealing Nuts			
1970–80	1	23	22–25	40–47	29–36	253	—	—	18	14	—	25	5
1970–71	2/1600	23	22–25	40–47	29–36	253	—	—	18	14	—	25	5
1972–81	2/1700, 1800, 2000	23	24	—	—	80	14	23	23	14	61	22	7–9
1970–73	3	23	22–25	40–47	94–108	253	—	—	18	14	—	25	5
1971–74	4	23	24	—	—	80	14	23	23	14	61	22	7–9

and line bored as a pair and, therefore, should always be replaced in pairs. When fitting them, it is necessary to coat only the mating surfaces with sealing compound and tighten them down to the correct torque. No gasket is used.

The pistons and cylinders are identical on any particular engine. However, it is not possible to interchange pistons and cylinders between engines. The four pistons each have three rings, two compression rings and one oil scraper. Each piston is attached to its connecting rod with a fully floating piston pin.

Each pair of cylinders shares a detachable cylinder head made of light aluminum alloy casting. The cylinder head contains the valves for both cylinders. Shrunk-in valve guides and valve seats are used.

NOTE: *Complete engine rebuilding procedures are given in the second half of this chapter.*

Engine Removal and Installation

Type 1, 2, and 3

The Volkswagen engine is mounted on the transmission, which in turn is attached to the frame. In the Type 1 and 2 models, there are two bolts and two studs attaching the engine to the transmission. Type 3 engines have an extra mounting at the rear of the engine. Type 3 engines with automatic transmissions have front and rear engine and transmission mounts. At the front, the gearbox is supported by the rear tubular crossmember; at the rear, a crossmember is bolted to the crankcase and mounted to the body at either end.

When removing the engine from the car, it is recommended that the rear of the car be about 4 ft off the ground. Remove the engine by bringing it out from underneath the car. Proceed with the following steps to remove the engine.

NOTE: *An easy way to prevent hooking up your automatic choke wire to the distributor and vice versa when installing the engine is to take the time to mark each wire and the terminal to which it is connected with masking tape, then coding each two pieces of tape 1, 2, 3, etc. When hooking up the wiring, simply match the pieces of tape. Or you can draw a diagram indicating the wire colors and the components to which they attach. Do the same with all*

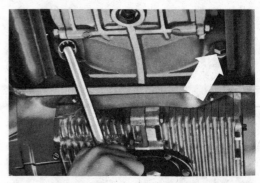

Removing lower engine mounting nuts

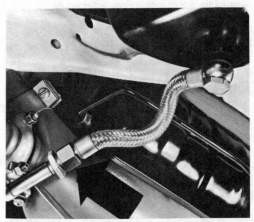

Disconnecting union nut between fluid reservoir and oil pump on Type 1 automatic stick shift models

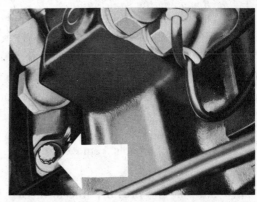

One of four 12 point bolts retaining torque converter to drive plate on Type 1 automatic stick shift models

vacuum hoses and you should have no problems installing the engine.

1. Disconnect the battery ground cable.
2. Disconnect the generator wiring.
3. Remove the air cleaner. On Type 1 and Type 2 engines, remove the rear engine

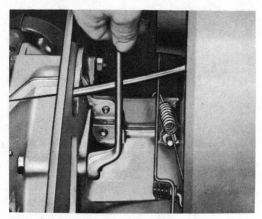

Removing upper engine mounting nuts

Retaining torque converter with strap

Type 3 engine mounts

Supporting transmission during engine installation

cover plate. On Type 2/1600 cc engines, remove the rear crossmember.

4. Disconnect the throttle cable and remove the electrical connections to the automatic choke, coil, electromagnetic cut-off-jet, the oil pressure sending unit, the backup light wiring at the right of the engine (Type 1), and all other interfering wiring.

NOTE: *Removing the throttle cable on the upright fan engine includes:*

a. Disconnecting the throttle cable from the carburetor;

b. Removing the spring retainer the spring cover and the spring;

c. Pulling the cable out from the transaxle side of the engine and;

d. Removing the cable guide.

5. Disconnect the fuel hose at the front engine cover plate and seal it to prevent leakage.

6. On Type 3 models, remove the oil dipstick and the rubber boot between the oil filter and the body.

7. Remove the cooling air intake bellows on Type 3 engines after loosening the clip that secures the unit.

8. On Type 3 models, remove the warm air hose.

9. On Type 3 fuel injected engines, remove and plug the pressure line to the left fuel distributor pipe and to the return line on the pressure regulator. Disconnect the fuel injection wiring harness.

10. Raise the car and support it with jackstands.

11. Remove the flexible air hoses between the engine and heat exchangers, disconnect the heater flap cables, remove the electrical heater fan hoses, if equipped, unscrew the two lower engine mounting nuts, and slide a

jack under the engine. On Type 2 engines, remove the two bolts from the rubber engine mounts located next to the muffler.

12. On Type 1 Automatic Stick Shift

models, disconnect the control valve cable and the manifold vacuum hoses. Disconnect the ATF suction line and plug it. On Type 3 fully automatic transmission models, disconnect the vacuum hose and the kick-down cable.

13. On all Automatic Stick Shift and fully automatic models, remove the four bolts from the converter drive plate through the holes in the transmission case. After the engine is removed, hold the torque converter on the transmission input shaft by using a strap bolted to the bellhousing.

14. Raise the jack until it just contacts the engine and have an assistant hold the two upper mounting bolts so that the nuts can be removed from the bottom. 1971 Type 2s have only an upper right-hand mount bolt.

NOTE: *1972 and later Type 2s have two top engine to transaxle bolts which also serve as top carrier bolts for the transaxle. The transaxle must be supported when these bolts are removed to prevent damage which could be caused by letting the unit hang. Many later model Type 1 and Type 2 vehicles have a captive left side top engine to transaxle nut which is reached from the transaxle side of the unit.*

15. When the engine mounts are disconnected and there are no remaining cables or wires left to be disconnected, move the engine toward the back of the car so that the clutch or converter plate disengages from the transmission.

16. Lower the engine out of the car.

17. Installation is the reverse of the above. When the engine is lifted into position, it should be rotated using the generator pulley so that the clutch plate hub will engage the transmission shaft splines. Tighten the upper mounting bolts first. Check the clutch, pressure plate, throwout bearing, and pilot bearing for wear.

On Type 3, synthetic washers are used to raise the engine about 3 mm when the rear engine mounting is attached and tightened. Use only enough washers in the rear mount so that the engine is lifted no more than 3 mm. Care should be used when installing the rear intake housing bellows of the Type 3 engine.

Type 4

1. Disconnect the battery.
2. Remove the cooling air bellows, warm air hoses, cooling air intake duct, and air cleaner. On sedans, remove the cooling air

Access hole for torque converter bolts—Type 4

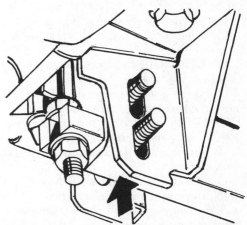

Engine carrier bolt location upon installation of engine—Type 4

fan. On station wagons, remove the dipstick tube rubber boot and the dipstick.

3. Disconnect the fuel injection wiring.
4. Disconnect the coil wires and remove the coil and its bracket.
5. Disconnect the oil pressure switch and the alternator wiring.
6. Disconnect the vacuum hose for the intake air distributor.
7. Disconnect the accelerator cable.
8. Working through the access hole at the upper right corner of the flywheel housing, remove the three screws which secure the torque converter to the drive plate. Remove the ATF oil dipstick and the rubber boot.
9. Remove the two upper engine mounting bolts.
10. Jack up the car and, working beneath the car, remove the muffler shield and the heat exchanger.

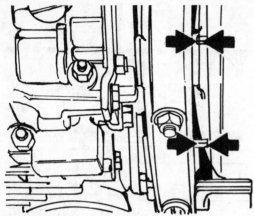

Checking that engine carrier is vertical and parallel to fan housing—Type 4

11. Disconnect the starter wiring.

12. Remove the heater booster exhaust pipe.

13. Remove the two lower engine mounting nuts.

14. Jack up the engine slightly and remove the four engine carrier screws.

NOTE: *Do not loosen the mountings on the body or the engine-transmission assembly will have to be recentralized in the chassis.*

15. Remove the engine from the car.

16. Reverse the removal procedures to install the engine. Install the engine on the lower engine mounting studs and then locate the engine in the engine carrier. When installing the engine in the carrier, lift the engine up so that the four screws are at the top of the elongated holes and tighten them in this position. If it is necessary to raise or lower the engine for adjustment purposes, use the threaded shaft. After the engine is installed, make sure that the rubber buffer is centered in the rear axle carrier. Make sure that the engine carrier is vertical and parallel to the engine fan housing. Readjust it if necessary by moving the brackets on the side members.

Cylinder Head

REMOVAL AND INSTALLATION

In order to remove the cylinder head from either pair of cylinders, it is necessary to remove the engine.

1. Remove the valve cover and gasket. Remove the rocker arm assembly. Unbolt the intake manifold from the cylinder head. The cylinder head is held in place by eight studs.

Since the cylinder head also holds the cylinders in place in the VW engine, and the cylinders in place in the VW engine, and the cylinders are not going to be removed, it will be necessary to hold the cylinders in place after the head is removed.

2. After the rocker arm cover, rocker arm retaining nuts, and rocker arm assembly have been removed, the cylinder head nuts can be removed and the cylinder head lifted off.

3. When reinstalling the cylinder head, the head should be checked for cracks both in the combustion chamber and in the intake and exhaust ports. Cracked heads must be replaced.

4. Spark plug threads should be checked. New seals should be used on the pushrod tube ends and they should be checked for proper seating.

5. The pushrod tubes should be turned so that the seam faces upward. In order to ensure perfect sealing, used tubes should be stretched slightly before they are reinstalled.

6. Install the cylinder head. Using new rocker shaft stud seals, install the pushrods and rocker shaft assembly.

NOTE: *Pay careful attention to the orientation of the shaft as described in the "Rocker Shaft" section.*

7. Torque the cylinder head in three stages. Adjust the valve clearance. Using a new gasket, install the rocker cover. It may be necessary to readjust the valves after the engine has been run a few minutes and allowed to cool.

VALVE SEATS

On all air-cooled VW engines, the valve seats are shrunk-fit into the cylinder head. This usually involves freezing the seat with a liquid nitrogen or some other refrigerant to about 200°F below zero, and heating up the cylinder head to approximately 400°F. Due to the extreme temperatures required to shrink-fit these items, and because of the extra care needed when working with metals at these extreme temperatures, it is advised that this operation be referred to an experienced repair shop.

CYLINDER HEAD OVERHAUL AND VALVE GUIDE REPLACEMENT

See the "Engine Rebuilding" section at the end of this chapter.

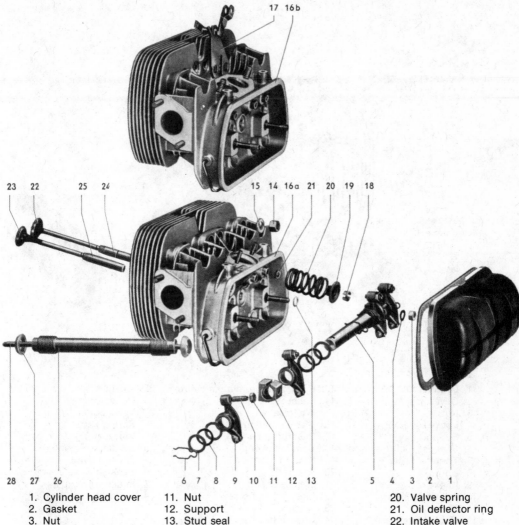

1. Cylinder head cover	11. Nut	20. Valve spring
2. Gasket	12. Support	21. Oil deflector ring
3. Nut	13. Stud seal	22. Intake valve
4. Spring washer	14. Nut	23. Exhaust valve
5. Rocker shaft	15. Washer	24. Intake valve guide
6. Clip	16a. Type 1, Type 2/1600 cylinder head	25. Exhaust valve
7. Thrust washer	16b. Type 3 cylinder head	26. Pushrod tube
8. Spring washer	17. Thermostat link	27. Sealing ring
9. Rocker arm	18. Valve cotter	28. Pushrod
10. Adjusting screw	19. Spring cap	

Cylinder head details—Types 1/1600, 2/1600 and 3/1600

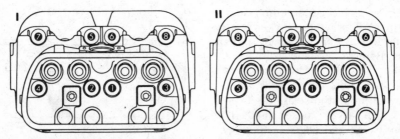

For 1600 cc engines, the cylinder head nuts should initially be tightened to 7 ft. lbs. in order I, then tightened to the recommended torque in order II

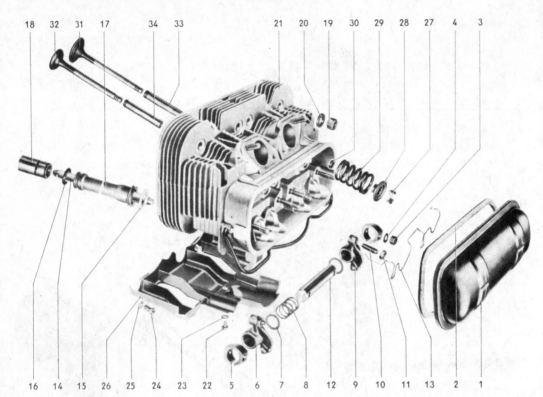

1. Cylinder head cover	13. Pushrod tube retaining wire	25. Washer
2. Cover gasket	14. Pushrods	26. Deflector plate
3. Nut	15. White sealing ring	27. Valve cotter
4. Lockwasher	16. Black sealing ring	28. Spring cap
5. Support	17. Pushrod tube	29. Valve spring
6. Exhaust rocker arm	18. Cam follower	30. Oil deflector ring
7. Thrust washer	19. Nut	31. Intake valve
8. Spring	20. Washer	32. Exhaust valve
9. Intake rocker arm	21. Cylinder head	33. Intake valve guide
10. Adjusting screw	22. Cheese head screw	34. Exhaust valve guide
11. Nut	23. Washer	
12. Rocker shaft	24. Cheese head screw	

Cylinder head details—types 2/1700, 2/1800, 2/2000 and type 4. 1978–81 type 2/2000 have hydraulic valve lifters in place of cam follower and use different rocker separator

Rocker Shafts

ROCKER SHAFT REMOVAL AND INSTALLATION

Before the valve rocker assembly can be reached, it is necessary to lever off the clip that retains the valve cover and then remove the valve cover. Remove the rocker arm retaining nuts, the rocker arm shaft, and the rocker arms. Remove the stud seals.

Before installing the rocker arm mechanism, be sure that the parts are as clean as possible. Install new stud seals. On Type 1, 2/1600, and 3, install the rocker shaft assembly with the chamfered edges of the rocker shaft supports pointing outward and the slots pointing upward. On Type 4 and Type

2/1700, 2/1800 and 2/2000 models, the chamfered edges must point outward and the slots must face downward. The pushrod tube retaining wire must engage the slots in the

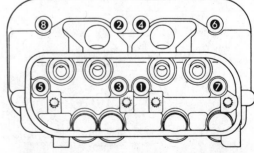

Cylinder head torque sequence—1700 cc, 1800 cc and 2000 cc

On Types 1, 2/1600 and 3, install the rocker shaft with the chamfer out and slots up

On Types 2/1700, 2/1800, 2/2000, and 4, install the rocker shaft with the chamfer out and the slots down

rocker arm shaft supports as well as the grooves in the pushrod tubes. Tighten the retaining nuts to the proper torque. Use only the copper colored nuts that were supplied with the engine. Make sure that the ball ends of the push rods are centered in the sockets of the rocker arms. Adjust the valve clearance on models without hydraulic lifters. Install the valve cover using a new gasket.

Intake Manifold

INTAKE MANIFOLD REMOVAL AND INSTALLATION

Single Carburetor Engines

1. Disconnect the battery.
2. Disconnect the generator wiring.
3. Remove the generator. It will be necessary to loosen the fan housing and tilt it back to gain clearance to remove the generator.
4. Disconnect the choke and the accelerator cable.
5. On some models it will be necessary to remove the carburetor from the manifold.
6. Unbolt the manifold from the cylinder

head and remove the manifold from the engine.
7. Reverse the above to install. Always use new gaskets.

Twin Carburetor Engines

1. Remove the carburetors as outlined in Chapter four.
2. Disconnect the tubes from the central idling system mixture distributor.
3. Disconnect all vacuum lines. Label them for purposes of installation.
4. Remove the nuts and bolts retaining the manifolds to the cylinder heads. Carefully lift off each manifold.
5. Reverse the above procedure to install, taking care to carefully clean all mating surfaces to the carburetors and cylinder heads. Always use new gaskets.

INLET MANIFOLD REMOVAL AND INSTALLATION

Fuel Injection Engines

1. Remove the air cleaner.
2. Remove the pressure switch which is mounted under the right pair of intake manifold pipes. Disconnect the injector wiring.
3. Remove the fuel injectors by removing the two nuts which secure them in place. On Type 3, do not separate the pair of injectors; they can be removed as a pair and must be left in the injector plate.
4. After removing the intake manifold outer cover plate, remove the two screws which secure the manifold inner cover plate.
5. The manifold may be removed by removing the two nuts and washers which hold the manifold flange to the cylinder head.
6. Installation is the reverse of the above. The inner manifold cover should be installed first, but leave the cover loose until the outer cover and manifold are in place. Always use new gaskets. See the following step for proper injector installation.
7. Connect the fuel hoses to the injectors, if removed, after assembling the injectors with the injector retainer plate in place. Make sure that the sleeves are in place on the injector securing studs. Carefully slip the injectors into the manifold and install the securing nuts. Never force the injectors in or out of the manifold. Reconnect the injector wiring.

Intake Air Distributor

REMOVAL AND INSTALLATION

Fuel Injected Engines

The intake air distributor is located at the center of the engines at the junction of the intake manifold pipes.

NOTE: *It is not necessary to remove the distributor if only the manifold pipes are to be removed.*

1. Remove the air cleaner and pressure switch which are located under the right pair of manifold pipes.
2. Push the four rubber hoses onto the intake manifold pipes.
3. Remove the accelerator cable and the throttle valve switch.
4. Disconnect the accelerator cable.
5. Disconnect the vacuum hoses leading to the ignition distributor and the pressure sensor and disconnect the hose running to the auxiliary air regulator.
6. Remove those bolts under the air distributor which secure the air distributor to the crankcase and remove the air distributor.
7. Installation is the reverse of removal.

Mufflers, Tailpipes, Heat Exchangers

REMOVAL AND INSTALLATION

Muffler, Type 1 Carbureted Engine and 2/1600

1. Working under the hood, disconnect the pre-heater hoses.
2. Remove the pre-heater pipe protection plate on each side of the engine. The plates are secured by three screws.
3. Remove the crankshaft pulley cover plate.
4. Remove the rear engine cover plate from the engine compartment. It is held in place by screws at the center, right, and left sides.
5. Remove the four intake manifold pre-heat pipe bolts. There are two bolts on each side of the engine.
6. Disconnect the warm air channel clamps at the left and right side of the engine.
7. Disconnect the heat exchanger clamps at the left and right side of the engine.
8. Remove the muffler from the engine.
9. Installation is the reverse of the above. Always use new gaskets to install the muffler.

Muffler, Type 1 Fuel Injected Engine

1. On vehicles with catalytic converters, simply unbolt the muffler from the converter and remove. It may be necessary to remove the tailpipe first to make room.
2. On vehicles without catalytic converters, unbolt the small EGR pipe (two bolts at each end), then unbolt the muffler from the heat exchangers.

Installation is the reverse of removal.

Muffler, Type 3

The muffler is secured to the heat exchangers with clamps and, on some models, to the body with bolts at the top and at the ends.

Muffler, Type 4, 2/1700, 2/1800, 2/2000

The muffler is secured to the left and/or right heat exchangers by three bolts or a muffler clamp. There is a bracket at one end of the muffler. Always use new gaskets when installing a new muffler.

Heat Exchangers, Type 1, 2/1600, and 3

1. Disconnect the air tube at the outlet end of the exchanger.
2. Remove the clamp which secures the muffler to the exchanger.
3. Loosen the clamp which secures the exchanger to the heater hose connection at the muffler.
4. Remove the nuts which secure the exchanger to the forward end of the cylinder head.
5. Remove the heater flap control wire.
6. Reverse the above to install. Always use new gaskets.

Heat Exchangers, Type 4, 2/1700, 2/1800, 2/2000

1. Disconnect the air hose at the outlet of each exchanger.
2. Disconnect the warm air tube at the outside end of the exchanger.
3. Disconnect the bolts or clamp which secures the exchangers to the muffler.
4. Remove the nuts at each exhaust port which secure the exchanger to the cylinder head.
5. Installation is the reverse of the above. Always use new gaskets.

Tailpipes, Type 1 and 2/1600

Loosen the clamps on the tailpipes and apply penetrating oil. Work the pipe side-to-side while trying to pull the tailpipe out of the muffler.

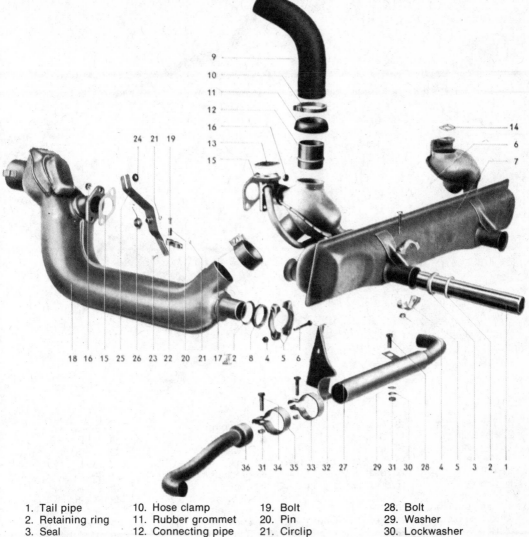

1. Tail pipe
2. Retaining ring
3. Seal
4. Nut
5. Clamp
6. Bolt
7. Muffler
8. Seal
9. Heater hose
10. Hose clamp
11. Rubber grommet
12. Connecting pipe
13. Gasket
14. Gasket
15. Gasket
16. Self-locking nut
17. Clamp
18. Heat exchanger
19. Bolt
20. Pin
21. Circlip
22. Link
23. Pin
24. Pin
25. Heater flap lever
26. Return spring
27. Damper pipe
28. Bolt
29. Washer
30. Lockwasher
31. Bolt
32. Damper pipe bracket
33. Bracket clamp
34. Bolt
35. Clamp
36. Tailpipe

Exploded view of exhaust system—1970–71 2/1600

NOTE: *It is often difficult to remove the tailpipes without damaging them.*

Tailpipe and Resonator, Type 3

Loosen the clamp at the resonator-to-muffler connection. Remove the bolt at the bend of the tailpipe and remove the resonator and tailpipe from the resonator, loosen the clamp which secures the tailpipe to the resonator and work them apart.

Tailpipe, Type 4, 2/1700, 2/1800, 2/2000

Remove the bolt which secures the pipe to the muffler. Remove the bolt which secures the pipe to the body and remove the pipe.

Pistons and Cylinders

Pistons and cylinders are matched according to their size. When replacing pistons and cyl-

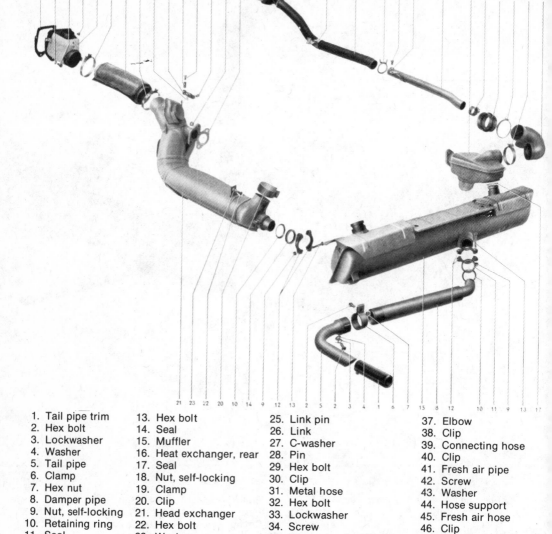

1. Tail pipe trim
2. Hex bolt
3. Lockwasher
4. Washer
5. Tail pipe
6. Clamp
7. Hex nut
8. Damper pipe
9. Nut, self-locking
10. Retaining ring
11. Seal
12. Clamp
13. Hex bolt
14. Seal
15. Muffler
16. Heat exchanger, rear
17. Seal
18. Nut, self-locking
19. Clamp
20. Clip
21. Head exchanger
22. Hex bolt
23. Washer
24. Flange gasket
25. Link pin
26. Link
27. C-washer
28. Pin
29. Hex bolt
30. Clip
31. Metal hose
32. Hex bolt
33. Lockwasher
34. Screw
35. Warm air mixer housing
36. Seal
37. Elbow
38. Clip
39. Connecting hose
40. Clip
41. Fresh air pipe
42. Screw
43. Washer
44. Hose support
45. Fresh air hose
46. Clip
47. Fresh air duct elbow

Exploded view of exhaust system—Type 3

inders, make sure that they are properly sized.

NOTE: *See the "Engine Rebuilding" section for cylinder refinishing.*

CYLINDER REMOVAL AND INSTALLATION

1. Remove the engine. Remove the cylinder head, pushrod tubes, and the deflector plate.

2. Slide the cylinder out of its groove in the crankcase and off of the piston. Try not to damage the cooling fins, as they chip easily. Matchmark the cylinders for reassembly.

The cylinders must be returned to their original bore in the crankcase. If a cylinder is to be replaced, it must be replaced with a matching piston.

3. Cylinders should be checked for wear and, if necessary, replaced with another matched cylinder and piston assembly of the same size.

4. Check the cylinder seating surface on the crankcase, cylinder shoulder and gasket for cleanliness and deep scores. When installing the cylinders, a new gasket, if required, should be fitted over the base of the cylinder and worked up to the crankcase-cyl-

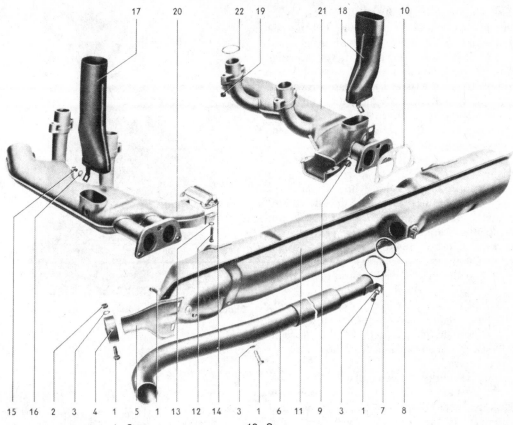

1. Screw
2. Nut
3. Spring washer
4. Clip
5. Bracket for tailpipe
6. Damper pipe
7. Seal
8. Sealing ring
9. Locknut
10. Gasket
11. Muffler
12. Screw
13. Spring washer
14. Heat exchange cover
15. Screw
16. Spring washer
17. Warm air fan left connection
18. Warm air fan right connection
19. Locknut
20. Left heat exchanger
21. Right heat exchanger
22. Sealing rings

Exploded view of exhaust system—Type 2/1700, Type 2/1800, Type 2/2000, and Type 4

Matchmarking pistons

Installing a cylinder

inder mating surface. These gaskets are usually made of paper, so be careful. Oil the gasket with regular engine oil after it is installed.

5. The piston, as well as the piston rings and pin must be oiled before reassembly.

6. Be sure that the ring gaps are of the correct dimension. Stagger the ring gaps around the piston, but make sure that the oil ring gap is positioned up when the pistons are in position on the connecting rods.

7. Turn the crankshaft until the intended piston is out as far as it can go, then fit the ring compressor, oil the cylinder walls and slide the cylinder onto the piston. Be careful that the other exposed piston skirts do not strike the crankcase when the crankshaft is turned. The bottoms of the cylinder barrels have a slight camfer to aid ring fitting. Make sure that the cylinder base gasket is in place on the cylinder barrel.

NOTE: *Use a ring compressor that pulls apart or you won't be able to get it off the piston once the cylinder barrel is over the rings. These are available at most automotive stores.*

8. Install the deflector plates.

9. Install the pushrod tubes using new gaskets. Install the pushrods. Make sure that the seam in the pushrod tube is facing upward.

10. Install the cylinder head.

PISTON REMOVAL AND INSTALLATION

NOTE: *See the "Engine Rebuilding" section for piston ring procedures.*

1. Remove the engine. Remove the cylinder head and, after matchmarking the cylinders, remove the cylinders.

NOTE: *You must remove both cylinder barrels from the bank to be worked on even if you are only removing one piston.*

2. Matchmark the pistons to indicate the cylinder number and which side points toward the flywheel.

3. Remove the circlips which retain the piston pin.

4. Heating the piston will aid in piston pin removal. To heat the piston, boil a clean rag in water and wrap it around the piston. You can fashion a pin remover by shaving an old piston pin down so that it will slide through the piston. Use it with a mallet to knock out the pin. Be sure to hold the piston when removing the pin so that the connecting rod is not bent.

5. Remove the piston from the connecting rod.

Checking piston ring end-gap

Checking piston ring side clearance

6. Before installing the pistons, they should first be cleaned and checked for wear. Remove the old rings. Clean the ring groove cleaner or a broken piece of ring. Clean the piston with solvent but do not use a wire brush or sand paper. Check for any cracks or scuff marks. Check the piston diameter with a micrometer and compare the readings to the specifications. If the running clearance between the piston and cylinder wall is 0.008 in. (0.2mm) or greater, the cylinder and piston should be replaced by a set of the same size grading. If the cylinder shows no sign of excessive wear or damage, it is permissible to install a new piston and rings of the appropriate size.

7. Place each ring in turn in its cylinder

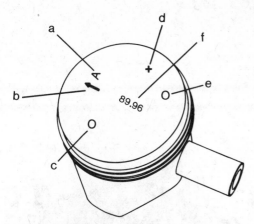

A. Corresponds to the index of the part number—serves as identifying mark
B. Arrow (indented or stamped on) must point toward flywheel
C. Paint spot indicates pistons which are of matching size (blue, pink, green)
D. Weight grading (+ or −)
E. Paint spot indicating weight grading (brown = − weight, grey = + weight)
F. Piston size in mm

Piston top markings—arrow (B) points toward flywheel

bore and check the piston ring endgap. If the gap is too large, replace the ring. If the gap is too narrow, file the end of the ring until the proper gap is obtained.

8. Insert the rings on the piston and check the ring side clearance. If the clearance is too large, replace the piston. Install the rings with the marking "Oben" or "Top" pointing upward.

9. If new rings are installed in a used piston, the ring ridge at the top of the cylinder bore must be removed with a ridge reamer.

10. Install a circlip on each piston on the side toward the flywheel, indicated by the arrow on the top of the piston. Install each piston so the arrow points toward the flywheel. If necessary, heat the piston to 75°C (167°F), then install the piston pin and fit the other circlip. Make sure the circlips are seated in their grooves properly.

11. Install the cylinders and the cylinder heads.

Crankcase

DISASSEMBLY AND ASSEMBLY

1. Remove the engine.
2. Remove the cylinder heads, cylinders, and pistons.
3. Remove the oil strainer, oil pressure switch, and the crankcase nuts. Remove the

flywheel and oil pump. The flywheel is held in place by the bolt, (Type 4 and 1972–81 Type 2 have five bolts), at the center of the flywheel. Matchmark the flywheel so that it can be replaced in the same position.

NOTE: *On manual transmission models, remove the clutch pressure plate and disc to expose the flywheel bolt(s).*

4. Keep the cam followers in the right crankcase half in position by using a retaining spring.

5. Clean the sludge off of the crankcase and locate *all* of the crankcase retaining nuts. Do not try to separate the halves until you are sure you have removed *all* of the nuts. Use a rubber hammer to break the seal between the crankcase halves.

CAUTION: *Never insert sharp metal tools, wedges, or any prying device between the crankcase halves. This will ruin the gasket surface and cause serious oil leakage.*

6. After the seal between the crankcase halves is broken, remove the right hand crankcase half, the crankshaft oil seal and the camshaft end plug. The camshaft and crankshaft can now be lifted out of the crankcase half.

7. Remove the cam followers (or lifters) bearing shells, and the oil pressure relief valve.

8. Before starting reassembly, check the crankcase for any damage or cracks.

9. Flush and blow out all ducts and oil passages. Check the studs for tightness. If the tapped holes are worn install a Heli-Coil®.

10. Install the crankshaft bearing dowel pins and bearing shells for the crankshaft and camshaft. Make sure the bearing shells are installed in the proper journal. See Crank-

Check dowel pins for tightness

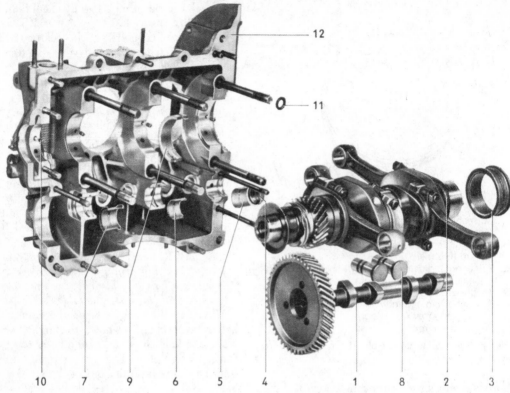

1. Camshaft
2. Crankshaft and connecting rods
3. Main bearing No. 1
4. Camshaft bore end cap
5. Camshaft No. 1 bearing shell
6. Camshaft No. 2 bearing shell
7. Left shell for camshaft No. 3 bearing (with thrust shoulder)
8. Cam follower
9. Crankshaft No. 2 bearing shell
10. Crankshaft bearing dowel pin
11. Crankcase joint seal
12. Left crankcase half

Exploded view of crankcase half assembly—Type 1, 2/1600, 3

shaft Removal and Installation, below, for crankshaft bearing placement.

11. Install the crankshaft and camshaft after the bearings have been well lubricated. When installing the camshaft and the crankshaft, make sure the timing marks are aligned. See Camshaft and Timing Gears Removal and Installation, below, for procedures.

12. Install the oil pressure relief valve.

13. Oil and install the cam followers.

NOTE: *To keep them from falling out during assembly, liberally coat them with white grease.*

14. Install the camshaft end plug using sealing compound.

15. Install the thrust washers and crankshaft oil seal. The oil seal must rest squarely on the bottom of its recess in the crankcase.

Tighten this nut first on Type 1, 2/1600, and 3 models

1. Camshaft
2. Crankshaft and connecting
   rod assembly
3. Main bearing No. 1
4. Main bearing No. 4
5. End cap for camshaft bore
6. Camshaft No. 1 bearing shell
7. No. 2 camshaft bearing
8. No. 3 camshaft bearing
   with shoulder for thrust
9. Crankshaft bearing dowel pin
10. No. 2 crankshaft bearing half
11. Left crankcase half

Exploded view of crankcase half assembly—Type 2/1700, 2/1800, 2/2000, and Type 4

The thrust washers at the flywheel end of the crankshaft are shims used to set the crankshaft end-play.

16. Spread a thin film of sealing compound on the crankcase joining faces and place the two halves together. Torque the nuts in several stages. Tighten the 8 mm nut located next to the 12 mm stud of the No. 1 crankshaft bearing first. As the crankcase

halves are being torqued, continually check the crankshaft for ease of rotation.

CAUTION: *Make sure the crankshaft bearings are seated correctly on their dowels or you could crack the bearings, the crankcase or both when tightening the crankcase nuts. See Crankshaft Removal and Installation for instructions.*

17. Crankshaft end-play is checked when

the flywheel is installed. It is adjusted by varying the number of thickness of the shims located behind the flywheel. Measure the end-play with a dial indicator mounted against the flywheel, and attached firmly to the crankcase.

Camshaft and Timing Gears

REMOVAL AND INSTALLATION

Removal of the camshaft requires splitting the crankcases. The camshaft and its bearing shells are then removed from the crankcase halves. Before reinstalling the camshaft, it should be checked for wear on the lobe surfaces and on the bearing surfaces. In addition, the riveted joint between the camshaft timing gear and the camshaft should be checked for tightness. The camshaft should be checked for a maximum runout of 0.0008 in. The timing gear should be checked for the correct tooth contact and for wear. If the camshaft bearing shells are worn or damaged, new shells should be fitted. The camshaft bearing shells should be installed with the tabs engaging the notches in the crankcase. It is usually a good idea to replace the bearing shells under any circumstances. Before installing the camshaft, the bearing journals and cam lobes should be generously coated with oil. When the camshaft is installed, care should be taken to ensure that the timing gear tooth marked (O) is located between the two teeth of the crankshaft timing gear marked with a center punch. The camshaft end-play is measured at the No. 3 bearing. End-play is 0.0015–0.005 in. (0.04–0.12 mm) and the wear limit is 0.006 in. (0.16 mm).

NOTE: *Camshaft gears are marked with a −1, 0, +1, etc., along their inner face to denote how much their pitch radius deviates from the standard pitch radius of 0. If your camshaft gear has 0 pitch deviation (i.e., if it is marked on its inner face with a "0"), do not confuse this mark with the zero shaped timing mark on the outer gear face.*

Crankshaft

CRANKSHAFT PULLEY REMOVAL AND INSTALLATION

On the Type 1 and 2/1600, the crankshaft pulley can be removed while the engine is still in the car. However, in this instance it is necessary for the rear cover plate of the engine to be removed. Remove the cover plate after taking out the screws in the cover plate below the crankshaft pulley. Remove the fan belt and the crankshaft pulley securing screw. Using a puller, remove the crankshaft pulley. The crankshaft pulley should be checked for proper seating and belt contact. The oil return thread should be cleaned and lubricated with oil. The crankshaft pulley should be installed in the reverse sequence. Check for oil leaks after installing the pulley.

On the Type 3, the crankshaft pulley can be removed only when the engine is out of the car and the muffler, generator, and cooling air intake housing are removed. After these parts have been removed, take out the plastic cap in the pulley. Remove the crankshaft pulley retaining bolt and remove the pulley.

Type 4 and Type 2/1700, 2/1800 and 2/2000, removal is the same as the Type 3. However, the pulley is secured by three socket head screws and a self locking nut.

Installation for Type 2/1700, 2/1800,

Aligning marks on timing gears

Type 2/1700, 2/1800, 2/2000 and Type 4 engine fan bolts

2/2000, 3 and 4 engines is the reverse of removal. When installing, use a new paper gasket between the fan and the crankshaft pulley. If shims are used, do not forget them. Don't use more than two shims. When inserting the pulley, make sure that the pin engages the hole in the fan. Ensure that the clearance between the generator belt and the intake housing is at least 4 mm and that the belt is parallel to the housing.

FLYWHEEL REMOVAL AND INSTALLATION

NOTE: *In order to remove the flywheel, the crankshaft will have to be prevented from turning. This may be accomplished on Type 1, 2/1600 and Type 3 models by using a 3 or 4 foot length of angle iron or thick stock sheet steel, such as an old fence post. Drill out two holes in the metal bar that correspond to two of the pressure plate retaining bolt holes. The metal bar is installed as per the accompanying illustration.*

Type 1, 2/1600, and 3

The flywheel is attached to the crankshaft with a gland nut and is located by four dowel pins. An oil seal is recessed in the crankcase casting at No. 1 main bearing. A needle bearing, which supports the main driveshaft, is located in the gland nut. Prior to removing the flywheel, it is necessary to remove it, using a 36 mm special wrench. Before removing the flywheel, matchmark the flywheel and the crankshaft.

Installation is the reverse of removal. Before installing the flywheel, check the flywheel teeth for any wear or damage. Check the dowel pins for correct fit in the crankshaft and in the flywheel. Adjust the crankshaft end-play and check the needle bearing in the gland nut for wear.

Type 2/1700, 2/1800, 2/2000 and 4

Removal and installation is similar to the Type 1, 2/1600, and 3 except that the flywheel is secured to the crankshaft by five socket head screws.

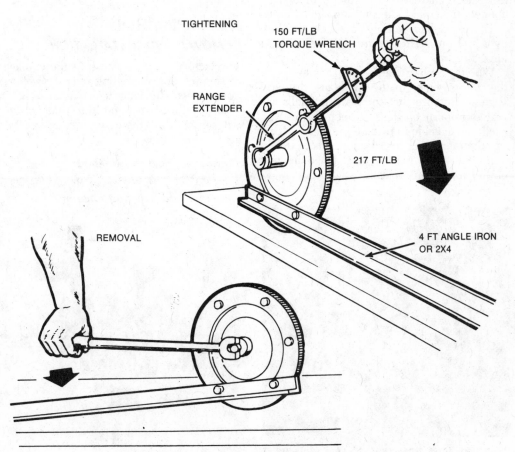

Removing/installing 1600 cc engine flywheel using special bar

CRANKSHAFT OIL SEAL (FLYWHEEL END) REPLACEMENT

This seal is removed after removing the flywheel. After the flywheel is removed, inspect the surface on the flywheel joining flange where the seal makes contact. If there is a deep groove or any other damage, the flywheel must be replaced. Remove the oil seal recess and coat it thinly with a sealing compound. Be sure that the seal rests squarely on the bottom of its recess. Make sure that the correct side of the seal is facing outward, that is, the lip of the seal should be facing the inside of the crankcase. Reinstall the flywheel after coating the oil seal contact surface with oil.

NOTE: *Be careful not to damage the seal when sliding the flywheel into place.*

CRANKSHAFT REMOVAL AND INSTALLATION

NOTE: *See the "Engine Rebuilding" section for crankshaft refinishing procedures.*

Removal of the crankshaft requires splitting the crankcase. After the crankcase is opened, the crankshaft can then be lifted out.

The crankshaft bearings are held in place by dowel pins. These pins must be checked for tightness.

When installing the bearings, make sure that the oil holes in the shells are properly aligned. Be sure that the bearing shells are seated properly on their dowel pins. Bearing shells are avilable in three undersizes. Measure the crankshaft bearing journals to determine the proper bearing size. Place one half of the No. 2 crankshaft bearing in the crankcase. Slide the No. 1 bearing on the crankshaft so that the dowel pin hole is toward the flywheel and the oil groove faces toward the fan. The No. 3 bearing is installed with the dowel pin hole facing toward the crankshaft web.

To remove the No. 3 main bearing, remove the distributor gear circlip and the distributor drive gear. Mild heat (176°F) must be applied to remove the gear. Next slide the spacer off of the crankshaft. The crankshaft timing gear should now be pressed off the crankshaft after mild heating. When the timing gear is reinstalled, the chamfer must face towards the No. 3 bearing. The No. 3 bearing can then be replaced. When removing and installing the gears on the crankshaft, be careful not to damage the No. 4 bearing journal.

When all of the crankshaft bearings are in place, lift the crankshaft and the connecting rod assembly into the crankcase and align the valve timing marks.

Install the crankcase half and reassemble the engine.

Connecting Rods

REMOVAL AND INSTALLATION

The factory suggests you split the crankcase to remove the connecting rods. However, if you're just checking your connecting rod bearings for wear, you can remove them without splitting the case. See the appropriate section, below.

Crankcase Splitting Method

NOTE: *See the "Engine Rebuilding" section for additional information.*

Removing burrs from rear oil seal housing in crankcase to ensure leak-free fit of oil seal

Forge marks on connecting rods must face up

Staking the connecting rod bolt

Tapping the connecting rod cap to relieve pretension

Measuring the connecting rod side clearance

After splitting the crankcase, remove the crankshaft and the connecting rod assembly. Remove the connecting rods, clamping bolts, and the connecting rod caps. Inspect the piston pin bushing. With a new bushing, the correct clearance is indicated by a light finger push fit of the pin at room temperature. Reinsert the new connecting rod bearings after all parts have been thoroughly cleaned. Assemble the connecting rods on the crankshaft, making sure that the rods are oriented properly on the crankshaft. The identification numbers stamped on the connecting rods and connecting rod caps must be on the same side. Note that the marks on the connecting rods are pointing upward, while the rods are pointing toward their respective cylinders. Lubricate the bearing shells before installing them.

Tighten the connecting rod bolts to the specified torque. A slight pre-tension between the bearing halves, which is likely to occur when tightening the connecting rod bolts, can be eliminated by gently striking the side of the bearing cap with a hammer. Do not install the connecting rod in the engine unless it swings freely on its journal. Using a peening chisel, secure the connecting rod bolts in place.

Failure to swing freely on the journal may be caused by improper side clearance, improper bearing clearance or failure to lubricate the rod before assembly.

Non-crankcase Splitting Method

NOTE: *See the "Engine Rebuilding" section for additional information.*

Remove the cylinder heads, cylinders and pistons. See above for procedures. Put a dab of grease in the end of a socket and, using an extension and ratchet, loosen and carefully remove the connecting rod nuts. The nuts face the piston side of the connecting rod. Turn the crankshaft as necessary to remove both nuts. Have an assistant hold the connecting rod cap from the other side of the engine and gently tap the cap bolts with a brass or plastic drift to separate the caps from the connecting rods. Pull the connecting rod out through the cylinder hole, then remove the cap. Be careful not to drop anything into the crankcase or you may have to split it after all. Reverse procedure to install. Install the connecting rods with the forged marks up: see illustration. Torque to proper specifications and using a small hammer, relieve pre-tension as instructed under Crankcase Splitting Method, above,

NOTE: *You will not be able to stake the nuts using this method, therefore it would be wise to apply Loctite® or an equivalent sealer to the threads.*

ENGINE LUBRICATION

OIL STRAINER REMOVAL AND INSTALLATION

The oil strainer can be easily removed by removing the retaining nuts, washers, oil strainer plate, strainer, and gaskets. The Type 2/1700, 2/1800, 2/2000 and Type 4 strainer is secured by a single bolt at the center of the strainer. Once taken out, the strainer must be thoroughly cleaned and all traces of old gaskets removed prior to fitting new ones. The suction pipe should be checked for tightness and proper position. When the strainer is installed, be sure that the suction pipe is correctly seated in the strainer. If necessary, the strainer may be bent slightly. The measurement from the strainer flange to the top of the suction pipe should be 10 mm. The measurement from the flange to the bottom of the strainer should be 6 mm. The cap nuts on Types 1, 2/1600, and 3 must not be overtightened. The Type 4 and Type 2/1700, 2/1800, 2/2000 have a spin-off replaceable oil filter as well as the strainer in the crankcase. The oil filter is located at the left rear corner of the engine.

OIL COOLER REMOVAL AND INSTALLATION

The Type 1 and 2/1600 oil cooler is located under the engine cooling fan housing at the left side of the engine. The Type 3 cooler is located at the same position but is mounted horizontally. The type 4 and Type 2/1700, 2/1800, 2/2000 coolers are mounted near the oil filter, at the left corner of the engine.

The oil cooler may be removed without taking the engine out of the car. On Types 1 and 2/1600, the engine fan housing must be

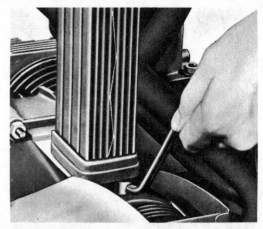

Removing oil cooler mounting using ring wrench—Type 1, 2/1600

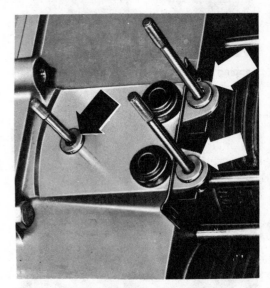

Oil cooler spacers on suitcase engines

removed. On the Type 3, the cooler is accessible through the left-hand cylinder cover plate. The Type 4 and Type 2/1700, 2/1800, 2/2000 cooler is accessible through the left side engine cowling, working either in the engine compartment or from underneath the car.

The oil cooler can be removed after the three retaining nuts have been taken off. The gaskets should be removed along with the cooler and replaced with new gaskets. If the cooler is leaking, check the oil pressure relief valve. The studs and bracket on the cooler should be checked for tightness. Make certain that the hollow ribs of the cooler do not touch one another. The cooler must not be clogged with dirt. Clean the contact surfaces on the crankcase, install new gaskets, and attach the oil cooler. Types 3 and 4, 2/1700, 2/1800 and 2/2000 have a spacer ring between the crankcase and the cooler at each securing screw. If these rings are omitted, the seals may be squeezed too tightly, resulting in oil stoppage and resultant engine damage. Use double retaining nuts and Loctite® on the cooler studs.

OIL PUMP REMOVAL AND INSTALLATION

On Types 1 and 2/1600, the pump can be removed while the engine is in the car, but it is first necessary to remove the cover plate, the crankshaft pulley, and the cover plate under the pulley. On Types 3, 4, 2/1700, 2/1800 and 2/2000, the oil pump can be taken out only after the engine is removed from the car and the air intake housing, the belt pulley fan housing, and fan are dismantled. On the Automatic Stick Shift models, the torque converter oil pump is driven by the engine oil pump.

On Type 1, 2/1600, and 3 remove the nuts from the oil pump cover and then remove the cover and its gasket. Remove the gears and take out the pump with a special extractor that pulls the body out of the crankcase. Care should be taken so as not to damage the inside of the pump housing.

Removing Type 1, 2/1600, and 3 oil pump

On Type 4, Type 2/1700, 2/1800, and 2/2000 engines, remove the four pump securing nuts and, prying on either side of the pump, pry the pump assembly out of the crankcase. To disassemble the pump, the pump cover must be pressed apart.

Prior to assembly, check the oil pump body for wear, especially the gear seating surface. If the pump body is worn, the result will be loss of oil pressure. Check the driven

Removing Type 2/1700, 2/1800, 2/2000 and 4 oil pump

gear shaft for tightness and, if necessary, peen it tightly into place or replace the pump housing. The gears should be checked for excessive wear, backlash, and end-play. Maximum end-play can be checked using a T-square and a feeler gauge. Check the mating surfaces of the pump body and the crankcase for damage and cleanliness. Install the pump into the crankcase with a new gasket. Do not use any sealing compound. Turn the camshaft several revolutions in order to center the pump body opposite the slot in the camshaft. On Type 1, 2/1600, and 3 the cover may now be installed. On Type 4, Type 2/1700, 2/1800, and 2/2000 models, the pump was installed complete. Tighten the securing nuts.

OIL PRESSURE RELIEF VALVE REMOVAL AND INSTALLATION

The oil pressure relief valve acts as a safety valve which opens when the oil pressure becomes too great. When the engine is cold, the oil is thick, which makes it easier for the oil pump to move it. This in turn creates greater oil pressure. On a cold engine, the oil pressure relief valve plunger is in its lowest position and allows only some of the oil to travel to lubrication points: the rest is fed back into the crankcase. This prevents the oil pressure from raising high enough to burst the seals in the oil cooler and elsewhere. As the engine warms, the plunger raises because the thinning oil doesn't have as much pressure as it did when cold, and more oil is directed toward the lubrication points.

The oil pressure relief valve is removed by unscrewing the end plug and removing the gasket ring, spring, and plunger. If the

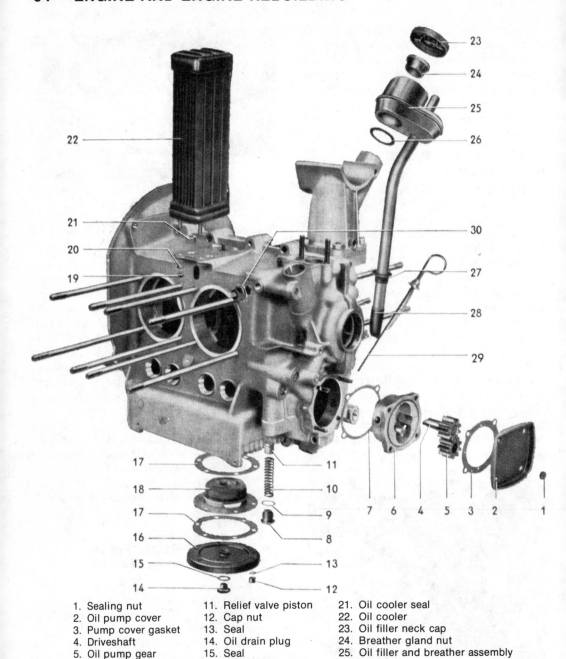

1. Sealing nut	11. Relief valve piston	21. Oil cooler seal
2. Oil pump cover	12. Cap nut	22. Oil cooler
3. Pump cover gasket	13. Seal	23. Oil filler neck cap
4. Driveshaft	14. Oil drain plug	24. Breather gland nut
5. Oil pump gear	15. Seal	25. Oil filler and breather assembly
6. Oil pump housing	16. Oil strainer cover	26. Seal
7. Housing gasket	17. Gasket	27. Grommet
8. Plug	18. Oil strainer	28. Breather rubber valve
9. Seal	19. Nut	29. Dipstick
10. Spring	20. Lockwasher	30. Oil pressure switch

Exploded view of lubrication system—Types 1, 2/1600

plunger sticks in its bore, it can be removed by screwing a 10 mm tap into it.

On 1600 cc engines, the valve is located to the left of the oil pump. On Automatic Stick Shift models, it is located on the oil pump housing. On 1700, 1800 and 2000 engines, the valve is located beside the oil filter.

Before installing the valve, check the plunger for any signs of seizure. If necessary, the plunger should be replaced. If there is

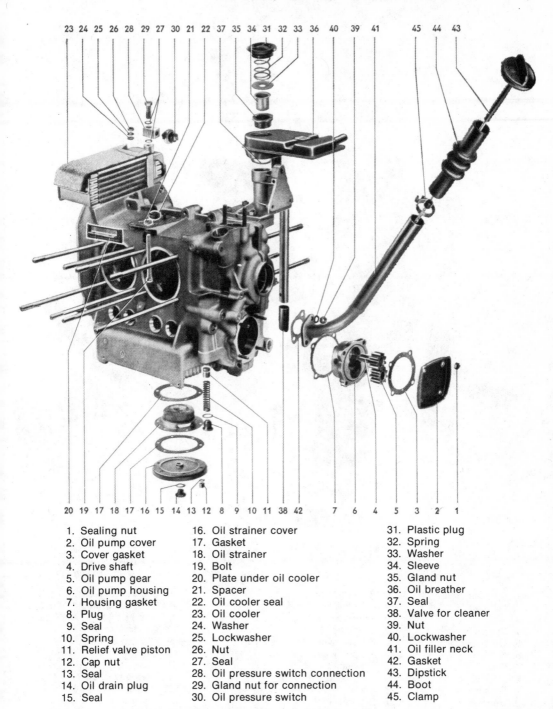

23 24 25 26 28 29 27 30 21 22 37 35 34 31 32 33 36 40 39 41 45 44 43

20 19 17 18 17 16 15 14 13 12 8 9 10 11 38 42 7 6 4 5 3 2 1

1. Sealing nut	16. Oil strainer cover	31. Plastic plug
2. Oil pump cover	17. Gasket	32. Spring
3. Cover gasket	18. Oil strainer	33. Washer
4. Drive shaft	19. Bolt	34. Sleeve
5. Oil pump gear	20. Plate under oil cooler	35. Gland nut
6. Oil pump housing	21. Spacer	36. Oil breather
7. Housing gasket	22. Oil cooler seal	37. Seal
8. Plug	23. Oil cooler	38. Valve for cleaner
9. Seal	24. Washer	39. Nut
10. Spring	25. Lockwasher	40. Lockwasher
11. Relief valve piston	26. Nut	41. Oil filler neck
12. Cap nut	27. Seal	42. Gasket
13. Seal	28. Oil pressure switch connection	43. Dipstick
14. Oil drain plug	29. Gland nut for connection	44. Boot
15. Seal	30. Oil pressure switch	45. Clamp

Exploded view of lubrication system—Type 3

any doubt about the condition of the spring, it should also be replaced. When installing the relief valve, be careful that you do not scratch the bore. Reinstall the plug with a new gasket.

Type 4 and Type 2/1700, 2/1800, 2/2000 engines have a second oil pressure relief valve located just to the right of, and below the oil filter.

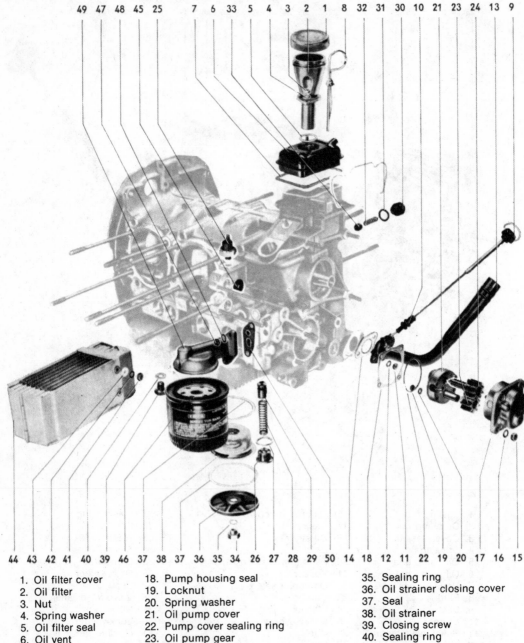

Exploded view of lubrication system—Types 2/1700, 2/1800, 2/2000 and Type 4

1. Oil filter cover
2. Oil filter
3. Nut
4. Spring washer
5. Oil filter seal
6. Oil vent
7. Seal
8. Oil dipstick
9. Dipstick
10. Bellows
11. Nut
12. Spring washer
13. Oil filler
14. Gasket
15. Nut
16. Spring washer
17. Oil pump housing

18. Pump housing seal
19. Locknut
20. Spring washer
21. Oil pump cover
22. Pump cover sealing ring
23. Oil pump gear
24. Driveshaft
25. Oil pressure switch
26. Screw
27. Sealing ring
28. Spring
29. Piston for oil relief valve
30. Screw
31. Sealing ring
32. Spring
33. Piston for oil pressure control valve
34. Nut

35. Sealing ring
36. Oil strainer closing cover
37. Seal
38. Oil strainer
39. Closing screw
40. Sealing ring
41. Nut
42. Spring washer
43. Washer
44. Oil cooler
45. Oil cooler sealing ring
46. Oil filter
47. Nut
48. Spring washer
49. Oil filter intermediate flange
50. Seal

vw803

Disassembling Type 2/1700, 2/1800, 2/2000 and 4 oil pump

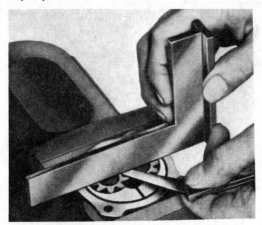

Checking oil pump end-play

HYDRAULIC VALVE LIFTERS

1978–81 Type 2 models are equipped with hydraulic lifters. No valve lash adjustment is required.

REMOVAL AND INSTALLATION

The lifters can be removed without removing the engine from the vehicle.

To remove the lifters, remove the rocker shafts with the rockers, withdraw the push rods and push rod tubes, then, using a magnetic probe, withdraw the lifters. Matchmark them with their respective cylinders to avoid confusion. Place the lifter with body down to avoid oil leak-out, thus making bleeding unnecessary before reinstallation.

Installation is the reverse of removal. When the rocker shafts and rockers are installed, set the adjusting screws in the rockers so that the ball shaped part is flush with the surface. Turn the crankshaft until cylinder no. 1 is at TDC compression stroke. Turn the adjusting screws so they just touch the valve stems, then turn them two turns clockwise and tighten the locknut. Adjust other cylinders in the same fashion.

NOTE: *Before installing make sure lifter is bled correctly by applying firm thumb pressure on the push rod socket. A resistance should be felt.*

BLEEDING HYDRAULIC LIFTERS

Fill a can with engine oil. Remove the lifter lockring, push rod socket, plunger, ball check valve with spring and plunger spring from the body. Be careful, the spring is very powerful! Place the lifter body in the can of oil so that it is completely submerged. Assemble the lifter except for the lockring and the pushrod socket. The lifter should be assembled while submerged in the oil. Open the valve with a suitable punch or scriber by pushing the punch down through the hole in the plunger to allow the oil to flow out of the lower part of the plunger. Insert the push rod socket in the lifter. Cut an old Type 1 push rod in half, then use it in conjunction with a press to slowly force down the push rod socket until the lock ring can be installed. The lifter must be submerged in oil the whole time.

1. Pulley bolt	16. Lockwasher	31. Spring
2. Dished washer	17. Outer fan cover	32. Washer
3. Crankshaft pulley	18. Reinforcement flange	33. Left cooling air regulator
4. Pulley nut	19. Inner fan cover	34. Right cooling air regulator
5. Special washer	20. Lockwasher	35. Cooling air regulator connecting rod
6. Rear pulley half	21. Nut	36. Washer
7. Spacer washer	22. Fan hub	37. Cheese head screw
8. V-belt	23. Shim	38. Lockwasher
9. Front pulley half	24. Fan	39. Washer
10. Woodruff key	25. Lockwasher	40. Connecting rod
11. Generator	26. Special nut	41. Thermostat bracket
12. Nut	27. Cheese head screw	42. Thermostat
13. Strap	28. Washer	43. Lockwasher
14. Bolt	29. Cheese head screw	44. Bolt
15. Bolt	30. Return spring	

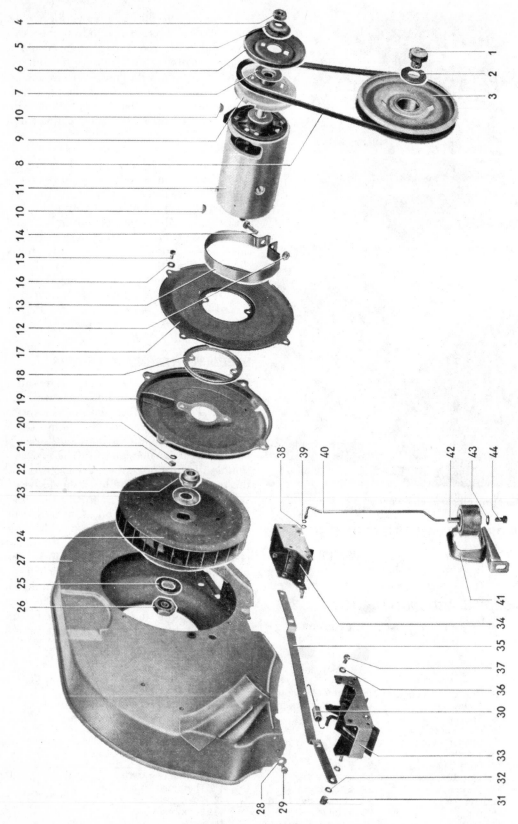

Exploded view of cooling system—Types 1 and 2/1600

1. Hose clip	20. Spacer washer	39. Washer
2. Bellows	21. Belt	40. Throttle valve shaft
3. Hose clip	22. Front pulley half	41. Left throttle valve
4. Hex bolt	23. Hex bolt	42. Right throttle valve
5. Lockwasher	24. Washer	43. Spring
6. Cooling air intake housing	25. Hex bolt	44. Lockwasher
7. Seal	26. Lockwasher	45. Valve rod
8. Rubber plug	27. Washer	46. Hex bolt
9. Cooling air intake housing cover	28. Engine mounting tube	47. Pin
10. Cap	29. Rear fan housing half	48. C-washer
11. Bolt	30. Fan	49. Washer
12. Lockwasher	31. Hex bolt	50. Intermediate lever
13. Crankshaft pulley	32. Washer	51. Connecting rod
14. Dowel pin	33. Front fan housing half	52. Thermostat
15. Shim	34. Nut	53. Washer
16. Gasket	35. Washer	54. Hex bolt
17. Pulley nut	36. Center support	55. Thermostat bracket
18. Special washer	37. Hex bolt	
19. Rear pulley half	38. Lockwasher	

Exploded view of cooling system—Type 3

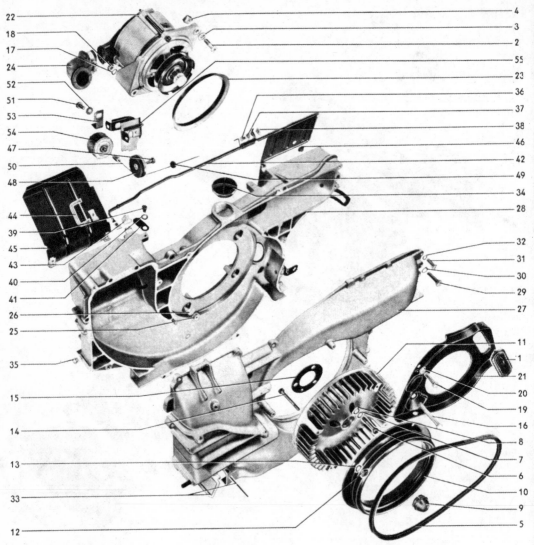

1. Cover plate insert
2. Socket head capscrew
3. Spring washer
4. Nut
5. Belt
6. Socket head capscrew
7. Spring washer
8. Flat washer
9. Cap
10. Crankshaft pulley
11. Fan
12. Nut
13. Spring nut
14. Socket head capscrew
15. Spacer
16. Bolt
17. Spring washer
18. Nut
19. Screw
20. Spring washer
21. Alternator cover plate
22. Alternator
23. Alternator sealing ring
24. Alternator elbow
25. Nut
26. Spring washer
27. Fan housing—rear half
28. Fan housing—front half
29. Bolt
30. Spring washer
31. Screw
32. Spring washer
33. Air non-return flap
34. Inspection hole cover
35. Plug
36. Bolt
37. Washer
38. Nut
39. Screw
40. Spring washer
41. Shaft retaining spring
42. Right flap and shaft
43. Bearing
44. Flap link
45. Left flap
46. Plug
47. Bolt
48. Cooling air control cable roller
49. Sealing washer
50. Cooling air control cable
51. Bolt
52. Washer
53. Thermostat washer
54. Thermostat
55. Thermostat bracket

Exploded view of cooling system—Types 2/1700, 2/1800, 2/2000 and Type 4

ENGINE COOLING

FAN HOUSING REMOVAL AND INSTALLATION

Type 1 and 2/1600

1. Remove the two heater hoses and the generator strap.
2. Pull out the lead wire from the coil. Remove the distributor cap and take off the spark plug connectors.
3. Remove the retaining screws that are located on both sides of the fan housing. Remove the rear hood.
4. Remove the outer half of the generator pulley and remove the fan belt.
5. Remove the thermostat securing screw and take out the thermostat.
6. Remove the lower part of the carburetor pre-heater duct.
7. The fan housing can now be removed with the generator. After removal, check the fan housing for damage and for loose air deflector plates.
8. Installation is the reverse of the above.
9. Make sure that the thermostat connecting rod is inserted into its hole in the cylinder head. The fan housing should be fitted properly on the cylinder cover plates so that there is no loss of cooling air.

FAN REMOVAL AND INSTALLATION

Type 1 and 2/1600

1. Remove the generator and fan assembly as described in the "Generator Removal and Installation' section.
2. While holding the fan, unscrew the fan retaining nut and take off the fan, spacer washers, and the hub.
3. To install, place the hub on the generator shaft, making sure that the woodruff key is securely positioned.
4. Insert the spacer washers. The clearance between the fan and the fan cover is 0.06–0.07 in. Place the fan into position and tighten its retaining nut. Correct the spacing by inserting the proper number of spacer washers. Place any extra washers between the lockwasher and the fan.
5. Reinstall the generator and the fan assembly.

Type 2/1700, 2/1800, 2/2000

1. On 1973–74 models, the air injection pump and related parts must first be removed. Loosen the air pump and remove the drive belt. Remove the pump and bracket retaining bolts and remove the air pump and retaining brackets. Unbolt and remove the extension shaft and pulley assembly from the fan and fan housing. Using a 12 point allen wrench, loosen the alternator drive belt adjusting bolt. Then, remove the timing scale, fan and crankshaft pulley assembly, and the alternator drive belt.
2. On models without the air injection pump, pry out the alternator cover insert, and, using a 12 point allen wrench, loosen the alternator adjusting bolt. Remove the alternator drive belt, the ignition timing scale and the grille over the fan. Remove the three socket head screws attaching the fan and crankshaft assembly to the crankshaft and remove the fan and pulley.
3. Disconnect the cooling air control cable at the flap control shaft.
4. On models so equipped, pull out the rubber elbow for the alternator from the front half of the fan housing.
5. Remove the four nuts retaining the fan housing to the engine crankcase. The assembled fan housing may then be removed by pulling it to the rear and off the engine. It is not necessary to separate the fan housing halves or remove the alternator to remove the fan housing.
6. Reverse the above procedure to install, taking care to adjust the alternator and air pump drive belts (1973–74 models) so that moderate thumb pressure deflects the belt about ½ in. when applied at a point midway between the longest run. Also, adjust the cooling air control cable as outlined in this section.

FAN HOUSING AND FAN REMOVAL AND INSTALLATION

Type 3

1. Remove the crankshaft pulley, the rear fan housing half, and the fan.
2. Unhook the linkage and spring at the right-hand air control flap.
3. Remove the screws for the front half of the housing and remove the housing.
4. Install the front half and ensure the correct sealing of the cylinder cover plates.
5. Replace and tighten the two lower mounting screws slightly.
6. Turn the two halves of the fan housing to the left until the crankcase half is contacted by the front lug.
7. Fully tighten the two lower mounting screws.

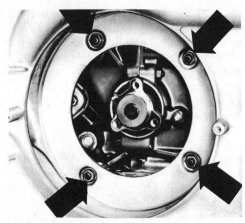

Type 3 fan housing nuts

8. Loosen the nuts at the breather support until it can be moved.

9. Insert and tighten the mounting screws of the upper fan housing half. Tighten the breather support nuts fully.

10. Connect the linkage and spring to the right-hand air control flap.

11. Install the fan and the rear half of the fan housing.

Type 4, Type 2/1700, 2/1800, 2/2000

1. Remove the engine. Remove the fan belt.

2. Remove the allen head screws and remove the belt pulley and fan as an assembly.

NOTE: *It is not necessary to remove the alternator to remove the fan housing.*

3. Remove the spacer and the alternator cover plate.

4. Disconnect the cooling air regulating cable at the shaft.

5. Remove the nuts and remove both halves of the fan housing at the same time.

6. Installation is the reverse of the above.

AIR FLAP AND THERMOSTAT ADJUSTMENT

Type 1 and 2/1600

1. Loosen the thermostat bracket securing nut and disconnect the thermostat from the bracket.

2. Push the thermostat upwards to fully open the air flaps.

3. Reposition the thermostat bracket so that the thermostat contacts the bracket at the upper stop, and then tighten the bracket nut.

4. Reconnect the thermostat to the bracket.

Type 3

1. Loosen the clamp screw on the relay lever.

2. Place the air flaps in the closed position. Make sure that the flaps close evenly. To adjust a flap, loosen its securing screw and turn it on its shaft.

3. With the flaps closed, tighten the clamp screw on the relay lever.

Type 4, Type 2/1700, 2/1800, 2/2000

1. Loosen the cable control.

2. Push the air flaps completely closed.

3. Tighten the cable control.

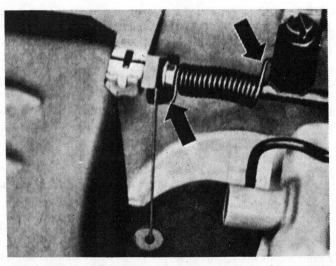

Type 2/1700, 2/1800, 2/2000, and Type 4 air flap cable control

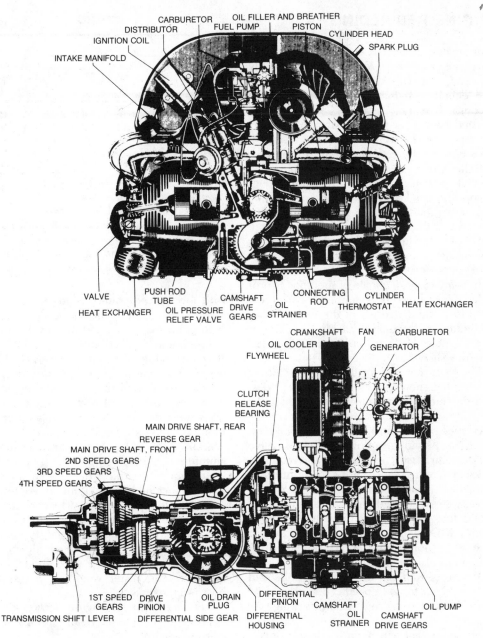

Type 1, 2/1600 upright fan engine and transaxle

ENGINE REBUILDING

This section describes, in detail, the procedures involved in rebuilding a horizontally opposed, air-cooled Volkswagen/Porsche four cylinder engine. It is divided into two sections. The first section, Cylinder Head Reconditioning, assumes that the cylinder head is removed from the engine, all manifolds and sheet metal shrouding is removed, and the cylinder head is on a workbench. The second section, Crankcase Reconditioning, covers the crankcase halves, the connecting rods, crankshaft, camshaft and lifters. It is assumed that the engine is mounted on a work stand (which can be rented), with the cylinder heads, cylinders, pistons, and all accessories removed.

In some cases, a choice of methods is provided. The choice of a method for a procedure is at the discretion of the user. It may be limited by the tools available to a user, or the proximity of a local engine rebuilding or machine shop.

The tools required for the basic rebuilding procedures should, with minor exceptions, be those included in a mechanic's tool kit: An accurate torque wrench (preferably a preset, click type), inside and outside micrometers, electric drill with grinding attachment, valve spring compressor, a set of taps and reamers, a valve lapping tool, and a dial indicator (reading in thousandths of an inch). Special tools, where required, are available from the major tool suppliers (i.e. Zelenda®, Craftsman®, K-D®, Snap-On®). The services of a competent automotive or aviation machine shop must also be readily available.

When assembling the engine, bolts and nuts with no torque specification should be tightened according to size and marking (see chart).

Any parts that will be in frictional contact must be pre-lubricated before assembly to provide protection on initial start-up. Many differnt pre-lubes are available and each mechanic has his own favorite. However, any product specifically formulated for this purpose, such as Vortex Pre-Lube®, STP®, Wynn's Friction Proofing®, or even a good grade of white grease may be used.

NOTE: *Do not use engine oil only, as its viscosity is not sufficient.*

Where semi-permanent (locked but removable) installation of nuts or bolts is required, the threads should be cleaned and coated

Metric

Bolt Diameter (mm)	Bolt Grade				Wrench Size (mm) Bolt and Nut
	5D	8G	10K	12K	
6	5	6	8	10	10
8	10	16	22	27	14
10	19	31	40	49	17
12	34	54	70	86	19
14	55	89	117	137	22
16	83	132	175	208	24
18	111	182	236	283	27
22	182	284	394	464	32
24	261	419	570	689	36

*—Torque values are for lightly oiled bolts.
CAUTION: Bolts threaded into aluminum require much less torque.

with locking compound. Studs may be permanently installed using a special compound such as Loctite® Stud and Bearing Mount.

Aluminum is used liberally in VW and Porsche engines due to its low weight and excellent heat transfer characteristics. Both the cylinder heads and the crankcase are aluminum alloy castings. However, a few precautions must be observed when handling aluminum alloy castings. However, a few precautions must be observed when handling aluminum engine parts:—Never hot-tank aluminum parts, unless the hot-tanking solution is specified for aluminum application (i.e. Oakite® Aluminum Cleaner 164, or ZEP® Hot Vat Aluminum Cleaner). Most hot-tanking solutions are used for ferrous metals only, and "cook" at much higher temperatures than the 175°F used for aluminum cleaners. The result would be a dissolved hear or crankcase.

—Always coat threads lightly with engine oil or anti-seize compound before installation, to prevent seizure.

—Never overtorque bolts or spark plugs in aluminum threads. Should stripping occur, threads can be restored using inserts such as the Heli-Coil®, K-D® Insert for Keenserts® kits.

To install a Heli-Coil® insert, tap drill the hole with the stripped threads to the specified size (see chart). If you are performing this operation on a spark plug hole with the head installed, coat the tap with wheel bearing grease to prevent aluminum shavings from falling into the combustion chamber (it will also help if the engine is rotated so that

Heli-Coil Specifications

| | Heli-Coil Insert | | | | | | |
Thread Size	Part No.	Insert Length (In.)	Drill Size	Tap Part No.	Insert Tool Part No.	Extracting Tool Part No.
1/2-20	1185-4	3/8	17/64 (.266)	4 CPB	528-4N	1227-6
5/16-18	1185-5	15/32	Q (.332)	5 CPB	528-5N	1227-6
3/8-16	1185-6	9/16	X (.397)	6 CPB	528-6N	1227-6
7/16-14	1185-7	21/32	29/64 (.453)	7 CPB	528-7N	1227-16
1/2-13	1185-8	3/4	33/64 (.516)	8 CPB	528-8N	1227-16

the exhaust valve of the subject cylinder is open, so that when the engine is initially started, if any chips did fall into the engine, they will be blown out the exhaust instead of scoring the cylinder walls, and, if compressed air is available, it may be applied through the spark plug hole and the chips blown out the exhaust port).

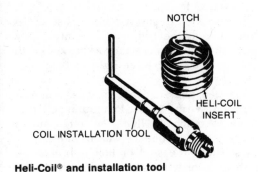

Heli-Coil® and installation tool

Heli-Coil® installation

NOTE: *Heli-Coil® tap sizes refer to the size thread being replaced, rather than the actual tap size.*

Using the specified tap, tap the hole for the Heli-Coil®. Place the insert on the proper installation tool (see chart). Apply pressure on the insert while winding it clockwise into the hole, until the top of the insert is one turn below the surface. Remove the installation tool and break the installation tang from the bottom of the insert by moving it up and down. If, for some reason, the

Heli-Coil® must be removed, tap the removal tool firmly into the hole, so that it engages the top thread, and turn the tool counterclockwise to extract the insert.

K-D® makes an insert specifically designed for the 14 mm spark plugs used in all VW's. The steel insert is 3/8 in. deep and has a lip which will seat the insert automatically to the correct depth. To install the K-D® insert, screw the combination reamer and tap into the damaged hole to ream the hole to the proper size and cut new threads for the insert. Then, screw the insert onto a spark plug, and torque the plug to 15–18 ft. lbs. to seat the insert.

NOTE: *Apply locking compound to the threads of the insert (cylinder head side) to make the installation permanent.*

Another spark plug insert that has come into favor is the Keenserts® insert. The special features of this type of insert are the locking keys and gas tight sealing ring. The Keenserts® kit consists of a ream and countersink tool, a tap 3/4–16 with pilot point, an installation tool (drift), and the inserts. To install a Keenserts® insert, the following procedure is used:

a. Ream and countersink the damaged spark plug hole.

b. Check the countersink depth. It should be 13/16 tool in until the stop comes into full contact with the head.

c. Tap the hole.

d. Select an insert. Mount the insert on the installation tool.

e. Rotate the tool and insert clockwise until the insert bottoms in the hole.

f. Drive the special anti-rotation keys into the head using the installation tool, sleeve, and a hammer.

g. Remove the installation tool. Check that the insert is flush with the cylinder

K-D® Tap/reamer and spark plug inserts

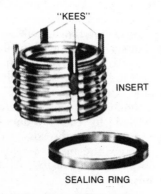

Keenserts® insert and sealing ring

head surface and that all keys have seated at the undercut portion of the insert.

h. To install the sealing ring, place it squarely around the top of the insert. Then, install a flat seated spark plug, with the plug gasket removed, and torque it to 35 ft. lbs. Remove the plug and check the seating of the ring. This should provide a gas tight seal, flush with the insert top.

i. Finally, install the spark plug with its gasket into the insert, and torque it to its normal 18 ft. lbs.

To remove a Keenserts® insert, use a $^{21}/_{32}$ drill through the center of the insert to a depth of ¼ in. Remove the locking keys with a punch and remove the insert with an E-Z out® tool.

Snapped bolts or studs may be removed using Vise-Grip® pliers. Penetrating oil (e.g. Liquid Wrench®, CRC®) will often aid in breaking the torque of frozen threads. In cases where the stud or bolt is broken off flush with, or below the surface, the following procedure may be used: Drill a hole (using a hardened bit) in the broken stud or

INSTALLATION TOOLS

REAM AND COUNTERSINK TOOL. Use this tool to remove the damaged threads, enlarge the hole to the proper size for tapping, and cut the counter-sink at the top of the hole to accommodate the sealing ring . . . in one operation. Ideally, it should be used in a drill press, however excellent results can be obtained with a hand-held electric drill. Keep the tool well lubricated to extend its life and prevent the adhesion of aluminum to the cutting edges.

TAP This is a conventional ¾-16 tap with a special "pilot point" to assure proper alignment with the newly prepared hole. Thorough lubrication will yield better threads and increase tap life.

INSTALLATION TOOL
This tool serves two purposes. It is used to thread the KEENSERTS insert into the cylinder head hole, and to drive the anti-rotation "KEES" into the cylinder head material surrounding the insert. As the insert is threaded into the hole, this tool acts as a depth-stop to assure that the top of the insert is automatically located flush with the upper surface of the cylinder head.

Keenserts® installation tools

bolt, about ½ of its diameter. Select a screw extractor (e.g. E-Z Out®) of the proper diameter, and tap it into the stud or bolt. Slowly turn the extractor counterclockwise to remove the stud or bolt.

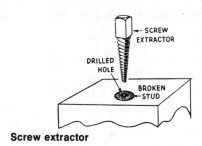

Screw extractor

Another process of checking for cracks is the Zyglo® process. This process does work with aluminum alloy. First the part is coated with a flourescent dye penetrant. Then the part is subjected to a blacklight inspection, under which cracks glow brightly, both at or below the surface.

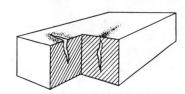

Magnaflux indication of cracks

One of the problems of small displacement, high-revving engines is that they are prone to developing fatigue cracks and other material flaws because they are highly stressed. One of the more popular procedures for checking metal fatigue and stress is Magnafluxing®. Magnafluxing® coats the part with fine magnetic particles, and subjects the part to a magnetic field. Cracks cause breaks in the magnetic field (even cracks below the surface not visible to the eye), which are outlined by the particles. However, since Magnafluxing® is a magnetic process, it applies only to ferrous metals (crankshafts, flywheels, connecting rods, etc.) It will not work with the aluminum heads and crankcases of these engines which are most prone to cracking.

A third method of checking for suspected cracks is the use of spot check dye. This method is quicker, and cheaper to perform, although hidden cracks beneath the surface may escape detection. First, the dye is sprayed onto the suspected area and wiped off. Then, the area is sprayed with a developer. The cracks will show up brightly.

If any of the threaded studs for the rocker arms or manifolds become damaged, and they are not broken off below the surface, they may be removed easily using the following procedure. Lock two nuts on the stud and unscrew the stud using the lower nut. It's as easy as that. Then, to make sure that the new stud remains in place, use locking compound on the threads.

Cylinder Head Reconditioning

Procedure	Method
Identify the valves: 8 7 6 5 4 3 2 1 **Cross-sectional view of valve and related parts**	Keep the valves in order, so that you know which valve (intake and exhaust) goes in which combustion chamber. If the valve faces are not full of carbon, you may number them, front to rear, with a permanent felt tip marker. 1. Cylinder head 2. Valve seat insert 3. Valve guide 4. Valve 5. Oil deflector ring (valve stem seal) 6. Valve keeper (key) 7. Valve spring 8. Valve spring cap (retainer)

Procedure	Method
Remove the valves and springs:	Using an appropriate valve spring compressor (see illustrations), compress the valve springs and lift out the keepers with needlenose pliers. Then, slowly release the compressor, and remove the valve, spring and spring retainer. On 1972 and earlier engines, a valve stem seal is used beneath the keepers which can be discarded. Check the keeper seating surfaces (see illustration) on the valve stem for burrs which may scratch the valve guide during installation of the valve. Remove any burrs with a fine file.

Lever-type valve spring compressor removing spring from 1600 cylinder head

This section assumes that the cylinder head is removed for this operation. However, if it is desired to remove the valve springs with the head installed, it will be necessary to screw a compressed air adaptor into the subject spark plug hole and maintain a pressure of 85 psi to keep the valve from dropping down.

Inspect the exhaust valves closely. More often than not, the cause of low compression is a burned exhaust valve. The classic burned valve is cracked on the valve face from the edge of the seat to the stem the way you could cut a pie. Remove all carbon, gum and varnish from the valve stem with a hardwood chisel, or with a wire brush and solvent (i.e. carburetor cleaner, lacquer thinner).

Overhead-type K-D® valve spring compressor

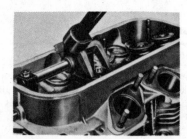

Lever-type valve spring compressor which pivots on bare rocker shaft to remove springs on 1700, 1800 and 200 cylinder heads

Lever-type valve spring compressor used in conjunction with compressed air chuck to remove springs with head installed—1600 shown

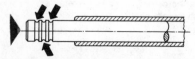

Valve keeper seating surfaces

Procedure	Method

Burned exhaust valve

Hot-tank the cylinder head:

Take the head(s) to an engine rebuilding or machine shop and have it (them) hot-tanked to remove grease, corrosion, carbon deposits and scale. NOTE: *Make sure that the hot tanking solution is designed to clean aluminum, not to dissolve it.*

After hot-tanking, inspect the combustion chambers (around the spark plug hole) and the exhaust ports for cracks (see illustration). Also, check the plug threads, manifold studs, and rocker arm studs for damage and looseness.

Cracks in combustion chamber adjoining spark plug hole

Degrease the remaining cylinder head parts:

Using solvent (i.e. Gunk® or Zep® carburetor cleaner), clean the rockers, rocker shafts, valve springs, spring retainers, keepers and the pushrods. You may also use solvent to clean the cylinder head although it will not clean as well as hot-tanking. Also clean the sheet metal shrouding at this time. Do not clean the pushrod tubes in solvent.

De-carbon the cylinder head:

Chip carbon away from the combustion chambers and exhaust ports using a chisel made of hardwood. Remove the remaining deposits with a stiff wire brush. You may also use a power brush (drill with wire attachment if you use a very light touch). Remember that you are working with a relatively soft metal (aluminum), and you do not want to grind into the metal. If you have access to a machine shop that works on aluminum heads, ask them about glass-beading the cylinder head.

Decarbonizing combustion chamber with power rotary wire brush

Procedure	Method
Check the valve stem-to-guide clearance (valve rock):  **Checking stem-to-guide clearance (valve rock) with dial gauge**	Clean the valve stem with lacquer thinner or carburetor cleaner to remove all gum and varnish. Clean the valve guides using solvent and an expanding wire-type valve guide cleaner or brass bristle brush. Mount a dial indicator to the head (see illustration) so that the gauge pin is at a 90° angle to the valve stem, up against the edge of the valve head. Insert the valve by hand so that the stem end is flush with the end of the guide. Move the valve off its seat, and measure the clearance by rocking the stem back and forth to actuate the dial indicator. Check the figure against specifications. Maximum rock should not exceed the wear limit. To check whether excessive rock is due to worn valve stems or guides (or both), one of two methods may be used. If a new valve is available, you may recheck the valve rock. If rock is still excessive the guide is at fault. Or, you may measure the old valve stem with a micrometer, and determine if it has passed its wear limit. In any case, most VW and Porsche mechanics will replace the exhaust valve and guides anyway, since they often wear out inside of 50,000 miles.

1600 Engines to '74

	Intake valve guide	Exhaust valve guide	Wear limit
Rock	.008–.009 in. (0.21–0.23 mm)	.011–.013 in. (0.28–0.32 mm)	.031 in. (0.8 mm)
Inside diameter	.3149–.3156 in. (8.00–8.02 mm)		.3172 in. (8.06 mm)

1700, 1800, 2000 Engines

	Intake valve guide	Exhaust valve guide	Wear limit
Rock	0.45 mm (.018 in.)		0.9 mm (.035 in.)
Inside diameter	8.00–8.02 mm (.3149–.3156 in.)	8.98–8.99 mm (.3534–.3538 in.)	8.06 or 9.06 mm (.3172 or .3566 in.)

Procedure	Method

1975–80 1600 Engines

	Intake valve guide	Exhaust valve guide	Wear limit
Rock	.008–.009 in. (0.21–0.23 mm)	.018 in. (0.45 mm)	.032 or .035 in. (0.8 or 0.9 mm)
Inside diameter	.3149–.3156 in. (8.00–8.02 mm)	.3534–.3538 in. (8.98–8.99 mm)	.3172 or 3566 in. (8.06 or 9.06 mm)

VW does not make available oversize valve stems to clean up excessive valve rock. Therefore, if excessive clearance is evident, replace the guides.

Knurling the valve guides:

Knurling is a process whereby metal is displaced and raised, thereby reducing clearance. It is a procedure used in engines where the guides are shrunk in making replacement a costly procedure. Although this operation can be performed on VW and Porsche engines, it is not recommended, since the exhaust guides will eventually need replacement anyway.

Replacing the valve guides:

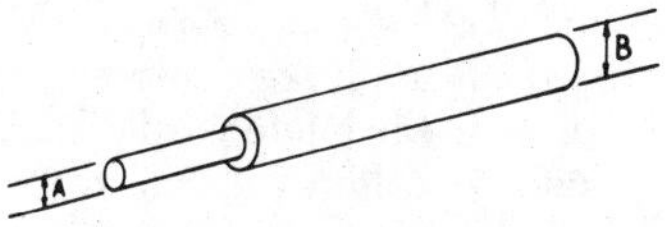

A-Valve guide I.D.
B-Slightly smaller than valve guide O.D.
Valve guide removal tool

The valve guides are a press fit into the head. NOTE: *If your replacement valve guides do not have a collar at the top, measure the distance the old guides protrude above the head.* Several different methods may be used to remove worn valve guides. One method is to press or tap the guides out of the head using a stepped drift (see illustration). The problem with this method is the risk of cracking the head. Another method, which reduces this risk, is to first drill out the guide about ⅔ of the length of the guide so that the walls of the guide at the top are paper thin ($1/32$ in. or so). This relieves most of the tension from the cylinder head guide bore, but still provides a solid base at the bottom of the guide to drift out the guide from the top. A third method of removing guides is to tap threads into the guide and pull it out from the top. After tapping the guide, place an old wrist pin (or some other type of sleeve) over the guide, so that the wrist pin rests squarely on the boss on the cylinder head around the guide. Then, take a long bolt (about 4 or 5 inches long with threads running all the way up to the bolt head) and thread a nut about half way up the bolt. Place a washer on top of the wrist pin (see illustration) and thread the bolt into the valve guide until the nut contacts the washer and wrist pin. Finally, screw the nut

Procedure

Method

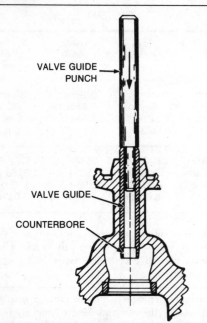

VALVE GUIDE PUNCH

VALVE GUIDE

COUNTERBORE

Cross-sectional view of valve guide and punch

Guide drilled out to relieve tension for removal

Tapping guide for removal using wrist pin method

down against the washer and wrist pin to pull out the guide.

If you are installing the guides without the aid of a press, using only hand tools, it will help to place the new valve guides in the freezer for an hour or so, and the clean, bare cylinder head in the oven at 350–400° F for ½ hour to 45 minutes. Controlling the temperature of the metals in this manner will slightly shrink the valve guides and slightly expand the guide bore in the cylinder head, allowing easier installation and lessening the risk of cracking the head in the process.

Most replacement valve guides, other than those manufactured by VW, have a collar at the top which provides a positive stop to seat the guides in the head. However, VW guides have no such collar. Therefore, on these guides, you will have to determine the height above the cylinder head boss that the guide must extend (about ¼ in.). Then, obtain a stack of washers, their inner diameter slightly larger than the outer diameter of the guide at the top of the guide. If the guide should extend ¼ in., use a ¼ in. thick stack of washers around the guide.

To install the valve guides in the head, use a collared drift, or a special valve guide installation tool of the proper outer diameter (see illustration). CAUTION: *If you have heated the head in the oven to aid installation, be extremely careful handling metal of this temperature. Use pot holders, or asbestos gloves with thick insulation. Do not set the head down on any surface that may be affected by the heat.* If the replacement guide is collared, drive in the guide until it seats against the boss on the cylinder head. If the guide is not collared, drive in the guide until the installation tool butts against the stack of washers (approx. ¼ in. thick) on the head. NOTE: *If you do not heat the head to aid installation, use penetrating lubricant in the guide bore, instead.*

Procedure	Method

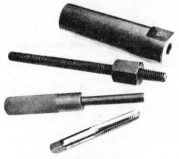

Valve guide removal kit

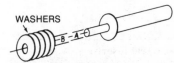

WASHERS

A-VALVE GUIDE I.D.
B-LARGER THAN THE VALVE GUIDE O.D.

Valve guide installation tool

Valve guide removal using long bolt, washer, nut, and wrist pin

Resurfacing (grinding) the valve face:

Using a valve grinding machine, have the valves resurfaced according to specifications (see chart).

Grinding a valve

Intake valves: 1600

A	B	C	D
1.259 in. (32.0 mm)	4.4 in. (112 mm)	.3130–3126 in. (7.95–7.94 mm)	44°

Exhaust valves: 1600

A	B	C	D
1.259 in. (32.0 mm)	4.4 in. (112 mm)	1970–'74 .3114–.3118 in. (7.91–7.92 mm)	45°
		1975–'76 .3500–.3510 in. (8.91–8.92 mm)	

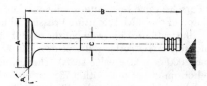

Critical valve dimensions (see chart)

1700, 1800, 2000	Intake valve	Exhaust valve
A (1700)	39.1–39.3 mm dia (1.5394–1.5472 in.)	32.7–33.0 mm dia (1.2874–1.2992 in.)

Procedure	Method

1700, 1800, 2000	Intake valve	Exhaust valve
A (1800)	41 mm dia (1.614 in.)	34 mm dia (1.338 in.)
A (2000)	37.5 mm dia (1.475 in.)	34 mm dia (1.338 in.)
B	116.8–117.3 mm (4.5984–4.6181 in.)	117.0–117.5 mm (4.6063–4.6260 in.)
C	7.94–7.95 mm dia (.3126–.3130 in.)	8.91–8.92 mm dia (.3508–.3512 in.)
D	29° 30'	45°

The valve stem tip should also be squared and resurfaced, by placing the stem in the V-block of the grinder, and turning it while pressing lightly against the grinding wheel. NOTE: *After grinding, the minimum valve head margin must be 0.50 mm (.020 in.). The valve head margin is the straight surface on the edge of the valve head, parallel with the valve stem.*

Replacing valve seat inserts:

This operation is not normally performed on VW and Porsche engines due to its expense and special shrink fit of the insert in the head. Usually, if the seat is destroyed, the head is also in bad shape (i.e. cracked, or hammered from a broken valve or piston). Some high-performance engine builders will replace the inserts to accommodate larger diameter valve heads. Otherwise, the operation will usually cost more than replacement of the head. Also, a replacement insert, if not installed correctly, could come out of the head, damaging the engine.

Resurfacing the valve seats:

Installing pilot in valve guide

Most valve seats can be reconditioned by resurfacing. This is done with a reamer or grinder. First, a pilot is installed in the valve guide (a worn valve guide will allow the pilot to wobble, causing an inaccurate seat cut). When using a reamer, apply steady pressure while rotating clockwise. The seat should clean up in about four complete turns, taking care to remove only as much metal as necessary. NOTE: *Never rotate a reamer counterclockwise.* When using a grinder, lift the cutting stone on and off the seat at approximately two cycles per second, until all flaws are removed.

It takes three separate cuts to recondition a VW or Porsche valve seat. After each cut, check the position of the valve seat using Prussian blue dye (see illustration). First, you cut the center of the seat using a 45° cutter (30° cutter on 1700, 1800 and 2000 cc intake valve seats). Then, you cut the bottom of the seat with a 75° cutter and narrow the top of the seat with a 15° stone. The center of the seat (seat width "a") must be maintained as per the following chart:

Procedure	**Method**

Cutting valve seat using reamer

Cutting valve seat using grinder

Engine	Intake	Exhaust
1600	.051–.063 in. (1.3–1.6 mm)	.067–.079 in. (1.7–2.0 mm)
1700, 1800, 2000	1.8–2.2 mm (.071–.087 in.)	2.0–2.5 mm (.079–.098 in.)

Equally as important as the width of the seat is its location in relation to the valve. Using a caliper, measure the distance between the center of the valve face on both sides of a valve. Then, place the caliper on the valve seat, and check that the pointers of the caliper locate in the center of the seat.

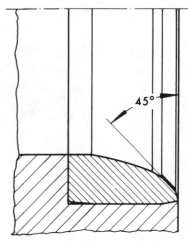

45° contact facing on seat of all 1600 valves and on 1700, 1800 and 2000 exhaust valves

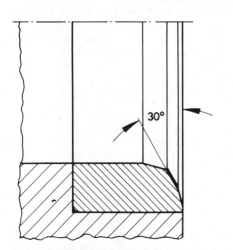

30° contact facing on seat of 1700, 1800 and 2000 intake valves

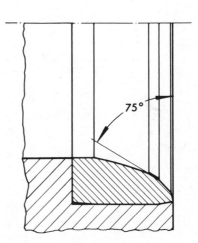

75° cut on lower edge of seat

Procedure	Method

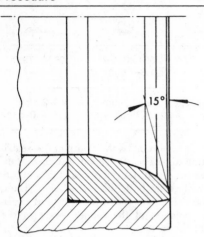

15° finish cut on upper (outer) edge of seat

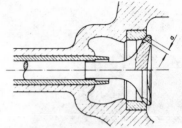

Seat contact width (dimension "a")

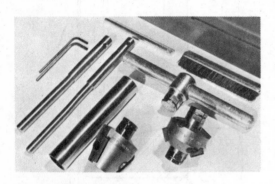

Valve seat reaming kit

Checking contact facing location and width

Checking valve seat concentricity:

In order for the valve to seat perfectly in its seat, providing a gas tight seal, the valve seat must be concentric with the valve guide. To check concentricity, coat the valve face with Prussian blue dye and install the valve in its guide. Applying light pressure, rotate the valve ¼ turn in its valve seat. If the entire valve seat face becomes coated, and the valve is known to be concentric, the seat is concentric.

Lapping the valves:

Hand lapping the valves

With accurately refaced valve seat inserts and new valves, it is not usually necessary to lap the valves. Valve lapping alone is not recommended for use as a resurfacing procedure.

Prior to lapping, invert the cylinder head, lightly lubricate the valve stem and install the valves in their respective guides. Coat the valve seats with fine Carborundum® grinding compound, and attach the lapping tool suction cup (moistened for adhesion) to the valve head. Then, rotate the tool (see illustration) between your palms, changing direction and lifting the tool often to prevent grooving. Lap the valve until a smooth, polished seat is evident. Finally,

Procedure	Method

Suction cup end of lapping tool on valve face

remove the tool and thoroughly wash away all traces of grinding compound. Make sure that no compound accumulates in the guides as rapid wear would result.

Check the valve springs:

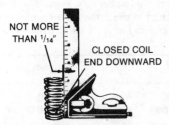

NOT MORE THAN 1/14″

CLOSED COIL END DOWNWARD

Checking valve spring free-length and squareness

Place the spring on a flat surface next to a square. Measure the height of the spring and compare that value to that of the other 7 springs. All springs should be the same height. Rotate the spring against the edge of the square to measure distortion. Replace any spring that varies (in both height and distortion) more than 1/16 in.

If you have access to a valve spring tester, you may use the following specifications to check the springs under a load (which is the only specification VW gives).

Type	Loaded length	Load
1600	1.2 in. (31.0 mm)	117.5–134.9 lb (53.2–61.2 kg)
1700, 1800, 2000	1.141 in. (29.0 mm)	168.0–186.0 lb (76.5–84.5 kg)

If any doubt exists as to the condition of the springs, and a spring tester is not available, replace them, they're cheap.

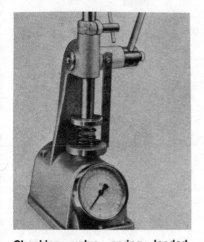

Checking valve spring loaded-length and tension

Install the valves:

Lubricate the valve stems with white grease (molybdenum-disulphide), and install the valves in their respective guides. Lubricate and install the valve stem seals (NOTE: *VW has not installed stem seals on new engines since 1972. The reason is, although the seals provide excellent oil control, the guides tend to run "dry" which only hastens their demise. This is especially true for exhaust valves which run at much greater temperatures*). Position the valve springs on the head. The spring is positioned with the closely coiled end facing the head.

Procedure	Method
	Check the valve stem keys (keepers) for burrs or scoring. The keys should be machined so that the valve may still rotate with the keys held together. Finally, install the spring retainers, compress the springs (using a valve spring compressor), and insert the keys using needlenose pliers or a special tool designed for this purpose. NOTE: *You can retain the keys with wheel bearing grease during installation.*
Inspect the rocker shafts and rocker arms:	Remove the rocker arms, springs and washers from the rocker shaft. NOTE: *Lay out the parts in the order they are removed.* Inspect the rocker arms for pitting or wear on the valve stem contact point, and check for excessive rocker arm bushing wear where the arm rides on the shaft. If the shaft is grooved noticeably, replace it. Use the following chart to check the rocker arm inner diameter and the rocker shaft outer diameter.

1700, 1800, 2000		1600
.7874–.7882 in. (20.00–20.02 mm)	rocker arms inner diameter (new)	.7086–.7093 in. (18.00–18.02 mm)
.7890 in. (20.04 mm)	wear limit	.710 in. (18.04 mm)
.7854–.7861 in. (19.95–19.97 mm)	rocker arm shaft outer diameter (new)	.7073–.7077 in. (17.97–17.98 mm)
.7846 in. (19.93 mm)	wear limit	.7066 in. (17.95 mm)

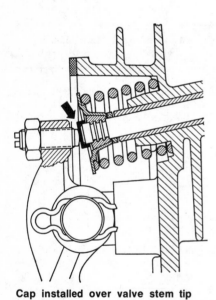

Cap installed over valve stem tip worn concave

Minor scoring may be removed with an emery cloth. If the valve stem contact point of the rocker arm is worn, grind it smooth, removing as little metal as necessary. If it is noticed at this point that the valve stem is worn concave where it contacts the rocker arm, and it is not desired to disassemble the valve from the head, a cap (see illustration) may be installed over the stem prior to installing the rocker shaft assembly.

Procedure	Method
Inspect the pushrods and pushrod tubes:	After soaking the pushrods in solvent, clean out the oil passages using fine wire, then blow through them to make sure there are no obstructions. Roll each pushrod over a piece of clean, flat glass. Check for runout. If a distinct, clicking sound is heard as the pushrod rolls, the rod is

Procedure	Method

Pushrod tube required length "a"

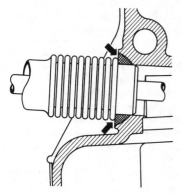

Silicone seal at pushrod tube ends

bent, necessitating replacement. All pushrods must be of equal length.

Inspect the pushrod tubes for cracks or other damage to the tube that would let oil out and dirt into the engine. The tubes on the 1600 engine are particularly susceptible to damage at the stretchable bellows. Also, on the 1600 engine, the tubes must be maintained at length "a" (see illustration) which is 190–191 mm or 7.4–7.52 in. If a tube is too short, it may be carefully stretched, taking care to avoid cracking. However, if the bellows are damaged or if a gritty, rusty sound occurs when stretching the tube, replace it. Always use new seals. When installing tubes in a 1600 engine, rotate the tubes so that the seams face upwards. When installing tubes in a 1700, 1800 or 2000 engine, make sure the retaining wire for the tubes engages the slots in the supports and rests on the lower edges of the tubes.

If, on an assembled, installed 1600 engine, it is desired to replace a damaged or leaky pushrod tube without pulling the engine, it may be accomplished using a "quick-change" pushrod tube available from several different specialty manufacturers. The special two-piece aluminum replacement tube is installed after removing the valve cover, rocker arm assembly and pushrod of the subject cylinder. The old tube is then pried loose with a screwdriver. Using new seals, the replacement tube is positioned between the head and crankcase, and expanded into place, via a pair of threaded, locking nuts.

Remove cover. Shove affected rocker arm to one side and pull out push rod.	Pry loose the damaged tube (don't lose seals from either end).	Using old seals, position new tube with gold end toward spark plug. Tighten.
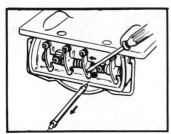		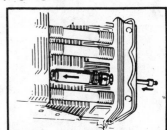

Quick-change tube installation

Crankcase Reconditioning

Procedure	Method
Disassembling crankcase:	See "Crankcase Disassembly and Assembly" earlier in this chapter.

Procedure	Method
Hot tank the crankcase:	Using only a hot-tanking solution formulated for aluminum or magnesium alloy, clean the crankcase to remove all sludge, scale, or foreign particles. You may also cold-tank the case, using a strong degreasing solvent, but you will have to use a brush and a lot of elbow grease to get the same results. After cleaning, blow out all oil passages with compressed air. Remove all old gasket sealing compound from the mating surfaces.
Inspect the crankcase:  Checking tightness of oil suction pipe	Check the case for cracks using the Zyglo or spot-check method described earlier in this section. Inspect all sealing or mating surfaces, especially along the crankcase seam, as the crankcase halves are machined in pairs and use no gasket. Check the tightness of the oil suction pipe. The pipe must be centered over the strainer opening. On 1600 engines, peen over the crankcase where the suction pipe enters the camshaft bearing web. Check all studs for tightness. Replace any defective studs as mentioned earlier in this section. Check all bearing bores for nicks and scratches. Remove light marks with a file. Deeper scratches and scoring must be removed by align boring the crankshaft bearing bores.
Align bore the crankcase:  Ridged main bearing bores prior to align boring	There are two surfaces on a VW crankcase that take quite a hammering in normal service. One is the main bearing saddles and the other the thrust flange of #1 bearing (at the flywheel end). Because the case is constructed of softer metal than the bearings, it is more malleable. The main bearing saddles are slowly hammered in by the rotation of the heavy crankshaft working against the bearings. This is especially true for an out-of-round crankshaft. The thrust flange of #1 main bearing receives its beating trying to control the end play of the crankshaft. This beating is more severe in cases of a driver with a heavy clutch foot. Popping the clutch bangs the pressure plate against the clutch disc, against the flywheel, against the crankcase flange, and finally against the thrust flange. All of this hammering leaves its mark on the case, but can be cleaned up by align boring. Most VW engine rebuilders who want their engines to stay together will align bore the case. This assures proper bearing bore alignment. Then, main bearings with the correct oversize outer diameter (and oversize thrust shoulder on #1) are installed. Also, as the split crankcase is constructed of light aluminum and magnesium alloy, it is particularly susceptible to warpage due to overheating. Align boring the case will clean up any bearing saddle misalignment due to warpage.

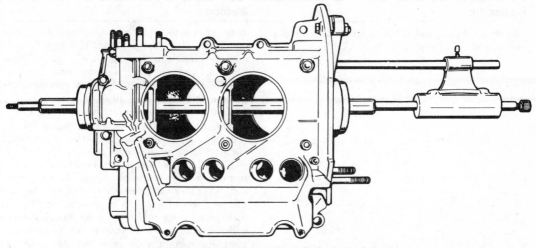

Align boring apparatus installed on crankcase

No. 1 main bearing thrust flange

Crankcase after align boring

Procedure	Method
Check connecting rod side clearance, and check connecting rods for straightness:	Before removing the connecting rods from the crankshaft, check the clearance between the rod and the crank throw using a feeler gauge. Replace any rod exceeding the wear limit. Proper side clearance (also known as end play or axial play) is .004–.016 in. (0.10–0.40 mm). Also, prior to removing the rods from the crankshaft, check them for straightness. This is accomplished easily using an old wrist pin, and sliding the wrist pin through each connecting rod (small end) in succession. Position each rod, in turn, so that as the pin begins to leave one rod, it is entering the next rod. Any binding indicates a scored wrist pin bushing or misaligned (bent) connecting rod. If the wrist pin absolutely will not slide from one adjacent rod to another, then you've got a really bent rod. Be ready for bent rods on any engine which has dropped a valve and damaged a piston.
Disassemble crankshaft:	Number the connecting rods (1 through 4 from the flywheel side) and matchmark their bearing halves. Remove the connecting rod retaining nuts (do not remove the bolts) from the bit end and remove the rods. Slide off the oil thrower (1600 only) and #4 main bearing. Slide off #1 main bearing from the flywheel end. Remove the snap-ring (circlip) using snap-ring pliers. #2 main bearing is the split type, each half of which should remain in its respective crankcase half. Using a large gear puller, or an arbor or hydraulic press, remove the distributor drive gear and crankshaft timing gear and spacer. Don't lose the woodruff key(s). NOTE: *The 1600 engine has two woodruff keys. The 1700, 1800 and 2000 engines have only one.* Finally, slide off #3 main bearing.
Inspect the crankshaft:	Clean the crankshaft with solvent. Run all oil holes through with a brass bristle brush. Blow them through with compressed air. Lightly oil the crankshaft to prevent rusting. Using a micrometer of known accuracy, measure the crankshaft journals for wear. The maximum wear limit for all journals is .0012 in. (0.03 mm). Check the micrometer reading against those specifications listed under "Crankshaft and Connecting Rod Specifications" which appears earlier in this chapter. Check the crankshaft runout. With main bearing journals #1 and #3 supported on V-blocks and a dial gauge set up perpendicular to the crankshaft, measure the runout at #2 and #4 main bearing journals. Maximum permissible runout is .0008 in. (0.02 mm). Inspect the crankshaft journals for scratches, ridges, scoring and nicks. All small nicks and scratches necessitate regrinding of the crankshaft at a machine shop. Journals worn to a taper or slightly out-of-round must also be reground. Standard undersizes are .010, .020, .030 in. (0.25, 0.50, 0.75 mm).

Procedure	Method

Inspect connecting rods:

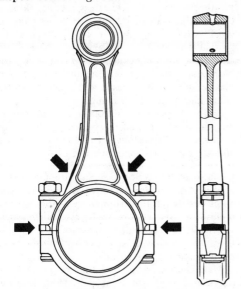

To lighten connecting rods, metal can be removed at the locations indicated by the arrows

Checking wrist pin fit

Check the connecting rods for cracks, bends and burns. Check the rod bolts for damage; replace any rod with a damaged bolt. If possible, take the rods to a machine shop and have them checked for twists and magnafluxed for hidden stress cracks. Also, the rods must be checked for straightness, using the wrist pin method described earlier. If you did not perform this check before removing the rods from the crankshaft, definitely do so before dropping the assembled crankshaft into the case.

Weigh the rods on a gram scale. On 1600 engines, the rods should all weigh within 10 grams (lightest to heaviest); on 1700, 1800 and 2000 engines, within 6 grams. All rods should ideally weigh the same. If not, find the lightest rod and lighten the others to match. Up to 8 grams of metal can be removed from a rod by filing or grinding at the low stress points shown in the illustration.

Check the fit of the wrist pin bushing. At 72° F, the pin should slide through the bushing with only light thumb pressure.

Check connecting rod bearing (oil) clearance:

It is always good practice to replace the connecting rod bearings at every teardown. The bearing size is stamped on the back of the inserts. However, if it is desired to reuse the bearings, two methods may be used to determine bearing clearance.

One tedious method is to measure the crankshaft journals using a micrometer to determine what size bearing inserts to use on reassembly (see Crankshaft and Connecting Rod Specifications) to obtain the required 0.0008–0.0027 in. oil clearance.

Another method of checking bearing clearance is the Plastigage method. This method can only be used on the split-type bearings and not on the ring-type bearings used to support the crankshaft. First, clean all oil from the bearing surface and crankshaft journal being checked. Plastigage is soluble in oil. Then, cut a piece of Plastigage the width of the rod bearing and insert it between the journal and bearing insert. NOTE: *Do not rotate the rod on the crankshaft.* Tighten the rod cap nuts to 22–25 ft-lbs. Remove the bearing

Procedure	Method
	insert and check the thickness of the flattened Plastigage using the Plastigage scale. Journal taper is determined by comparing the width of the Plastigage strip near its ends. To check for journal eccentricity, rotate the crankshaft 90° and retest. After checking all four connecting rod bearings in this manner, remove all traces of Plastigage from the journal and bearing. Oil the crankshaft to prevent rusting. If the oil clearance is .006 in. (0.15 mm) or greater, it will be necessary to have the crankshaft ground to the nearest undersize (.010 in.) and use oversize connecting rod bearings.
Check main bearing (oil) clearance:	It is also good practice to replace the main bearings at every engine teardown as their replacement cost is minimal compared to the replacement cost of a crankshaft or short block. However, if it becomes necessary to reuse the bearings, you may do so after checking the bearing clearance. Main bearings #1, 3 and 4 are ring-type bearings that slip over the crankshaft. These bearings cannot be checked using the Plastigage method. Only the split-type #2 main bearing can be checked using Plastigage. However, since this involves bolting together and unbolting the crankcase halves several times, it is not recommended. Therefore, the main bearings are checked using a micrometer. Use the following chart to determine if the bearing (oil) clearance exceeds its wear limit.

Main Bearing Clearance

	New	Wear limit
Crankshaft bearings 1 + 3 (1600 engine)	0.04–0.10 mm (.0016–.004 in.)	0.18 mm (.007 in.)
Crankshaft bearings 1 + 3 (1700, 1800, 2000 engine)	0.05–0.10 mm (.002–.004 in.)	0.18 mm (.007 in.)
Crankshaft bearing 2 (all models)	0.03–0.09 mm (.001–.0035 in.)	0.17 mm (.0067 in.)
Crankshaft bearing 4 (all models)	0.05–0.10 mm (.002–.004 in.)	0.19 mm (.0075 in.)

Never reuse a bearing that shows signs of wear, scoring or blueing. If the bearing clearance exceeds its wear limit, it will be necessary to regrind the crankshaft to the nearest undersize and use oversize main bearings.

Procedure	Method
Clean and inspect the camshaft: **Camshaft lobe measurement**  **Checking camshaft run-out**  **Checking axial play of camshaft and timing gear**	Degrease the camshaft using solvent. Clean out all oil holes and blow through with compressed air. Visually inspect the cam lobes and bearing journals for excessive wear. The edges of the camshaft lobes should be square. Slight damage can be removed with silicone carbide oilstone. To check for lobe wear not visible to the eye, mike the camshaft diameter from the tip of the lobe to base (distance A) and then mike the diameter of the camshaft at a 90° angle to the previous measurement (distance B) (see illustration). This will give you camshaft lift. Measure lift for each lobe. If any lobe differs more than .025 in., replace the camshaft. Check the camshaft for runout. Place the #1 and #3 journals in V-blocks and rest a dial indicator on #2 journal. Rotate the camshaft and check the reading. Runout must not exceed 0.0015 in. (0.04 mm). Repair is by replacement. Check the camshaft timing gear rivets for tightness. If any of the gear rivets are loose, or if the gear teeth show a poor contact pattern, replace the camshaft and timing gear assembly. Check the axial (end) play of the timing gear. Place the camshaft in the left crankcase half. The wear limit is .0063 in. (0.16 mm). If the end play is excessive, the thrust shoulder of #3 camshaft bearing is probably worn, necessitating replacement of the cam bearings.
Check the camshaft bearings:  **Camshaft bearing inserts**	The camshaft bearings are the split-type. #3 camshaft bearing has shoulders on it to control axial play. Since there is no load on the camshaft, the bearings are not normally replaced. However, if the bearings are scored or imbedded with dirt, if the camshaft itself is being replaced, or if the thrust shoulders of #3 bearing are worn (permitting excessive axial play), the bearings should be replaced. In all cases, clean the bearing saddles and check the oil feed holes for cleanliness. Make sure that the oil holes for the bearing inserts align with those in the crankcase. Coat the bearing surfaces with prelube.

Procedure	Method
Check the lifters (tappets): 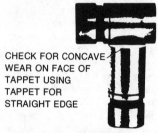 CHECK FOR CONCAVE WEAR ON FACE OF TAPPET USING TAPPET FOR STRAIGHT EDGE **Checking lifter face for wear**	Remove all gum and varnish from the lifters using a tooth brush and carburetor cleaner. The cam following surface of the lifters is slightly convex when new. In service, this surface will wear flat which is OK to reinstall. However, if the cam following surface of the lifter is worn concave, the lifter should be replaced. To check this, place the cam following surface of one lifter against the side of another (as illustrated), using the one lifter as a straightedge. After checking, coat the lifters with oil to prevent rusting.
Assemble crankshaft:	NOTE: *All dowel pin holes in the main bearings must locate to the flywheel end of the bearing saddles.* Coat #3 main bearing journal with assembly lubricant. Slide the #3 bearing onto the pulley side of the crankshaft and install the large woodruff key in its recess (the hole in the bearing should be nearest to the flywheel end of the crankshaft). In the meantime, heat both the crankshaft timing gear and distributor drive gears to 176° F in an oil bath. If a hydraulic or an arbor press is available, press on the timing gear, taking care to keep the slot for the woodruff key aligned, the timing marks facing away from the flywheel, and the chamfer in the gear bore facing #3 main bearing journal. CAUTION: *Use protective gloves when handling the heated gears.* NOTE: *Be careful not to scratch the crankshaft journals.* Or, if a press is not available, you may drive on the gear using a 2 in. diameter length of pipe and a hammer, taking care to protect the flywheel end of the crankshaft with a piece of wood. The woodruff key must lie flat in its recess. Then, slide on the spacer ring and align it with the woodruff key. On 1600 engines, install the smaller woodruff key. Now, press or drive on the distributor drive gear in the same manner as the crankshaft timing gear. Make sure it seats against the spacer ring. Install the snap-ring (circlip) using snap-ring pliers. Take care not to scratch #4 main bearing journal. Prelube main bearings #1 and #4 and slide them on the crankshaft. On 1600 engines, install the oil slinger, concave side out. NOTE: *Make sure crankshaft timing gear and distributor drive gear fit snugly on the crankshaft once they return to room temperature.* Install the bearing inserts for the connecting rods and rod caps by pressing in on bearing ends with both thumbs. Make sure the tangs fit in the notches. Don't press in the middle as the inserts

Procedure	Method
	may soil or crack. Prelube the connecting rod bearings and journals. Then, install the connecting rods on the crankshaft, making sure the forge marks are up (as they would be installed in the crankcase [3, 1, 4, 2 from flywheel end]), and the rod and bearing cap matchmarks align. Use new connecting rod nuts. After tightening the nuts, make sure that each rod swings freely 180° on the crankshaft by its own weight. NOTE: *A slight pretension (binding) of the rod on the crankshaft may be relieved by lightly rapping on the flat side of the big end of the rod with a hammer.* If the connecting rod nuts are not of the self-locking type (very rare), peen the nuts into the slot on the rods to lock them in place and prevent the possibility of throwing a rod.

Installing crankshaft and camshaft:

Aligning timing marks

Camshaft end plug installation

Pencil mark a line on the edge of each ring-type main bearing to indicate the location of the dowel pin hole. Install the lower half of #2 main bearing in the left side of the crankcase so that the shell fits securely over its dowel pin. Prelube the bearing surface.

Lift the crankshaft by two of the connecting rods and lower the assembly into the left crankcase halve. Make sure the other connecting rods protrude through their corresponding cylinder openings. Then, rotate each ring-type main bearing (#1, then #3, then #4) until the pencil marks made previously align with the center of the bearing bore. As each bearing is aligned with its dowel pin, a distinctive click should be heard and the crankshaft should be felt dropping into position. After each bearing is seated, you should not be able to rock any of the main bearings or the crankshaft in the case. Just to be sure, check the bearing installation by placing the other half of #2 main bearing over the top of its crankshaft journal. If the upper half rocks, the bearing or bearings are not seated properly on their dowels. Then, install the other half of #2 main bearing in the right crankcase halve. Prelube the bearing surface.

Rotate the crankshaft until the timing marks (twin punch marks on two adjacent teeth) on the timing gear point towards the camshaft side of the case. Lubricate and install the lifters. Coat the lifters for the right half of the case with grease to keep them from falling out during assembly. Coat the camshaft journals and bearing surfaces with assembly lubricant. Install the camshaft so that the single timing mark (0) on the camshaft timing gear aligns (lies between) with the two on the crankshaft timing gear. This is critical as it establishes valve timing.

Install the camshaft end plug using oil-resistant sealer. On cars with manual transmission, the hollow end of the plug faces in towards the engine. On cars equipped with automatic or automatic stick shift transmission, the hollow end

Procedure	Method
	faces out towards the front of the car to provide clearance for the torque converter drive plate retaining bolts. The timing gear mesh is correct if the camshaft does not lift from its bearings when the crankshaft is rotated backwards (opposite normal direction of rotation).
Check timing gear backlash: **Checking timing gear backlash**	Mount a dial indicator to the crankcase with its stem resting on a tooth of the camshaft gear. Rotate the gear until all slack is removed, and zero the indicator. Then, rotate the gear in the opposite direction until all slack is removed and record gear backlash. The reading should be between .000 and .002 in. (0.00 and 0.05 mm).
Assembling crankcase: **Installing crankcase stud seals**	See "Crankcase Assembly and Disassembly" earlier in this chapter. Use the following installation notes; a. Make sure all bearing surfaces are pre-lubed. b. Always install new crankcase stud seals. c. Apply only non-hardening oil resistant sealer to all crankcase mating surfaces. d. Always use new case nuts. Self-sealing nuts must be installed with the red coated side down. e. All small crankcase retaining nuts are first torqued to 10 ft-lbs, then 14 ft-lbs. All large crankcase retaining nuts are torqued to 20 ft-lbs, then 25 ft-lbs (except self-sealing large nuts [red plastic insert], which are torqued to a single figure of 18 ft lbs). Use a criss-cross torque sequence. On 1700, 1800 and 2000 engines, you will have to keep the long case bolt heads from turning. f. While assembling the crankcase halves, always rotate the crankshaft periodically to check for binding. If any binding occurs, immediately disassemble and investigate the case. Usually, a main bearing has come off its dowel pin, or maybe you forgot to align bore that warped crankcase.
Check crankshaft end-play:	After assembling the case, crankshaft end-play can be checked. End-play is controlled by the thickness of 3 shims located between the flywheel and #1 main bearing flange. End-play is checked with the flywheel installed as follows. Attach a dial indicator to the crankcase with the stem positioned on the face of the flywheel. Move the flywheel in and out and check the reading. End-play should be between .003–.005

Procedure	Method

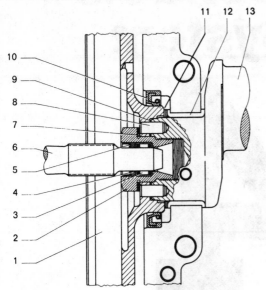

1. Flywheel
2. Gland nut
3. Needle bearing
4. Felt ring
5. Retaining ring
6. Rear driveshaft
7. Lockwasher
8. Dowel pin
9. Rubber sealing ring
10. Crankshaft oil seal
11. Shims
12. Crankshaft bearing
13. Crankshaft

Cross-section of 1600 flywheel, crankshaft, oil seal, and related parts

in. (0.07–0.13 mm). The wear limit is .006 in. (0.15 mm).

To adjust end-play, remove the flywheel and reinstall, this time using only two shims. Remeasure the end-play. The difference between the second reading and the .003–.005 in. figure is the required thickness of the third shim. Shims come in the following sizes;

0.24 mm—.0095 in.
0.30 mm—.0118 in.
0.32 mm—.0126 in.
0.34 mm—.0134 in.
0.36 mm—.0142 in.
0.38 mm—.0150 in. (1700, 1800 and 2000 only)

Checking crankshaft end-play

Emission Controls and Fuel System

EMISSION CONTROLS

Crankcase Ventilation System

All models are equipped with a crankcase ventilation system. The purpose of the crankcase ventilation system is twofold. It keeps harmful vapors from escaping into the atmosphere and prevents the buildup of crankcase pressure. Prior to the 1960s , most cars employed a vented oil filler cap and road draft tube to dispose of crankcase vapor. The crankcase ventilation systems now in use are

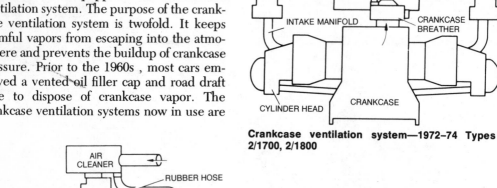

Crankcase ventilation system—1972–74 Types 2/1700, 2/1800

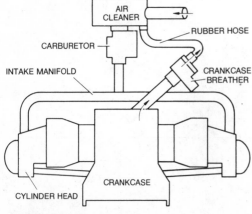

Crankcase ventilation system—1970–74 Types 1, 2/1600

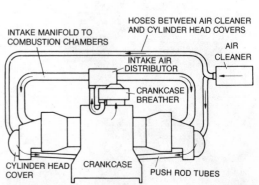

Crankcase ventilation system—Types 3 and 4

an improvement over the old method and, when functioning properly, will not reduce engine efficiency.

Type 1 and 2 carbureted engine crankcase vapors are recirculated from the oil breather through a rubber hose to the air cleaner. The vapors then join the air/fuel mixture and are burned in the engine. Fuel injected cars mix crankcase vapors into the air/fuel mixture to be burned in the combustion chambers. Fresh air is forced through the engine to evacuate vapors and recirculate them into the oil breather, intake air distributor, and then to be burned.

CRANKCASE VENTILATION SYSTEM SERVICE

The only maintenance required on the crankcase ventilation system is a periodic check. At every tune-up, examine the hoses for clogging or deterioration. Clean or replace the hoses as required.

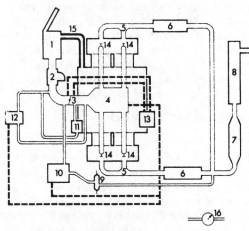

1. Air cleaner
2. Air sensor
3. Throttle valve
4. Intake air distributor
5. Exhaust manifold
6. Heat exchanger
7. Catalytic converter
8. Muffler
9. EGR filter
10. EGR valve
11. Auxiliary air regulator
12. Throttle switch
13. Ignition distributor
14. Fuel injector
15. Crankcase ventilation
16. Indicator light for EGR

Exhaust and air lines

- - - - - - - - - -
Control lines (vacuum)

1975 and later Type 1 and Type 2 emission control systems

Evaporative Emission Control System

Required by law since 1971, this system prevents raw fuel vapors from entering the atmosphere. The various systems for different models are similar. They consist of an expansion chamber, activated charcoal filter, and connecting lines. Fuel vapors are vented to the charcoal filter where hydrocarbons are deposited on the element. The engine fan forces fresh air into the filter when the engine is running. The air purges the filter and the hydrocarbons are forced into the air cleaner to become part of the air/fuel mixture and burned.

EVAPORATIVE EMISSION CONTROL SERVICE

See Chapter One under "Routine Maintenance."

Air Injection System 1973–74

Type 2 vehicles are equipped with the air injection system, or air pump as it is sometimes called. In this system, an engine driven air pump delivers fresh air to the engine exhaust ports. The additional air is used to promote after-burning of any unburned mixture as it leaves the combustion chamber. In addition, the system supplies fresh air to the intake manifold during gear changes to provide more complete combustion of the air/fuel mixture.

Check the air pump belt tension and examine the hoses for deterioration as a regular part of your tune-up procedure.

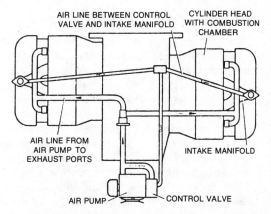

Air injection (exhaust manifold afterburning) system—1973 Type 2/1700

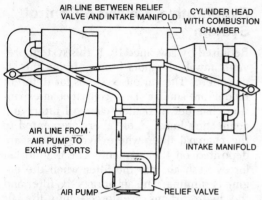

Air injection (exhaust manifold afterburning) system—1974 Type 2/1800

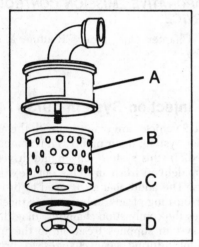

A. Housing
B. Filter element
C. Washer
D. Wingnut

Type 2 air pump filter

AIR INJECTION SYSTEM SERVICE

The only maintenance required for the system is an air pump belt tension check at 6,000 mile intervals and an air pump filter element replacement at 18,000 mile or 2 year intervals. See Chapter One for the belt tension check.

The air pump filter element is located in a housing adjacent to the pump. To remove the element, loosen the hose clamp and disconnect the filter housing from the pump. Then, loosen the wing nut and draw out the element. Never attempt to clean the old element. Install a new paper element and assemble the filter housing.

Exhaust Gas Recirculation System

In order to control exhaust emissions of oxides of nitrogen (NO_x), an exhaust gas recirculation (EGR) system is employed on 1972 Type 1 and Type 3 models equipped with automatic transmission and sold in California, on 1973 Type 1 and Type 3 models equipped with automatic transmission sold nationwide, on all 1973 and later Type 2 models, on all 1974 Type 4 models equipped with automatic transmission, and on all 1974 and later Type 1 models. The system lowers peak flame temperature during combustion by introducing a small (about 10%) percentage of relatively inert exhaust gas into the intake charge. Since the exhaust gas contains little or no oxygen, it cannot react with nor influence the air/fuel mixture. However, the exhaust gas does (by volume) take up space in the combustion chambers (space that would otherwise be occupied by a heat-producing, explosive air/fuel mixture), and does serve to lower peak combustion chamber temperature. The amount of exhaust gas directed to the combustion chambers is infinitely variable by means of a vacuum operated EGR valve. For system specifics, see the vehicle type breakdown under "General Description."

GENERAL DESCRIPTION

Type 1

For 1972, EGR is used only on automatic stick shift models sold in California. Exhaust gas is drawn from the left hand rear exhaust flange and then cooled in a cooling coil. From here, the gas is filtered in a cyclone filter and finally channelled to the intake manifold, via the EGR valve. The valve permits exhaust gas recirculation during part throttle applications, but not during idling or wide open throttle.

All 1973 models (nationwide) equipped with the automatic stick shift transmission use an EGR system. As in '72, the gas is drawn from the left rear exhaust flange. However, instead of the cooling coil and cyclone filter, a replaceable element type filter is used. The remainder of the system remains unchanged from 1972.

All 1974 Type 1 cars, regardless of equipment, are equipped with EGR. The system uses the element type filter and EGR valve which recirculates exhaust gases during part throttle applications as before. However, to improve driveability, all California models

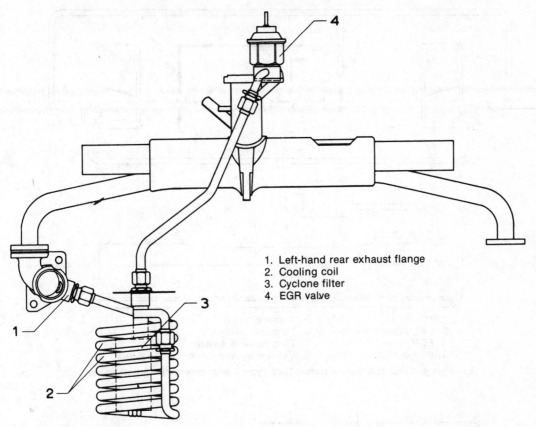

1. Left-hand rear exhaust flange
2. Cooling coil
3. Cyclone filter
4. EGR valve

Exhaust gas recirculation system—1972 Type 1 automatic stick shift sold in California

use a two stage EGR valve (one stage in the 49 states), and California models equipped with an automatic use an electric throttle valve switch to further limit exhaust gas recirculation to part throttle applications (EGR permitted only between 12° to 72° on a scale of 90° throttle valve rotation).

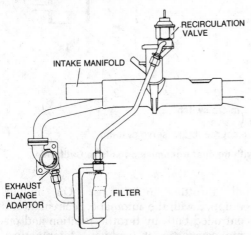

Exhaust gas recirculation system—1973–74 Type 1

EGR is installed on all 1975–80 models. All applications use the element type filter and single stage EGR valve. Recirculation occurs during part throttle applications as before. The system is controlled by a throttle valve switch which measures throttle position, and an intake air sensor which reacts to engine vacuum. 1977 and later Type 1s destined for California are equipped with a mechanically operated EGR valve. A rod is attached to the throttle valve lever and operates the throttle position. No exhaust gases are recirculated at or near full throttle or at closed throttle. Beginning in 1975, an odometer actuated EGR reminder light (on the dashboard) is used to inform the driver that it is time to service the EGR system. The reminder light measures elapsed mileage and lights at 15,000 mile intervals. A reset button is located behind the switch.

Type 2

Type 2 models use an EGR system beginning in 1973. All models use two valves; one at each manifold. Exhaust gas is taken from the

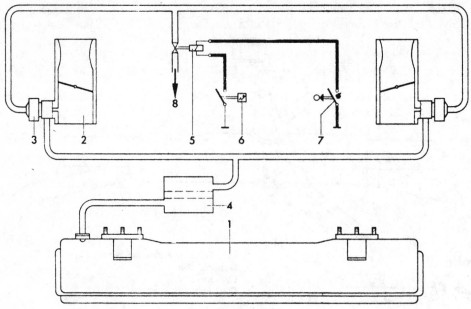

1. Muffler
2. Left intake manifold
3. EGR valve (2)
4. Element filter
5. Two-way valve
6. Temperature switch
7. Throttle valve switch
8. Vacuum source (brake servo system)

Exhaust gas recirculation system—1973 Type 2 with automatic transmission

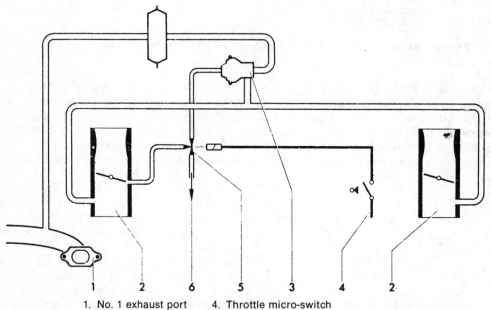

1. No. 1 exhaust port
2. Intake manifolds
3. EGR valve
4. Throttle micro-switch
5. Two-way valve
6. Vacuum source (brake servo system)

Exhaust gas recirculation system—1974 Type 2 with manual transmission sold in California

muffler, cleaned in a replaceable type filter, then directed to both intake manifolds, via the EGR valves. On models equipped with manual transmission, recirculation is vacuum controlled and occurs *both* during part *and* full throttle applications. On models equipped with the automatic, recirculation is controlled both by throttle position and engine compartment (ambient) temperature. When the ambient temperature exceeds 54°

F, a sensor switch (located above the battery) opens, permitting EGR during part throttle applications.

All 1974 Type 2 models use EGR, but there are three different systems used. All models use one central EGR valve. Exhaust gas is taken from #4 exhaust port, cleaned in an element type filter, and then directed to both intake manifolds via the single EGR valve. Models equipped with manual transmission and sold in the 49 states use a single stage EGR valve which allows recirculation according to the vacuum signal in the left carburetor during part throttle applications. Models equipped with manual transmission and sold in California use a two stage EGR valve which recirculates exhaust gases during part throttle openings in two steps. During the first stage, EGR is controlled by the vacuum in the left carburetor. The second stage controls EGR according to the throttle position of the right carburetor. Finally, all models equipped with automatic transmission (nationwide) use a single stage EGR valve which controls recirculation according to throttle valve position and engine cooling

air temperature. When the cooling system air reaches 185° F, a sensor switch (located between the coil and distributor) opens, permitting EGR during part throttle applications.

All 1975–81 Type 2 models utilize an EGR system. A single stage EGR valve and element type filter are used on all applications. Recirculation occurs during part throttle opening and is controlled by engine vacuum, throttle position and engine compartment temperature. At or near full throttle and when the throttle is closed, a solenoid is activated by the throttle valve switch which cuts off the vacuum supply and stops the recirculation of exhaust gases. At 15,000 mile intervals, a dash mounted EGR service reminder light is activated to warn the driver that EGR service is now due. A reset button is located behind the switch.

Type 3

EGR is first used in the 1972 Type 3 models destined for California and equipped with automatic transmission. Exhaust gas is drawn from the front right hand exhaust flange to

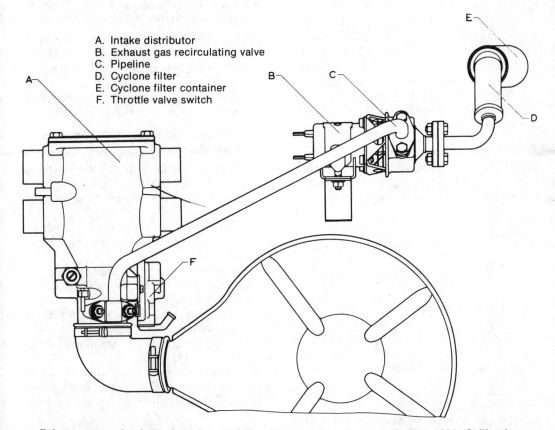

A. Intake distributor
B. Exhaust gas recirculating valve
C. Pipeline
D. Cyclone filter
E. Cyclone filter container
F. Throttle valve switch

Exhaust gas recirculation system—1972 Type 3 with automatic transmission sold in California

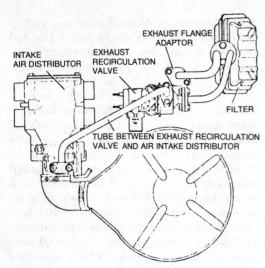

Exhaust gas recirculation system—1973 Type 3 with automatic transmission

the EGR valve via a container and cyclone filter. The EGR valve then delivers the exhaust gases to the intake air distributor under part throttle (not full throttle or idling) conditions when the ambient air temperature reaches 65° F *and* only first or second gears are selected.

All 1973 Type 3 models equipped with automatic transmission use an EGR system. The exhaust gases are cleaned in a replaceable element type filter in 1973 instead of the cyclone filter and container of the previous year. The EGR valve then delivers the gases according to an electromagnetic valve which permits recirculation above 54° F.

Type 4

EGR appears only on 1974 models (nationwide) equipped with automatic transmission. On this system, exhaust gas is drawn from

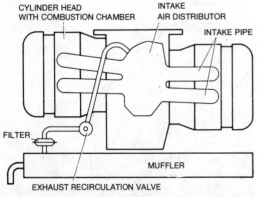

Exhaust gas recirculation system—1974 Type 4 with automatic transmission

the muffler to a single EGR valve via an element type filter. The gases are delivered to the intake air distributor under part throttle conditions.

EGR VALVE SERVICE

The EGR valve should be checked every 15,000 miles and the filter cleaned (cyclone type) or replaced (element type).

EGR VALVE CHECKING

1972–74 Type 1 (Except 1974 California Models)

1. With the engine idling at operating temperature (176° F), pull off the vacuum hose from the EGR valve and push on the black hose from the intake air preheating thermostat instead.

2. If the idle speed drops off sharply or stalls, recirculation is taking place and the valve is OK. If, however, the idle speed does not change, the EGR valve is faulty or a hose is cracked or blocked.

3. Replace the vacuum hoses to their original locations.

1974 Type 1 California and 1974 Type 2 Manual Transmission California Models

On these 1974 California models, a two-stage EGR valve with a visible pin is used. To check the valve operation, simply make sure that the pin moves in and out relative to engine rpm. If the pin does not move, check the hoses and/or replace the EGR valve.

1975–80 Type 1 Except 1977 and Later California Models

1. Start the engine and pull the electrical connector off the EGR valve vacuum unit (the disk-shaped unit located near the ignition coil).

2. This should make the engine slow down or stall, which means exhaust gases are being recirculated.

3. If no engine speed change occurs, stop the engine, then return the ignition key to the ON (not START) position.

4. Connect a test light across the terminals of the connector cable, then move the throttle valve by hand from idle position to about mid-speed range.

5. If the test light goes off when the throttle is moved out of idle position but lights at idle or full throttle position, replace the EGR valve.

6. If the test light does not light at all,

there is probably trouble with the wiring or the throttle valve switch, which is located to the left of the alternator

Type 1 1977 and Later California Models

Remove the E-clip connecting the operating rod from the throttle to the EGR valve. Start the engine and allow it to idle. Manually operate the EGR valve: the engine should slow down or stop when the EGR valve is opened. If no speed change occurs, check the EGR pipe for clogging or replace the EGR valve.

ADJUSTING

1. Idle the engine at 800–950 rpm.
2. Loosen both locknuts on the rod and shorten the length of the rod by turning it.
3. The idle should drop suddenly, indicating the EGR valve has opened. From this position lengthen the rod 1½ turns ($1^5{}_6$ turns 1979–80), using the pin in the center of the rod for orientation.
4. Tighten the locknuts.

1973 Type 2

1. Remove the EGR valve.
2. Inspect the valve for cleanliness.
3. Check the valve for freedom of movement by pressing in on the valve pin.
4. Connect the valve to the vacuum hose of another engine or vacuum source and start the engine. At 1500–2000 rpm the valve pin should be pulled in and when the speed is reduced it should return to its original position. Replace the EGR valve if it doesn't operate correctly.
5. Replace the washer and install the valve.
6. Repeat this operation on the second valve.

1974 Type 2 w/Manual Transmission (Except California Models)

1. With the engine idling at operating temperature, pull off the vacuum hose at the tee-fitting for the EGR valve and push on the hose from the flow valve of the air pump to the fitting instead.
2. If idle speed drops sharply or stalls, the valve is OK. If the rpm does not change, a hose is blocked or the valve is faulty.
3. Replace the hoses to their original locations.

1975 and Later Type 2

This procedure is the same as 1975–80 Type 1 Except 1977 and Later California, except

that the EGR valve is located approximately on top of No. 4 cylinder. A long feed pipe connects the EGR valve with the throttle valve housing. The throttle valve switch is located at the bottom of the throttle valve housing and is difficult to see without removing the housing. The switch is black, rectangular and has an electrical connector plugged into it.

1972–73 Type 3

1. Remove the EGR valve.
2. Reconnect the vacuum hose and place the valve on the base.
3. Start the engine. If it doesn't stall, the vacuum line between the valve base and the intake manifold is clogged and must be cleaned.
4. Run the engine at 2000–3000 rpm. The closing pin of the EGR valve should pull in 0.15 in. (4 mm) and immediately return to its original position at idle. Replace the EGR valve if it doesn't operate correctly.
5. Install the EGR valve using new seals.

1974 Type 4 Automatic Transmission

1. Run the engine at idle.
2. At the EGR valve, disconnect the hose that runs to the throttle valve housing.
3. Disconnect the hose that runs to the idle speed regulator from the "T" pipe located in front of the intake manifold, and connect the hose from the EGR valve to the "T" pipe. Hold the idle speed regulator plunger back with your hand to prevent it from raising the idle speed.
4. If the engine speed drops or the engine stalls, the EGR valve is working. If nothing happens, either the EGR valve is defective or the lines are clogged.

Catalytic Converter System

All 1975–81 Type 1 and 2 models sold in California and 1977–81 models sold in the other 49 states are equipped with a catalytic converter. The converter is installed in the exhaust system, upstream and adjacent to the muffler.

Catalytic converters change noxious emissions of hydrocarbons (HC) and carbon monoxide (CO) into harmless carbon dioxide and water vapor. The reaction takes place inside the converter at great heat using platinum and palladium metals as the catalyst. If the engine is operated on lead-free fuel, they are designed to last 50,000 miles before replacement.

1979–81 Type 2 models sold in California are equipped with an oxygen sensor system installed in the exhaust pipe on the left side of the engine in back of the catalytic converter. At temperatures above 575° F and for various compositions of gases, the sensor sends a signal to the AFC control unit which then corrects fuel injector operating time to insure accurately metered fuel/air mixture and keep the exhaust emissions within the legal limits. The sensor is coupled to a throttle valve switch which disconnects the sensor signal during full throttle. At all other times (except during engine warm up) the sensor is in operation.

The sensor must be replaced every 30,000 miles. A light on the speedometer lights at 30,000 mile intervals to alert you that sensor service is needed. After the service is done, reset the sensor light by pushing the button on the control box which is connected to the speedometer cable and is usually located behind the dash.

Deceleration Control

All 1975 and later Type 1 and Type 2 manual transmission models, Type 2 automatic transmission models after chassis No. 226 2 077 583, and Type 3 and 4 California manual transmission models are equipped with vacuum operated deceleration valves. The deceleration valve prevents an overly rich mixture from reaching the exhaust. During deceleration, the valve opens, allowing air to by-pass the throttle plate and enter the combustion chamber, thereby leaning the air/fuel mixture. Type 2 automatic transmission models up to chassis No. 226 2 077 583 and Type 3 and 4 California automatic transmission models have electrically operated deceleration valves which are activated by the transmission.

CHECKING THE DECELERATION VALVE
Vacuum Type

The deceleration valve on the Type 1 is located on the engine compartment hood left hinge mounting. It is at the center front of the engine between the fuel injection intake air sensor on the Type 2 (don't confuse it with the EGR canister).

A faulty deceleration valve will cause engine speed to be higher than normal at idle. To test the valve, pinch shut the large fabric covered hose leading into the air cleaner. If the idle speed drops, the valve is faulty and should be replaced.

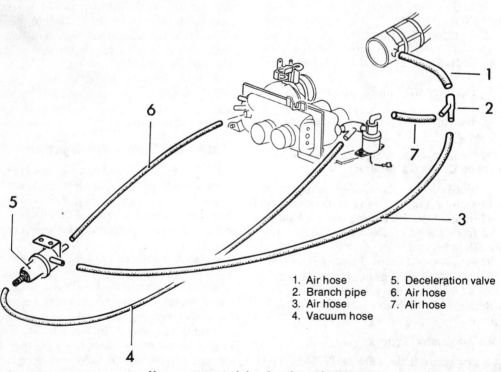

1. Air hose	5. Deceleration valve
2. Branch pipe	6. Air hose
3. Air hose	7. Air hose
4. Vacuum hose	

Vacuum operated deceleration valve

Electrical Type

1. From under the vehicle, remove the wire from the automatic transmission fluid pressure switch which runs to the deceleration valve. The valve is located on the intake air distributor.

2. Turn the ignition On, and ground the disconnected wire against the transmission housing or the chassis frame.

3. An audible click should be heard. If not, replace the deceleration valve or the automatic transmission fluid pressure switch.

Electrically operated deceleration valve

Throttle Valve Positioner

All 1970–71 Type 1 and 2/1600 models equipped with manual transmission, and 1972 Type 1 models with manual transmission sold in California use a throttle valve positioner to hold the throttle butterfly slightly open during deceleration to prevent an excessively rich mixture from reaching the combustion chambers. The throttle valve positioner consists of two parts connected by a hose. The operating part is mounted on the carburetor, connected to the throttle valve arm. It regulates fast idle speed. The control section (altitude corrector) is located at the left side of the engine compartment. It controls throttle valve closing time.

ADJUSTMENT

NOTE: *The car should first be warmed to operating temperature (122–158°F) for this adjustment. Make sure the choke plate is open.*

1. Hook up a tachometer (0–3000 rpm sweep minimum) to the engine with the positive lead to the distributor side of the coil and the negative lead to a good ground. You will also need a stop watch or a good wristwatch with a second hand.

CAUTION: *Keep yourself, any clothing, jewelry, your hair, or tools, etc. well clear*

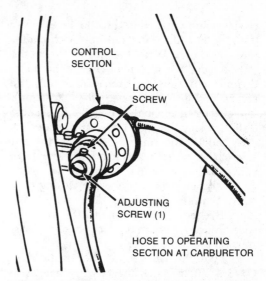

CONTROL SECTION

LOCK SCREW

ADJUSTING SCREW (1)

HOSE TO OPERATING SECTION AT CARBURETOR

1970–72 throttle valve positioner adjustment showing adjusting screw (1) on control section (altitude corrector) located at left rear of engine compartment on Type 1 and 2/1600 models

Operating section of 1970–72 two-piece throttle valve positioner showing mounting screws and hose connections

of the engine belts and pulleys. Make sure you are in a well ventilated area.

2. Start the engine and let it idle in neutral. Make a check of the fast idle speed by pulling the fast idle lever back so that it contacts the lever stop on the carburetor. The tachometer should read 1450–1650 rpm. If the fast idle is not within specifications, turn the adjusting screw (on the lever stop) as required. Disconnect the tachometer.

3. Take the car for a warmup drive. Recheck the fast idle as in steps 1 and 2. The tachometer reading should not exceed 1700 rpm.

4. Now, make a check of the throttle valve

closing time. Pull the throttle lever away from the fast idle lever until the tachometer reads 3000 rpm. While keeping an eye on the second hand of your watch, release the throttle lever and check the time elapsed until the engine reaches idle speed (800–900 rpm). The closing time should be 2.5–4.5 seconds. If the closing time is not within specifications, adjust the control section at the left side of the engine compartment. After loosening the lock screw, turn the adjusting screw (1) clockwise to increase closing time and counterclockwise to decrease closing time. Recheck the adjustment. If it is within specifications, tighten the lock screw and disconnect the tachometer.

5. Take the car for another test drive. Once again, recheck the closing time as in step 4. The closing time now must not exceed 6 seconds. If it does, go back to step 4.

If, after several attempts, the positioner does not consistently operate correctly, check the hoses for looseness or cracks, then check the diaphragm unit for clogging or diaphragm malfunction.

If the diaphragm unit (the part that is attached to the carburetor) is replaced, the pull rod on the new unit must be adjusted. After installing the new unit, adjust the rod by loosening both lock nuts on the rod and turning the middle part to either extend or shorten the length. When the throttle valve is closed, the fast idle lever (inner lever) must not touch either the carburetor body or the throttle valve lever (when the choke is fully open).

FUEL SYSTEM

Understanding the Fuel system

An automotive fuel system consists of everything between the fuel tank and the carburetor or fuel injection unit. This includes the tank itself, all the lines, one or more fuel filters, a fuel pump (mechanical or electric), and the carburetor or fuel injection unit.

With the exception of the carburetor or fuel injection unit, the fuel system is quite simple in operation. Fuel is drawn from the tank through the fuel line by the fuel filter, and from there to the carburetor where it is distributed to the cylinders.

FUEL TANK

Normally, fuel tanks are located at the rear of the vehicle, although on most rear-engined cars, they are located at the front. The tank itself also contains a fuel gauge sending unit, and a filler tube. In most tanks, there is also a screen of some sort in the bottom of the tank near the pickup to filter out impurities. Since the advent of emission controls, tanks are equipped with a control system to prevent fuel vapor from being discharged into the atmosphere. A vent line in the tank which is connected to a filter in the engine compartment. Vapors from the tank are trapped in the filter canister, where they are routed back to the fuel tank, making the system a closed loop. All the fumes are prevented from escaping to the atmosphere. These systems also require the use of a special gas cap which makes an airtight seal.

FUEL PUMP

There are two types of fuel pumps in general use; the mechanical pump and the electric pump. Mechanical pumps are the more common of the two, used on nearly all American cars. Electric pumps are used on all fuel-injected cars (and some carburetor-equipped cars, such as the Vega) in addition to seeing wide use on a number of imported cars.

Mechanical fuel pumps are usually mounted on the side of the block and operated by an eccentric on the engine's camshaft. A pump rocker arm rests against the camshaft eccentric and as the camshaft rotates, causes the rocker arm to rock back and forth. Inside the fuel pump, the rocker arm is connected to a flexible diaphragm. A spring is mounted under the diaphragm to maintain pressure on the diaphragm. As the rocker arm rocks, it pulls the diaphragm down and then releases it. Once the diaphragm is released, the spring pushes it back up. This continual diaphragm motion causes a partial vacuum and pressure in the space above the diaphragm. The vacuum sucks the fuel from the tank and the pressure pushes it toward the carburetor.

As a general rule, mechanical fuel pumps are quite dependable. When trouble does occur, it is usually caused by a cracked or broken diaphragm, which will not draw sufficient fuel. Occasionally, the pump arm or spring will become so worn that the fuel pump can no longer produce an adequate supply of fuel, but this condition can be easily checked. Older fuel pumps are rebuildable, but late-model pumps have a crimped edge and must be replaced if defective.

There are two general types of electric fuel

pumps in use today. The impeller type pump uses a vane or impeller which is driven by an electric motor. These pumps are often mounted in the fuel tank, though they are sometimes found below or beside the tank.

The bellows-type pump, is becoming rare. The bellows pump ordinarily is mounted in the engine compartment and contains a flexible metal bellows operated by an electromagnet.

Most electric fuel pumps are not rebuildable and if defective must be replaced. Minor service is usually confined to checking electrical connections and checking for a blown fuse.

FUEL FILTERS

In addition to the screen located in the bottom of the fuel tank, all fuel systems have at least one other filter located somewhere between the fuel tank and the carburetor. On some models, the filter is part of the fuel pump itself, on others it is located in the fuel line, and still others locate the filter in the carburetor inlet or the carburetor body itself.

The fuel filter is usually a paper or bronze element which screens out impurities in the fuel, before it has a chance to reach the carburetor. If you replace the fuel filter, you'll be amazed at the bits of sediment and dirt trapped by the filter.

CARBURETOR

The carburetor is the most complex part of the entire fuel system. Carburetors vary greatly in construction, but they all operate basically the same way; their job is to supply the correct mixture of fuel and air to the engine in response to varying conditions.

Despite their complexity in operation, carburetors function because of a simple physical principle—the venturi principle. Air is drawn into the engine by the pumping action of the pistons. As the air enters the top of the carburetor, it passes through a venturi, which is nothing more than a restriction in the throttle bore. The air speeds up as it passes through the venturi, causing a slight drop in pressure. This pressure drop pulls fuel from the float bowl through a nozzle into the throttle bore, where it mixes with the air and forms a fine mist, which is distributed to the cylinders through the intake manifold.

There are six different systems (fuel/air circuits) in a carburetor that make it work; the Flat system, Main Metering system, Idle and Low-Speed system, Accelerator Pump system, Power system, and the Choke system. The way these systems are arranged in the carburetor determines the carburetor's size and shape.

It's hard to believe that the little single-barrel carburetor used on 4 or 6 cylinder engins have all the same basic systems as the enormous 4-barrel's used on V8 engines. Of course, the 4-barrels have more throttle bores ("barrels") and a lot of other hardware you won't find on the little single-barrels. But basically, all carburetors are similar, and if you understand a simple single-barrel, you can use that knowledge to understand a 4-barrel. If you'll study the explanations of the various systems on this page, you'll discover that carburetors aren't as tricky as you thought they were. In fact, they're fairly simple, considering the job they have to do.

It's important to remember that carburetors seldom give trouble during normal operation. Other than changing the fuel and air filters and making sure the idle speed and mixture are ok at every tune-up, there's not much maintenance you can perform on the average carburetor.

Mechanical Fuel Pump

All 1970–74 Type 1 and 2 models utilize a mechanical fuel pump. The pump is located to the left of the generator/alternator on Type 1 and 2/1600 models, and located next to the flywheel on dual carburetor Type 2 models. On Type 1 and 2/1600 models the pump is pushrod operated by an eccentric on the distributor driveshaft. On Type 2/1700 and 2/1800 twin carb models the pump is operated by a pushrod which rides on a camshaft eccentric.

REMOVAL AND INSTALLATION

Types 1, 2/1600

1. Disconnect the fuel lines at the pump and plug them to prevent leakage.

2. Remove the two securing nuts.

3. Remove the fuel pump. If necessary, the pushrod, gaskets, and intermediate flange may also be removed.

4. When installing the fuel pump, it is necessary to check the fuel pump pushrod stroke. This is done by measuring the distance that the pushrod projects above the intermediate flange when both gaskets are in place. The rod must project ½ inch. If not, remove or insert enough bottom gaskets under the flange until it does.

Carburetor Operating Principles

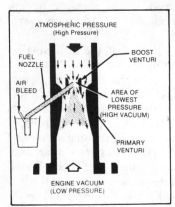

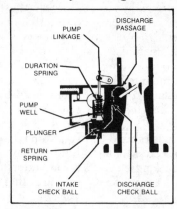

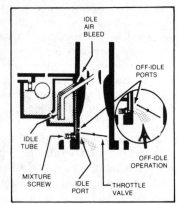

The venturi principle in operation. The pumping action of the pistons creates a vacuum which is amplified by the venturi in the carburetor. This pressure drop will pull fuel from the float bowl through the fuel nozzle. Unfortunately, there is not enough suction present at idle or low speed to make this system work, which is why the carburetor is equipped with an idle and low speed circuit

Accelerator pump system. When the throttle is opened, the air flowing through the venturi starts flowing faster almost immediately, but there is a lag in the flow of fuel out of the main nozzle. The result is that the engine runs lean and stumbles. It needs an extra shot of fuel just when the throttle is opened. This shot is provided by the accelerator pump, which is nothing more than a little pump operated by the throttle linkage that shoots a squirt of fuel through a separate nozzle into the throat of the carburetor

Idle and low-speed system. The vacuum in the intake manifold at idle is high because the throttle is almost completely closed. This vacuum is used to draw fuel into the engine through the idle system and keep it running. Vacuum acts on the idle jet (usually a calibrated tube that sticks down into the main well, below the fuel level) and sucks the fuel into the engine. The idle mixture screw is there to limit the amount of fuel that can go into the engine

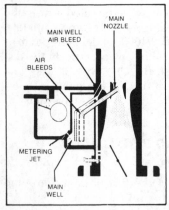

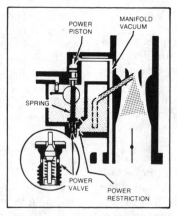

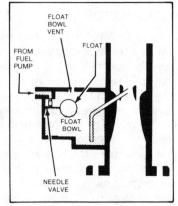

The main metering system may be the simplest system of all, since it is simply the venturi principle in operation. At cruising speeds, the engine sucks enough air to constantly draw fuel through the main fuel nozzle. The main fuel nozzle or jet is calibrated to provide a metering system. The metering system is necessary to prevent an excess amount of fuel flowing into the intake manifold, creating an overly rich mixture

Power circuit. The main metering system works very well at normal engine loads, but when the throttle is in the wide-open position, the engine needs more fuel to prevent detonation and give it full power. The power system provides additional fuel by opening up another passage that leads to the main nozzle. This passageway is controlled by a power valve

Float circuit. When the fuel pump pushes fuel into the carburetor, it flows through a seat and past a needle which is a kind of shutoff valve. The fuel flows into the float bowl and raises a hinged float so that the float arm pushes the needle into the seat and shuts off the fuel. When the fuel level drops, the float drops and more fuel enters the bowl. In this way, a constant fuel supply is maintained

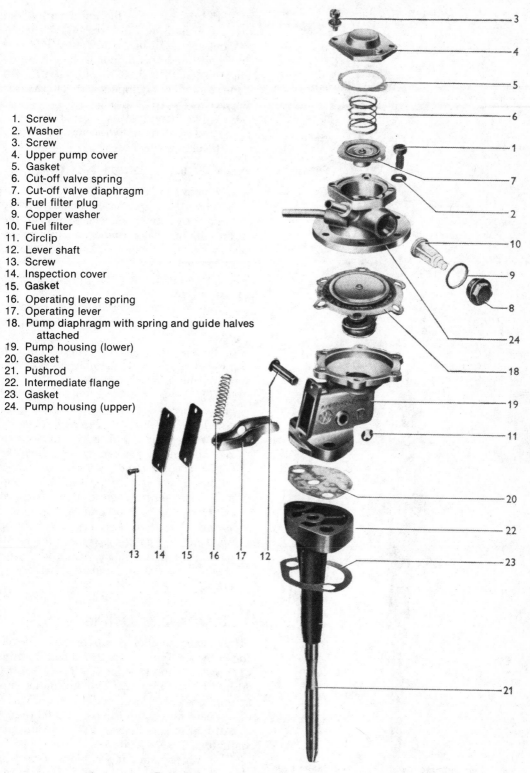

1. Screw
2. Washer
3. Screw
4. Upper pump cover
5. Gasket
6. Cut-off valve spring
7. Cut-off valve diaphragm
8. Fuel filter plug
9. Copper washer
10. Fuel filter
11. Circlip
12. Lever shaft
13. Screw
14. Inspection cover
15. **Gasket**
16. Operating lever spring
17. Operating lever
18. Pump diaphragm with spring and guide halves attached
19. Pump housing (lower)
20. Gasket
21. Pushrod
22. Intermediate flange
23. Gasket
24. Pump housing (upper)

Exploded view of fuel pump—1970 Type 1

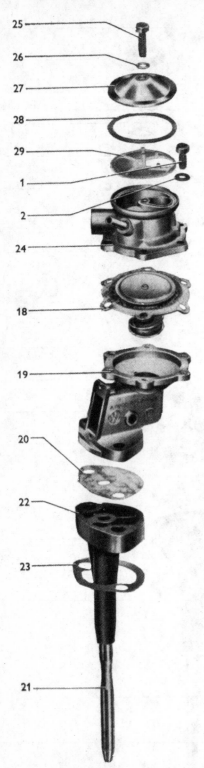

25
26
27
28
29
1
2
24
18
19
20
22
23
21

18. Pump diaphragm with
     spring and guide
     halves attached
21. Pushrod
22. Intermediate flange

27. Fuel filter cover
28. Fuel filter cover
     gasket
29. Fuel filter screen

Exploded view of fuel pump—1970 Type 2

5. Fill the cavity in the lower part of the fuel pump housing with grease. Total push-rod length is 4.252 in. for all Type 2/1600 and for Type 1 models equipped with generators. Pushrod length is 3.937 in. for all 1973–74 Type 1 models equipped with alternators. Replace any worn pushrod.

6. Using new gaskets, install the fuel pump and tighten the two securing nuts.

7. Install the fuel hoses.

Types 2/1700 and 2/1800 Twin Carb

1. Remove the engine.

2. Once the engine is removed, remove the upper and lower deflector plates and the carburetor preheater connection to gain access to the pump mounting bolts (adjacent to the flywheel).

3. Disconnect and plug the fuel lines to the carburetors.

4. Remove the two retaining bolts and lift off the fuel pump, gaskets and intermediate flange.

5. Reverse the above procedure to install, using new gaskets. Remember to coat the pushrod and lever with grease.

NOTE: *Prior to installation of the fuel pump, check the action of the camshaft eccentric driven pushrod. Install just the intermediate flange on the engine with 2 gaskets underneath and one on top. Turn the engine over by hand until the pushrod is on the highest point of the camshaft eccentric. Then, measure the distance between the tip of the pushrod and the top gasket surface. Adjust, as necessary, to 0.2 in. by removing or installing gaskets under the intermediate flange. Total pushrod length should be 5.492 in. minimum. Replace, if worn.*

TESTING AND ADJUSTING

The maximum fuel pump pressure developed by the Type 1 and 2/1600 fuel pump is 3-5 psi at 3,400 rpm for the Type 1 (4,000 rpm for the Type 2). The maximum fuel pump pressure developed by the Type 2 Twin carb fuel pump is 5 psi at 3800 rpm.

All fuel pumps deliver 400 cc of fuel per minute at 38000–4000 rpm.

The only adjustment possible is performed by varying the thickness of the fuel pump flange gaskets. Varying the thickness of the gaskets will change the stroke of the fuel pump pushrod. This adjustment is not meant to compensate for a pump in bad condition;

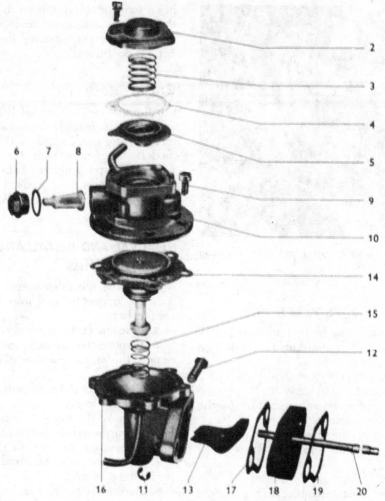

1. Screw
2. Cover
3. Cut-off diaphragm spring
4. Cut-off diaphragm gasket
5. Cut-off diaphragm
6. Plug
7. Washer
8. Filter
9. Screw
10. Pump upper part
11. Circlip
12. Lever shaft
13. Pump lever
14. Diaphragm and spring
15. Diaphragm spring
16. Pump lower part
17. Gasket
18. Intermediate
19. Gasket
20. Push rod

Exploded view of fuel pump—1972-74 Type 2 twin carb

therefore, do not attempt to vary the height of the pushrod to any great extent.

The fuel pumps used on 1970 Type 1 and 2 models, and 1972-74 Type 2 models may be disassembled for cleaning or repairs. All other mechanical pumps are permanently sealed and must be replaced if found defective.

Electric Fuel Pump

All Type 3 and Type 4 models, as well as 1975 and later Type 1 and Type 2 models have an electric pump. The fuel pump is located near the front axle on Types 1, 3, and 4, and near the fuel tank on Type 2.

Electric fuel pump showing fuel filter mounting bracket

REMOVAL AND INSTALLATION

1. Disconnect the fuel pump wiring. Pull the plug from the pump but do not pull on the wiring.
2. Disconnect the fuel hoses and plug them to prevent any leakage.
3. Remove the two nuts which secure the pump and then remove the pump.
4. Reconnect the fuel pump hoses and wiring and install the pump on the vehicle.

ADJUSTMENTS

Electric fuel pump pressure is 28 psi. Fuel pump pressure is determined by a pressure regulator which diverts part of the fuel pump output to the gas tank when 28 psi is reached. The regulator, located on the engine firewall,

Fuel injection fuel pressure regulator with locknut and adjusting screw (small arrow) at left end of regulator

has a screw and lock nut on its end. Loosen the lock nut and adjust the screw to adjust the pressure. Do not force the screw in or out if it does not turn.

Carburetors

Carburetors are used on all 1970–74 Type 1 and 2 models. A single downdraft unit is used on all Type 1 models and on 1970–71 Type 2 models. Beginning with the 1972 model year, the Type 2 utilizes twin carburetion. The type of carburetor used (34 PICT-3, etc.) is stamped on the float bowl and should be clearly visible.

REMOVAL AND INSTALLATION

Type 1 and 2/1600

1. Remove the air cleaner.
2. Disconnect the fuel hose. Plug it to prevent leakage.
3. Disconnect the vacuum hoses.
4. Remove the automatic choke cable and remove the wire for the electromagnetic pilot jet.
5. Disconnect the accelerator cable at the throttle valve lever.
6. Remove the two nuts securing the carburetor on the intake manifold and then remove the carburetor from the engine.
7. Using a new gasket, install the carburetor on the manifold.
8. Reconnect the fuel and vacuum hoses, the automatic choke cable, and the wiring for the pilot jet.
9. Reconnect the throttle cable and adjust it so that at full throttle there is a gap of 0.04 in. between the throttle lever and its stop on the lower portion of the carburetor body.

NOTE: *Open the throttle valve by hand and tighten the adjustment screw, then have an assistant open the throttle and recheck the adjustment.*

Type 2/1700 and 2/1800 Twin Carb

1. Remove the air cleaner.
2. Disconnect and plug the fuel line(s).
3. Disconnect the electrical leads for the automatic choke, pilot jet cut-off valve, and idle mixture cut-off valve.
4. If removing the left carburetor, disconnect the vacuum line (2), the idle mixture line for the central idling system, and the idle air intake line from the top of the carburetor.
5. Remove the linkage cross shaft bracket retaining bolt (3). Disconnect the return

Type 2 twin carb. connections for left carburetor

spring and the pull rod and release the linkage from both carburetors.

6. Remove the carburetor retaining nuts and remove the carburetor(s).

7. Reverse the above procedure to install, taking care to use new gaskets. After installation, synchronize the carburetors as outlined under "Fuel Adjustments" in Chapter Two.

THROTTLE LINKAGE ADJUSTMENT

Single and Twin Carburetor Models

1. Have an assistant hold the accelerator pedal to the floor at wide open throttle. Measure the distance between the throttle

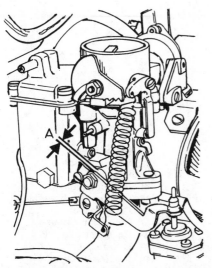

Full throttle clearance (distance "a") should be 0.04 in. on Type 1 and 2/1600 engines, and 0.04–0.06 in. on Type 2/1700 and 2/1800 engines

valve lever and the stop on the carburetor body. Proper distance (a) is 0.04 in. minimum.

2. To adjust, loosen the cable adjusting screw found in the bottom on the throttle lever.

3. The throttle lever has a rigid cylinder attached to its end. Move the rigid portion in or out of the end of the throttle lever to obtain the proper adjustment and tighten the adjusting screw. The proper adjustment is reached when there is a gap of 0.04 in. (single carb) or 0.04–0.06 in (twin carb) between the throttle valve lever and its stop on the lower portion of the carburetor body. See the note at the end of the "Carburetor Removal and Installation" procedure.

FLOAT AND FUEL LEVEL ADJUSTMENT

NOTE: *The carburetor must be on a level surface to obtain an accurate reading.*

A properly assembled carburetor has a preset float level. For the float level to be correct the fiber washer under the needle valve seat must be installed and be of the proper thickness. See the "Carburetor Specifications Chart."

The only way to adjust the float level, if it is absolutely necessary, and still retain proper seating of the needle in the needle valve seat, is to vary the thickness of the fiber washer beneath the seat.

Washers are available in thicknesses of 0.50 mm, 0.80 mm, 1.00 mm, and 1.50 mm.

THROTTLE VALVE GAP

Type 2 34 PDSIT 2/3 Carburetors

CARBURETOR REMOVED

NOTE: *The choke valve must be closed for proper adjustment.*

1. Remove the carburetor from the car.

2. Loosen the two nuts (A) on the automatic choke connecting rod and insert a wire gauge or drill between the throttle valve and the side of the venturi. The gauge should be .024 in. for 1972–73 models and .028 in. for 1974.

3. Move the two nuts (A) up or down on the connecting rod until the throttle valve gap is adjusted and tighten the two nuts (A).

CARBURETOR INSTALLED

1. Back out the idle speed screw until the throttle valve is completely closed.

2. Turn the idle speed screw until it just touches the throttle lever.

Carburetor Overhaul

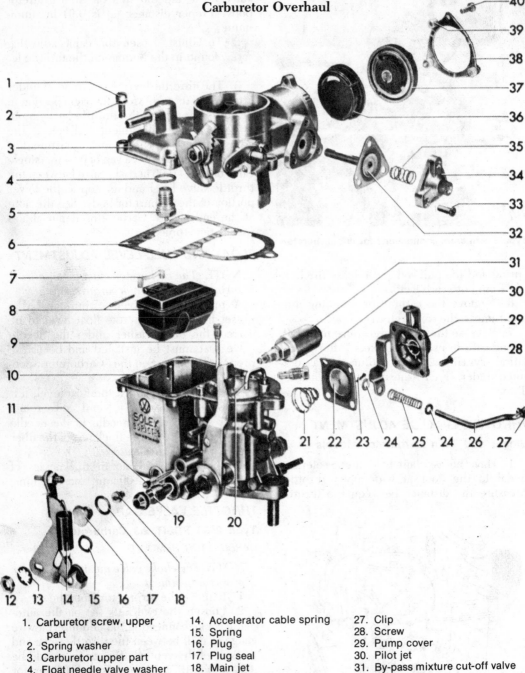

1. Carburetor screw, upper part
2. Spring washer
3. Carburetor upper part
4. Float needle valve washer
5. Float needle valve
6. Washer
7. Float pin retainer
8. Float and pin
9. Air correction jet
10. Carburetor lower part
11. Volume control screw
12. Nut
13. Lock washer
14. Accelerator cable spring
15. Spring
16. Plug
17. Plug seal
18. Main jet
19. By-pass air screw
20. Accelerator pump injector tube
21. Pump diaphragm spring
22. Pump diaphragm
23. Cotter pin
24. Washer
25. Connecting rod spring
26. Connecting rod
27. Clip
28. Screw
29. Pump cover
30. Pilot jet
31. By-pass mixture cut-off valve
32. Vacuum diaphragm
33. Screw
34. Vacuum diaphragm cover
35. Vacuum diaphragm spring
36. Cap (plastic)
37. Automatic choke
38. Cover retaining ring
39. Cover spacer
40. Retaining ring screw

Exploded view of Solex 30 PICT-3 carburetor used on 1970 Type 1 and 2/1600 models

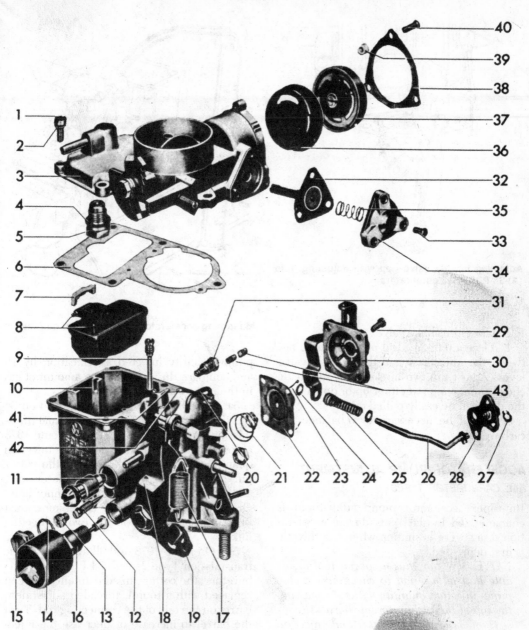

1. Carburetor screw,
   upper part
2. Spring washer
3. Carburetor upper part
4. Float needle valve
   washer
5. Float needle valve
6. Washer
7. Float pin retainer
8. Float and pin
9. Air correction jet and
   emulsion tube
10. Carburetor lower part
11. By-pass screw
12. Volume control screw

13. Main jet
14. Plug washer
15. Plug
16. By-pass air cut-off
    valve
17. Return spring
18. Fast idling lever
19. Throttle valve lever
    and stop screw
20. Accelerator pump
    injection pipe
21. Diaphragm spring
22. Accelerator pump
    diaphragm
23. Cotter pin

24. Washer
25. Connecting rod
    spring
26. Connecting rod
27. Clip
28. Bell crank lever
29. Countersunk head
    screw
30. Pump cover
31. Pilot jet
32. Vacuum-diaphragm
33. Countersunk head
    screw
34. Vacuum diaphragm
    cover

35. Vacuum diaphragm
    spring
36. Plastic cap
37. Insert with spring
    and heater element
38. Cover retaining
    ring
39. Retaining ring
    spacer
40. Retaining ring screw
41. Pilot air drilling
42. Auxiliary air drilling
43. Auxiliary fuel jet and
    plug

Exploded view of Solex 34 PICT-3 carburetor used on 1971–74 Type 1 and 1971 Type 2/1600 models

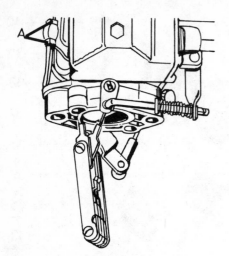

Adjusting throttle valve gap with adjusting nuts (A)-34 PDSIT 2/3 carburetors

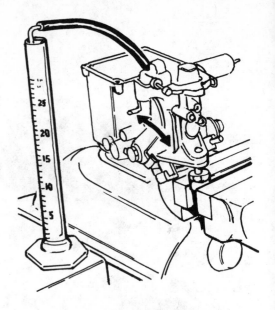

Measuring accelerator pump injection quantity

3. Close the choke valve.

4. Place a 0.09 in. drill or wire gauge between the idle screw and the throttle valve lever. Adjust the two nuts on the automatic choke connecting rod either up or down until the drill can be easily pulled out.

5. It will be necessary to rebalance the carburetors.

ACCELERATOR PUMP ADJUSTMENT

ALL CARBURETOR TYPES

Improper accelerator pump adjustment is characterized by flat spots during acceleration or a severe hesitation when the throttle is first depressed.

NOTE: *VW now has a special tool available that allows you to check accelerator pump injection quantity without removing the top of the carburetor (air horn). It consists of a measuring glass, and injection pipe and a choke plate retainer. The part number is VW 119.*

1. Remove the carburetor from the engine and remove the upper half of the carburetor.

2. Support the carburetor securely in a vise without damaging the carburetor body.

3. Fill the float chamber with gasoline and attach a rubber tube to the injector tube. Place the open end of the tube into a milliliter measuring tube.

4. Move the throttle lever several strokes until all of the air is forced out of the tube. Move the throttle lever an additional ten full strokes and measure the quantity of gas in the measuring tube. Multiply the accelerator

pump quantity injected specification by 10 and compare this figure to the amount of gas in the measuring tube.

5a. On 30 PICT-3 carburetors, and on 34 PDSIT 2/3 carburetors used on manual transmission Type 2s and on 1972 and some 1973 automatic transmission Type 2s, the injection quantity is decreased by moving the cotter pin on the connecting link to the outer hole, and increased by moving it to the inner hole. On dual carburetors, both cotter pins must be in the same holes on the two connecting links.

5b. On some 1973 and all 1974 automatic transmission Type 2s with 34 PDSIT 2/3 carburetors, the cotter pin adjustment has been replaced with a round, threaded adjustment barrel on the end of the connecting rod. Turn the barrel to increase or decrease the injection quantity. The 1974 automatic transmission Type 2 with 34 PDIST 2/3 carburetors also has a thermal valve screwed into the bottom part of the carburetor housing to the side of the accelerator pump. This valve regulates the amount of fuel injected by the accelerator pump according to carburetor body temperature. When temperature is below 70°F, the valve is closed and allows 1.5 cc of fuel to be injected on each stroke. Above 70°F, the valve opens, allowing only about half as much fuel on each stroke, the rest being routed back into the float bowl. When measuring full injection quantity, make sure carburetor body temperature is below 60°F.

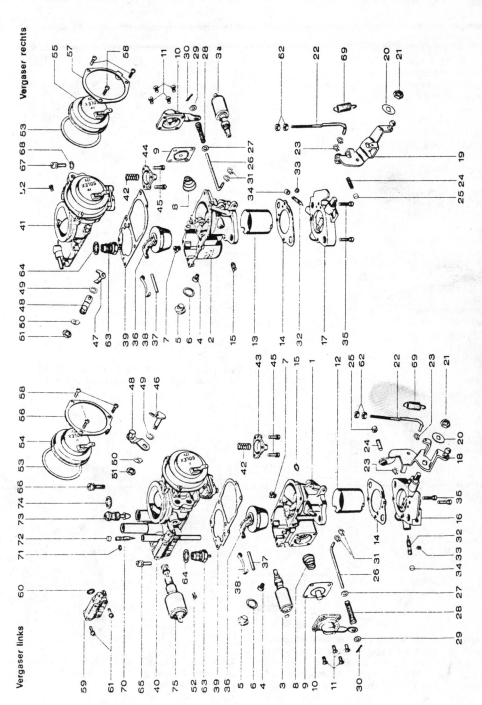

Exploded view of Solex 34 PDSIT 2/3 carburetors used on 1972-74 2/1700, 2/1800 models

1. Carburetor body—34 PDSIT-2
2. Carburetor body—34 PDSIT-3
3. Electromagnetic idling cutoff valve—34 PDSIT-2
3a. Electromagnetic idling cutoff valve—34 PDSIT-3
4. Main jet
5. Main jet cover plug
6. Main jet cover plug seal
7. Air correction jet
8. Pump diaphragm spring
9. Pump diaphragm
10. Accelerator pump cover
11. Screws
12. Venturi—34 PDSIT-2
13. Venturi—34 PDSIT-3
14. Throttle body gasket
15. Venturi setscrew
16. Throttle body—34 PDSIT-2
17. Throttle body—34 PDSIT-3
18. Throttle arm—34 PDSIT-2
19. Throttle arm—34 PDSIT-3
20. Special washer
21. Nut
22. Connecting rod
23. Circlip
24. Throttle valve opening adjusting screw
25. Plug
26. Connecting link
27. Washer
28. Connecting link
29. Washer
30. Cotter pin
31. Circlip
32. Idle mixture screw
33. O-ring
34. Plug
35. Throttle body screws
36. Float
37. Float pin
38. Float pin retainer
39. Gasket
40. Carburetor upper part (air horn with idle mixture enrichment—34 PDSIT-2
41. Carburetor upper part (air horn)—34 PDSIT-3
42. Vacuum diaphragm spring
43. Vacuum diaphragm cover—34 PDSIT-2
44. Vacuum diaphragm cover—34 PDSIT-3
45. Screws
53. Choke heating element gasket
54. Choke heating element—34 PDSIT-2
55. Choke heating element—34 PDSIT-3
56. Choke cover retaining ring—34 PDSIT-2
57. Choke cover retaining ring—34 PDSIT-3
58. Screws
59. Idle mixture enrichment unit
60. O-ring
61. Screws
62. Connecting rod locknuts
63. Float valve
64. Float valve washer
65. Screws
66. Screws
67. Screws
68. Washer
69. Throttle return spring
70. Idle mixture screw
71. O-ring
72. Plug
73. Idle speed adjusting screw
74. O-ring
75. Central idling system electromagnetic cutoff valve
Vergaser links—left carburetor (34 PDSIT-2)
Vergaser rechts—right carburetor (34 PDSIT-3)

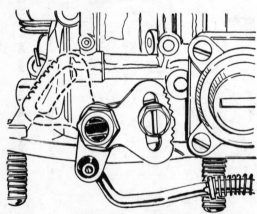

Accelerator pump injection quantity adjusting segment for 1973–74 Type 1 models with alternator. Dotted line shows position of adjusting segment for 1971–73 Type 1 models with generator (Solex 34 PICT-3)

Accelerator pump injection quantity adjusting nut for 1973–74 Type 1 models sold in California (Solex 34 PICT-4)

5c. On 34 PICT-3 carburetors, the injection quantity is decreased by loosening the retaining screw and turning the adjusting lever clockwise, and increased by loosening the retaining screw and turning the adjusting lever counterclockwise. Tighten the adjusting screw after adjusting.

5d. On 34 PICT-4 carburetors (used on 1973–74 Type 1 models sold in California) the injection quantity is adjusted by turning the adjusting screw (spring loaded) on the pump operating rod. The 1974 California models of these carburetors also have the partial fuel cutoff mentioned in step 5b for 1974 Type 2 automatic transmission with 34 PDSIT 2/3 carburetor. Make sure carburetor body temperature is below 60°F before checking full injection quantity.

FAST IDLE ADJUSTMENT

The fast idle speed is adjusted by means of a screw located at the upper end of the throttle valve arm. This screw rests against a cam with steps cut into its edge.

To adjust the fast idle, start the engine and rotate the cam so that the fast idle screw is resting against the highest step on the fast idle cam. The fast idle speed should be 1450–1650 rpm. Turn the fast idle screw either in or out until the proper idle speed is obtained.

On dual carburetor engines it is necessary to adjust the fast idle on only the left carbure-tor. There is a direct connection between the two carburetors and if the left carburetor is adjusted the right will automatically be adjusted.

ACCELERATOR CABLE REPLACEMENT

1. Disconnect the cable from the accelerator pedal.
2. Disconnect the cable from the throttle lever.
3. Pull the cable from the accelerator pedal end and then remove it from the car.
4. Grease the cable before sliding it into its housing.
5. Slide the cable into its housing and push it through its guide tubes. It may be necessary to raise the car and start the cable into the segments of guide tube found under the car.
6. Install one cable end into the accelerator cable. Slip the other end into the throttle valve lever and adjust the cable.

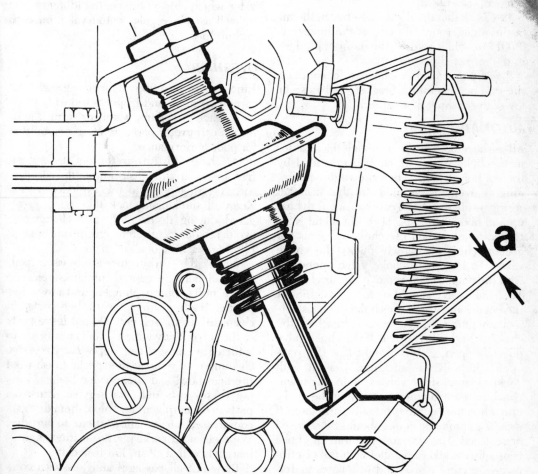

Dashpot adjustment on 1972–74 Type 1 models. Distance "A" is 0.040 in.

NOTE: *Make sure that the rubber boot at the rear end of the cable is properly seated so that water will not enter the guide tubes.*

DASHPOT ADJUSTMENT

1972–74 Type 1 with Manual Transmission

NOTE: *The car must be fully warmed up and the choke plate open.*

1. Check that the distance (a) between the tip of the dashpot and the throttle lever is 0.040 in. with the dashpot plunger fully retracted and the throttle fully closed on the warm running position of the fast idle cam.
2. To adjust, loosen the two locknuts on the dashpot mounting bracket, and raise or lower the dashpot as needed.

1972–74 Type 2 Twin Carb

NOTE: *This adjustment is required only if the dashpot has been removed or the linkage disassembled.*

1. Check that the distance between the tip of the plunger and the tab on the linkage is 0.0015 in. while holding the dashpot plunger in the retracted position.
2. To adjust, loosen the two locknuts on the dashpot mounting bracket, and raise or lower the dashpot as required.

AUTOMATIC CHOKE

All carburetor equipped models have automatic choke valves which are controlled by the ignition switch. When the engine is running, current is applied to the bi-metal spring inside the choke case causing it to heat up and bend. One end of the bi-metal is attached to a lever on the choke valve: as the bi-metal bends it slowly opens the choke valve. To check the choke valve operation, with the engine cold, remove the air cleaner. The choke valve should be fully closed. Start the engine and watch the choke valve: as normal operating temperature is reached the choke should slowly open. If the choke valve does not open, give it a slight tap. If it pops open, the valve is sticking: spray it with choke cleaner. If the valve still doesn't open, check to see if current is reaching the choke unit when the engine is initially turned on. If it is, the automatic choke should be checked or replaced. The wire to the automatic choke is usually hooked in parallel with the electromagnetic cutoff valve and originates at terminal 15 of the ignition coil.

ELECTROMAGNETIC CUTOFF VALVE (ANTI-DIESELING SOLENOID)

This valve prevents the engine from "running on" or dieseling after the ignition key is turned off. The unit consists of a small plunger connected to a solenoid. While the engine is running, current is applied to the valve which causes the solenoid to pull the plunger back. When the plunger is pulled back it allows fuel to flow into the idling system of the carburetor; when the plunger is let forward it cuts off fuel flow. See the exploded views of the carburetors to locate the electromagnetic cutoff valve.

This unit is usually trouble free, however, if it does go faulty it can cut off the entire idling system, causing the car to stall when idling but to run if the accelerator pedal is used. The unit simply unscrews. The wiring on the valve is usually hooked in parallel with the automatic choke and originates at terminal 15 of the ignition coil. Type 2 models with dual carburetors have an extra cutoff valve which cuts off the central idling system as well as one regular cutoff valve on each carburetor.

OVERHAUL

Efficient carburetion depends greatly on careful cleaning and inspection during overhaul, since dirt, gum, water, or varnish in or on the carburetor parts are often responsible for poor performance.

Overhaul your carburetor in a clean, dust-free area. Carefully disassemble the carburetor, referring often to the exploded views. Keep all similar and look-alike parts segregated during disassembly and cleaning to avoid accidental interchange during assembly. Make a note of all jet sizes.

When the carburetor is disassembled, wash all parts (except diaphragms, electric choke units, pump plunger, and any other plastic, leather, fiber, or rubber parts) in clean carburetor solvent. Do not leave parts in the solvent any longer than is necessary to sufficiently loosen the deposits. Excessive cleaning may remove the special finish from the float bowl and choke valve bodies, leaving these parts unfit for service. Rinse all parts in clean solvent and blow them dry with compressed air to allow them to air dry. Wipe clean all cork, plastic, leather, and fiber parts with a clean, lint-free cloth.

Blow out all passages and jets with compressed air and be sure that there are no re-

CHILTON'S
FUEL ECONOMY
& TUNE-UP TIPS

55 WAYS TO IMPROVE FUEL ECONOMY

Tune-up • Spark Plug Diagnosis • Emission Controls

Fuel System • Cooling System • Tires and Wheels

General Maintenance

CHILTON'S FUEL ECONOMY & TUNE-UP TIPS

Fuel economy is important to everyone, no matter what kind of vehicle you drive. The maintenance-minded motorist can save both money and fuel using these tips and the periodic maintenance and tune-up procedures in this Repair and Tune-Up Guide.

There are more than 130,000,000 cars and trucks registered for private use in the United States. Each travels an average of 10-12,000 miles per year, and, and in total they consume close to 70 billion gallons of fuel each year. This represents nearly ⅔ of the oil imported by the United States each year. The Federal government's goal is to reduce consumption 10% by 1985. A variety of methods are either already in use or under serious consideration, and they all affect you driving and the cars you will drive. In addition to "down-sizing", the auto industry is using or investigating the use of electronic fuel delivery, electronic engine controls and alternative engines for use in smaller and lighter vehicles, among other alternatives to meet the federally mandated Corporate Average Fuel Economy (CAFE) of 27.5 mpg by 1985. The government, for its part, is considering rationing, mandatory driving curtailments and tax increases on motor vehicle fuel in an effort to reduce consumption. The government's goal of a 10% reduction could be realized — and further government regulation avoided — if every private vehicle could use just 1 less gallon of fuel per week.

How Much Can You Save?

Tests have proven that almost anyone can make at least a 10% reduction in fuel consumption through regular maintenance and tune-ups. When a major manufacturer of spark plugs sur-

TUNE-UP

1. Check the cylinder compression to be sure the engine will really benefit from a tune-up and that it is capable of producing good fuel economy. A tune-up will be wasted on an engine in poor mechanical condition.

2. Replace spark plugs regularly. New spark plugs alone can increase fuel economy 3%.

3. Be sure the spark plugs are the correct type (heat range) for your vehicle. See the Tune-Up Specifications.

Heat range refers to the spark plug's ability to conduct heat away from the firing end. It must conduct the heat away in an even pattern to avoid becoming a source of pre-ignition, yet it must also operate hot enough to burn off conductive deposits that could cause misfiring.

The heat range is usually indicated by a number on the spark plug, part of the manufacturer's designation for each individual spark plug. The numbers in bold-face indicate the heat range in each manufacturer's identification system.

Manufacturer	Typical Designation
AC	R **45** TS
Bosch (old)	WA **145** T30
Bosch (new)	HR **8** Y
Champion	RBL **15** Y
Fram/Autolite	4**15**
Mopar	P-**62** PR
Motorcraft	BRF-**42**
NGK	BP **5** ES-15
Nippondenso	W **16** EP
Prestolite	14GR **5** 2A

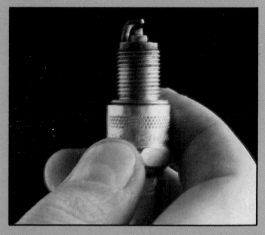

Periodically, check the spark plugs to be sure they are firing efficiently. They are excellent indicators of the internal condition of your engine.

On AC, Bosch (new), Champion, Fram/Autolite, Mopar, Motorcraft and Prestolite, a higher number indicates a hotter plug. On Bosch (old), NGK and Nippondenso, a higher number indicates a colder plug.

4. Make sure the spark plugs are properly gapped. See the Tune-Up Specifications in this book.

5. Be sure the spark plugs are firing efficiently. The illustrations on the next 2 pages show you how to "read" the firing end of the spark plug.

6. Check the ignition timing and set it to specifications. Tests show that almost all cars have incorrect ignition timing by more than 2°.

MMT Fouled

APPEARANCE: Spark plugs fouled by MMT (Methycyclopentadienyl Maganese Tricarbonyl) have reddish, rusty appearance on the insulator and side electrode.

CAUSE: MMT is an anti-knock additive in gasoline used to replace lead. During the combustion process, the MMT leaves a reddish deposit on the insulator and side electrode.

RECOMMENDATION: No engine malfunction is indicated and the deposits will not affect plug performance any more than lead deposits (see Ash Deposits). MMT fouled plugs can be cleaned, regapped and reinstalled.

High Speed Glazing

APPEARANCE: Glazing appears as shiny coating on the plug, either yellow or tan in color.

CAUSE: During hard, fast acceleration, plug temperatures rise suddenly. Deposits from normal combustion have no chance to fluff-off; instead, they melt on the insulator forming an electrically conductive coating which causes misfiring.

RECOMMENDATION: Glazed plugs are not easily cleaned. They should be replaced with a fresh set of plugs of the correct heat range. If the condition recurs, using plugs with a heat range one step colder may cure the problem.

Ash (Lead) Deposits

APPEARANCE: Ash deposits are characterized by light brown or white colored deposits crusted on the side or center electrodes. In some cases it may give the plug a rusty appearance.

CAUSE: Ash deposits are normally derived from oil or fuel additives burned during normal combustion. Normally they are harmless, though excessive amounts can cause misfiring. If deposits are excessive in short mileage, the valve guides may be worn.

RECOMMENDATION: Ash-fouled plugs can be cleaned, gapped and reinstalled.

Detonation

APPEARANCE: Detonation is usually characterized by a broken plug insulator.

CAUSE: A portion of the fuel charge will begin to burn spontaneously, from the increased heat following ignition. The explosion that results applies extreme pressure to engine components, frequently damaging spark plugs and pistons.

Detonation can result by over-advanced ignition timing, inferior gasoline (low octane) lean air/fuel mixture, poor carburetion, engine lugging or an increase in compression ratio due to combustion chamber deposits or engine modification.

RECOMMENDATION: Replace the plugs after correcting the problem.

Photos Courtesy Champion Spark Plug Co.

EMISSION CONTROLS

13. Be aware of the general condition of the emission control system. It contributes to reduced pollution and should be serviced regularly to maintain efficient engine operation.

14. Check all vacuum lines for dried, cracked or brittle conditions. Something as simple as a leaking vacuum hose can cause poor performance and loss of economy.

15. Avoid tampering with the emission control system. Attempting to improve fuel econ-

FUEL SYSTEM

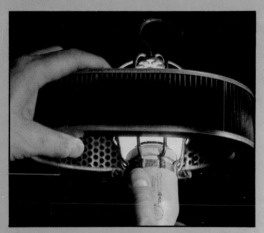

Check the air filter with a light behind it. If you can see light through the filter it can be reused.

Extremely clogged filters should be discarded and replaced with a new one.

18. Replace the air filter regularly. A dirty air filter richens the air/fuel mixture and can increase fuel consumption as much as 10%. Tests show that ⅓ of all vehicles have air filters in need of replacement.

19. Replace the fuel filter at least as often as recommended.

20. Set the idle speed and carburetor mixture to specifications.

21. Check the automatic choke. A sticking or malfunctioning choke wastes gas.

22. During the summer months, adjust the automatic choke for a leaner mixture which will produce faster engine warm-ups.

COOLING SYSTEM

29. Be sure all accessory drive belts are in good condition. Check for cracks or wear.

30. Adjust all accessory drive belts to proper tension.

31. Check all hoses for swollen areas, worn spots, or loose clamps.

32. Check coolant level in the radiator or expansion tank.

33. Be sure the thermostat is operating properly. A stuck thermostat delays engine warm-up and a cold engine uses nearly twice as much fuel as a warm engine.

34. Drain and replace the engine coolant at least as often as recommended. Rust and scale

TIRES & WHEELS

38. Check the tire pressure often with a pencil type gauge. Tests by a major tire manufacturer show that 90% of all vehicles have at least 1 tire improperly inflated. Better mileage can be achieved by over-inflating tires, but never exceed the maximum inflation pressure on the side of the tire.

39. If possible, install radial tires. Radial tires deliver as much as ½ mpg more than bias belted tires.

40. Avoid installing super-wide tires. They only create extra rolling resistance and decrease fuel mileage. Stick to the manufacturer's recommendations.

41. Have the wheels properly balanced.

veyed over 6,000 cars nationwide, they found that a tune-up, on cars that needed one, increased fuel economy over 11%. Replacing worn plugs alone, accounted for a 3% increase. The same test also revealed that 8 out of every 10 vehicles will have some maintenance deficiency that will directly affect fuel economy, emissions or performance. Most of this mileage-robbing neglect could be prevented with regular maintenance.

Modern engines require that all of the functioning systems operate properly for maximum efficiency. A malfunction anywhere wastes fuel. You can keep your vehicle running as efficiently and economically as possible, by being aware of your vehicle's operating and performance characteristics. If your vehicle suddenly develops performance or fuel economy problems it could be due to one or more of the following:

PROBLEM	POSSIBLE CAUSE
Engine Idles Rough	Ignition timing, idle mixture, vacuum leak or something amiss in the emission control system.
Hesitates on Acceleration	Dirty carburetor or fuel filter, improper accelerator pump setting, ignition timing or fouled spark plugs.
Starts Hard or Fails to Start	Worn spark plugs, improperly set automatic choke, ice (or water) in fuel system.
Stalls Frequently	Automatic choke improperly adjusted and possible dirty air filter or fuel filter.
Performs Sluggishly	Worn spark plugs, dirty fuel or air filter, ignition timing or automatic choke out of adjustment.

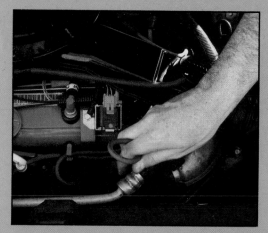

Check spark plug wires on conventional point type ignition for cracks by bending them in a loop around your finger.

Be sure that spark plug wires leading to adjacent cylinders do not run too close together. (Photo courtesy Champion Spark Plug Co.)

7. If your vehicle does not have electronic ignition, check the points, rotor and cap as specified.

8. Check the spark plug wires (used with conventional point-type ignitions) for cracks and burned or broken insulation by bending them in a loop around your finger. Cracked wires decrease fuel efficiency by failing to deliver full voltage to the spark plugs. One misfiring spark plug can cost you as much as 2 mpg.

9. Check the routing of the plug wires. Misfiring can be the result of spark plug leads to adjacent cylinders running parallel to each other and too close together. One wire tends to pick up voltage from the other causing it to fire "out of time".

10. Check all electrical and ignition circuits for voltage drop and resistance.

11. Check the distributor mechanical and/or vacuum advance mechanisms for proper functioning. The vacuum advance can be checked by twisting the distributor plate in the opposite direction of rotation. It should spring back when released.

12. Check and adjust the valve clearance on engines with mechanical lifters. The clearance should be slightly loose rather than too tight.

SPARK PLUG DIAGNOSIS

Normal

APPEARANCE: This plug is typical of one operating normally. The insulator nose varies from a light tan to grayish color with slight electrode wear. The presence of slight deposits is normal on used plugs and will have no adverse effect on engine performance. The spark plug heat range is correct for the engine and the engine is running normally.

CAUSE: Properly running engine.

RECOMMENDATION: Before reinstalling this plug, the electrodes should be cleaned and filed square. Set the gap to specifications. If the plug has been in service for more than 10-12,000 miles, the entire set should probably be replaced with a fresh set of the same heat range.

Oil Deposits

APPEARANCE: The firing end of the plug is covered with a wet, oily coating.

CAUSE: The problem is poor oil control. On high mileage engines, oil is leaking past the rings or valve guides into the combustion chamber. A common cause is also a plugged PCV valve, and a ruptured fuel pump diaphragm can also cause this condition. Oil fouled plugs such as these are often found in new or recently overhauled engines, before normal oil control is achieved, and can be cleaned and reinstalled.

RECOMMENDATION: A hotter spark plug may temporarily relieve the problem, but the engine is probably in need of work.

Incorrect Heat Range

APPEARANCE: The effects of high temperature on a spark plug are indicated by clean white, often blistered insulator. This can also be accompanied by excessive wear of the electrode, and the absence of deposits.

CAUSE: Check for the correct spark plug heat range. A plug which is too hot for the engine can result in overheating. A car operated mostly at high speeds can require a colder plug. Also check ignition timing, cooling system level, fuel mixture and leaking intake manifold.

RECOMMENDATION: If all ignition and engine adjustments are known to be correct, and no other malfunction exists, install spark plugs one heat range colder.

Carbon Deposits

APPEARANCE: Carbon fouling is easily identified by the presence of dry, soft, black, sooty deposits.

CAUSE: Changing the heat range can often lead to carbon fouling, as can prolonged slow, stop-and-start driving. If the heat range is correct, carbon fouling can be attributed to a rich fuel mixture, sticking choke, clogged air cleaner, worn breaker points, retarded timing or low compression. If only one or two plugs are carbon fouled, check for corroded or cracked wires on the affected plugs. Also look for cracks in the distributor cap between the towers of affected cylinders.

RECOMMENDATION: After the problem is corrected, these plugs can be cleaned and reinstalled if not worn severely.

omy by tampering with emission controls is more likely to worsen fuel economy than improve it. Emission control changes on modern engines are not readily reversible.

16. Clean (or replace) the EGR valve and lines as recommended.

17. Be sure that all vacuum lines and hoses are reconnected properly after working under the hood. An unconnected or misrouted vacuum line can wreak havoc with engine performance.

23. Check for fuel leaks at the carburetor, fuel pump, fuel lines and fuel tank. Be sure all lines and connections are tight.

24. Periodically check the tightness of the carburetor and intake manifold attaching nuts and bolts. These are a common place for vacuum leaks to occur.

25. Clean the carburetor periodically and lubricate the linkage.

26. The condition of the tailpipe can be an excellent indicator of proper engine combustion. After a long drive at highway speeds, the inside of the tailpipe should be a light grey in color. Black or soot on the insides indicates an overly rich mixture.

27. Check the fuel pump pressure. The fuel pump may be supplying more fuel than the engine needs.

28. Use the proper grade of gasoline for your engine. Don't try to compensate for knocking or "pinging" by advancing the ignition timing. This practice will only increase plug temperature and the chances of detonation or pre-ignition with relatively little performance gain.

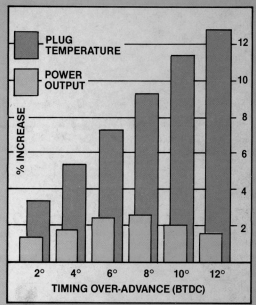

Increasing ignition timing past the specified setting results in a drastic increase in spark plug temperature with increased chance of detonation or preignition. Performance increase is considerably less. (Photo courtesy Champion Spark Plug Co.)

that form in the engine should be flushed out to allow the engine to operate at peak efficiency.

35. Clean the radiator of debris that can decrease cooling efficiency.

36. Install a flex-type or electric cooling fan, if you don't have a clutch type fan. Flex fans use curved plastic blades to push more air at low speeds when more cooling is needed; at high speeds the blades flatten out for less resistance. Electric fans only run when the engine temperature reaches a predetermined level.

37. Check the radiator cap for a worn or cracked gasket. If the cap does not seal properly, the cooling system will not function properly.

42. Be sure the front end is correctly aligned. A misaligned front end actually has wheels going in differed directions. The increased drag can reduce fuel economy by .3 mpg.

43. Correctly adjust the wheel bearings. Wheel bearings that are adjusted too tight increase rolling resistance.

Check tire pressures regularly with a reliable pocket type gauge. Be sure to check the pressure on a cold tire.

GENERAL MAINTENANCE

Check the fluid levels (particularly engine oil) on a regular basis. Be sure to check the oil for grit, water or other contamination.

A vacuum gauge is another excellent indicator of internal engine condition and can also be installed in the dash as a mileage indicator.

44. Periodically check the fluid levels in the engine, power steering pump, master cylinder, automatic transmission and drive axle.

45. Change the oil at the recommended interval and change the filter at every oil change. Dirty oil is thick and causes extra friction between moving parts, cutting efficiency and increasing wear. A worn engine requires more frequent tune-ups and gets progressively worse fuel economy. In general, use the lightest viscosity oil for the driving conditions you will encounter.

46. Use the recommended viscosity fluids in the transmission and axle.

47. Be sure the battery is fully charged for fast starts. A slow starting engine wastes fuel.

48. Be sure battery terminals are clean and tight.

49. Check the battery electrolyte level and add distilled water if necessary.

50. Check the exhaust system for crushed pipes, blockages and leaks.

51. Adjust the brakes. Dragging brakes or brakes that are not releasing create increased drag on the engine.

52. Install a vacuum gauge or miles-per-gallon gauge. These gauges visually indicate engine vacuum in the intake manifold. High vacuum = good mileage and low vacuum = poorer mileage. The gauge can also be an excellent indicator of internal engine conditions.

53. Be sure the clutch is properly adjusted. A slipping clutch wastes fuel.

54. Check and periodically lubricate the heat control valve in the exhaust manifold. A sticking or inoperative valve prevents engine warm-up and wastes gas.

55. Keep accurate records to check fuel economy over a period of time. A sudden drop in fuel economy may signal a need for tune-up or other maintenance.

strictions or blockages. Never use wire or similar tools to clean jets, fuel passages, or air bleeds. Clean all jets and valves separately to avoid accidental interchange.

Check all parts for wear or damage. If wear or damage is found, replace the defective parts. Especially check the following:

1. Check the float needle and seat for wear. If wear is found, replace the complete assembly.

2. Check the float hinge pin for wear and the float(s) for dents or distortion. Replace the float if fuel has leaked into it.

3. Check the throttle and choke shaft bores for wear or an out-of-round condition. Damage or wear to the throttle arm, shaft, or shaft bore will often require replacement of the throttle body. These parts require a close tolerance of fit; wear may allow air leakage, which could affect starting and idling.

NOTE: *Throttle shafts and bushings are not included in overhaul kits. They can be purchased separately.*

4. Inspect the idle mixture adjusting needles for burrs or grooves. Any such condition requires replacement of the needle, since you will not be able to obtain a satisfactory idle.

5. Test the accelerator pump check valves. They should pass air one way but not the other. Test for proper seating by blowing and sucking on the valve. Replace the valve if necessary. If the valve is satisfactory, wash the valve again to remove breath moisture.

6. Check the bowl cover for warped surfaces with a straightedge.

7. Closely inspect the valves and seats for wear and damage, replacing as necessary.

8. After the carburetor is assembled, check the choke valve for freedom of operation.

Carburetor overhaul kits are recommended for each overhaul. These kits contain all gaskets and new parts to replace those that deteriorate most rapidly. Failure to replace all parts supplied with the kit (especially gaskets) can result in poor performance later.

Some carburetor manufacturers supply overhaul kits of three basic types: minor repair; major repair; and gasket kits. Basically, they contain the following:

Minor Repair Kits:
• All gaskets
• Float needle valve
• Volume control screw
• All diaphragms
• Spring for the pump diaphragm

Major Repair Kits:
• All jets and gaskets
• All diaphragms
• Float needle valve
• Volume control screw
• Pump ball valve
• Main jet carrier
• Float
Gasket Kits:
• All gaskets

After cleaning and checking all components, reassemble the carburetor, using new parts and referring to the exploded view. When reassembling, make sure that all screws and jets are tight in their seats, but do not overtighten as the tips will be distorted. Tighten all screws gradually in rotation. Do not tighten needle valves into their seats; uneven jetting will result. Always use new gaskets. Be sure to adjust the float level when reassembling.

Fuel Injection

NON-AIR FLOW CONTROLLED

The Bosch Electronic fuel injection system used on all Type 3 models, and on 1971–74 Type 4 models (except 1974 models equipped with an automatic), consists of two parts. One part consists of the actual injection components: the injectors, the fuel pump, pressure regulator, and related wiring and hoses. The second part consists of the injection controls and engine operating characteristics sensors: a manifold vacuum sensor that monitors engine load, trigger contacts used to determine when and which pair of injectors will operate, three temperature sensors used to control air fuel mixture enrichment, a cold starting valve for additional cold starting fuel enrichment, a throttle valve switch used to cut off fuel during deceleration, and the brain box used to analyze information about engine operating characteristics and, after processing this information, to control the electrically operated injectors.

It is absolutely imperative that no adjustments other than those found in the following pages be performed. The controls for this fuel injection system are extremely sensitive and easily damaged when subject to abuse. Never attempt to test the brain box without proper training and the proper equipment. The dealer is the best place to have any needed work performed.

CAUTION: *Whenever a fuel injection component is to be removed or installed,*

Carburetor Specifications—Types 1 and 2
(All measurements are in metric units)

Year	Type Common Designation	Engine Code	Carburetor (Solex)	Venturi Diameter (mm)	Main Jet	Air Correction Jet	Pilot Jet	Aux Fuel Jet	Aux Air Jet	Power Fuel Jet	Needle Valve Washer Thickness (mm)	Accelerator Pump Injection Quantity (cc^3 stroke)	Throttle Valve Gap (mm)	Fuel Level (mm)
1970	1/1600, 2/1600	B	30 PICT-3	24	x112.5	125Z-MT 140Z-AT 140Z-Bus	65	45.0	130	100/100	1.5	1.05–1.35	—	19.5–20.5–
1971	1/1600	AE	34 PICT-3	26	x130	75Z/80Z	g60	47.5	90	100/100	0.5	1.45–1.75	—	17–19
	2/1600	AE	34 PICT-3	26	x125	60Z	g57.5	42.5	90	95/95	0.5	1.45–1.75	—	17–19
1972	1/1600	AE	34 PICT-3	26	x130	75Z/80Z	g60	47.5	90	100/100	0.5	1.45–1.75	—	17–19
	1/1600	AH (Calif only)	34 PICT-3	26	x127.5/x130	75Z/80Z	g55	42.5	90	100	0.5	1.3–1.6	—	17–19
	2/1700 Twin carb	CB	Left 34 PDSIT-2	26	x137.5	155	55	45.0	0.7	—	0.5	0.8–1.0	0.6	12–14
			Right 34 PDSIT-3	26	x137.5	155	55	—	—	—	0.5	0.8–1.0	0.6	12–14
1973	1/1600	AK	34 PICT-3	26	x127.5/x127.5	75Z/80Z	g55	42.5	90	100	0.5	1.3–1.6	—	17–19

Year	Engine/Disp	Code	Carburetor											
	1/1600	AH, AM (Calif only)	34 PICT-4	26	×112.5	75Z/70Z	g55	42.5	90	100	0.5	1.3–1.6	—	17–19
	2/1700 Twin carb	CB (man trans)	Left 34 PDSIT-2	26	×130	140	55	45.0	0.7	—	1.0	0.6–0.8	0.6	12–14
			Right 34 PDSIT-3	26	×130	140	55	—	—	—	1.0	0.6–0.8	0.6	12–14
	2/1700 Twin carb	CD (AT)	Left 34 PDSIT-2	26	×132.5	155	50	45.0	0.7	—	1.0	0.7–1.2	0.6	12–14
			Right 34 PDSIT-3	26	×132.5	155	50	—	—	—	1.0	0.7–1.2	0.6	12–14
1974	1/1600	AK	34 PICT-3	26	×127.5/×127.5	75Z/80Z	g55	42.5	90	100	0.5	1.3–1.6	—	17–19
	1/1600	AH, AM (Calif only)	34 PICT-4	26	×127.5	75Z-MT 70Z-AT	g55	42.5	90	100	0.5	1.1②	—	17–19
	2/1800 Twin carb	AW	Left 34 PDSIT-2	26	×130	175	52.5	45.0	0.7	—	1.0	1.5①	0.7	12–14
			Right 34 PDSIT-3	26	×130	175	52.5	—	—	—	1.0	1.5①	0.7	12–14
1975–81	Air flow controlled electronic fuel injection													

MT—Manual Transmission
AT—Automatic Transmission
—Not Applicable
① Engine below 70°F: 0.7cc, Engine Above 75°F.
② Engine Above 75°F: 1.7cc, Engine below 70°F.

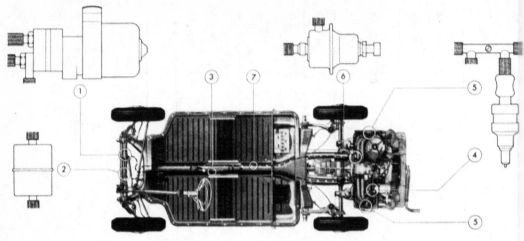

1. Fuel pump
2. Fuel filter
3. Pressure line
4. Ring main

5. Injectors
6. Pressure regulator
7. Return line (not pressurized)

Location of fuel injection components—Type 3

the battery should be disconnected and the ignition turned OFF.

It is not recommended that the inexperienced mechanic work on any portion of the fuel injection system.

AIR FLOW CONTROLLED

1974 Type 4 models equipped with automatic transmission, as well as all 1975–81 Type 1 and Type 2 models, are equipped with an improved system known as the Air Flow Controlled Electronic Fuel Injection System. With this system, some of the electronic sensors and wiring are eliminated, and the control box is smaller. Instead fuel is metered according to intake air flow.

The system consists of the following components;

Intake air sensor—measures intake air volume and temperature and sends voltage signals to the control unit (brain box). It also controls the electric fuel pump by shutting it off when intake air stops. It is located between the air cleaner and the intake air distributor.

Ignition contact breaker points—these are the regular points inside the distributor. When the points open, all four injectors are triggered. The points also send engine speed signals to the control unit. No separate triggering contacts are used.

Throttle valve switch—provides only for full load enrichment. This switch is not adjustable.

Temperature sensor I—senses intake temperature as before. It is now located in the intake air sensor.

Temperature sensor II—senses cylinder head temperature as before.

Control unit (brain box—contains only 80 components compared to the old system's 300.

Pressure regulator—is connected by a vacuum hose to the intake air distributor and is no longer adjustable. It adjusts fuel pressure according to manifold vacuum.

Auxiliary air regulator—provides more air during cold warmup.

ELECTRONIC CONTROL (BRAIN) BOX

All work concerning the brain box is to be performed by the dealer. Do not remove the brain box and take it to a dealer because the dealer will not be able to test it without the vehicle. Do not disconnect the brain box unless the battery is disconnected and the ignition is OFF.

FUEL INJECTORS

There are two types of injectors. One type is secured in place by a ring that holds a single injector. The second type of injector is secured to the intake manifold in pairs by a common bracket.

Checking Fuel Injector Operation

When the engine fails to run or runs erratically, always check the ignition system before

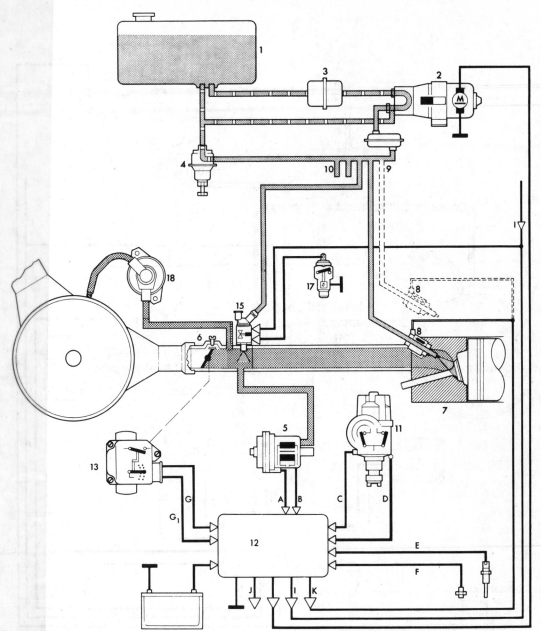

1. Fuel tank
2. Fuel pump
3. Fuel filter
4. Pressure regulator
5. Pressure sensor
6. Intake air distributor
7. Cylinder head
8. Injectors
9. Fuel distributor pipe
10. Fuel distributor pipe with connection for cold starting device
11. Distributor with trigger contacts (distributor contact I, distributor contact II)
12. Control unit
13. Throttle valve switch with acceleration enrichment

15. Cold starting valve
17. Thermostat for cold starting device
18. Auxiliary air regulator
A + B. from pressure sensor (load condition signal)
C + D. from distributor contacts (engine speed and releasing signal)
E + F. from temperature sensors (warmup signal)
G. from throttle valve switch (fuel supply cut-off when coasting)
G1. Acceleration enrichment
I. from starter, terminal 50 solenoid switch (signal for enrichment mixture when starting)
J. to the injectors, cylinders 1 and 4
K. to the injectors, cylinders 2 and 3

Schematic of electronic fuel injection system—1970 and later 49 states models, 1970–71 California models

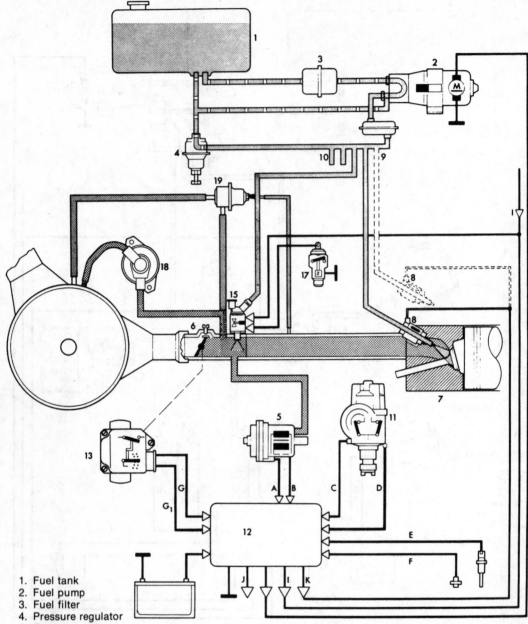

1. Fuel tank
2. Fuel pump
3. Fuel filter
4. Pressure regulator
5. Pressure sensor
6. Intake air distributor
7. Cylinder head
8. Injectors
9. Fuel distributor pipe
10. Fuel distributor pipe with connection for cold starting device
11. Distributor with trigger contacts (contacts I and II)
12. Electronic control unit
13. Throttle valve switch with acceleration enrichment
14. Pressure switch
15. Cold starting valve
17. Thermostat for cold starting device
18. Auxiliary air regulator
19. Deceleration mixture control valve

autom. = electromagnetic
manual = pneumatic

A + B. from pressure sensor (load condition signal)
C + D. from distributor contacts (engine speed and releasing signal)
E + F. from temperature sensors (warmup signal)
G. from throttle valve switch (full throttle signal. Type 3 only)
G 1. Acceleration enrichment
I. from starter, terminal 50 solenoid switch (signal for enrichment mixture when starting)
J. to injectors, cylinders 1 and 4
K. to the injectors, cylinders 2 and 3

Schematic of electronic fuel injection system—1972–74 California models

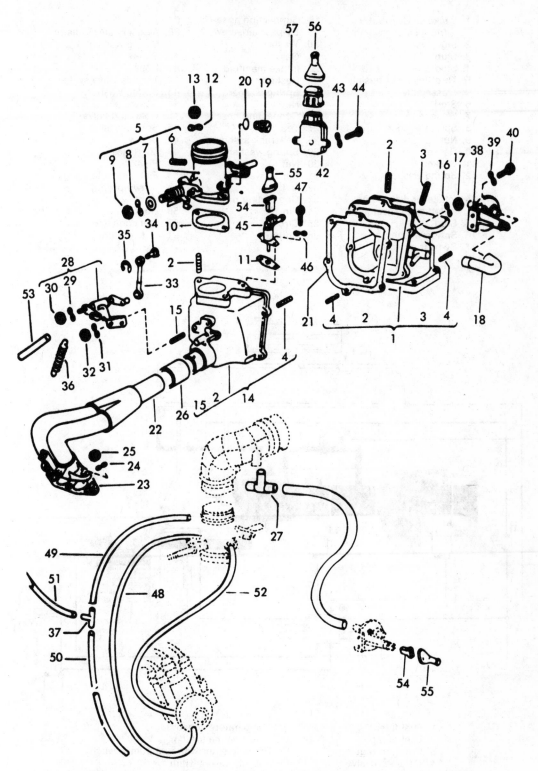

Airflow controlled fuel injection system—1975–80 Type 1 shown, Type 2 similar

1. Intake air distributor
   (right-side) assembly
2. Stud
3. Stud
4. Stud
5. Throttle valve housing
   assembly
6. Stud
7. Washer
8. Spring washer
9. Nut
10. Gasket
11. Gasket
12. Spring washer
13. Nut
14. Intake air distributor
    (left-side) assembly
15. Stud
16. Spring washer
17. By-pass air screw

18. Connecting hose
19. By-pass air screw
20. Washer
21. Gasket
22. Intake manifold
23. Gasket
24. Spring washer
25. Nut
26. Connecting hose
27. Tee
28. Bellcrank assembly
29. Spring washer
30. Nut
31. Spring washer
32. Nut
33. Connecting rod
34. Pin
35. Circlip
36. Spring

37. Tee
38. Auxiliary air regulator
39. Spring washer
40. Screw
41. Hose
42. Throttle valve switch
43. Spring washer
44. Screw
45. Cold-start valve
46. Spring washer
47. Screw
48–52. Hoses
53. Pipe
54. Flat connector plug
    (two-prong)
55. Boot
56. Boot
57. Flat connector plug
    (five-prong)

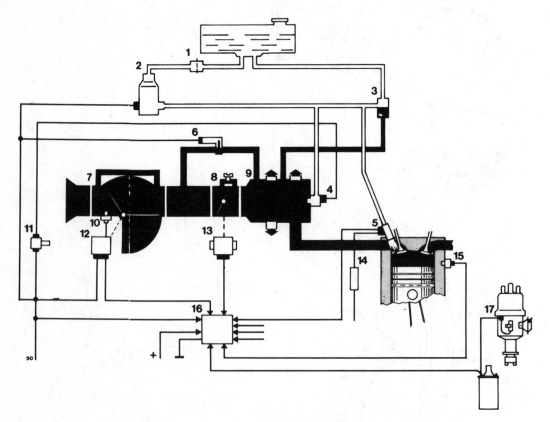

1. Fuel filter
2. Fuel pump
3. Pressure regulator
4. Cold-start valve
5. Injector
6. Auxiliary air regulator
7. Intake air sensor
8. Throttle valve housing
9. Intake air distributor
10. Temperature sensor I
11. Thermo-time switch
12. Potentiometer with fuel pump switch
13. Throttle valve switch
14. Resistor
15. Temperature sensor II
16. Control unit
17. Ignition contact breaker points

Schematic of airflow controlled electronic fuel injection system—1975–81 models

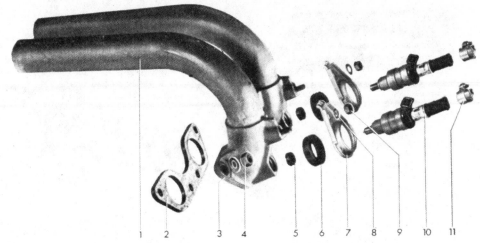

1. Intake manifold
2. Intake manifold gasket
3. Lockwasher
5. Inner sealing bushing
6. Outer sealing bushing
7. Retainer
8. Lockwasher
9. Nut
10. Fuel injector
11. Hose connection with clamp

Individually mounted fuel injectors

assuming that the problem lies under that inscrutable tangle known as the fuel injection system. If the ignition system is functioning correctly, remove the injectors from the engine, leaving the fuel lines and wiring connected to them. Disconnect the high tension cable from the ignition coil to prevent the engine from starting and have an assistant engage the starter briefly.

NOTE: *See precautions in Chapter Two for electronic ignition.*

CAUTION: *Raw fuel will be sprayed from the injectors if they are working, so have container ready and do not smoke.*

If a cone-shaped mist of fuel sprays in pulses from all of the injectors, they are working properly. If one or more injectors fail to spray, check the fuel injection signal.

To check for injector leakage, wipe the tips of the injectors dry with a clean, lint-free rag, then turn the ignition to ON (not START). If the injector tips become wet with fuel but do not drip more than one or two drops per minute, it is a good possibility that the pressure regulator is set too high; if the injector loses more than one or two drops per minute, the injector is faulty and should be replaced.

Checking the Fuel Injector Signal

NOTE: *You will need a mechanic's stethoscope to perform the second part of this test.*

Unplug the electrical connector on the fuel injector and connect the leads of a test light to the two terminals of the connector. Disconnect the ignition coil high tension cable to prevent the engine from starting and have an assistant engage the starter.

NOTE: *See Precautions in Chapter Two for electronic ignition.*

The test light should blink, indicating the pulses of the injector.

Reconnect all fuel injector connections and run the engine. Place the end of the stethoscope on the fuel injector body. You should hear a clicking sound indicating that the injector is working properly. Failure to hear a clicking sound or hearing a sound different from the rest of the injectors probably indicates a faulty injector.

Removal and Installation

SINGLE INJECTORS

1. Remove the nut which secures the injector bracket to the manifold.

2. If the injector is not going to be replaced, do not disconnect the fuel line. Disconnect the injector wiring.

3. Gently slide the injector bracket up the injector and pull the injector from the intake manifold. Be careful not to damage the inner and outer rubber sealing rings. These sealing rings are used to seal the injector to the manifold and must be replaced if they show any sign of deterioration.

4. Installation is the reverse of removal.

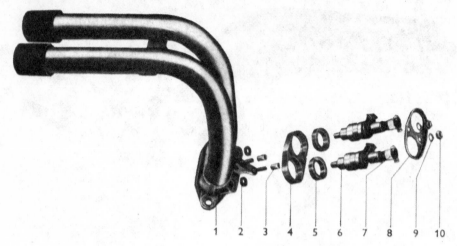

1. Intake manifolds with injector seats
2. Injector inner locating sealing bushings
3. Sleeves
4. Injector plate
5. Injector outer locating bushings
6. Electromagnetic fuel injector
7. Hose connection with clamp
8. Injector retainer
9. Lockwasher
10. Nut

Paired fuel injectors

Be careful not to damage the injector tip or contaminate the injector with dirt.

PAIRED INJECTORS

1. Disconnect the injector wiring.

2. Remove the two nuts which secure the injector bracket to the manifold. Slide the bracket up the injector. Do not disconnect the fuel lines if the injector is not going to be replaced.

3. Gently slide the pair of injectors out of their bores along with the rubber sealing rings, injector plate, and the inner and outer injector locating bushings. It may be necessary to remove the inner bushings from the intake manifold after the injectors are removed since they sometimes lodge within the manifold.

NOTE: *There are two sleeves that fit over the injector bracket studs. Be careful not to lose them.*

4. Upon installation, place the injector bracket, the outer locating bushings, the injector plate, and the inner locating bushings on the pair of injectors in that order.

5. Gently slip the injector assembly into the manifold and install the bracket nuts. Be careful not to damage the injector tips or contaminate the injectors with dirt.

6. Reconnect the injector wiring.

THROTTLE VALVE SWITCH

Removal and Installation

1. Remove the air filter.

2. The switch is located on the throttle valve housing. Disconnect the throttle valve return spring.

3. Remove the throttle valve assembly but do not disconnect the bowden wire for the throttle valve or the connecting hoses to the ignition distributor.

Throttle valve switch—1971 Type 4 shown. Note securing screws (a) and direction of adjustment (b)

Throttle valve switch—1970–72 Type 3, 1972–74 Type 4

Cold start valve location—Type 1. Thermo-time switch is mounted near it

4. Remove the throttle valve switch securing screws and remove the switch.

5. Reverse the above steps to install. It will be necessary to adjust the switch after installation.

Adjustment (Non-Air Flow Controlled Only)

The throttle valve switch is used to shut off the fuel supply during deceleration. The switch is supposed to operate when the throttle valve is opened 2°. A degree scale is stamped into the attachment plate for adjustment purposes.

1. Completely close the throttle valve.

2. Loosen the switch attaching screws and turn the switch carefully to the right until it hits its stop.

3. Turn the switch slowly to the left until it can be heard to click and then note the position of the switch according to the degree scale.

4. Continue to turn the switch another 2°. The distance between any two marks on the degree scale is 2°.

5. Tighten the screws and recheck the adjustment.

COLD START VALVE

The cold start valve is located on the air intake distributor and is held by two screws. The cold start valve operates only when the engine and the outside air are cold. It injects fuel into the air intake distributor for several seconds when the starter is engaged and then shuts off. If the valve is not working, it will be very difficult to start the engine; if the valve is leaking, it could cause flooding while starting, especially if the engine is hot. The cold start valve is controlled by a thermo-time switch or, on some models, a thermostat. Power for the valve is fed from terminal 50 of the starter.

Checking Cold Start Valve Leakage

Remove the cold start valve from the engine after disconnecting the electrical connector. Tape the connector's end to prevent sparks. Leave the fuel line attached. Disconnect the high tension ignition coil wire to prevent the engine from starting and have an assistant engage the starter while you hold the valve nozzle up in a rag.

NOTE: *See precautions in Chapter two for electronic ignitions.*

If fuel forms on the nozzle and begins to drip off, the valve is leaking and should be replaced, or fuel pressure is too high.

CAUTION: *Fuel might be expelled from the valve, so do not smoke and do not allow any electrical connections (coil wire, etc.) to cause sparks.*

Checking Cold Start Valve Operation

1. Remove the cold start valve from the engine leaving the fuel line attached.

2. Remove the high tension wire from the middle of the ignition coil and put tape over the coil terminal to prevent sparks.

NOTE: *See precautions in Chapter two for electronic ignition.*

3. If you haven't done so already, disconnect the electrical connector from the cold start valve.

4. Have a container ready to catch gasoline and using a jumper wire, connect one of the terminals on the cold start valve to ground. Connect the other terminal of the cold start valve to terminal 15 of the ignition coil using another jumper cable.

5. Point the nozzle of the cold start valve into the container and have an assistant turn the ignition to the ON position.

CAUTION: *Be careful not to allow the jumper wires to touch each other and do not smoke, as fuel will be expelled from the valve if it is working.*

6. A spray of fuel should come from the valve while the ignition is on. If not, the cold start valve is not working correctly.

7. Reconnect the cold start valve electrical connection. Turn the ignition to ON. If the cold start valve injects fuel with the ignition in the ON (not START) position, there is a good possibility that the cold start valve wire that belongs on terminal 50 of the starter has been mistakingly connected to terminal 30.

This test has been for the cold start valve itself, not the other components of the cold start system (thermo-time valve, relay, etc.). If your vehicle still starts hard on cold mornings, the problem could be with the thermo-time switch (thermo-switch on some models). It is best to let your dealer troubleshoot these components.

TRIGGER CONTACTS (NON-AIR FLOW CONTROLLED ONLY)

Removal and Installation

The trigger contacts are located in the base of the distributor and are secured by two screws. These contacts are supplied in pairs

Removing trigger contacts—Non-airflow controlled only

and are not adjustable. Do not attempt to replace just one set of contacts.

One set of contacts controls a pair of injectors and tells the injectors when to fire.

FUEL PRESSURE REGULATOR

Removal and Installation

Disconnect the hoses from the regulator and remove the regulator from its bracket. The fuel pump pressure is adjustable; however, lack of fuel pressure is usually due to other defects in the system and the regulator should be adjusted only as a last resort.

Adjustment (Non-Air Flow Controlled Only)

1. Remove the air cleaner.
2. Connect a fuel pressure gauge as shown.
3. Start the engine and operate at idle.
4. Loosen locknut "A" and adjust fuel pressure to 28 psi with screw "B."

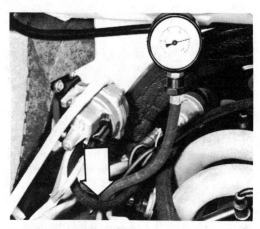

Fuel pressure regulator test gauge installation

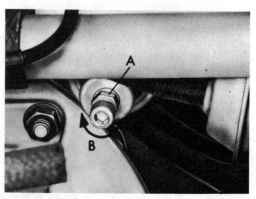

Fuel pressure regulator adjustment—Type 3

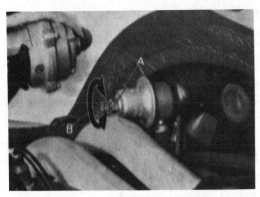

Fuel pressure regulator adjustment—Type 4

TEMPERATURE SENSORS I AND II

Removal and Installation

The air temperature sensor is located in the air distributor housing and may be unscrewed from the housing. The second temperature switch is located in the cylinder head on the left side and senses cylinder

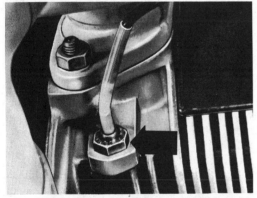

Cylinder head temperature sensing switch

Thermo (air temperature) switch location—Type 1

head temperature. It is removed with a special wrench. To test these switches, attach an ohmmeter and measure the resistance of the switch as the temperature is raised gradually to 212°. As the temperature rises, the resistance of the first switch should drop from about 200 ohms to 80 ohms. The cylinder head switch resistance should drop from about 1700 ohms to 190 ohms at 212°.

The third switch is actually a thermoswitch and is an ON/OFF type switch. Below 41° it is ON to activate the cold starting valve. The switch is located next to the distributor and may be removed with a 24 mm wrench.

PRESSURE SENSOR (NON-AIR FLOW CONTROLLED ONLY)

Removal and Installation

The sensor is secured to the firewall by two screws. Remove the screws and disconnect the wiring.

Remove the pressure connection and immediately plug the connection into the sensor. Always keep the connection plugged as the bellows inside the sensor is sensitive to the smallest pieces of dirt. Reverse the above steps to install.

Do not disassemble the sensor. There are no adjustments possible.

NOTE: *Do not reverse the square electrical plug when reconnecting the sensor wiring.*

Pressure sensor retaining screws—Type 3 and 4 only

IDLE SPEED REGULATOR

1975–76 Type 2, 1971 and later Type 4, with Automatic Transmission

NOTE: *An illustration of this device can be seen at the end of Chapter 2, "Tune-up",* with the caption *"Idling speed regulator dashpot adjustment . . ."*

This vacuum operated assembly slightly opens the throttle when the transmission is put in drive to prevent the engine from stalling under the load.

To test, adjust the regulator as described in Chapter 2 "Tune-up". When the plunger clearance is correct, pull the vacuum hose off the idle speed regulator: the plunger should extend and open the throttle slightly. When you reconnect the hose, the plunger should pull back. If not, check the hose for blockage or rips, or replace the regulator.

AUXILIARY AIR REGULATOR

The auxiliary air regulator lets extra air into the intake manifold during engine warm-up which allows the engine to run smoothly while it is cold. As the engine warms up, a rotary valve inside the air regulator twists shut slowly, cutting off more and more air intake until almost none is passing through the unit.

To test the auxiliary air regulator, the engine must be cold. Unplug the fabric covered air intake hose (not the one that leads into the intake air distributor). There should be suction at the hose. Cover the hose: engine speed should drop. After a reasonable amount of time (time will be longer in cold weather), the suction should diminish until it is almost nonexsistant. If the regulator does not close at all, disconnect its electrical connector and connect a test light to the terminals of the connector (not the regulator). With the engine running the test light should light. If it does, the auxiliary air regulator is probably defective.

TROUBLESHOOTING

There are very few items to check without the special tester used by the dealer.

It is possible to check the fuel pressure by

Auxiliary air regulator—Type 4. Automatic Transmission Type 3 regulator similar

inserting a fuel pressure gauge in the line after the pressure regulator. Insert the gauge using a T-fitting. Turn on the key and check the pressure. If the pressure is low, check for leaking injectors, restricted lines, clogged fuel filters, damaged pressure regulator, bad fuel pump, water in the gas and resultant corrosion of the injectors, or a leaking or jammed cold start valve.

Fuel Tank
REMOVAL AND INSTALLATION
Type 1, Type 3, Type 4

1. Disconnect the battery ground cable.
2. Drain the fuel from the tank.
3. Detach the fuel line and the wires from the sending unit, after removing the luggage compartment liner.
4. Remove the ventilation hoses from the fuel tank.
5. Loosen the hose clamps on the filler neck hose and remove the hose.
6. Remove the bolts from the four fuel tank retaining plates. Lift off the retaining plates and remove the tank from the car.
7. Installation is the reverse of removal.

Type 2 Through 1979

1. On all models except the pick-up truck, remove the engine. See Chapter 3 for procedures. On 1972 and later models, it is possible to remove the rear panel without removing the engine, but it is a tight squeeze.
2. If not done already, disconnect the battery cable and drain the fuel from the tank.
3. Remove the screws from the bulkhead behind the fuel tank (enclosed models) or from the panels in the lower storage compartment (pick-up truck models).
4. Disconnect the fuel filler hose and all lines and hoses. Plug the fuel lines.
5. Remove the fuel tank hold down straps and remove the tank toward th engine compartment (enclosed models) or through the lower storage compartment (pick-up trucks).
6. Installation is the reverse of removal.

Type 2 1980–81

The fuel tank is located behind the front axle assembly. It can be removed from beneath the vehicle after being drained by removing all hoses and wiring, then removing the two braces from beneath the tank and any other retaining bolts.

Chassis Electrical

HEATER

The only Volkswagens with an electric heater blower fan are the Type 2/1700/1800/2000 through 1979 and the Type 4, which also comes standard with an auxilliary gas heating system. The 1980 Type 2 heater fan is driven by the alternator. Do not confuse the fresh air circulation fan used on many Type 3 models and all 1971 and later Super Beetles and Type 1 Convertibles and all 1976 and later standard Type 1 models, with a heater blower fan, as the fresh air fan circulates only fresh, unheated air through the vehicle.

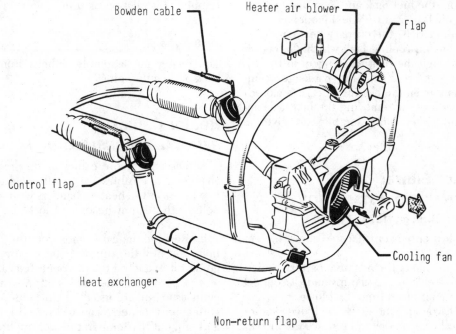

Bowden cable

Heater air blower

Flap

Control flap

Cooling fan

Heat exchanger

Non-return flap

Type 2 heater components

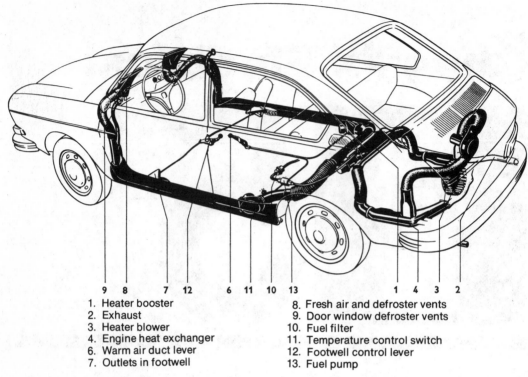

1. Heater booster
2. Exhaust
3. Heater blower
4. Engine heat exchanger
6. Warm air duct lever
7. Outlets in footwell
8. Fresh air and defroster vents
9. Door window defroster vents
10. Fuel filter
11. Temperature control switch
12. Footwell control lever
13. Fuel pump

Type 4 heater components

The auxiliary gas heating system on the Type 4 switches on when the engine is not producing enough heat for the passenger compartment. The gas heater runs on gasoline from the fuel tank and is available as an option on Type 2 and Type 3 models.

On all models, the primary heat circulator is the engine cooling fan, which directs air flow through the heat exchangers in the exhaust system and into the passenger compartment when the heating ducts are closed.

Procedures for removing the heat exchangers and heater duct assemblies are given in Chapter 3.

Heater Blower

REMOVAL AND INSTALLATION

Type 2 Through 1979, Type 4

The heater blower is located above the engine.

1. Disconnect the negative battery cable.

2. Loosen the two clamps and disconnect the warm air hoses from the blower.

3. Disconnect and mark the blower motor electrical connections and remove the blower housing retaining screws or nuts.

4. Remove the blower housing.

5. To remove the blower motor and fan from the housing, remove the three screws in the blower end plate and remove the assembly. Installation is the reverse of removal.

1980 Type 2

The heater fan assembly unbolts from the back of the alternator.

Heater Cables

REMOVAL AND INSTALLATION

1. Disconnect the cables at the heat exchangers. The cables are usually held in the flap levers at the heat exchangers with sleeve bolts with 10 mm heads and locked with 9 mm head nuts.

2. Remove the cable ends from the sleeve bolts and pull the rubber boots off the cable guide tubes and off the disconnected cables.

3. Disconnect the cables at the heater controls. They are usually held by pins with cotter pin retainers. You will have to unbolt and pull out the temperature control lever to unfasten the cables on Types 1, 3, and 4. On

the Type 2, disconnect the cables from the temperature control lever on the dash.

4. Remove the cables by pulling them out from the heater control side.

5. Feed new cables into the guide tubes at the heater controls after you have sprayed them completely with silicone to prevent rust and wear.

WINDSHIELD WIPERS

Blade and Arm

REMOVAL AND INSTALLATION

To remove the wiper blade, turn the blade at an angle to the arm, then move the blade down so its spring clip moves off the hook in the arm and remove the blade. Reverse to install.

To remove the arm, on models before 1973, remove the cap nut where the arm attaches to the windshield wiper drive shaft and lift off the arm. On 1973 and later models, the retaining nut is covered by a plastic cap. Remove the cap, remove the nut and remove the arm. When installing wiper arms, make sure they park at the bottom of the swept area and that they cover the entire swept area when in operation.

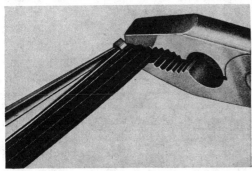

To remove rubber insert, squeese tabs at open end of blade and remove insert

Motor

REMOVAL AND INSTALLATION

Type 1

1. Disconnect the battery ground cable.
2. Remove the wiper arms.
3. Remove the wiper bearing nuts as well as the washers. Take off the outer bearing seals.
4. On Super Beetle and convertible 1973–80, remove the screws holding the cover of the fresh air box in the luggage com-

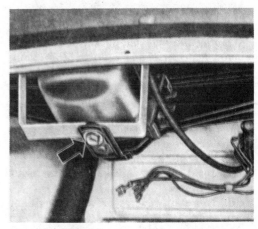

Type 1 wiper motor and frame removal

partment, remove the cover and remove the plastic rain cover, if necessary. On all other models, remove the back of the instrument panel from the luggage compartment.

5. On all except 1973–80 Super Beetle and Convertible, remove the fresh air box/rain drain by removing the three screws at the top and the nut at the bottom; next remove the glove box and the right side air vent.

6. Disconnect the wiper motor wiring harness and remove the screw which secures the wiper frame to the body.

7. Remove the frame and motor with the linkage.

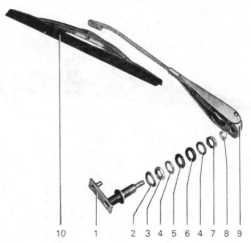

1. Wiper shaft with crank
2. Spring washer
3. Brass nut
4. Washer
5. Inner bearing seal
6. Outer bearing seal
7. Nut
8. Wiper shaft seal
9. Bracket and arm
10. Windshield wiper blade

Type 1 wiper motor linkage

NOTE: *The ball joints at the ends of the linkage may be slipped apart by gently popping the ball and socket apart with a screwdriver. Always lubricate the joints upon reassembly.*

8. Remove the lock and spring washers from the motor drive shaft and remove the connecting rod. Matchmark the motor and frame to ensure proper realignment when the motor is reinstalled.

9. Remove the nut located at the base of the motor driveshaft, and remove the motor from the frame.

10. To install, reverse the above steps and heed the following reminders.

11. The pressed lug on the wiper frame must engage the groove in the wiper bearing. Make sure that the wiper spindles are perpendicular to the plane of the windshield.

12. Check the linkage bushings for wear.

13. The hollow side of the links must face toward the frame with the angled end of the driving link toward the right bearing.

14. The inner bearing seal should be placed so that the shoulder of the rubber molding faces the wiper arm.

Type 2

1. Disconnect the ground wire from the battery.

2. Remove both wiper arms.

3. Remove the bearing cover and nut.

Type 2 wiper motor location

4. Remove the heater branch connections under the instrument panel.

5. Disconnect the wiper motor wiring.

6. Remove the wiper motor securing screw and remove the motor.

7. Reverse the above steps to install.

Type 3

1. Disconnect the negative battery cable.

2. Remove the ashtray and glove compartment.

3. Remove the fresh air controls.

4. Remove the cover for the heater and water drainage hoses.

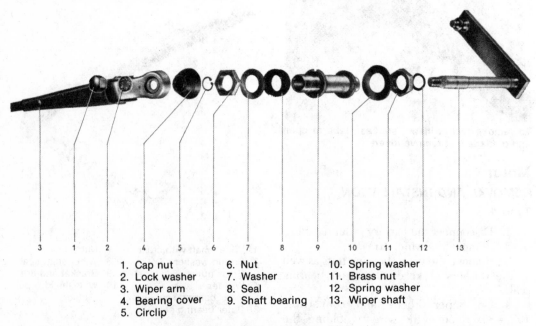

1. Cap nut
2. Lock washer
3. Wiper arm
4. Bearing cover
5. Circlip
6. Nut
7. Washer
8. Seal
9. Shaft bearing
10. Spring washer
11. Brass nut
12. Spring washer
13. Wiper shaft

Type 2 and Type 4 wiper motor linkage

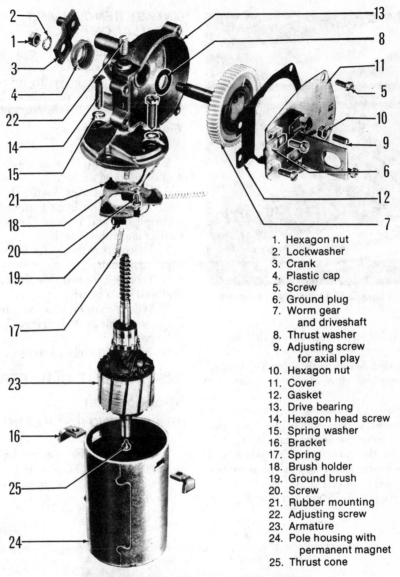

1. Hexagon nut
2. Lockwasher
3. Crank
4. Plastic cap
5. Screw
6. Ground plug
7. Worm gear
   and driveshaft
8. Thrust washer
9. Adjusting screw
   for axial play
10. Hexagon nut
11. Cover
12. Gasket
13. Drive bearing
14. Hexagon head screw
15. Spring washer
16. Bracket
17. Spring
18. Brush holder
19. Ground brush
20. Screw
21. Rubber mounting
22. Adjusting screw
23. Armature
24. Pole housing with
    permanent magnet
25. Thrust cone

Wiper motor disassembled—Types 1 and 3

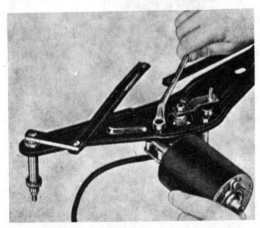

Removing Type 3 wiper motor from bracket

5. Disconnect the motor wiring.

6. Remove the wiper arms.

7. Remove the bearing covers and nuts, washers, and outer bearing seals.

8. Remove the wiper motor securing screws and remove the motor.

9. Reverse the above steps to install.

Type 4

1. Disconnect the negative battery cable.

2. Remove the wiper arms.

3. Remove the bearing cover and remove the nut under it.

4. Remove the steering column cover and the hoses running between the fresh air control box and the vents.

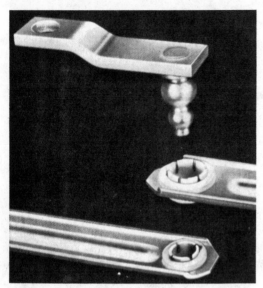

Typical wiper linkage ball joint—Type 4 shown

5. Remove the clock but do not disconnect the wiring.

6. Remove the left fresh air and defroster vent. Disconnect the air hose from the vent.

7. Disconnect the wiring for the motor at the windshield wiper switch. Remove the ground wire from the motor gear cover.

8. Remove the motor securing screw and remove the motor frame and motor assembly downward and to the right.

9. Reverse the above steps to install.

LINKAGE REMOVAL AND INSTALLATION

The windshield wiper linkage is secured at the ends by a ball and socket type joint. The ball and joint may be gently pried apart with the aid of a screwdriver. Always lubricate the joints with grease before assembly.

Wiper Arm Shaft

1. Remove the wiper arm.

2. Remove the bearing cover or the shaft seal depending on type.

3. On Type 4, remove the shaft circlip.

4. Remove the large wiper shaft bearing securing nut and remove the accompanying washer and rubber seal.

5. Disconnect the wiper linkage from the wiper arm shaft.

6. Working from inside the car, slide the shaft out of its bearing.

NOTE: *It may be necessary to lightly tap the shaft out of its bearing. Use a soft face hammer.*

7. Reverse the above steps to install.

INSTRUMENT CLUSTER

Speedometer

REMOVAL AND INSTALLATION
All Except Type 2

1. Disconnect the negative battery cable.

NOTE: *On the Type 3, it is necessary to remove the fuse panel to gain access to the speedometer.*

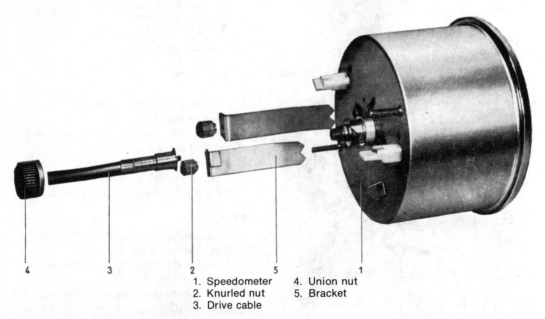

1. Speedometer
2. Knurled nut
3. Drive cable
4. Union nut
5. Bracket

Speedometer and brackets—Type 1 Beetle

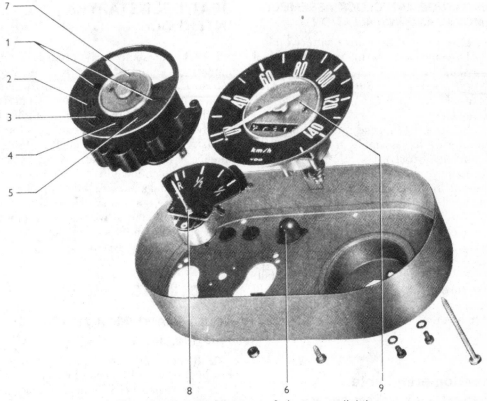

1. Turn signal warning lights
2. Generator warning light
3. High beam warning light
4. Parking light warning light
5. Oil pressure warning light
6. Instrument lighting
7. Warning light holder
8. Fuel gauge
9. Speedometer

Instrument cluster—1970–72 Type 2

2. Disconnect the speedometer light bulb wires.

3. Unscrew the knurled nut which secures the speedometer cable to the back of the speedometer. Pull the cable from the back of the speedometer.

4. Using a 4 mm allen wrench, remove the two knurled nuts which secure the speedometer brackets. Remove the brackets.

5. Remove the speedometer from the dashboard by sliding it out toward the steering wheel.

6. Reverse the above steps to install. Before fully tightening the nuts for the speedometer brackets, make sure the speedometer is correctly positioned in the dash.

Type 2 through 1979

1. Disconnect the negative battery cable.

2. Remove the fresh air control lever knobs.

3. Remove the Phillips head screws at the four corners of the instrument pane, being careful not to lose the spring clips on 1973 and later models.

4. Disconnect the speedometer cable.

5. Lift the instrument panel out of the dash far enough to disconnect the wiring, then remove the instrument panel. Remove the two long screws, separate the panel halves, then remove the screws and remove the speedometer. Installation is the reverse of removal.

Type 2 1980–81

1. Remove the upper dashboard cover. The cover simply pulls off. Disconnect the negative battery cable.

2. Remove retaining screws and disconnect all switches from the instrument panel. Squeeze the tabs on the switches to remove.

3. Disconnect the speedometer cable, all electrical connections, then remove the instrument panel. The speedometer can now be removed from the panel.

Installation is the reverse of removal.

FUEL GAUGE AND CLOCK ASSEMBLY REMOVAL AND INSTALLATION

1. Disconnect the negative battery cable.

2. Disconnect the wiring from the back of the assembly.

NOTE: *On the Type 3 it is necessary to remove the fuse panel to gain access to this assembly.*

3. Remove the knurled nuts and brackets which secure the assembly in the dash. Use a 4 mm allen wrench.

4. Remove the assembly by gently sliding it toward the steering wheel and out of the dash.

5. The fuel gauge is secured into the base of the clock by two screws. Remove the screws and slip the fuel gauge out of the clock.

6. Reverse the above steps to install. Make sure the clock and fuel gauge assembly is properly centered in the dash before fully tightening the nuts.

Speedometer Cable

REMOVAL AND INSTALLATION

1. Unscrew the cable from the back of the speedometer.

2. At the left front wheel, pry off the circlip retaining the square end of the speedometer shaft to the wheel bearing dust cap.

3. Pull the cable out of the back of the steering knuckle from under the car. With the circlip removed, the cable should pull right out. Pull the cable out of its holding grommets and remove.

Installation is the reverse of removal.

Ignition Switch

Ignition switch removal and installation is covered in Chapter 7.

SEAT BELT/STARTER INTERLOCK

All 1974 and some early production 1975 models are equipped with a seat belt/starter interlock system to prevent the driver and front seat passenger (if applicable) from starting the engine without first buckling his/her seat belts. The proper sequence is; sit in the seat(s), buckle up, start the engine. If this sequence is not followed, a warning system is activated which includes a "fasten belts" visual display and a buzzer. If the engine should stall with the ignition switch turned on, the car may be restarted within three minutes. Late production 1975 models are not equipped with this system.

HEADLIGHTS

REMOVAL AND INSTALLATION

Type 1, 2, and 3

1. Remove the screw which secures the headlight ring and remove the ring.

2. The sealed beam is held in place by a ring secured by three screws. Remove the screws and the ring. Do not confuse the headlight aiming screws with the screws for the ring. There are only two screws used for aiming.

3. Pull the wiring off the back of the sealed beam and remove the beam.

4. Reverse the above steps to install.

Type 4

This is the same procedure as above except that the headlight ring is secured by two screws.

FUSES

All major circuits are protected from overloading or short circuiting by fuses. A 12 po-

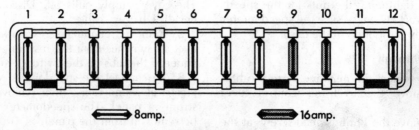

➡ 8amp.   ➡ 16amp.

Typical fuse box layout

Fuses

Type 1

Circuit	Fuse
Left parking, side marker, and tail lights	8 amps
Right parking, side marker, and tail lights	8 amps
Left low beam	8 amps
Right low beam	8 amps
Left high beam	8 amps
Right high beam, high beam indicator	8 amps
License plate light	8 amps
Emergency flasher system	8 amps
Interior lights	16 amps
Windshield wiper, rear window defogger, fresh air fan	16 amps
Horn, stop lights, ATF warning light	8 amps
Fuel gauge, turn signals, brake warning light, oil pressure, turn signal and generator warning lights	8 amps

Type 2

Circuit	Fuse.
Left tail and side marker lights	8 amps
Right tail and marker lights, license light, parking lights	8 amps
Left low beam	8 amps
Right low beam	8 amps
Left high beam, high beam indicator	8 amps
Right high beam	8 amps
Accessories	8 amps
Emergency flasher, front interior light	8 amps ①
Rear interior light, buzzer alarm, auxiliary heater	16 amps
Windshield wipers, rear window defogger	16 amps
Turn signals, warning lamps for alternator, oil pressure, fuel gauge, kickdown, and back-up lights	8 amps
Horn, stop lights, brake warning light	8 amps

Type 3

Circuit	Fuse
Right tail light, license plate light, parking and side marker light, luggage compartment light	8 amps
Left tail light	8 amps
Left low beam	8 amps
Right low beam	8 amps
Left high beam, high beam indicator	8 amps
Right high beam	8 amps
Electric fuel pump	8 amps
Emergency flasher, interior light	8 amps
Buzzer	16 amps
Windshield wipers, fresh air fan, rear window defogger	16 amps
Stop lights, turn signals, horn, brake warning light, back-up lights	8 amps
Accessories	8 amps

Type 4

Circuit	Fuse
Parking lights, left tail and left rear side marker lights	8 amps
Right tail light, right rear side marker light, license plate light, selector lever console light	8 amps
Left low beam	8 amps
Right low beam	8 amps
Left high beam	8 amps
Right high beam, high beam indicator	8 amps
Fuel pump	
Interior light, emergency flasher, buzzer	
Cigarette lighter, heater	16 amps
Window wiper, fresh air fan, heater, rear window defogger	16 amps
Turn signals, back-up lights, warning lights for alternator, oil pressure, fuel gauge	8 amps
Horn, brake warning light, stop lights	8 amps

① 1980–81—16 amp

sition fusebox is located beneath the dashboard near the steering column, or located in the luggage compartment on some air conditioned models.

When a fuse blows, the cause should be investigated. Never install a fuse of a larger capacity than specified (see "Fuse Specifications"), and never use a foil or a bolt or nail in place of a fuse. However, always carry a few spares in case of emergency. There are 10 8 amp (white) fuses and two 16 amp (red) fuses in the VW fusebox. Circuits number 9 and 10 use the 16 amp fuses. To replace a fuse, pry off the clear plastic cover for the fusebox and depress a contact at either end of the subject fuse.

WIRING DIAGRAMS

Wiring diagrams have been left out of this book. As cars have become more complex, and available with longer and longer option lists, wiring diagrams have grown in size and complexity also. It has become virtually impossible to provide a readable reproduction in a reasonable number of pages.

Clutch and Transaxle

6

TRANSAXLE

All of the Volkswagens covered in this manual are equipped with transaxles so named because the transmission gears and the axle gears are contained in the same housing. On manual and automatic stickshift VWs, the transmission part of assembly shares the same hypoid gear oil as the rear axle part. Automatic transaxles use ATF Dexron® in the transmission part, and hypoid gear oil in the rear axle.

All transaxles are mounted in a yoke at the rear of the car and bolt up to the front of the engine.

The transaxle case is constructed of aluminum alloy.

MANUAL TRANSAXLE

All manual transaxles employ four forward speeds and a reverse. All forward speeds have synchromesh engagement. The gears are helical and in constant mesh. Gear selection is accomplished by a floor-mounted lever working through a shift rod contained in the frame tunnel. The final drive pinion and ring gear are also helical cut.

MANUAL TRANSAXLE REMOVAL AND INSTALLATION

1. Disconnect the negative battery cable.
2. Remove the engine.
3. Remove the socket head screws which secure the drive shifts to the transmission. Remove the bolts from the transmission end first and then remove the shafts.

NOTE: *It is not necessary to remove the drive shafts entirely from the car if the car does not have to be moved while the transaxle is out.*

Socket-head screws retaining driveshafts

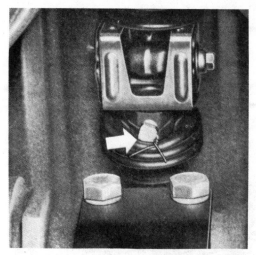

Shift linkage setscrew—Type 2 has one at front also

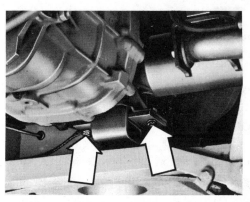

Front transaxle mounting bolts

4. Disconnect the clutch cable from the clutch lever and remove the clutch cable and its guide tube from the transaxle. Loosen the square head bolt at the shift linkage coupling located near the rear of the transaxle. Slide the coupling off the inner shift lever. There is an access plate under the rear seat to reach the coupling on Type 1 and 3. It is necessary to work under the car to reach the coupling on Type 2 models.

5. Disconnect the starter wiring.

6. Disconnect the back-up light switch wiring.

7. Remove the front transaxle mounting bolts.

8. Support the transaxle with a jack and remove the transmission carrier bolts.

NOTE: *1972 and later Type 2s have two upper carrier bolts which also join the engine to the transmission. The transmission must be supported when these bolts are re-*

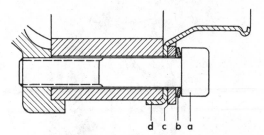

a. Socket head screws   c. Spacer
b. Lockwasher   d. Protective cap

Drive axle bolt and washer positioning

moved to prevent damage which could be caused by letting the unit hang.

9. Carefully lower the jack and remove the transaxle from the car.

10. To install, jack the transaxle into position and loosely install the bolts.

11. Tighten the transmission carrier bolts first, then tighten the front mounting nuts.

12. Install the drive shaft bolts with new lock washers. The lock washers should be positioned on the bolt with the convex side toward the screw head.

13. Reconnect the wiring, the clutch cable, and the shift linkage.

NOTE: *It may be necessary to align the transmission so that the drive shaft joints do not rub the frame.*

14. Install the engine.

AUTOMATIC STICK SHIFT TRANSAXLE

An automatic clutch control three speed transmission (transaxle) has been available on the Type 1. It is known as the Automatic Stick Shift.

It consists of a three speed gear box connected to the engine through a hydrodynamic torque converter. Between the converter and gearbox is a vacuum-operated clutch, which automatically separates the power flow from the torque converter while in the process of changing gear ratios.

While the torque converter components are illustrated here, the picture is for familiarization purposes only. The unit cannot be serviced. It is a welded unit, and must be replaced as a complete assembly.

The power flow passes from the engine via converter, clutch and gearbox to the final drive, which, as with the conventional gearbox, is located in the center of the transmission housing.

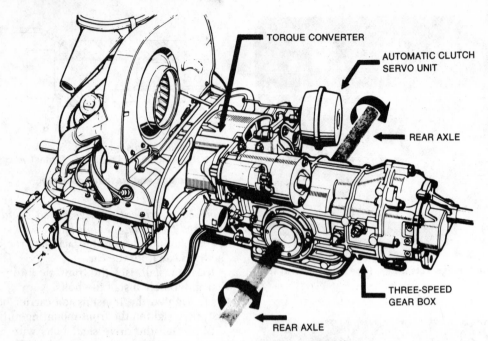

TORQUE CONVERTER

AUTOMATIC CLUTCH
SERVO UNIT

REAR AXLE

THREE-SPEED
GEAR BOX

REAR AXLE

Basic components of automatic stick shift

The converter functions as a conventional clutch for starting and stopping. The shift clutch serves only for engaging and changing the speed ranges. Frictionwise, it is very lightly loaded.

There is an independent oil supply for the converter provided by an engine driven pump and a reservoir. The converter oil pump, driven off the engine oil pump, draws fluid from the reservoir and drives it around a circuit leading through the converter and back to the reservoir.

This circuit also furnishes cooling for the converter fluid.

OPERATION

The control valve is activated by a very light touch to the top of the shift selector knob which, in turn, is connected to an electromagnet. It has two functions.

At the beginning of the selection process, it has to conduct the vacuum promptly from the intake manifold to the clutch servo, so

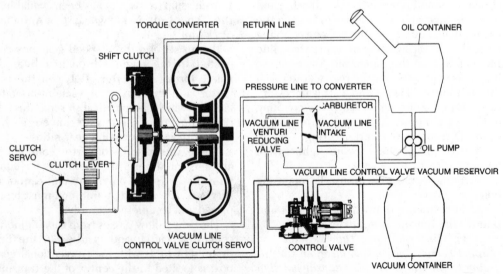

TORQUE CONVERTER   RETURN LINE   OIL CONTAINER

SHIFT CLUTCH

PRESSURE LINE TO CONVERTER

CARBURETOR

VACUUM LINE
VENTURI
REDUCING
VALVE

VACUUM LINE
INTAKE

OIL PUMP

CLUTCH
SERVO

CLUTCH LEVER

VACUUM LINE CONTROL VALVE VACUUM RESERVOIR

VACUUM LINE
CONTROL VALVE CLUTCH SERVO

CONTROL VALVE

VACUUM CONTAINER

Automatic stick shift vacuum circuits

that the shift clutch disengages at once, and thus interrupts the power flow between converter and transmission. At the end of the selection process, it must, according to driving conditions, automatically ensure that the shift clutch engages at the proper speed. It may neither slip nor engage too harshly. The control valve can be adjusted for this purpose.

As soon as the selector lever is moved to the engaged position, the two contacts in the lever close the circuit. The electromagnet is then under voltage and operates the main valve. By this means the clutch servo is connected to the engine intake manifold, and at the same time the connection to the atmosphere is closed. In the vacuum space of the servo system, a vacuum is built up, the diaphragm of the clutch servo is moved by the difference with atmospheric pressure and the shift clutch is disengaged via its linkage. The power flow to the gearbox is interrupted and the required speed range can be engaged. The process of declutching, from movement of the selector lever up to full separation of the clutch, lasts about 1/10 sec. The automatic can, therefore, declutch faster than would be possible by means of a foot-operated clutch pedal.

When the selector lever is released after changing the speed range, the switch interrupts the current flow to the electro-magnet, which then returns to its rest position and closes the main valve. The vacuum is reduced by the reducing valve and the shift clutch re-engages.

Clutch engagement takes place, quickly or slowly, according to engine loading. The clutch will engage suddenly, for example, at full throttle, and can transform the full drive moment into acceleration of the car. Or, this can be effected slowly and gently if the braking force of the engine is to be used on overrun. In the part-load range, too, the duration of clutch re-engagement depends on the throttle opening, and thus the depression in the carburetor venturi.

Vanes on the outside of the converter housing aid in cooling. In the case of abnormal prolonged loading, however (lugging a trailer over mountain roads in second or third speed), converter heat may exceed maximum permissible temperature. This condition will cause a red warning light to function in the speedometer.

There is also a starter locking switch. This, combined with a bridging switch, is operated by the inner transmission shift lever. It performs two functions:

1. With a speed range engaged, the electrical connection to the starter is interrupted. The engine, therefore, can only be started in neutral.
2. The contacts in the selector lever are not closed in the neutral position. Instead, the bridging switch transmits a voltage to the electromagnets of the control valve. This ensures that the spearator clutch is also disengaged in the neutral shifter position.

AUTOMATIC STICK SHIFT TRANSAXLE REMOVAL AND INSTALLATION

1. Disconnect the negative battery cable.
2. Remove the engine.
3. Make a bracket to hold the torque converter in place. If a bracket is not used, the converter will slide off the transmission input shaft.
4. Detach the gearshift rod coupling.
5. Disconnect the drive shafts at the transmission end. If the driveshafts are not going to be repaired, it is not necessary to detach the wheel end.
6. Disconnect the drive ATF hoses from the transmission. Seal the open ends. Disconnect the temperature switch, neutral safety switch, and the back-up light switch.
7. Pull off the vacuum servo hose.
8. Disconnect the starter wiring.
9. Remove the front transaxle mounting nuts.
10. Loosen the rear transaxle mounting bolts. Support the transaxle and remove the bolts.
11. Lower the axle and remove it from the car.
12. With the torque converter bracket still in place, raise the axle into the car.
13. Tighten the nuts for the front transmission mounting. Insert the rear mounting bolts but do not tighten them at this time.
14. Replace the vacuum servo hose.
15. Connect the ATF hoses, using new washers. The washers are seals.
16. Connect the temperature switch and starter cables.
17. Install the driveshafts, using new washers. Turn the convex sides of the washers toward the screw head.
18. Align the transaxle so that the inner drive shaft joints do not rub on the frame fork and then tighten the rear mounting bolts.
19. Insert the shift rod coupling, tighten the screw, and secure it with wire.

20. Remove the torque converter bracket, and install the engine.

21. After installing the engine, bleed the ATF lines if return flow has not started after 2–3 minutes.

Drive Shaft and Constant Velocity Joint

REMOVAL AND INSTALLATION

1. Remove the bolts which secure the joints at each end of the shaft, tilt the shaft down, and remove the shaft.

2. Loosen the clamps which secure the rubber boot to the axle and slide the boot back on the axle.

3. Drive the stamped steel cover off of the joint with a drift.

NOTE: *After the cover is removed, do not tilt the ball hub as the balls will fall out of the hub.*

4. Remove the circlip from the end of the axle and press the axle out of the joint.

5. Reverse the above steps to install. The position of the dished washer is dependent on the type of transmission. On automatic transmissions, it is placed between the ball hub and the circlip. On manual transmissions, it is placed between the ball hub and the shoulder on the shaft. Be sure to pack the joint with grease.

NOTE: *The chamfer on the splined inside diameter of the ball hub faces the shoulder on the driveshaft.*

CONSTANT VELOCITY JOINT OVERHAUL

The constant velocity joint (CV joint) must be disassembled to remove and replace old grease and to inspect. The individual pieces of the CV joint are machined matched; in the event that some part of the joint is bad, the entire joint (not including the axle shaft) must be replaced.

1. Remove the CV joint from the axle shaft as described above.

2. Pivot the ball hub and ball cage out of the joint until they are at a ninety degree angle to the case, and pull the ball hub and cage out as an assembly.

3. Press the balls out of the cage.

4. Align the two grooves and take the ball hub out of the cage.

5. Check the outer race, ball hub, ball cage and balls for wear and pitting. Check the ball cage for hairline cracks. Signs of

Turn ball hub and cage 90° from case to remove

Align the two grooves and take ball hub out of cage

polishing indicating the tracks of the ball bearings is no reason for replacement.

To assemble:

6. Fit the ball hub into the cage. It doesn't matter which way the hub is installed. Press in the ball bearings.

7. Fit the hub assembly into the outer race at a ninety degree angle to the outer race. When inserting, make sure that a wide separation between ball grooves on the outer race ("a" in the illustration) and a narrow separation between ball grooves on the hub ("b" in the illustration) are together when the hub and cage assembly is swung into the outer race (direction of arrow in illustration).

8. When pivoting the ball hub and cage assembly into the outer race, the hub should be pivoted out of the cage so that the balls

Installing ball hub and cage—swing in direction of arrow. See text.

Hub pivoted out of cage so balls will fit in grooves

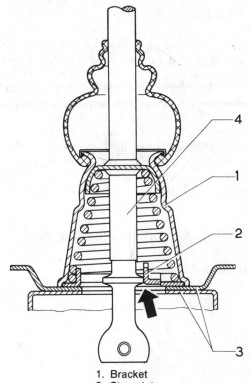

1. Bracket
2. Stop plate
3. Floor plate
4. Gear lever

Manual shifter—arrow points to stop plate

spread apart enough to fit into the ball grooves.

9. Press the cage firmly down until the hub swings fully into position.

10. Pack the unit completely with axle grease. The joint is properly assembled when the ball hub can be moved over the full range of axial movement by hand.

SHIFT LINKAGE ADJUSTMENT

The Volkswagen shift linkage is not adjustable. When shifting becomes difficult or there is an excessive amount of play in the linkage, check the shifting mechanism for worn parts. Make sure the shift linkage coupling is tightly connected to the inner shift lever located at the rear of the transaxle under a plate below the rear seat on Types 1, 3, 4. On Type 2, Check the set screw where the front shift rod connects to the center section below the passenger compartment, and the rear setscrew where the linkage goes into the transaxle. Worn parts may be found in the shift lever mechanism and the supports for the linkage rod sometimes wear out.

The gear shift lever can be removed after the front floor mat has been lifted. After the two retaining screws have been removed from the gear shift lever ball housing, the gear shift lever, ball housing, rubber boot, and spring are removed as a unit.

CAUTION: *Carefully mark the position of the stop plate and note the position of the turned up ramp at the side of the stop plate. Normally the ramp is turned up and on the right hand side of the hole.*

Installation is the reverse of removal. Lubricate all moving parts with grease. Test the gear shift pattern. If there is difficulty in shifting, adjust the stop plate back and forth in its slotted holes.

CLUTCH

The clutch used in all models is a single dry disc mounted on the flywheel with a diaphragm spring type pressure plate. The release bearing is the ball bearing type and does not require lubrication. On Types 1, 2 (except Vanagon), and 3, the clutch is engaged mechanically via a cable which attaches to the clutch pedal. On the Type 4 and the Vanagon, the clutch is engaged hydraulically, using a clutch pedal operated master cylinder and a bell housing mounted slave cylinder.

CLUTCH ASSEMBLY REMOVAL AND INSTALLATION

Manual Transmission

1. Remove the engine.
2. Remove the pressure plate securing bolts one turn at a time until all spring pressure is released.
3. Remove the bolts and remove the clutch assembly.

NOTE: *Notice which side of the clutch disc faces the flywheel and install the new disc in the same direction.*

4. Before installing the new clutch, check the condition of the flywheel. It should not have excessive heat cracks and the friction surface should not be scored or warped. Check the condition of the throw out bearing. If the bearing is worn, replace it.
5. Lubricate the pilot bearing in the end of the crankshaft with grease.
6. Insert a pilot shaft, used for centering the clutch disc, through the clutch disc and place the disc against the flywheel. The pilot shaft will hold the disc in place.
7. Place the pressure plate over the disc and loosely install the bolts.

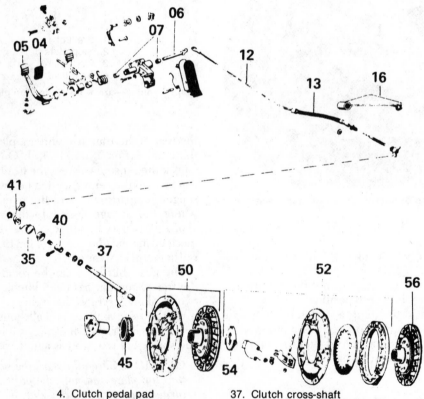

4. Clutch pedal pad
5. Clutch pedal
6. Clutch pedal shaft
7. Bushings for pedal cluster
12. Clutch cable
13. Clutch cable sleeve
16. Angle plate for clutch cable
35. Clutch return spring
37. Clutch cross-shaft
40. Bushing—operating shaft
41. Clutch operating lever
45. Clutch release bearing
50. Clutch
52. Pressure plate
54. Clutch release plate
56. Clutch disc

Exploded view of manual transaxle clutch system components—Types 1, 2 and 3

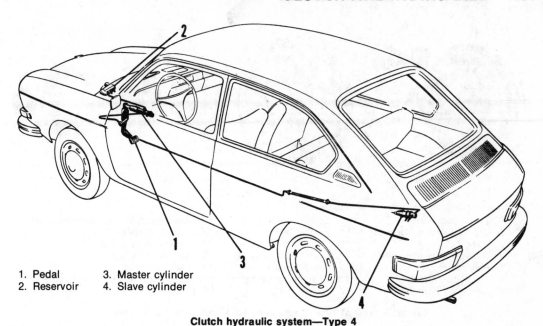

1. Pedal
2. Reservoir
3. Master cylinder
4. Slave cylinder

Clutch hydraulic system—Type 4

NOTE: *Make sure the correct side of the clutch disc is facing outward. The disc will rub the flywheel if it is incorrectly positioned.*

8. After making sure that the pressure plate aligning dowels will fit into the pressure plate, gradually tighten the bolts.

9. Remove the pilot shaft and reinstall the engine.

10. Adjust the clutch pedal free-play.

Automatic Stick Shift

1. Disconnect the negative battery cable.
2. Remove the engine.

3. Remove the transaxle.

4. Remove the torque converter by sliding it off of the input shaft. Seal off the hub opening.

5. Mount the transaxle in a repair stand or on a suitable bench.

6. Loosen the clamp screw and pull off the clutch operating lever. Remove the transmission cover.

7. Remove the hex nuts between the clutch housing and the transmission case.

NOTE: *Two nuts are located inside the differential housing.*

8. The oil need not be drained if the

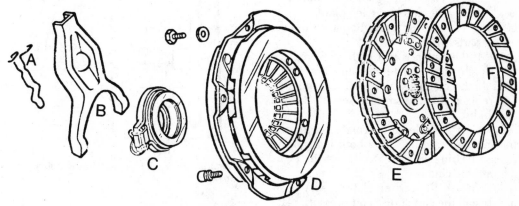

A. Retaining spring
B. Clutch operating lever
C. Release bearing
D. Pressure plate
E. Clutch plate
F. Clutch plate lining

Type 4 clutch and pressure plate assembly. Clutch face (F) is normally attached to clutch plate (E)

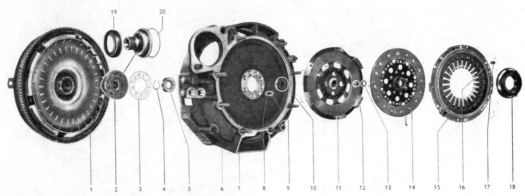

1. Torque converter
2. One-way clutch support
3. Gasket
4. Circlip for carrier plate
5. Ball bearing
6. O-ring for stud
7. Converter housing
8. Spring washer
9. Socket head screw
10. Seal
11. Clutch carrier plate
12. Needle bearing
13. Seal/carrier plate
14. Clutch plate
15. Diaphragm clutch pressure plate
16. Spring washer
17. Socket head screw
18. Release bearing
19. Seal/converter
20. O-ring/one-way clutch support

Exploded view of Type 1 automatic stick shift clutch assembly

clutch is removed with the cover opening up and the gearshift housing breather blocked.

9. Pull the transmission from the clutch housing studs.

10. Turn the clutch lever shaft to disengage the release bearing.

11. Remove both lower engine mounting bolts.

12. Loosen the clutch retaining bolts gradually and alternately to prevent distortion. Remove the bolts, pressure plate, clutch plate, and release bearing.

13. Do not wash the release bearing. Wipe it dry only.

14. Check the clutch plate, pressure plate, and release bearing for wear and damage. Check the clutch carrier plate, needle bearing, and seat for wear. Replace the necessary parts.

15. If the clutch is wet with ATF, replace the clutch carrier plate seal and the clutch disc. If the clutch is wet with transmission oil, replace the transmission case seal and clutch disc.

16. Coat the release bearing guide on the transmission case neck and both lugs on the release bearing with grease. Insert the bearing into the clutch.

17. Grease the carrier plate needle bearing. Install the clutch disc and pressure plate using a pilot shaft to center the disc on the flywheel.

18. Tighten the pressure plate retaining bolts evenly and alternately. Make sure that

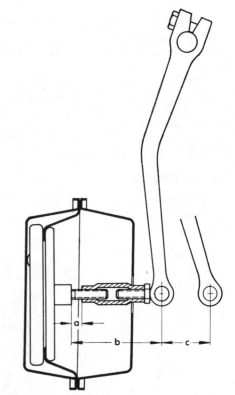

Automatic stick shift clutch basic adjusting dimensions

the release bearing is correctly located in the diaphragm spring.

19. Insert the lower engine mounting bolts from the front. Replace the sealing

rings if necessary. Some units have aluminum sealing rings and cap nuts.

20. Push the transmission onto the converter housing studs. Insert the clutch lever shaft behind the release bearing lugs. Push the release bearing onto the transmission case neck. Tighten the bolts which hold the clutch housing to the transmission case.

21. Install the clutch operating lever.

22. It is necessary to adjust the basic clutch setting. The clutch operating lever should contact the clutch housing. Tighten the lever clamp screw slightly.

23. First adjust dimension (a) to 0.335 in. Adjust dimension (b) to 3.03 in. Finally adjust dimension (c) to 1.6 in. by repositioning the clutch lever on the clutch shaft. Tighten the lever clamp screw.

24. Push the torque converter onto the support tube. Insert it into the turbine shaft by turning the converter.

25. Check the clutch play after installing the transaxle and engine.

CLUTCH CABLE ADJUSTMENT

Manual Transmission—Types 1, 2, 3

1. Check the clutch pedal travel by measuring the distance the pedal travels toward the floor until pressure is exerted against the clutch. The distance is ⅜ to ¾ in.

2. To adjust the clutch, jack up the rear of the car and support it on jackstands.

3. Remove the left rear wheel.

4. Adjust the cable tension by turning the wing nut on the end of the clutch cable. Turning the wing nut counterclockwise decreases pedal free-play, turning it clockwise increases free-play.

5. When the adjustment is completed, the wings of the wing nut must be horizontal so that the lugs on the nut engage the recesses in the clutch lever.

6. Push on the clutch pedal several times and check the pedal free-play.

7. Install the wheel and lower the car.

Automatic Stick Shift—Type 1

The adjustment is made on the linkage between the clutch arm and the vacuum servo unit. To check the clutch play:

1. Disconnect the servo vacuum hose.

2. Measure the clearance between the upper edge of the servo unit mounting bracket and the lower edge of the adjusting turnbuckle. If the clearance (e) is 0.16 in. or more, the clutch needs adjustment.

Clutch pedal free-play (travel) is distance "a"

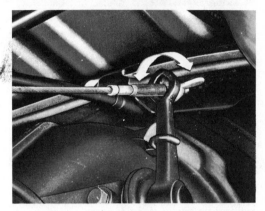

Wing nut for manual transaxle clutch cable adjustment

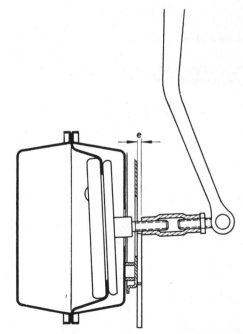

Checking clutch adjustment—Automatic Stick Shift

Adjusting automatic stick shift clutch—distance "d" is 0.25 in., measured between the locknut and the turnbuckle

Speed of engagement adjusting screw (arrow)

3. Reconnect the vacuum hose.

To adjust the clutch:

1. Disconnect the servo vacuum hose.

2. Loosen the turnbuckle locknut and back it off completely to the lever arm. Then turn the servo turnbuckle against the locknut. Now back off the turnbuckle 5–5½ turns. The distance between the locknut and the turnbuckle should be 0.25 in.

3. Tighten the locknut against the adjusting sleeve.

4. Reconnect the vacuum hose and road test the vehicle. The clutch is properly adjusted when Reverse gear can be engaged silently and the clutch does not slip on acceleration. If the clutch arm contacts the clutch housing, there is no more adjustment possi- ble and the clutch plate must be replaced.

The speed of engagement of the Automatic Stick Shift clutch is regulated by the vacuum operated valve rather than by the driver's foot. The adjusting screw is on top of the valve under a small protective cap. Adjust the valve as follows:

1. Remove the cap.

2. To slow the engagement, turn the adjusting screw ¼–½ turn clockwise. To speed engagement, turn the screw counterclockwise.

3. Replace the cap.

4. Test operation by shifting from Second to First at 44 mph without depressing the accelerator. The shift should take exactly one second to occur.

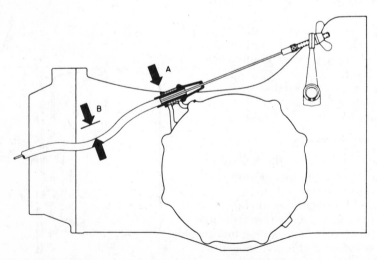

For smooth clutch action on Type 1 models, dimension "B" should be 1.0–1.7 in. Adjust cable to provide slight sag at point "B" by installing washers at point "A"

CLUTCH CABLE REPLACEMENT

Types 1, 2, and 3

1. Jack up the car and remove the left rear wheel.

2. Disconnect the cable from the clutch operating lever.

3. Remove the rubber boot from the end of the guide tube and off the end of the cable.

4. On Type 1, unbolt the pedal cluster and remove it from the car. It will also be necessary to disconnect the brake master cylinder push rod and throttle cable from the pedal cluster. On Type 2, remove the cover under the pedal cluster, then remove the pin from the clevis on the end of the clutch cable. On Type 3, remove the frame head cover and remove the pin from the clevis on the end of the clutch cable.

5. Pull the cable out of its guide tube from the pedal cluster end.

6. Installation is the reverse of the above. NOTE: *Grease the cable before installing it and readjust the clutch pedal free-play.*

Clutch Master Cylinder

REMOVAL AND INSTALLATION

Type 4

1. Siphon the hydraulic fluid from the master cylinder (clutch) reservoir.

2. Pull back the carpeting from the pedal area and lay down some absorbent rags.

3. Pull the elbow connection from the top of the master cylinder.

4. Disconnect and plug the pressure line from the rear of the master cylinder.

5. Remove the master cylinder mounting bolts and remove the cylinder to the rear.

6. Reverse the above procedure to install, taking care to bleed the system and adjust pedal free-play.

Type 2 (Vanagon)

1. Remove the lower front bulkhead paneling.

2. Remove the cover over the brake master cylinder by grasping the top cover to the instrument cover at the two notches at the front and pulling it off.

3. Disconnect and plug the reservoir hose and the clutch line from the master cylinder.

4. Disconnect the clevis pin on the master cylinder push rod.

5. Remove the two bolts and remove the master cylinder.

6. Installation is the reverse of removal. When attaching the push rod, play between the push rod and the piston in the master cylinder must be 0.020 in. maximum. Adjust if necessary.

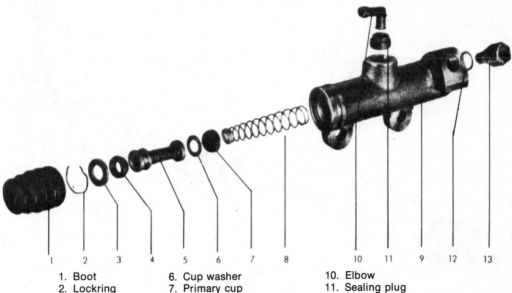

1. Boot
2. Lockring
3. Stop ring
4. Secondary cup
5. Piston
6. Cup washer
7. Primary cup
8. Spring and spring plate
9. Cylinder
10. Elbow
11. Sealing plug
12. Seal
13. Residual pressure valve

Exploded view of Type 4 master cylinder

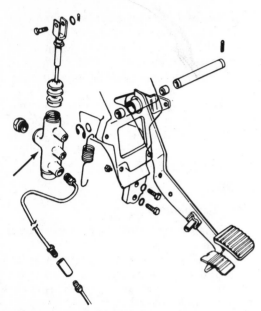

Vanagon clutch master cylinder

Clutch Slave Cylinder
REMOVAL AND INSTALLATION
Type 4

1. Locate the slave cylinder on the bell housing.

2. Disconnect and plug the pressure line from the slave cylinder.

3. Disconnect the return spring from the pushrod.

4. Remove the retaining circlip from the boot and remove the boot.

5. Remove the circlip and slide the slave cylinder rearwards from its mount.

6. Remove the spring clip from the mount.

7. Reverse the above procedure to install, taking care to bleed the system and adjust pedal free-play.

Type 2 (Vanagon)

The slave cylinder is mounted on a bracket on the left side of the transaxle.

1. Jack up the vehicle and support it on stands.

2. Disconnect the clutch line and plug it to prevent fluid leakage.

3. Remove the pushrod from the clutch lever socket ball.

4. Remove the two bolts and nuts and remove the slave cylinder.

Installation is the reverse of removal. The bleeder screw is located at the top of the cylinder.

1. Pushrod
2. Retaining ring
3. Boot
4. Retaining ring
5. Lockspring
6. Piston
7. Cup
8. Cylinder
9. Bleeder valve
10. Cap

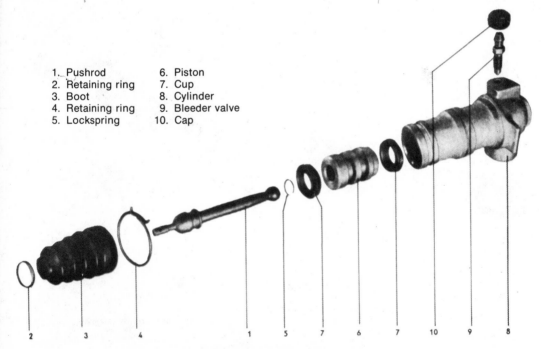

Exploded view of Type 4 slave cylinder

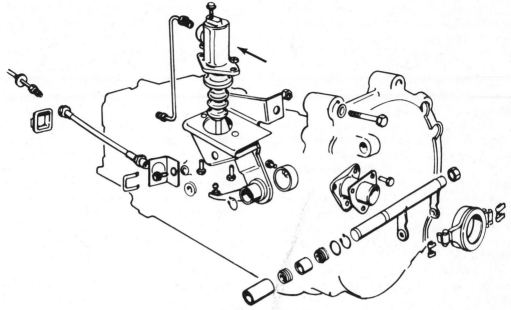

Vanagon clutch slave cylinder

CLUTCH SYSTEM BLEEDING AND ADJUSTMENT

Type 4, Vanagon

NOTE: *Perform steps 1–4 only for Vanagon.*

Whenever air enters the clutch hydraulic system due to leakage, or if any part of the system is removed for service, the system must be bled. The hydraulic system uses high quality brake fluid meeting SAE J1703 or DOT 3 or DOT 4 specifications. Brake fluid is highly corrosive to plant finishes and care should be exercised that no spillage occurs. The procedure is as follows;

1. Top up the clutch fluid reservoir and make sure the cap vent is open.

2. Locate the slave cylinder bleed nipple and remove all dirt and grease from the valve. Attach a hose to the nipple and submerge the other end of the hose in a jar containing a few inches of clean brake fluid.

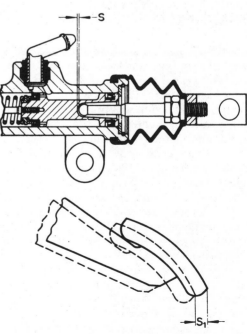

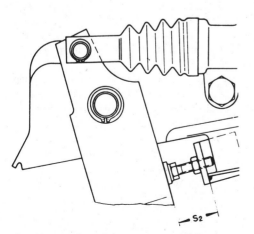

Adjusting clutch pedal stop screw—Type 4

Adjusting clutch pedal free-play—Type 4

3. Find a friend to operate the clutch pedal. When your friend depresses the clutch pedal slowly to the floor, open the bleeder valve about one turn. Have your friend keep the pedal on the floor until you close the bleeder valve. Repeat this operation several times until no air bubbles are emitted from the tube.

NOTE: *Keep a close check on the fluid level in the fluid reservoir. Never let the level fall below the ½ full mark.*

4. After bleeding, discard the old fluid and top up the reservoir.

5. The clutch pedal should have a free-play of 0.20–0.28 in., and a 7 in. total travel. If either of the above are not to specifications, adjust the master cylinder as follows. (Steps 6–9).

6. Loosen the master cylinder pushrod locknut and shorten the pushrod length slightly.

7. Loosen the master cylinder bolts and push the cylinder as far forward as it will go. Retighten the bolts.

8. Remove the rubber cap from the clutch pedal stop screw and adjust distance S2 to 0.89 in. Install the rubber cap.

9. Then lengthen the pushrod as necessary to obtain a pedal free-play of 0.20–0.28 in. Tighten the pushrod locknut.

10. Road-test the car.

FULLY AUTOMATIC TRANSAXLE

A fully automatic transmission (transaxle) is available on Type 3 models, available on all 1971–74 Type 4 models, and 1973 and later Type 2 models. 1976–81 Type 2s are equipped with a different transmission which is basically the same as the one used in the VW Rabbit, although the final drive section is the same as the one used on all other models in this book. Both units consist of an automatically shifted three speed planetary transmission and torque converter.

The torque converter is a conventional three-element design. The three elements are an impeller (driving member), a stator (reaction member), and the turbine (driven member). Maximum torque multiplication, with the vehicle starting from rest, is two and one-half to one. Maximum converter efficiency is about 96 percent.

The automatic transmission is a planetary unit with three forward speeds which engage automatically depending on engine loading and road speed. The converter, planetary unit, and control system are incorporated together with the final drive in a single housing. The final drive is located between the converter and the planetary gearbox.

The transmission control system includes a gear type oil pump, a centrifugal governor which regulates shift points, a throttle modulator valve which evaluates engine loading according to intake manifold pressure, and numerous other regulating components assembled in the transmission valve body.

Power flow passes through the torque converter to the turbine shaft, then to the clutch drum attached to the turbine shaft, through a clutch to a sungear. The output planet carrier then drives the rear axle shafts via the final drive.

Transmission ranges are Park, Reverse, Neutral, Drive (3), Second (2), and First (1).

AUTOMATIC TRANSMISSION REMOVAL AND INSTALLATION

NOTE: *The engine and transmission must be removed as an assembly on the Type 4 and Type 2/1700, 2/1800, 2/2000.*

1. Remove the battery ground cable.

2. On the sedan, remove the cooling air intake duct with the heating fan and hoses. Remove the cooling air intake connection and bellows, then detach the hoses to the air cleaner.

3. On the station wagons, remove the warm air hoses and air cleaner. Remove the boot between the dipstick tube and the body and the boot between the oil filler neck and the body. Disconnect the cooling air bellows at the body.

4. Disconnect the wires at the regulator and the alternator wires at the snap-connector located by the regulator. Disconnect the auxiliary air regulator and the oil pressure switch at the snap connectors located by the distributor.

5. Disconnect the fuel injection wiring on Type 3 and 4 models. There are 12 connections and they are listed as follows:

  a. Fuel injector cylinder 2, 2-pole, protective gray cap;

  b. Fuel injector cylinder 1, 2-pole, protective black cap;

  c. Starter, 1-pole, white;

  d. Throttle valve switch, 4-pole;

  e. Distributor, 3 pole;

  f. Thermo switch, 1-pole, white;

  g. Cold start valve, 3-pole;

h. Temperature sensor crankcase, 2-pole;

i. Ground connection, 3-pole, white wires;

j. Temperature sensor for the cylinder head, 1-pole;

k. Fuel injector cylinder 3, 2-pole, protective black cap;

l. Fuel injector cylinder 4, 2-pole, protective gray cap.

6. Disconnect the accelerator cable.

7. Disconnect the right fuel return line.

8. Raise the car.

9. Disconnect the warm hoses from the heat exchangers.

10. Disconnect the starter wires and push the engine wiring harness through the engine cover plate.

11. Disconnect the fuel supply line and plug it.

12. Remove the heater booster exhaust pipe.

13. Remove the rear axles and cover the ends to protect them from dirt.

14. Remove the selector cable by unscrewing the cable sleeve.

15. Remove the wire from the kickdown switch.

16. Remove the bolts from the rubber transmission mountings, taking careful note of the position, number, and thickness of the spacers that are present.

CAUTION: *These spacers must be reinstalled exactly as they were removed. Do not detach the transmission carrier from the body.*

17. Support the engine and transmission assembly in such a way that it may be lowered and moved rearward at the same time.

18. Remove the engine carrier bolts and the engine and transmission assembly from the car.

NOTE: *The top carrier bolts on the Type 2 are the top engine to transmission bolts. Be sure to support the engine/transmission assembly before completely removing the bolts.*

19. Matchmark the flywheel and the torque converter and remove the three attaching bolts.

20. Remove the engine-to-transmission bolts and separate the engine and transmission.

CAUTION: *Exercise care when separating the engine and transmission as the torque converter will easily slip off the input shaft if the transmission is tilted downward*

Type 2/1700, 2/1800, 2/2000 and Type 4 engine carrier bolts positioned at the tops of their elongated holes

21. Installation is as follows. Install and tighten the engine-to-transmission bolts after aligning the match marks on the flywheel and converter.

22. Making sure the match marks are aligned, install the converter-to-flywheel bolts.

23. Make sure the rubber buffer is in place and the two securing studs do not project more than 0.7 in. from the transmission case.

24. Tie a cord to the slot in the engine compartment seal. This will make positioning the seal easier.

25. Lift the assembly far enough to allow the accelerator cable to be pushed through the front engine cover.

26. Continue lifting the assembly into place. Slide the rubber buffer into the locating tube in the rear axle carrier.

27. Insert the engine carrier bolts and raise the engine until the bolts are at the top of their elongated slots. Tighten the bolts.

NOTE: *A set of three gauges must be obtained to check the alignment of the rubber buffer in its locating tube. The dimensions are given in the illustration as is the measuring technique. The rubber buffer is centered horizontally when the 11 mm gauge can be inserted on both sides. The buffer is located vertically when the 10 mm gauge can be inserted on the bottom side and the 12 mm gauge can be inserted on the top side. See Steps 28 and 29 for adjustment procedure.*

28. Install the rubber transmission mount bolts with spacers of the correct thickness.

a. 5.095 in.   c. 0.590 in.
b. 0.472 in.   d. 0.393, 0.433, and 0.472 in.

Buffer alignment gauges

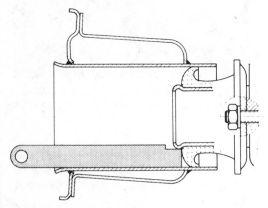

Measuring technique for centering the buffer

The purpose of the spacers is to center the rubber buffer vertically in its support tube. The buffer is not supposed to carry any weight; it absorbs torsional forces only.

29. To locate the buffer horizontally in its locating tube, the engine carrier must be vertical and parallel to the fan housing. It is adjusted by moving the engine carrier bolts in elongated slots. Further travel may be obtained by moving the brackets attached to the body. It may be necessary to adjust the two rear suspension wishbones with the center of the transmission after the rubber buffer is horizontally centered. Take the car to a dealer or alignment specialist to align the rear suspension.

30. Adjust the selector level cable.

31. Connect the wire to the kickdown switch.

32. Install the rear axles. Make sure the lockwashers are placed with the convex side out.

33. Reconnect the fuel hoses and heat exchanger hoses. Install the pipe for the heater booster.

34. Lower the car and pull the engine compartment seal into place with the cord.

35. Reconnect the fuel injection and engine wiring. Push the starter wires through the engine cover plate and connect the wires to the starter.

Checking position of engine carrier

36. Install the intake duct with the fan and hoses, also the cooling air intake.

PAN REMOVAL AND INSTALLATION

1. Some models have a drain plug in the pan. Remove the plug and drain the transmission oil. On models without the plug, loosen the pan bolts 2–3 turns and lower one corner of the pan to drain the oil.

2. Remove the pan bolts and remove the pan from the transmission.

NOTE: *It may be necessary to tap the pan with a rubber hammer to loosen it.*

3. Use a new gasket and install the pan. Tighten the bolts loosely until the pan is properly in place, then tighten the bolts fully, moving in a diagonal pattern.

NOTE: *Do not overtighten the bolts.*

4. Refill the transmission with ATF.

5. At 5 minute intervals, retighten the pan bolts two or three times.

FILTER SERVICE

The Volkswagen automatic transmission has a filter screen secured by a screw to the bottom of the valve body. Remove the pan and remove the filter screen from the valve body.

CAUTION: *Never use a cloth that will leave the slightest bit of lint in the transmission when cleaning transmission parts. The lint will expand when exposed to transmission fluid and clog the valve body and filter.*

Clean the filter screen with compressed air. 1976–81 Type 2s have a non-cleanable filter which must be replaced with a new one if ATF fluid is very dirty.

FRONT (SECOND) BAND ADJUSTMENT
Except 1976–81 Type 2

Tighten the front band adjusting screw to 7 ft. lbs. Then loosen the screw and tighten it to 3.5 ft. lbs. From this position, loosen the screw exactly 1¾ to 2 turns and tighten the lock nut.

1976–81 Type 2

Only the second band is adjustable on this transmission. The adjuster is located on the passenger side of the transmission beside the gear selector lever. It is held by a locknut. The transmission must be horizontal when the band is adjusted or the band could jam. Tighten the adjusting screw to 7 ft. lbs., then loosen it and tighten it to 3.5 ft. lbs. From this position loosen it exactly 2½ turns and tighten the locknut.

REAR (FIRST) BAND ADJUSTMENT
Except 1976–81 Type 2

Tighten the rear band adjusting screw to 7 ft. lbs. Then loosen the screw and retighten it to 3.5 ft. lbs. From this position, loosen the screw exactly 3¼ to 3½ turns and tighten the lock nut.

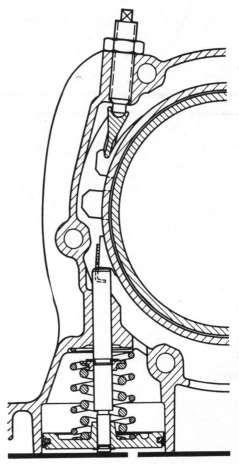

Front band assembly—adjustment screw at the top

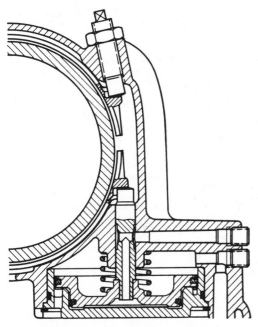

Rear band assembly—adjustment screw at the top

KICKDOWN SWITCH ADJUSTMENT
Except 1976–81 Type 2, All Type 4

1. Disconnect the accelerator cable return spring.

2. Move the throttle to the fully open position. Adjust the accelerator cable to give 0.02–0.04 in. clearance between the stop and the end of the throttle valve lever.

3. When the accelerator cable is adjusted and the throttle is moved to the fully open position, the kickdown switch should click. The ignition switch must be ON for this test.

4. To adjust the switch, loosen the switch securing screws and slide the switch back and forth until the test in Step 3 is satisfied.

5. Reconnect the accelerator cable return spring.

1976–81 Type 2

1. Press the accelerator pedal fully to the floor (kickdown position).

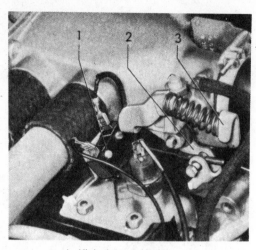

1. Kick-down switch
2. Accelerator cable lever
3. Throttle valve lever

Kick-down switch

2. In this position, the play at the operating lever on the transmission should be 0.04–0.08 in.

3. If not, adjust at the retaining screw on the accelerator pedal.

Clamp securing shift linkage rod halves

Type 4

The Type 4 switch is located in the accelerator pedal pod. On some models it can be adjusted by moving it on its mount. Adjust so that kickdown solenoid in transmission can be heard to click when the accelerator is to the floor.

SHIFT LINKAGE ADJUSTMENT

Make sure the shifting cable is not kinked or bent and that the linkage and cable are properly lubricated.

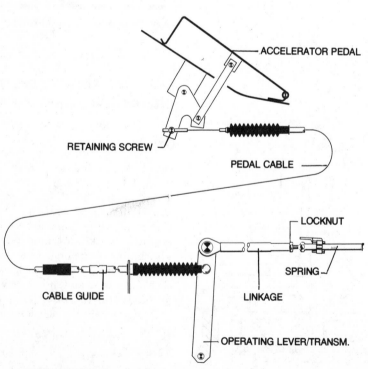

1976–81 Type 2 kickdown adjustment. Operating lever is on transmission. Linkage then goes from operating lever to throttle valve on engine

Pressing transmission lever rearward against its stop. Lever is below operating lever on 1976–81 Type 2

1. Move the gear shift lever to the Park position.

2. Loosen the clamp which holds the front and rear halves of the shifting rod together. Loosen the clamping bolts on the transmission lever.

3. Press the lever on the transmission rearward as far as possible. Spring pressure will be felt. The manual valve must be on the stop in the valve body.

4. Holding the transmission lever against its stop, tighten the clamping bolt.

5. Holding the rear shifting rod half, push the front half forward to take up any clearance and tighten the clamp bolt.

6. Test the shift pattern.

Suspension and Steering

FRONT SUSPENSION— TORSION BAR TYPE

Type 1 Beetle, 1970 Beetle Convertible, Type 1 Karmann Ghia, Type 2 Through 1979, Type 3

Each front wheel rotates on a ball joint mounted spindle. The spindle is suspended independently by a pair of torsion bars.

The principle of torsion bars is that of springing action taking place via twisting of the bars. When a front wheel goes up or down, the torsion bars are twisted, causing a downward or upward force in the opposite direction.

The supporting part of the Volkswagen front axle is the axle beam, which is two rigidly joined tubes attached to the frame with four screws. At each end of the tubes there is a side plate designed to provide additional strength and serve as the upper mounting point for the shock absorbers. Because the front axle is all-welded, it is replaced as a unit whenever damaged.

TORSION BAR REMOVAL AND INSTALLATION

1. Jack up the car and remove both wheels and brake drums.

2. Remove the ball joint nuts and remove the left and right steering knuckles. A forked ball joint removing tool is available at an auto parts store.

   CAUTION: *Never strike the ball joint stud.*

3. Remove those arms attached to the torsion bars on one side only. To remove the arms, loosen and remove the arm setscrew and pull the arm off the end of the torsion bar.

4. Loosen and remove the set-screw which secures the torsion bar to the torsion bar housing.

5. Pull the torsion bar out of its housing.

6. To install, carefully note the number of leaves and the position of the countersink marks for the torsion bar and the torsion arm.

7. Align the countersink mark in the center of the bar with the hole for the set-screw and insert the torsion bar into its housing. Install the set-screw. Install the torsion arm.

8. Reverse Steps 1–3 to complete.

TORSION ARM REMOVAL AND INSTALLATION

1. Jack up the car and remove the wheel and tire.

2. Remove the brake drum and the steering knuckle.

3. If the lower torsion arm is being re-

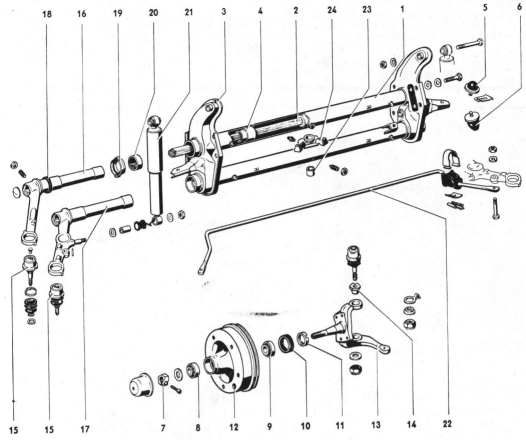

1. Front axle beam
2. Torsion bar
3. Side plate
4. Torsion arm bush
5. Upper rubber buffer
6. Lower rubber buffer
7. Clamp nut for wheel bearing adjustment
8. Outer front wheel bearing
9. Inner front wheel bearing
10. Front wheel bearing seal
11. Spacer ring
12. Brake drum
13. Steering knuckle
14. Eccentric bush for camber adjustment
15. Ball joint
16. Upper torsion arm
17. Lower torsion arm
18. Seal for torsion arm
19. Seal retainer
20. Torsion arm needle bearing
21. Shock absorber
22. Stabilizer
23. Swing lever shaft bush
24. Swing lever stop

Exploded view of front torsion bar suspension—Type 2 through 1979

moved, disconnect the stabilizer bar. To remove the stabilizer bar clamp, tap the wedge shaped keeper toward the outside of the car or in the direction the narrow end of the keeper is pointing.

4. On Type 1 and 2, back off on the set-screw locknut and remove the set-screw. On Type 3, remove the bolt and keeper from the end of the torsion bar.

5. Slide the torsion arm off the end of the torsion bar.

6. Reverse the above steps to install. Check the camber and toe-in settings.

SHOCK ABSORBER REMOVAL AND INSTALLATION

1. Remove the wheel and tire.

2. Remove the nut from the torsion arm stud and slide the lower end of the shock off of the stud.

3. Remove the nut from the shock absorber shaft at the upper mounting and remove the shock from the vehicle.

4. The shock is tested by operating it by hand. As the shock is extended and compressed, it should operate smoothly over its

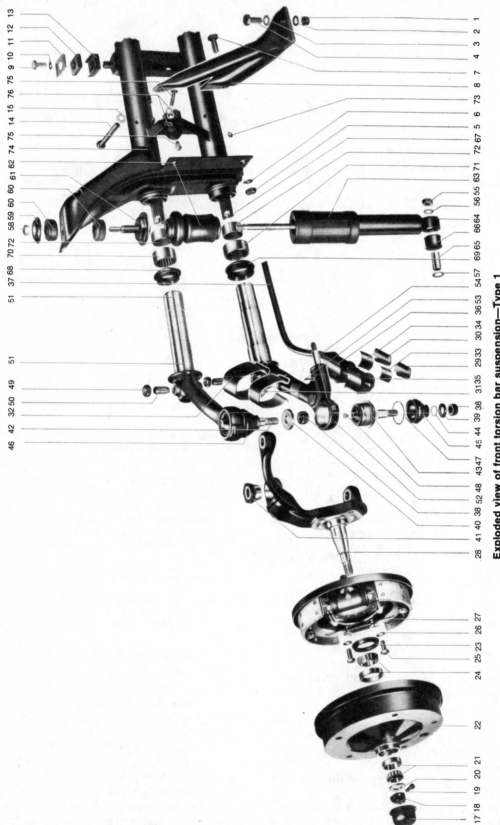

Exploded view of front torsion bar suspension—Type 1

1. Nut
2. Spring washer
3. Washer
4. Bolt
5. Nut
6. Spring washer
7. Bolt
8. Support for axle
9. Bolt
10. Spring washer
11. Plate
12. Rubber packing, upper
13. Rubber packing, lower
14. Bolt
15. Spring washer
16. Lockwasher
17. Dust cap
18. Clamp nut for wheel bearing
19. Socket hd. screw for clamp nut
20. Thrust washer
21. Outer tapered roller bearing
22. Brake drum
23. Oil seal
24. Inner tapered roller bearing
25. Bolt
26. Spring washer

27. Front wheel brake and locking plate
28. Steering knuckle
29. Retainer, small
30. Retainer, large
31. Clip, small
30. Retainer, large
31. Clip, small
32. Clip, large
33. Plate, small
34. Plate, large
35. Rubber mounting, small
36. Rubber mounting, large
37. Stabilizer bar
38. Self-locking nut
39. Washer, small
40. Washer, large
41. Eccentric bushing for camber adjustment
42. Upper ball joint
43. Lower ball joint
44. Ring for rubber boot
45. Boot for lower joint
46. Boot for upper joint
47. Ring for rubber boot
48. Plug
49. Locknut

50. Setscrew for torsion bar
51. Torsion arm, upper
52. Torsion arm, lower
53. Pin
54. Pin for shock absorber
55. Nut
56. Lockwasher
57. Lockwasher
58. Nut
59. Plate for damper bushing
60. Damper bushing
61. Pin for buffer
62. Buffer
63. Tube
64. Shock absorber
65. Sleeve for rubber rushing
66. Rubber bushing
67. Torsion bar—10 leaf
68. Seal for upper torsion arm
69. Seal for lower torsion arm
70. Needle bearing, upper
71. Needle bearing, lower
72. Metal bushing for torsion arms
73. Grease fitting
74. Axle beam
75. Bolt

entire stroke with an even pressure. Its damping action should be clearly felt at the end of each stroke. If the shock is leaking slightly, the shock need not be replaced. A shock that has had an excessive loss of fluid will have flat spots in the stroke as the shock is compressed and extended. That is, the pressure will feel as though it has been suddenly released for a short distance during the stroke.

5. Installation is the reverse of Steps 1–3.

BALL JOINT INSPECTION

A quick initial inspection can be made with the vehicle on the ground. Grasp the top of the tire and vigorously pull the top of the tire in and out. Test both sides in this manner. If the ball joints are excessively worn, there will be an audible tap as the ball moves around in its socket. Excess play can sometimes be felt through the tire.

A more rigorous test may be performed by jacking the car under the lower torsion arm and inserting a lever under the tire. Lift up gently on the lever so as to pry the tire upward. If the ball joints are worn, the tire will move upward ⅛–¼ in. or more. If the tire displays excessive movement, have an assistant inspect each joint, as the tire is pryed upward, to determine which ball joint is defective.

BALL JOINT REPLACEMENT

1. Jack up the car and remove the wheel and tire.

2. Remove the brake drum and disconnect the brake line from the backing plate.

3. Remove the nut from each ball joint stud and remove the ball joint stud from the steering knuckle. Remove the steering knuckle from the car. A ball joint removal tool is available at an auto parts store. Do not strike the ball joint stud.

4. Remove the torsion arm from the torsion bar.

5. Remove the ball joint from the torsion arm by pressing it out.

6. Press a new ball joint in, making sure that the square notch in the joint is in line with the notch in the torsion arm eye.

NOTE: *Ball joints are supplied in different sizes designated by V-notches in the ring around the side of the joint. When replacing a ball joint, make sure that the new part has the same number of V-notches. If*

Notch in ball joint indicating that it is oversized

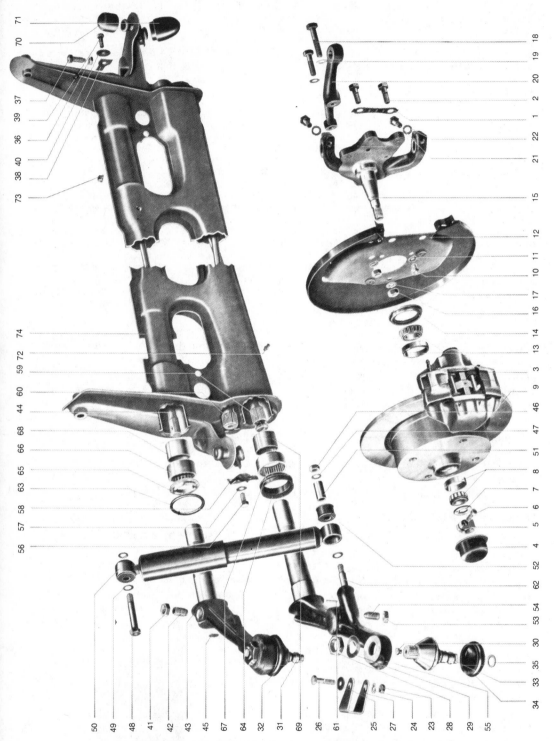

Exploded view of front torsion bar suspension—Type 3

1. Lockplate
2. Screw
3. Caliper
4. Dust cap
5. Clamp nut
6. Screw
7. Thrust washer
8. Bearing
9. Brake disc
10. Screw
11. Lockwasher
12. Backing plate
13. Bearing
14. Oil seal
15. Steering knuckle
16. Nut
17. Lockwasher
18. Screw
19. Lockwasher

20. Steering arm
21. Screw
22. Lockwasher
23. Nut
24. Lockwasher
25. Washer
26. Screw
27. Stop
28. Nut
29. Lockwasher
30. Plug
31. Upper ball joint
32. Seal
33. Lower ball joint
34. Seal
35. Retaining ring
36. Nut
37. Screw
38. Lockplate

39. Screw
40. Washer
41. Locknut
42. Set screw
43. Upper torsion arm
44. Stabilizer
45. Sealing washer
46. Nut
47. Lockwasher
48. Screw
49. Lockwasher
50. Shock absorber
51. Sleeve
52. Bushing
53. Nut
54. Set screw
55. Lower torsion arm
56. Screw

57. Lockwasher
58. Retainer
59. Torsion arm, left
60. Torsion arm, right
61. Dowel pin
62. Pin
63. Seal
64. Seal
65. Axial ring
66. Needle bearing
67. Needle bearing
68. Bushing
69. Bushing
70. Buffer
71. Buffer
72. Grease fitting
73. Grease fitting
74. Front axle beam

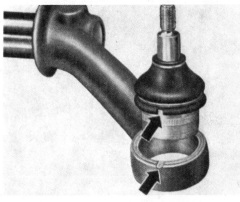

Align square notch in ball joint with notch in torsion arm upon installation

it has no notches, the replacement joint should have no notches.

7. Reverse Steps 1–4 to complete the installation.

FRONT SUSPENSION—STRUT TYPE

Type 1 Super Beetle, Super Beetle Convertible, and Type 4

Each wheel is suspended independently on a shock absorber strut surrounded by a coil spring. The strut is located at the bottom by a track control arm and a ball joint, and at the top by a ball bearing which is rubber mounted to the body. The benefits of this type of suspension include a wider track, a very small amount of toe-in and camber change during suspension travel, and a reduced turning circle. The strut front suspension requires no lubrication. It is recommended, however, that the ball joint dust seals be checked every 6,000 miles and the ball joint play every 30,000 miles.

SUSPENSION STRUT REMOVAL AND INSTALLATION

1. Jack up the car and remove the wheel and tire.
2. If the left strut is to be removed, remove the speedometer cable from the steering knuckle.
3. Disconnect the brake line from the bracket on the strut.
4. At the base of the strut, bend down the locking tabs for the three bolts and remove the bolts.
5. Push down on the steering knuckle and pull the strut out of the knuckle.
6. Remove the three nuts which secure the top of the strut to the body. Before removing the last nut, support the strut so that it does not fall out of the car.
7. Reverse the above steps to install the strut. Always use new nuts and locking tabs during installation.

TRACK CONTROL ARM REMOVAL AND INSTALLATION

1. Remove the ball joint stud nut and remove the stud from the control arm.
2. Disconnect the stabilizer bar from the control arm.
3. Remove the nut and eccentric bolt at the frame. This is the pivot bolt for the control arm and is used to adjust camber.
4. Pull the arm downward and remove it from the vehicle.
5. Reverse the above steps to install.

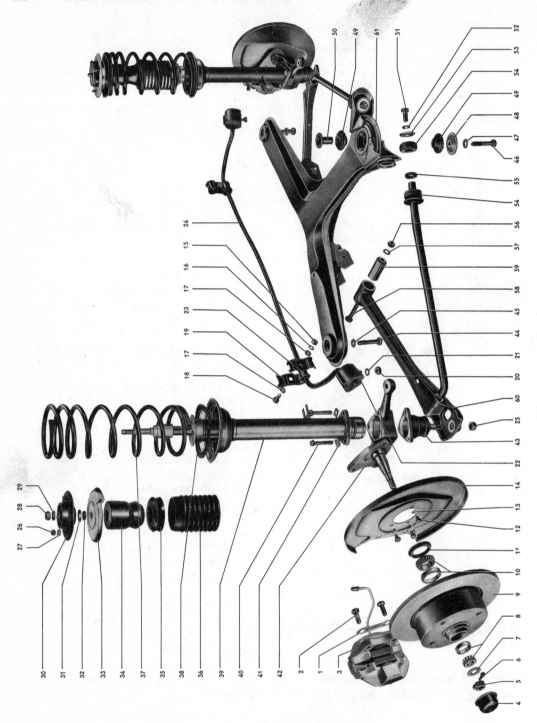

Exploded view of front strut suspension—Type 4

1. Lockplate
2. Bolt
3. Caliper
4. Hub cap
5. Wheel bearing locknut
6. Allen screw for locknut
7. Thrust washer
8. Outer taper roller bearing
9. Brake disc
10. Inner taper roller bearing
11. Oil seal
12. Bolt
13. Spring washer
14. Splash shield for disc
15. Nut
16. Spring washer
17. Washer
18. Bolt
19. Clamp for stabilizer bar
20. Nut
21. Spring washer
22. Stabilizer mounting for control arm

23. Rubber bushing for clamp
24. Stabilizer bar
25. Self-locking nut
26. Self-locking nut
27. Washer
28. Self-locking nut
29. Washer, small
30. Suspension strut bearing
31. Sealing plate
32. Spacer ring
33. Spring plate
34. Rubber stop for shock absorber
35. Retaining ring for protective tube
36. Protective tube for shock absorber
37. Coil spring
38. Damping ring, coil spring
39. Shock absorber
40. Bolt
41. Lockwasher
42. Steering knuckle

43. Ball joint
44. Bolt
45. Lockwasher
46. Bolt
47. Lockwasher
48. Seat for damping ring
49. Damping ring for front axle carrier
50. Spacer sleeve
51. Bolt
52. Spring washer
53. Plate for damping ring
54. Damping ring for radius rod
55. Locating ring for radius rod
56. Nut
57. Spring washer
58. Bolt
59. Bushing for track control arm
60. Track control arm
61. Front axle carrier

1. Suspension strut
2. Track control arm
3. Stabilizer
4. Steering gear
5. Tie-rods
6. Idler arm and bracket
7. Safety steering column
8. Frame head

1971–80 Type 1 Super Beetle and Convertible, front suspension and steering

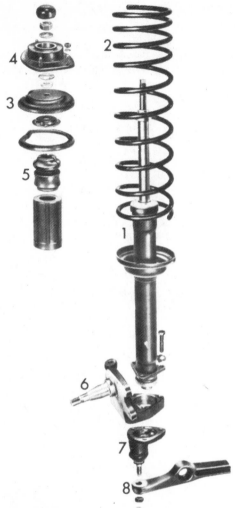

Compressing coil spring of strut suspension

1. Shock absorber
2. Coil spring
3. Spring plate
4. Strut bearing
5. Hollow rubber spring
6. Steering knuckle
7. Ball joint
8. Track control arm

Type 1 Super Beetle and Convertible front strut details

Make sure the groove in the stabilizer bar bushing is horizontal.

6. Realign the front end.

SHOCK ABSORBER REMOVAL AND INSTALLATION

In this type suspension system, the shock absorber is actually the supporting vertical member.

1. Remove the strut as outlined above.

2. It is necessary to disassemble the strut to replace the shock absorber. To remove the spring, it must be compressed. The proper type compressor is available at an auto parts store.

3. Remove the nut from the end of the shock absorber shaft and slowly release the spring. The strut can now be disassembled. Testing is the same as the torsion bar shock absorber.

4. Reverse the above steps to install.

BALL JOINT INSPECTION

Vehicles with strut suspension have only one ball joint on each side located at the base of the strut in the track control arm.

Raise the car and support it under the frame. The wheel must be clear of the ground.

With a lever, apply upward pressure to the track control arm. Apply the pressure gently and slowly; it is important that only enough pressure is exerted to check the play in the ball joint and not compress the suspension.

Using a vernier caliper, measure the distance between the control arm and the lower edge of the ball joint flange. Record the reading. Release the pressure on the track control arm and again measure the distance between the control arm and the lower edge of the ball joint flange. Record the reading. Subtract the higher reading from the lower reading. If the difference is more than 0.10 in., the ball joint should be replaced.

NOTE: *Remember that even in a new joint there will be measurable play because the ball in the ball joint is spring loaded.*

BALL JOINT REPLACEMENT

1. Jack up the car and remove the wheel and tire.

2. Remove the nut from the ball joint stud and remove the stud from the track control arm.

3. Bend back the locking tab and remove the three ball joint securing screws.

4. Pull the track control arm downward and remove the ball joint from the strut.

5. Reverse the above steps to install.

FRONT SUSPENSION—SPRING ON LOWER ARM

1980–81 Type 2 (Vanagon)

The front suspension consists of upper and lower control arms, a separate upper coil spring/shock absorber mount, steering knuckle and attaching ball joints and a strut arm mounted on the lower control arm for stability.

COIL SPRING REMOVAL AND INSTALLATION

1. Jack up the front of the vehicle and support it on stands, then remove the wheel. Remove the shock absorber.

2. Compress the coil spring using a spring compressor.

3. Disconnect the stabilizer bar from the strut.

4. Measure the distance from the end of the outer nut on the strut to the tip of the strut itself, then remove the strut. This measurement is later used during installation to align the strut.

5. After the strut is removed from the lower control arm, you should be able to pull the lower ball joint to control arm attachment out of the control arm.

6. Remove the coil spring.

To install:

7. Seat the compressed coil spring on its cushions, making sure the grooves for the spring ends are in the correct positions.

8. Reverse remaining procedures to install. When installing strut, adjust the outside nut so that it conforms to the measurement made in step 4.

SHOCK ABSORBER REMOVAL AND INSTALLATION

1. Jack the front of the vehicle and remove the front wheel.

2. Loosen and remove the single retaining nut at the top of the coils spring/shock absorber upper mount.

3. Remove the through bolt which retains the bottom of the shock absorber to the lower control arm and pull the shock absorber out through the bottom of the lower control arm.

4. Reverse the procedure to install.

BALL JOINT REMOVAL AND INSTALLATION

Upper Ball Joint

1. Raise the vehicle and support it on jack stands, then remove the wheel.

2. Place a jack under the lower control arm as close to the steering knuckle as possible and jack up just enough to put a slight load on the coil spring.

3. Loosen the steering knuckle to ball joint nut but do not remove completely.

4. Free the ball joint from the steering knuckle using a ball joint removal tool, then remove the nut.

5. Remove the two upper ball joint to upper control arm bolts and remove the ball joint.

6. Reverse procedure to install. Check wheel alignment.

Lower Ball Joint

1. Jack up the front of the vehicle and support it on stands, then remove the wheel.

2. Place a jack under the lower control arm as close to steering knuckle as possible and put a slight load on the coil spring by jacking up the jack.

3. Disconnect the brake caliper hose from the caliper, and remove the brake caliper and rotor if they are in the way.

4. Loosen the upper ball joint to steering knuckle to ball joint nut, but do not remove it. Free the upper ball joint from the steering knuckle and remove the nut.

5. Remove the lower ball joint to lower control arm nut and free the ball joint from the control arm using a ball joint removal tool. Remove the steering knuckle.

6. Press the ball joint off the steering knuckle.

7. Press a new ball joint in place on knuckle, observing any alignment marks on the ball joint and the knuckle.

8. Reverse the procedure to install. Bleed the brakes.

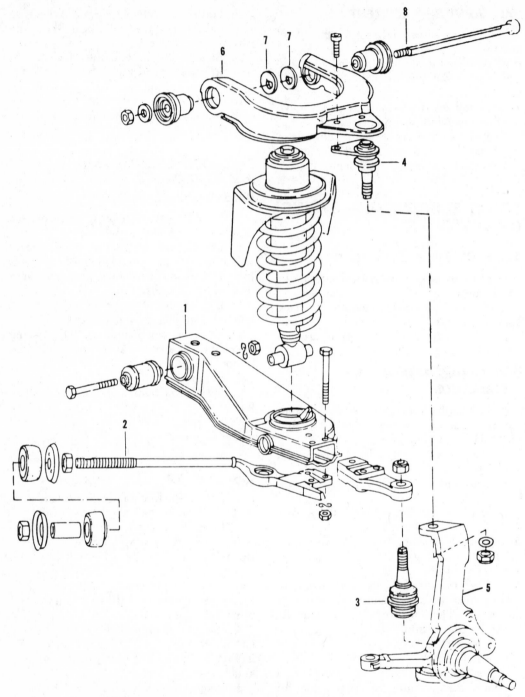

1. Lower control arm
2. Strut
3. Lower ball joint
4. Upper ball joint
5. Steering knuckle
6. Upper control arm
7. Camber adjuster cam
8. Upper control arm through bolt and camber adjuster

Front suspension, 1980–81 Type 2. Stabilizer bar which bolts into strut not shown

UPPER CONTROL ARM REMOVAL AND INSTALLATION

1. Jack up the vehicle and remove the front wheel.
2. Place a jack under the lower control arm and raise to put a slight load on the coil spring.
3. Free the upper ball joint from the steering knuckle.
4. Remove the upper control arm to frame mounting bolt and remove the control arm.
5. Reverse procedure to install. Check and adjust wheel alignment.

LOWER CONTROL ARM REMOVAL AND INSTALLATION

1. Jack up the vehicle and remove the wheel.
2. Remove the coil spring. See above for procedures.
3. Remove the lower control arm to frame mounting bolt and remove the control arm.
4. Reverse procedures to install.

Front End Alignment—All Types

CASTER ADJUSTMENT

Caster is the forward or backward tilt of the spindle. Forward tilt is negative caster and backward tilt is positive caster. Caster is not

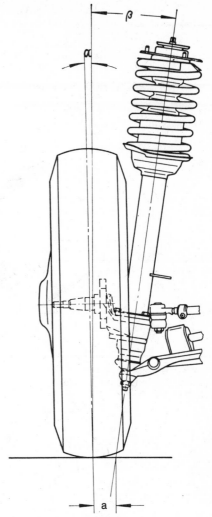

Angle α = camber
Angle β = steering pivot angle
a = steering roll radius

Camber angle—strut suspension shown

adjustable on torsion bar or the strut suspensions. A slight caster adjustment can be made on the 1980–81 Type 2 Vanagon by moving the nuts on the end of the front suspension strut.

CAMBER ADJUSTMENT

Camber is the tilt of the top of the wheel, inward or outward, from true vertical. Outward tilt is positive, inward tilt is negative.

Torsion Bar Suspension

The Upper ball joint on each side is mounted in an eccentric bushing. The bushing has a hex head and it may be rotated in either direction using a wrench.

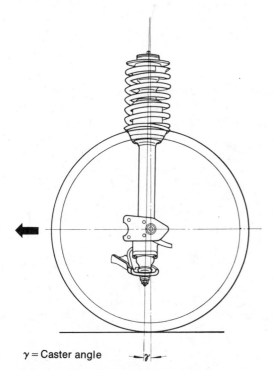

γ = Caster angle

Caster angle—strut suspension shown

Wheel Alignment Specifications

| | | Front Axle | | | | | Rear Axle | | |
| | | Caster | | Camber | | | Camber | | |
Year	Model	Range (deg)	Pref Setting (deg)	Range (deg)	Pref Setting (deg)	Toe-in (in. or degrees)	Range (deg)	Pref Setting (deg)	Toe-in (deg)
1970–77	Type 1	±1°	+3° 20'	±20'	+30'	+0.071– +0.213	±40'	−1°	0' ± 15'
1971–80	Type 1 ①	±35'	+2°	+20'	+1°	+0.071– +0.213	±40'	−1°	0' ± 15'
1970–79	Type 2	±40'	+3°	±20'	+40'	0.0– +0.136	±30'	−50'	+10' ± 20'
1980–81	Type 2 ③	±15'	7° 15'	±30'	0	+40'	±30'	−50'	0° ± 10'
1970–73	Type 3	±40'	+4°	±20'	+1° 20'	+0.118	±40'	−1° 20'	0' ± 15' ②
1971–74	Type 4	±35'	+1° 45'	+25' −30'	+1° 10'	+0.024– +0.165	±30'	−1°	+10' ± 15'

①Super Beetle and Convertible
②Squareback given; Sedan 5' ± 15'
③Vehicle empty

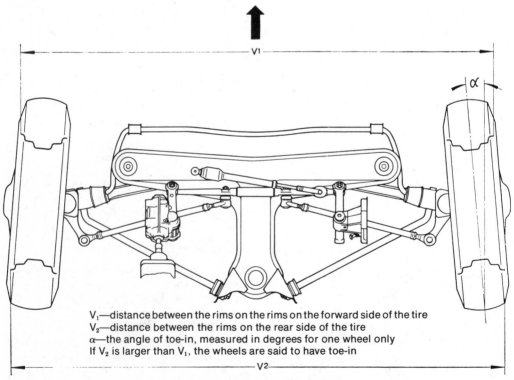

V₁—distance between the rims on the rims on the forward side of the tire
V₂—distance between the rims on the rear side of the tire
α—the angle of toe-in, measured in degrees for one wheel only
If V₂ is larger than V₁, the wheels are said to have toe-in

Toe-in—strut suspension shown

Strut Suspension

The track control arm pivots on an eccentric bolt. Camber is adjusted by loosening the nut and rotating the bolt.

Spring on Lower Arm

Camber is adjusted by turning the upper control arm mounting bolt, which causes the two cams on the upper control arm to force the arm in or out.

TOE-IN ADJUSTMENT

Toe-in is the adjustment made to make the front wheels point slightly into the front. Toe-in is adjusted on all types of front suspensions by adjusting the length of the tie-rod sleeves.

REAR SUSPENSION— DIAGNONAL ARM TYPE

Types 1, 2 through 1979, and 3

The rear wheels of Types 1, 2, and 3 models are independently sprung by means of torsion bars. The inside ends of the torsion bars are anchored to a body crossmember via a splined tube which is welded to the frame. The torsion bar at each side of the rear suspension has a different number of splines at each end. This makes possible the adjustment of the rear suspension.

On Type 3 models, an equalizer bar, located above the rear axle, is used to aid the handling qualities and lateral stability of the rear axle. This bar also acts progressively to soften bumps in proportion to their size.

SHOCK ABSORBER REMOVAL AND INSTALLATION

The shock absorber is secured at the top and bottom by a through bolt. Raise the car and remove the bolts. Remove the shock absorber from the car.

DIAGONAL ARM REMOVAL AND INSTALLATION

1. Remove the wheel shaft nuts. CAUTION: *Do not raise the car to remove the nuts. They can be safely removed only if the weight of the car is on its wheels.*
2. Disconnect the driveshaft of the side to be removed.
3. Remove the lower shock absorber mount. Raise the car and remove the wheel and tire.

Unloaded Rear Tension Bar Settings

Type	Model	Transmission	Setting	Range
1	all	all	20° 30'	+ 50'
2	221, 223, 226	Manual	21° 10'	+ 50'
2	222	Manual	23°	+ 50'
2 ③	221, 223	all	20°	+ 50'
2 ④	222	all	23°	+ 50'
3	311	Manual	23°	+ 50'
3	311	Automatic	24°	+ 50'
3	361	all	21° 30'	+ 50'

③ From chassis 212 2 000 001 (1972-up)
④ From chassis 212 2 000 001 (1972-up)

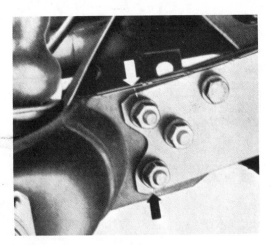

Marking diagonal arm and torsion bar for alignment

Diagonal arm pivot bolt—both spacer washers on the outside

1. Frame or sub-frame
2. Diagonal arm (complete)
3. Double spring plate
4. Torsion bar
5. Rubber bushing, inner left
6. Rubber bushing, outer
7. Cover for spring plate hub
8. Bolt
9. Lockwasher
10. Fitted bolt
11. Spacer
12. Bolt
13. Washer
14. Lockwasher
15. Bolt
16. Nut
17. Shock absorber
18. Rubber stop
19. Bolt
20. Bolt
21. Lockwasher
22. Nut

Exploded view of diagonal arm rear suspension—Type 1 shown

4. Remove the brake drum, disconnect the brake lines and emergency brake cable, and remove the backing plate.

5. Matchmark the torsion bar plate and the diagonal arm with a cold chisel.

6. Remove the four bolts and nuts which secure the plate to the diagonal arm.

7. Remove the pivot bolts for the diagonal arm and remove the arm from the car.

NOTE: *Take careful note of the washers at the pivot bolts. These washers are used to determine alignment and they must be put back in the same place.*

8. Remove the spring plate hub cover.

9. Using a steel bar, lift the spring plate off of the lower suspension stop.

10. On Type 1, remove the five bolts at the front of the fender. On all others, remove the cover in the side of the fender.

11. Remove the spring plate and pull the torsion bar out of its housing.

NOTE: *There are left and right torsion bars designated by an (L) or (R) on the end face. (Coat any rubber bushings with talcum powder upon installation. Do not use graphite, silicon, or grease.*

12. To install, insert the torsion bar, outer bushing, and spring plate. Make sure that the marks you made earlier line up.

13. Using two bolts, loosely secure the spring plate hub cover. Place a thick nut between the leaves of the spring plate.

14. Lift the spring plate up to the lower suspension stop and install the remaining bolts into the hub cover. Tighten the hub cover bolts.

15. Install the diagonal arm pivot bolt and washers and peen it with a chisel. There must always be at least one washer on the outside end of the bolt.

16. Align the chisel marks and attach the diagonal arm to the spring plate.

17. Install the backing plate, parking brake cable, and brake lines.

18. Reconnect the shock absorber. Install the brake drum and wheel shaft nuts.

19. Reconnect the driveshaft. Bleed the brakes.

20. Install the wheel and tire.

21. Check the suspension alignment.

REAR SUSPENSION—COIL SPRING AND TRAILING ARM TYPE

Type 4

The rear wheels of Type 4 models are independently sprung by means of coil springs and trailing arms. The shock absorbers mount inside the coil springs. Each coil spring and shock absorber mounts between the trailing arm and a sheet metal shock tower. Each trailing arm pivots on a body crossmember.

SHOCK ABSORBER REMOVAL AND INSTALLATION

The shock absorber is the lower stop for the suspension.

CAUTION: *The A-arm must be securely supported when the shock absorber is disconnected to prevent the spring tension from being released suddenly.*

Leaving the car on the ground or raising the car and securely supporting the A-arm, remove the lower shock absorber through bolt. To gain access to the upper shock mounting, remove the access panel for each shock located at the sides of the rear luggage shelf. Remove the self locking nut from the shock absorber shaft and remove the shock. Installation is the reverse of removal.

TRAILING ARM REMOVAL AND INSTALLATION

1. Raise the car and place it on jackstands. Securely block up the A-arm.

CAUTION: *The A-arm must be securely supported when the shock absorber is disconnected to prevent the spring tension from being released suddenly. The shock absorber is the lower stop for the suspension.*

2. Disconnect the driveshaft.

3. Disconnect the handbrake cable at the brake lever and remove it.

4. Disconnect the brake lines and the stabilizer bar if equipped.

5. With the vehicle on the ground or the A-arm securely supported, remove the lower shock absorber mounting bolt.

6. Slowly release the A-arm and remove the coil springs.

7. Mark the position of the brackets or the eccentric bolts, whichever are removed, with a chisel. Remove the nuts which secure the brackets in the rear axle carrier, or the pivot bolts in the bonded rubber bushings, and remove the A-arm.

8. Loosely install the A-arm. If the pivot bolts were removed, install them loosely. If the eccentric bolts and brackets were removed, install them, aligning the chisel marks, and then tighten them.

9. Insert the coil spring and slowly compress it into place. Install the lower shock absorber mount.

1980–81 Type 2 (Vanagon)

The suspension is basically the same as the Type 4 except the shock absorber is not mounted inside the coil spring.

SHOCK ABSORBER REMOVAL AND INSTALLATION

See Type 4 shock absorber removal and installation for procedures observe the CAUTION. The shock absorber is not mounted inside the spring, but behind it. Remove the shock absorber retaining bolts and remove.

TRAILING ARM REMOVAL AND INSTALLATION

Procedures are the same as for Type 4, except: when removing the trailing arm, remove it at the bushing bolts.

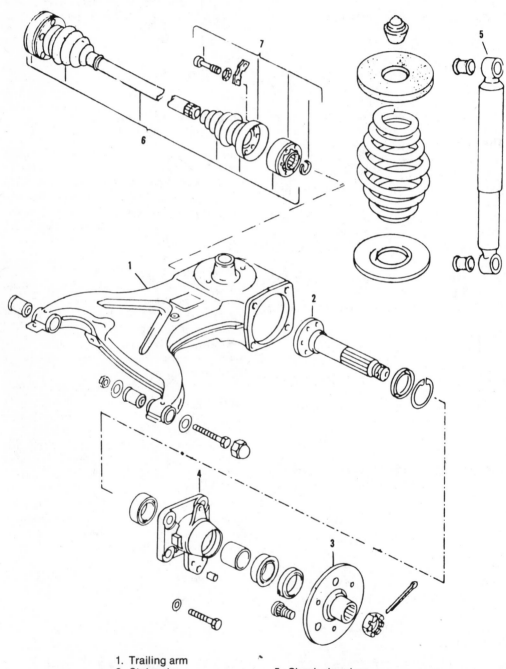

1. Trailing arm
2. Stub axle
3. Wheel hub
4. Wheel bearing housing

5. Shock absorber
6. Axle shaft
7. Constant velocity joint

1980 Type 2 rear suspension

Rear Suspension Adjustments

Type 1, Diagonal Arm Suspension

The only adjustment is the toe-in adjustment. The adjustment is performed by varying the number of washers at the diagonal arm pivot. There must always be one washer located on the outboard side of the pivot.

Type 2 Through 1979, 3, Diagonal Arm Suspension

The transmission and engine assembly position in the vehicle is adjustable. It is necessary that the assembly be correctly centered before the suspension is aligned. It may be adjusted by moving the engine and transmission brackets in their elongated slots.

The distance between the diagonal arms may be adjusted by moving the washers at the A-arm pivots. The washers may be positioned only two ways. Either both washers on the outboard side of the pivot or a single washer on each side of the pivot. To adjust the distance, position the diagonal arms and move the washers in the same manner at both pivots.

The wheel track angle may be adjusted by moving the diagonal arm flange in the elongated slot in the spring plate.

The toe-in is adjusted by positioning the washers and the diagonal arm pivot.

Type 4, A-Arm Suspension

The toe-in is adjusted by the eccentric A-arm pivot bolts.

The rubber buffer centralization procedure is given in the "Type 4 Transaxle (Automatic) Removal and Installation" procedure.

The track width can be adjusted by loosening the A-arm mounting bracket bolts and moving the brackets in or out to the proper position.

Type 4 Engine and Transmission Assembly Centering Specifications

Offset between vehicle center and engine/transmission unit center	1.0 in.
Center of left measuring hole to center of right measuring hole	44.3 ± 0.04 in.
Center of left measuring hole to center of rib on transmission	23.1 ± 0.02 in.
Center of right measuring hole to Center of rib on transmission	21.2 ± 0.02 in.

STEERING

STEERING WHEEL REMOVAL AND INSTALLATION

1. Disconnect the negative battery cable.
2. Remove the center emblem. This emblem will gently pry off the wheel, or is attached by screws from the back of the steering wheel.
3. Remove the nut from the steering shaft. This is a right-hand thread.

NOTE: *Mark the steering shaft and steering wheel so that the wheel may be installed in the same position on the shaft.*

4. Using a steering wheel puller, remove the wheel from the splined steering shaft. Do not strike the end of the steering shaft.
5. Reverse the above steps to install. Make sure to align the match marks made on the steering wheel and steering shaft. The gap between the turn signal switch housing and the back of the wheel is 0.08–0.12 in. (distance "a").

Steering wheel removal—Type 2 shown

TURN SIGNAL SWITCH REMOVAL AND INSTALLATION

1. Disconnect the negative battery cable.
2. Remove the steering wheel.
3. Remove the four turn signal switch securing screws.
4. Disconnect the turn signal switch wiring plug under the steering column.
5. Pull the switch and wiring guide rail up and out of the steering column.
6. Reverse the above steps to install. Make sure the spacers located behind the switch, if installed originally, are in position. The distance between the steering wheel and

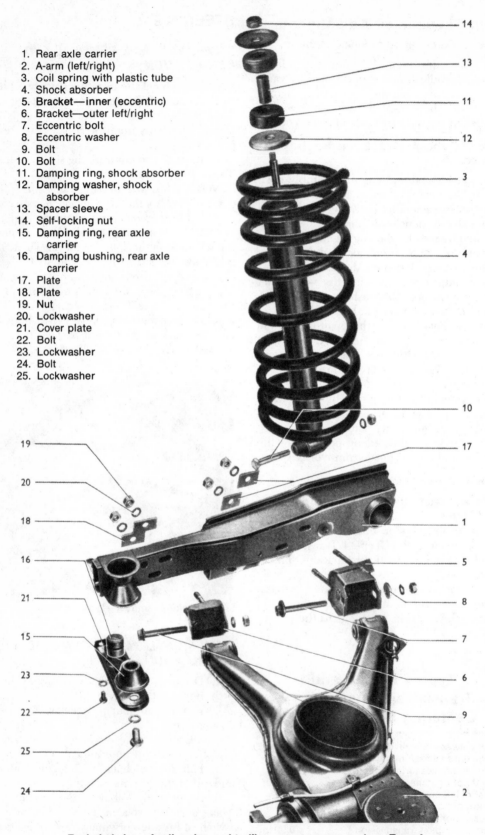

1. Rear axle carrier
2. A-arm (left/right)
3. Coil spring with plastic tube
4. Shock absorber
5. Bracket—inner (eccentric)
6. Bracket—outer left/right
7. Eccentric bolt
8. Eccentric washer
9. Bolt
10. Bolt
11. Damping ring, shock absorber
12. Damping washer, shock absorber
13. Spacer sleeve
14. Self-locking nut
15. Damping ring, rear axle carrier
16. Damping bushing, rear axle carrier
17. Plate
18. Plate
19. Nut
20. Lockwasher
21. Cover plate
22. Bolt
23. Lockwasher
24. Bolt
25. Lockwasher

Exploded view of coil spring and trailing arm rear suspension—Type 4

the steering column housing is (distance "a") 0.08–0.12 in. Install the switch with the lever in the central position.

Ignition Switch

SWITCH REMOVAL AND INSTALLATION

1. Disconnect the steering column wiring at the block located behind the instrument panel and pull the column wiring harness into the passenger compartment.

2. Remove the steering wheel.

3. Remove the circlip on the steering shaft.

4. Disconnect the negative battery cable.

5. Insert the key and turn the switch to the ON position. On Type 3 vehicles it is necessary to remove the fuse box.

6. Remove the three securing screws and slide the switch assembly from the steering column tube.

NOTE: *It is not necessary to remove the turn signal switch at this time. If it is necessary to remove the switch from the housing, continue with the disassembly procedure.*

7. Remove the turn signal switch.

8. After removing the wiring retainer, press the ignition switch wiring block upward and out of the housing and disconnect the wiring.

9. Remove the lock cylinder and the steering lock mechanism.

10. Remove the ignition switch screw and pull the ignition switch rearward.

11. Reverse the above steps to install. When reinstalling the turn signal switch, make sure the lever is in the center position.

NOTE: *The distance (a) between the steering wheel and the ignition switch housing is 2–3 mm (0.08–0.12 in.).*

Correct distance (a) between ignition switch housing and steering wheel is 0.08–0.12 in.

IGNITION LOCK CYLINDER REMOVAL AND INSTALLATION

1. Proceed with Steps 1–8 in the "Ignition Switch" procedure.

2. With the key in the cylinder and turned to the ON position, pull the lock cylinder out far enough so the securing pin can be depressed through a hole in the side of the lock cylinder housing. Use a steel wire to depress the pin.

3. As the pin is depressed, pull the lock cylinder out of its housing.

4. To install the lock cylinder, gently push the cylinder into its housing. Make sure the pin engages correctly and that the retainer fits easily in place. Do not force any parts together; when they are correctly aligned, they will fit easily together.

NOTE: *On many 1976 and later Type 1s, and many Type 2s, the release hole was not drilled by the factory. Using the illustrations, drill your own release hole with a 1/8 in. drill bit.*

Removing turn signal switch

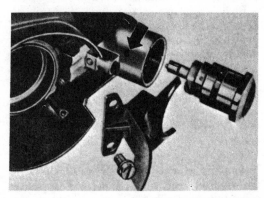

Access hole for depressing lock cylinder retaining pin

Type 2 drilling measurement for release pin. "a" equals 13mm (0.51 in.)

Removing tie-rod end stud with ball joint puller

Type 1 drilling measurements for release pin. "a" and "b" equal 11mm (7/16 in.)

STEERING LINKAGE REMOVAL AND INSTALLATION

All tie-rod ends are secured by a nut which holds the tapered tie-rod end stud into a matching tapered hole. There are several ways to remove the tapered stud from its hole after the nut has been removed.

First, there are several types of removal tools available from auto parts stores. These tools include directions for their use. One of the most commonly available tools is the fork shaped tool which is a wedge that is forced under the tie-rod end. This tool should be used with caution because instead of removing the tie-rod end from its hole it may pull the ball out of its socket, ruining the tie-rod end.

It is also possible to remove the tie-rod end by holding a heavy hammer on one side of the tapered hole and striking the opposite side of the hole sharply with another hammer. The stud will pop out of its hole.

CAUTION: *Never strike the end of the tie-rod end stud. It is impossible to remove the tie-rod end in this manner.*

Once the tie-rod end stud has been removed, turn the tie-rod end out of the adjusting sleeve. On the pieces of the steering linkage that are not used to adjust the toe-in, the tie-rod end is welded in place and it will be necessary to replace the whole assembly.

When reassembling the steering linkage, never put lubricant in the tapered hole.

MANUAL STEERING GEAR ADJUSTMENT

There are three types of adjustable steering gear units. The first type is the roller type, identified by the square housing cover secured by four screws, one at each corner. The second type is the worm and peg type, identified by an assymetric housing cover with the adjusting screw located at one side of the housing cover. The third type is the rack and pinion type used on 1975 Super Beetles, and 1975 and later Convertibles.

Worm and Roller Types—Types 1, 3, 4 and 1973–79 Type 2 Models

Disconnect the steering linkage from the pitman arm and make sure the gearbox mounting bolts are tight. Have an assistant rotate the steering wheel so that the pitman arm moves alternately 10° to the left and then 10° to the right of the straight ahead position. Turn the adjusting screw in until no further play can be felt while moving the pitman arm. Tighten the adjusting screw locknut and recheck the adjustment.

Worm and Peg Type—1970–72 Type 2 Models

Have an assistant turn the steering wheel back and forth through the center position several times. The steering wheel should turn through the center position without any noticeable binding.

Adjusting worm and peg steering gear—worm and roller type similar

To adjust, turn the adjusting screw inward while the assistant is turning the steering wheel. Turn the screw in until the steering begins to tighten up. Back out the adjusting screw until the steering no longer binds while turning through the center point and tighten the adjusting screw locknut.

The adjustment is correct when there is no binding and no perceptible play.

Rack and Pinion Type—1975 Type 1 Super Beetle and 1975–80 Convertible

The steering gear requires adjustment if it begins to rattle noticeably. First, remove the access cover in the spare tire well. Then, with the car standing on all four wheels, turn the adjusting screw in by hand until it contacts the thrust washer. While holding the screw in this position, tighten the locknut.

The adjustment is correct when there is no binding and the steering self-centers properly.

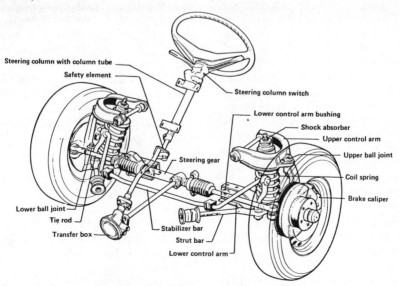

1. Side member
2. Bracket-to-side member bolts 4.5 mkg (32 ft. lbs.)
3. Steering gear-to-bracket bolts 2.5 mkg (18 ft. lbs.)
4. Adjusting screw

Type 1 rack and pinion steering details—1975 La Grande Bug (Super Beetle) and 1975–79 Convertible

Steering column with column tube
Safety element
Steering column switch
Lower control arm bushing
Shock absorber
Upper control arm
Upper ball joint
Steering gear
Coil spring
Brake caliper
Lower ball joint
Tie rod
Transfer box
Stabilizer bar
Strut bar
Lower control arm

Vanagon front suspension and steering

Brakes

BRAKE SYSTEM

Understanding the Brakes

HYDRAULIC SYSTEM

Hydraulic system are used to actuate the brakes of all modern automobiles. The system transports the power required to force the frictional surfaces of the braking system together from the pedal to the individual brake units at each wheel. A hydraulic system is used for two reasons. First, fluid under pressure can be carried to all parts of an automobile by small hoses—some of which are flexible—without taking up a significant amount of room or posing routing problems. Second, a great mechanical advantage can be given to the brake pedal end of the system, and the foot pressure required to actuate the brakes can be reduced by making the surface area of the master cylinder pistons smaller than that of any of the pistons in the wheel cylinders or calipers.

The master cylinder consists of a fluid reservoir and either a single or double cylinder and piston assembly. Double type master cylinders are designed to separate the front and rear braking systems hydraulically in case of a leak.

Steel lines carry the brake fluid to a point on the vehicle's frame near each of the vehi-

cle's wheels. The fluid is then carried to the slave cylinders by flexible tubes in order to allow for suspension and steering movements.

In drum brake systems, the slave cylinders are called wheel cylinders. Each wheel cylinder contains two pistons, one at either end, which push outward in opposite directions. In disc brake systems, the slave cylinders are part of the calipers. One or four cylinders are used to force the brake pads against the disc, but all cylinders contain one piston only. All slave cylinder pistons employ some type of seal, usually made of rubber, to minimize the leakage of fluid around the piston. A rubber dust boot seals the outer end of the cylinder against dust and dirt. The boot fits around the outer end of the piston on disc brake calipers, and around the brake actuating rod on wheel cylinders.

The hydraulic system operates as follows: When at rest, the entire system, from the piston(s) in the master cylinder to those in the wheel cylinders or calipers, is full of brake fluid. Upon application of the brake pedal, fluid trapped in front of the master cylinder piston(s) is forced through the lines to the slave cylinders. Here, it forces the pistons outward, in the case of drum brakes, and inward toward the disc, in the case of disc brakes. The motion of the pistons is opposed by return springs mounted outside the cylinders in drum brakes, and by internal springs or spring seals, in disc brakes.

Upon release of the brake pedal, a spring located inside the master cylinder immediately returns to the master cylinder piston(s) to the normal position. The pistons contain check valves and the master cylinder has compensating ports drilled in it. These are uncovered as the pistons reach their normal position. The piston check valves allow fluid to flow toward the wheel cylinders or calipers as the pistons withdraw. Then, as the return springs force the brake pads or shoes into the released position, the excess fluid returns to the master cylinder fluid reservoir through the compensating ports. It is during the time the pedal is in the released position that any fluid that has leaked out of the system will be replaced through the compensating ports.

Dual circuit master cylinders employ two pistons, located one behind the other, in the same cylinder. The primary piston is actuated directly by mechanical linkage from the brake pedal. The secondary piston is actuated by fluid trapped between the two pistons. If a leak develops in front of the secondary piston, it moves forward until it bottoms against the front of the master cylinder, and the fluid trapped between the pistons will operate the rear brakes. If the rear brakes develop a leak, the primary piston will move forward until direct contact with the secondary piston takes place, and it will force the secondary piston to actuate the front brakes. In either case, the brake pedal moves farther when the brakes are applied, and less braking power is available.

All dual-circuit systems use a distributor switch to warn the driver when only half of the brake system is operational. This switch is located in a valve body which is mounted on the firewall or the frame below the master cylinder. A hydraulic piston receives pressure from both circuits, each circuit's pressure being applied to one end of the piston. When the pressures are in balance, the piston remains stationary. When one circuit has a leak, however, the greater pressure in that circuit during application of the brakes will push the piston to one side, closing the distributor switch and activating the brake warning light.

In disc brake systems, this valve body also contains a metering valve and, in some cases, a proportioning valve. The metering valve keeps pressure from traveling to the disc brakes on the front wheels until the brake shoes on the rear wheels have contacted the drums, ensuring that the front brakes will never be used alone. The proportioning valve throttles the pressure to the rear brakes so as to avoid rear wheel lock-up during very hard braking.

These valves may be tested by removing the lines to the front and rear brake systems and installing special brake pressure testing gauges. Front and rear system pressures are then compared as the pedal is gradually depressed. Specifications vary with the manufacturer and design of the brake system.

Brake system warning lights may be tested by depressing the brake pedal and holding it while opening one of the wheel cylinder bleeder screws. If this does not cause the light to go on, substitute a new lamp, make continuity checks, and, finally, replace the switch as necessary.

The hydraulic system may be checked for leaks by applying pressure to the pedal gradually and steadily. If the pedal sinks very slowly to the floor, the system has a leak. This is not to be confused with a springy or spongy feel due to the compression of air within the lines. If the system leaks, there will be a gradual change in the position of the pedal with a constant pressure.

Check for leaks along all lines and at wheel cylinders. If no external leaks are apparent, the problem is inside the master cylinder.

DISC BRAKES

Instead of the traditional expanding brakes that press outward against a circular drum, disc brake systems utilize a cast iron disc with brake pads positioned on either side of it. Braking effect is achieved in a manner similar to the way you would squeeze a spinning phonograph record between your fingers. The disc (rotor) is a one-piece casting with cooling fins between the two braking surfaces. This enables air to circulate between the braking surfaces making them less sensitive to heat buildup and more resistant to fade. Dirt and water do not affect braking action since contaminants are thrown off by the centrifugal action of the rotor or scraped off by the pads. Also, the equal clamping action of the two brake pads tends to ensure uniform, straightline stops. All disc brakes are inherently self-adjusting.

There are three general types of disc brake:

1) A fixed caliper, four-piston type.
2) A floating caliper, single piston type.
3) A sliding caliper, single piston type.

The fixed caliper design uses two pistons mounted on either side of the rotor (in each side of the caliper). The caliper is mounted rigidly and does not move.

The sliding and floating designs are quite similar. In fact, these two types are often lumped together. In both designs, the pad on the inside of the rotor is moved into contact with the rotor by hydraulic force. The caliper, which is not held in a fixed position, moves slightly, bringing the outside pad into contact with the rotor. There are various methods of attaching floating calipers. Some pivot at the bottom or top, and some slide on mounting bolts. In any event, the end result is the same.

DRUM BRAKES

Drum brakes employ two brake shoes mounted on a stationary backing plate. These shoes are positioned inside a circular cast iron drum which rotates with the wheel assembly. The shoes are held in place by springs; this allows them to slide toward the drums (when they are applied) while keeping the linings and drums in alignment. The shoes are actuated by a wheel cylinder which is mounted at the top of the backing plate. When the brakes are applied, hydraulic pressure forces the wheel cylinder's two actuating links outward. Since these links bear directly against the top of the brake shoes, the tops of the shoes are then forced outward against the inner side of the drum. This action forces the bottoms of the two shoes to contact the brake drum by rotating the entire assembly slightly (known as servo action). When pressure within the wheel cylinder is relaxed, return springs pull the shoes back away from the drum.

Most modern drum brakes are designed to self-adjust themselves during application when the vehicle is moving in reverse. This motion causes both shoes to rotate very slightly with the drum, rocking an adjusting lever, thereby causing rotation of the adjusting screw by means of a star wheel.

POWER BRAKE BOOSTERS

Power brakes operate just as standard brake systems except in the actuation of the master cylinder pistons. A vacuum diaphragm is lo-cated on the front of the master cylinder and assists the driver in applying the brakes, reducing both the effort and travel he must put into moving the brake pedal.

The vacuum diaphragm housing is connected to the intake manifold by a vacuum hose. A check valve is placed at the point where the hose enters the diaphragm housing, so that during periods of low manifold vacuum brake assist vacuum will not be lost.

Depressing the brake pedal closes off the vacuum source and allows atmospheric pressure to enter on one side of the diaphragm. This causes the master cylinder pistons to move and apply the brakes. When the brake pedal is released, vacuum is applied to both sides of the diaphragm, and return springs return the diphragm and master cylinder pistons to the released position. If the vacuum fails, the brake pedal rod will butt against the end of the master cylinder actuating rod, and direct mechanical application will occur as the pedal is depressed.

The hydraulic and mechanical problems that apply to conventional brake systems also apply to power brakes, and should be checked for if the tests below do not reveal the problem.

Test for a system vacuum leak as described below:

1. Operate the engine at idle with the transmission in Neutral without touching the brake pedal for at least one minute.

2. Turn off the engine, and wait one minute.

3. Test for the presence of assist vacuum by depressing the brake pedal and releasing it several times. Light application will produce less and less pedal travel, if vacuum was present. If there is no vacuum, air is leaking into the system somewhere.

Test for system operation as follows:

1. Pump the brake pedal (with engine off) until the supply vacuum is entirely gone.

2. Put a light, steady pressure on the pedal.

3. Start the engine, and operate it at idle with the transmission in Neutral. If the system is operating, the brake pedal should fall toward the floor if constant pressure is maintained on the pedal.

Power brake systems may be tested for hydraulic leaks just as ordinary systems are tested, except that the engine should be idling with the transmission in Neutral throughout the test.

Brake Adjustment

All models are equipped with dual hydraulic brake systems in accordance with federal regulations. In case of a hydraulic system failure, ½ braking efficiency will be retained.

All type 1 models (except the Karmann Ghia), and 1970 Type 2 models are equipped with front drum brakes. Discs are used at the front of all Type 1 Karmann Ghias, 1971–81 Type 2 models, and all Type 3 and 4 models. All models use rear drum brakes.

Disc brakes are self adjusting and cannot be adjusted by hand. As the pads wear, they will automatically compensate for the wear by moving closer to the disc, maintaining the proper operating clearance.

Drum brakes, however, must be manually adjusted to take up excess clearance as the shoes wear. To adjust drum brakes, both front and rear, it is necessary to jack up the car and support it on a jackstand. The wheel must spin freely. On the backing plate there are four inspection holes with a rubber plug in each hole. Two of the holes are for checking the thickness of the brake lining and the other two are used for adjustment.

NOTE: *There is an adjustment for each brake shoe. That means that on each wheel it is necessary to make two adjustments, one for each shoe on that wheel.*

Remove the adjustment hole plugs and, using a screwdriver or brake adjusting tool, insert the tool into the hole. Turn the star wheel until a slight drag is noticed as the wheel is rotated by hand. Back off on the star wheel 3–4 notches so that the wheel turns freely. Perform the same adjustment on the other shoe.

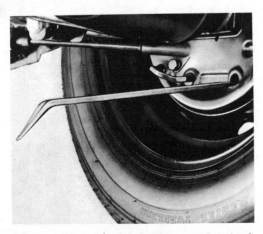

Brake adjusting spoon inserted into hole in backing plate—rear drum brake shown

NOTE: *One of the star wheels in each wheel has left-hand threads and the other star wheel has right-hand threads.*

Repeat the above procedure on each wheel with drum brakes.

HYDRAULIC SYSTEM

Master Cylinder
REMOVAL AND INSTALLATION

NOTE: *The brake master cylinder on the 1980 Type 2 (Vanagon) is located under the dash. Remove the bottom and top dash covers for access.*

1. Drain the brake fluid from the master cylinder reservoir.

CAUTION: *Do not get any brake fluid on the paint, as it will dissolve the paint.*

2. On Type 3, remove the master cylinder cover plate.

3. Pull the plastic elbows out of the rubber sealing rings on the top of the master cylinder, if equipped, or unfasten the fluid pipe seat nuts.

4. Remove the two bolts which secure the master cylinder to the frame and remove the cylinder. Note the spacers on the Type 1 between the frame and the master cylinder.

5. To install, bolt the master cylinder to the frame. Do not forget the spacers on the Type 1.

6. Lubricate the elbows with brake fluid and insert them into the rubber seals.

7. If necessary, adjust the brake pedal free travel. On Type 1, 3, and 4, adjust the length of the master cylinder pushrod so that there is a 5–7 mm of brake pedal free-play before the pushrod contacts the master cylinder piston. On Type 2, the free-play is properly adjusted when the length of the pushrod, measured between the ball end and the center of the clevis pin hole, is 4.17 in.

8. Refill the master cylinder reservoir and bleed the brakes.

MASTER CYLINDER OVERHAUL

1. Remove the master cylinder from the car.

2. Remove the rubber sealing boot.

3. Remove the stop screw and sealing ring on the top of the unit.

4. Insert a screwdriver in the master cylinder piston, exert inward pressure, and remove the snap-ring from its groove in the end of the unit. The internal parts are spring

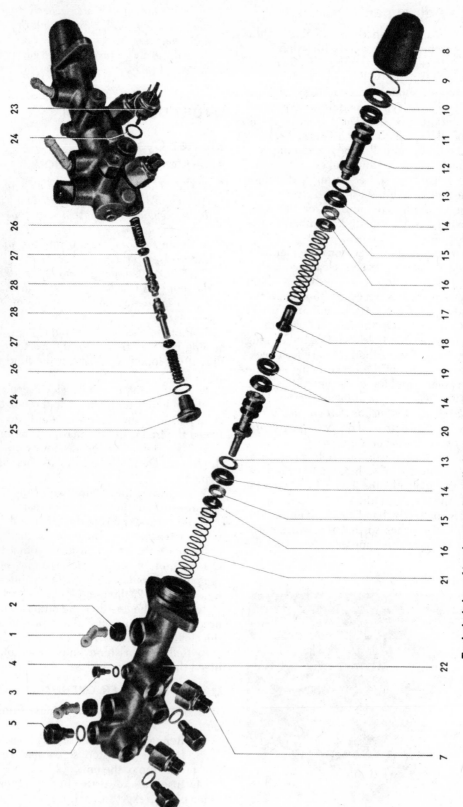

Exploded view of tandem master cylinder—parts 8 through 12 used only on non-vacuum booster models.
Parts 24 through 28 operate warning light switch and are not used on all models

1. Elbow
2. Sealing plug
3. Stop screw
4. Seal
5. Residual pressure valve
6. Sealing ring
7. Brake light switch
8. Rubber boot
9. Lockring
10. Stop washer
11. Secondary cup
12. Rear brake circuit piston
13. Cup washer
14. Cup
15. Support washer
16. Spring retainer
17. Rear brake circuit spring
18. Stop sleeve
19. Stroke limiting screw
20. Front brake circuit piston
21. Front brake circuit spring
22. Master cylinder housing
23. Warning light switch
24. Seal
25. Plug
26. Spring
27. Cup
28. Piston

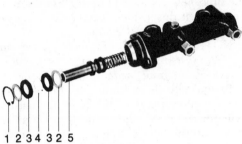

1. Circlip
2. Stop washer
3. Seal cup
4. Plastic washer
5. Pushrod

Sealing parts on vacuum booster equipped models

loaded and must be kept from flying out when the snap-ring is removed.

5. Carefully remove the internal parts of the unit and make note of their order and the orientation of the internal parts. If parts remain in the cylinder bore, they may be removed with a wire hook or very gentle application of low pressure air to the stop screw hole. Cover the end of the cylinder bore with a rag and stand away from the open end of the bore when using compressed air.

6. Use alcohol or brake fluid to clean the master cylinder and its parts.

7. It may be necessary to hone the cylinder bore, or clean it by lightly sanding it with emery cloth. Clean thoroughly after honing

1. Retaining ring
2. Circlip
3. Air connection
4. Boot
5. Sealing ring
6. Cap
7. Damping ring
8. Filter

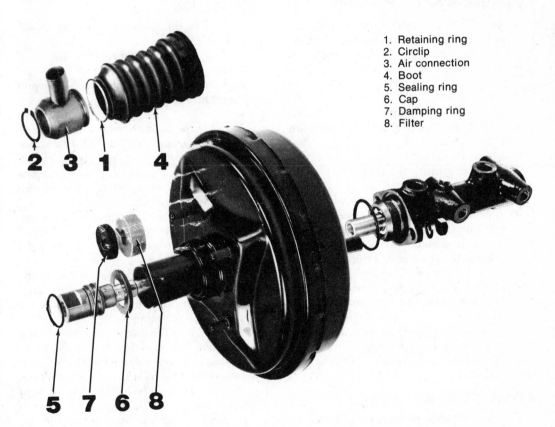

Exploded view of 1971–79 Type 2 brake servo

or sanding. Lubricate the bore with brake fluid before reassembly.

8. Holding the master cylinder with the open end downward, place the cup washer, primary cup, support washer, spring retainer, and spring onto the front brake circuit piston and insert the piston vertically into the master cylinder bore.

9. Assemble the rear brake circuit piston, cup washer, primary cup, support washer, spring retainer, stop sleeve, spring, and stroke limiting screw and insert the assembly into the master cylinder.

10. Install the stop washer and snapring.

11. Install the stop screw and seal, making sure the hole for the screw is not blocked by the piston. If the hole is blocked, it will be necessary to push the piston further in until the screw can be turned in.

NOTE: *1971–79 Type 2 vehicles have a brake servo and the order of assembly of the additional seals is illustrated.*

12. Install the master cylinder and bleed the brakes.

Hydraulic System Bleeding

The hydraulic brake system must be bled any time one of the lines is disconnected or air enters the system. This may be done manually or by the pressure method.

PRESSURE BLEEDING

1. Clean the top of the master cylinder, remove the caps, and attach the pressure bleeding adapter.

2. Check the pressure bleeder reservoir for correct pressure and fluid level, then open the release valve.

3. Fasten a bleeder hose to the wheel cylinder bleeder nipple and submerge the free end of the hose in a transparent receptacle. The receptacle should contain enough brake fluid to cover the open end of the hose.

4. Open the wheel cylinder bleeder nipple and allow the fluid to flow until all bubbles disappear and an uncontaminated flow of fluid exists.

5. Close the nipple, remove the bleeder hose, and repeat the procedure on the other wheel cylinders or brake calipers are equipped.

MANUAL BLEEDING

This method requires two people: one to depress the brake pedal and the other to open the bleeder nipples.

1. Remove the reservoir caps and fill the reservoir.

2. Attach a bleeder hose and a clear container as outlined in the pressure bleeding procedure.

3. Have the assistant depress the brake pedal to the floor several times and then have him hold the pedal to the floor. With the pedal to the floor, open the bleeder nipple until the fluid flow ceases and then close the nipple. Repeat this sequence until there are no more air bubbles in the fluid.

NOTE: *As the air is gradually forced out of the system, it will no longer be possible to force the brake pedal to the floor.*

Periodically check the master cylinder for an adequate supply of fluid. Keep the master cylinder reservoir full of fluid to prevent air from entering the system. If the reservoir does run dry during bleeding, it will be necessary to rebleed the entire system.

FRONT DISC BRAKES

BRAKE PAD REMOVAL AND INSTALLATION

1. Loosen but do not remove the reservoir cover.

2. Jack up the car and remove the wheel and tire.

3. Using a punch, remove the two pins which retain the disc brake pads in the caliper.

NOTE: *If the pads are to be reused, mark the pads to insure that they are reinstalled in the same caliper and on the same side of the disc. Do not invert the pads. Changing pads from one location to another can cause uneven braking.*

4. If the pads are not going to be reused, force a wedge between the disc and the pad and pry the piston back into the caliper as far as possible.

5. Using compressed air, blow away the brake dust. Pull the old pad out of the caliper and insert a new one, taking care to note the position of the retaining plate.

NOTE: *On ATE and many Teves disc brakes, before inserting the brake pads, make sure the relieved part of the piston is in the correct position to accept the retaining plate. In the illustration, the sides of the retaining plate "b" fit into the relieved area while the circular part of the plate "a" fits in the piston's center. On some Type 2s and other models, the retaining plate is*

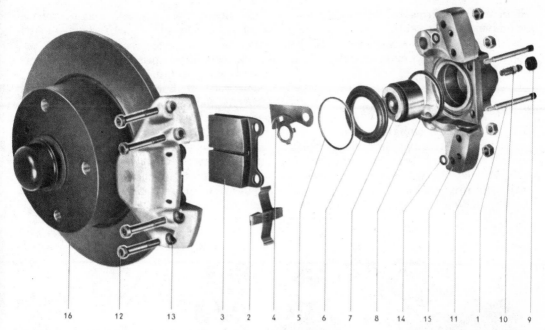

1. Friction pad retaining pin
2. Spreader spring
3. Friction pad
4. Piston retaining plate
5. Clamp ring
6. Seal
7. Piston
8. Rubber seal
9. Dust cap
10. Bleeder valve
11. Nut
12. Cheese head screw
13. Caliper outer housing
14. Seal
15. Caliper inner housing
16. Brake disc

Exploded view of ATE disc brake components—Teves components similar

simply a flat piece of metal with two notches which fit into the relieved areas in the piston. The relieved side of the piston should face against (away from) the rotation direction of the wheel when the car is going forward.

When installing retaining plate, make sure circular part "a" fits piston center and that retaining plate fits down behind relieved parts "b" of piston. If not, shift piston with pliers. Some models have flat retainer plate with indents which fit at "b"

6. Now insert the wedge between the disc and pad on the opposite side and force that piston into the caliper. Remove the old pad and insert a new one.

7. If the old pads are to be reused, it is not necessary to push the piston into the caliper. Pull the pads from the caliper and reinstall the pads when necessary.

8. Install a new brake pad spreader spring and insert the retaining pins. Be careful not to shear the split clamping bushing from the pin. Insert the pin from the inside of the caliper and drive it to the outside.

9. Pump the brake pedal several times to take up the clearance between the pads and the disc before driving the car.

10. Install the wheel and tire and carefully road test the car. Apply the brakes gently for first 500 to 1000 miles to properly break in the pads and prevent glazing them.

BRAKE CALIPER REMOVAL AND INSTALLATION

1. Jack up the car and remove the wheel and tire.

2. Remove the brake pads.

3. Disconnect the brake line from the caliper.

4. Remove the two bolts which secure the

caliper to the steering knuckle and remove the caliper from the vehicle.

5. Reverse the above steps to install the caliper and bleed the brakes after the caliper is installed.

BRAKE CALIPER OVERHAUL

Clean all parts in alcohol or brake fluid.

1. Remove the caliper from the vehicle.
2. Remove the piston retaining plates.
3. Pry out the seal spring ring using a small screwdriver. Do not damage the seal beneath the ring.

4. Remove the seal with a plastic or hard rubber rod. Do not use sharp edged or metal tools.

5. Rebuild one piston at a time. Securely clamp one piston in place so that it cannot come out of its bore. Place a block of wood between the two pistons and apply air pressure to the brake fluid port.

CAUTION: *Use extreme care with this technique because the piston can fly out of the caliper with tremendous force.*

6. Remove the rubber seal at the bottom of the piston bore using a rubber or plastic tool.

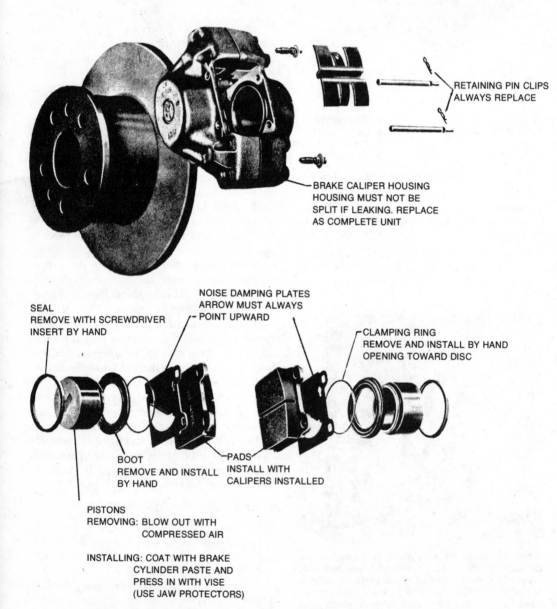

RETAINING PIN CLIPS
ALWAYS REPLACE

BRAKE CALIPER HOUSING
HOUSING MUST NOT BE
SPLIT IF LEAKING. REPLACE
AS COMPLETE UNIT

NOISE DAMPING PLATES
ARROW MUST ALWAYS
POINT UPWARD

SEAL
REMOVE WITH SCREWDRIVER
INSERT BY HAND

CLAMPING RING
REMOVE AND INSTALL BY HAND
OPENING TOWARD DISC

BOOT
REMOVE AND INSTALL
BY HAND

PADS
INSTALL WITH
CALIPERS INSTALLED

PISTONS
REMOVING: BLOW OUT WITH
COMPRESSED AIR

INSTALLING: COAT WITH BRAKE
CYLINDER PASTE AND
PRESS IN WITH VISE
(USE JAW PROTECTORS)

Exploded view of Girling disc brake components—1975 and later Type 2 shown

7. Check the bore and piston for wear, rust, and pitting.

8. Install a new seal in the bottom of the bore and lubricate the bore and seal with brake fluid.

9. Gently insert the piston, making sure it does not cock and jamb in the bore.

NOTE: *When installing pistons on ATE and Teves calipers, make sure the relieved part of the piston is in the correct position to accept the retaining plate for the brake pads. See brake pad removal and installation for more information and illustration.*

10. Install the new outer seal and new spring ring.

11. Install the piston retaining plate.

12. Repeat the above procedure on the other piston. Never rebuild only one side of a caliper.

BRAKE DISC REMOVAL AND INSTALLATION

1. Jack up the car and remove the wheel and tire.

2. Remove the caliper.

3. On Type 2, remove the three socket head bolts which secure the disc to the hub and remove the disc from the hub. Sometimes the disc is rusted to the hub. Spray penetrating oil on the seam and tap the disc with a lead or brass hammer. If it still does not come off, screw three 8 mm by 40 screws into the socket head holes. Tighten the screws evenly and pull the disc from the hub.

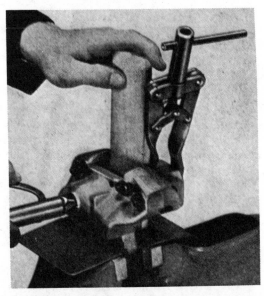

Clamping a piston in place and applying compressed air to the brake hose port

4. Type 1, 3, and 4, remove the wheel bearing cover. On the left side it will be necessary to remove the small clip which secures the end of the speedometer cable to the cover.

5. Loosen the nut clamp, unscrew the wheel bearing nut and remove the nut and outer wheel bearing.

6. Pull the disc off of the spindle.

7. To remove the wheel bearing races, see the "Wheel Bearing Removal and Installation" procedure.

8. Installation is the reverse of the above. Make sure the wheel bearing is properly adjusted.

BRAKE DISC INSPECTION

Visually check the rotor for excessive scoring. Minor scores will not affect the performance; however, if the scores are over $1/32$ in., it is necessary to replace the disc or have it resurfaced. The disc must be 0.02 in. over the wear limit to be resurfaced. The disc must be free of surface cracks and discoloration (heat bluing). Hand spin the disc and make sure that it does not wobble from side to side.

Front Wheel Bearings
REMOVAL AND INSTALLATION

1. Jack up the car and remove the wheel and tire.

2. Remove the caliper and disc (if equipped with disc brakes) or brake drum.

3. To remove the inside wheel bearing, pry the dust seal out of the hub with a screwdriver. Lift out the bearing and its inner race.

4. To remove the outer race for either the inner or outer wheel bearing, insert a long punch into the hub opposite the end from which the race is to be removed. The race rests against a shoulder in the hub. The shoulder has two notches cut into it so that it is possible to place the end of the punch directly against the back side of the race and drive it out of the hub.

5. Carefully clean the hub.

6. Install new races in the hub. Drive them in with a soft faced hammer or a large piece of pipe of the proper diameter. Lubricate the races with a light coating of wheel bearing grease.

7. Force wheel bearing grease into the sides of the tapered roller bearings so that all the spaces are filled.

1. Speedometer cable circlip
2. Hub cap dust cover
3. Clamp nut allen screw
4. Wheel bearing clamp nut
5. Thrust washer
6. Outer taper roller bearing
7. Brake drum

8. Drum seal (grease)
9. Inner taper roller bearing
10. Bolt
11. Spring washer
12. Front brake unit
13. Steering knuckle

Exploded view of Type 1 front wheel roller bearings

8. Place a small amount of grease inside the hub.

9. Place the inner wheel bearing into its race in the hub and tap a new seal into the hub. Lubricate the sealing surface of the seal with grease.

10. Install the hub on the spindle and install the outer wheel bearing.

11. Adjust the wheel bearing and install the dust cover.

12. Install the caliper (if equipped with disc brakes).

ADJUSTMENT

The bearing may be adjusted by feel or by a dial indicator.

To adjust the bearing by feel, tighten the adjusting nut so that all the play is taken up in the bearing. There will be a slight amount of drag on the wheel if it is hand spun. Back off fully on the adjusting nut and retighten very lightly. There should be no drag when the wheel is hand spun and there should be no perceptible play in the bearing when the wheel is grasped and wiggled from side to side.

To use a dial indicator, remove the dust cover and mount a dial indicator against the hub. Grasp the wheel at the side and pull the wheel in and out along the axis of the spindle. Read the axial play on the dial indicator. Screw the adjusting nut in or out to obtain 0.001–0.005 in. of axial play. Secure the adjusting nut and recheck the axial play.

FRONT DRUM BRAKES

BRAKE DRUM REMOVAL AND INSTALLATION

1. Jack up the car and remove the wheel and tire.

2. On the left side, remove the clip which secures the speedometer cable to the wheel bearing dust cover. Remove the dust cover.

3. Loosen the nut clamp, remove the wheel bearing adjusting nut and slide the brake drum off of the spindle. It may be necessary to back off on the brake shoe star wheels so that there is enough clearance to remove the drum.

4. Installation is the reverse of removal. Adjust the wheel bearings after installing the drum.

CAUTION: *Do not forget to readjust the brake shoes if they were disturbed during removal.*

Front wheel brake

Rear wheel brake

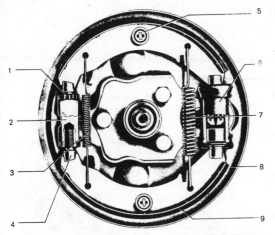

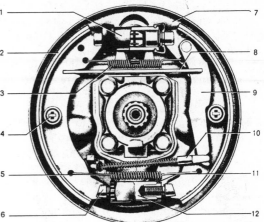

FRONT
1. Adjusting screw
2. Anchor block
3. Front return spring
4. Adjusting nut
5. Guide spring with cup and pin
6. Cylinder
7. Rear return spring

8. Back plate
9. Brake shoe with lining

REAR
1. Cylinder
2. Brake shoe with lining
3. Upper return spring
4. Spring with cup and pin

5. Lower return spring
6. Adjusting screw
7. Back plate
8. Connecting link
9. Lever
10. Brake cable
11. Adjusting nut
12. Anchor block

Front and rear drum brakes—Type 1

BRAKE DRUM INSPECTION

If the brake drums are scored or cracked, they must be replaced or machined. If the vehicle pulls to one side or exhibits a pulsating braking action, the drum is probably out of round and should be checked at a machine shop. The drum may have a smooth even surface and still be out of round. The drum should be free of surface cracks and dark spots.

The notched adjusters must be positioned as shown

BRAKE LINING REMOVAL AND INSTALLATION

Type 1

1. Jack up the car and remove the wheel and tire.
2. Remove the brake drum.
3. Remove the small disc and spring which secure each shoe to the backing plate.
4. Remove the two long springs between the two shoes.
5. Remove the shoes from the backing plate.
6. If new shoes are being installed, remove the adjusters in the end of each wheel cylinder and screw the star wheel up against the head of the adjuster. When inserting the adjusters back in the wheel cylinders, notice that the slot in the adjuster is angled and must be positioned as illustrated.
7. Position new shoes on the backing plate. The slot in the shoes and the stronger return spring must be at the wheel cylinder end.
8. Install the disc and spring which secure the shoe to the backing plate.
9. Install the brake drum and adjust the wheel bearing.

Type 2

1. Remove the brake drum.
2. Pry the rear brake shoe out of the adjuster, as illustrated, and detach the return springs. Remove the forward shoe.
3. If new shoes are to be installed, screw the star wheel up against the head of the adjuster.
4. Install the rear brake shoe.
5. Attach the return spring to the front brake shoe and then to the rear shoe.
6. Position the front brake shoe in the slot of the adjusting screw and lever it into position in the same manner as it was removed. Make sure that the return springs do not touch the brake line between the upper and lower wheel cylinders.
7. Install the brake-drum and adjust the wheel bearings.

WHEEL CYLINDER REMOVAL AND INSTALLATION

1. Remove the brake shoes.
2. On Type 1, disconnect the brake line from the rear of the cylinder. On Type 2, disconnect the brake line from the rear of the cylinder and transfer line from the front of the cylinder.
3. Remove the bolts which secure the cylinder to the backing plate and remove the cylinder from the vehicle.
4. Reverse the above steps to install and bleed the brakes.

WHEEL CYLINDER OVERHAUL

1. Remove the wheel cylinder.
2. Remove the brake adjusters and remove the rubber boot from each end.
NOTE: *The Type 2 cylinder has only one rubber boot, piston, and cup. The rebuilding procedures are the same.*
3. On Type 1, push in on one of the pistons to force out the opposite piston and rubber cup. On Type 2, remove the piston and cup by blowing compressed air into the brake hose hole.
4. Wash the pistons and cylinder in clean brake fluid or alcohol.
5. Inspect the cylinder bore for signs of pitting, scoring, and excessive wear. If it is badly scored or pitted, the whole cylinder should be replaced. It is possible to remove the glaze and light scores with crocus cloth or a brake cylinder hone. Before rebuilding the cylinder, make sure the bleeder screw is free. If the bleeder is rusted shut or broken off, replace the entire cylinder.
6. Dip the new pistons and rubber cups in brake fluid. Place the spring in the bore and insert the rubber cups into the bore against the spring. The concave side of the rubber cup should face inward.
7. Place the pistons in the bore and install the rubber boot.
8. Install the cylinder and bleed the brakes after the shoes and drum are in place. Make sure that the brakes are adjusted.

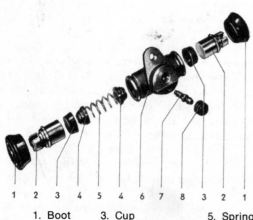

1. Boot	3. Cup	5. Spring
2. Piston	4. Cup expander	6. Housing
7. Bleeder valve	9. Adjusting nut	
8. Dust cap	10. Adjusting screw	

Front wheel cylinders disassembled—Type 1 (left) and Type 2 (right)

REAR DRUM BRAKES

BRAKE DRUM REMOVAL AND INSTALLATION

Type 1, 2, 3

1. With the wheels still on the ground, remove the cotter pin from the slotted nut on the rear axle and remove the nut from the axle. This isn't as easy as it sounds. You'll need a very long breaker bar or metal pipe for this operation.

CAUTION: *Make sure the emergency brake is now released.*

2. Jack up the car and remove the wheel and tire.

3. The brake drum is splined to the rear axle and the drum should slip off the axle. However, the drum sometimes rusts on the splines and it is necessary to remove the drum using a puller.

4. Before installing the drum, lubricate the splines. Install the drum on the axle and tighten the nut on the axle to 217 ft. lbs. Line up a slot in the nut with a hole in the axle and insert a cotter pin. Never loosen the nut to align the slot and hole.

Removing rear drum with puller—Types 1, 2 and 3

Type 4

The drum is held in place by the wheel lugs. Jack up the car and remove the wheel and tire. After the wheel is removed, there are two small screws that secure the drum to the hub and they must be removed before the drum will slip off the hub.

Tightening rear axle nut (36 mm or 1$^{7}/_{16}$ in.) to 217 ft. lbs. using 0–150 ft. lb. torque wrench and half-length adaptor (a 3 or 4 foot metal pipe will do nicely)

INSPECTION

Inspection is the same as given in the "Front Drum Brake" section.

BRAKE LINING REMOVAL AND INSTALLATION

1. Remove the brake drum.
2. Remove both shoe retaining springs.
3. Disconnect the lower return spring.
4. Disconnect the hand brake cable from the lever attached to the rear shoe.
5. Remove the upper return spring and clip.
6. Remove the brake shoes and connecting link.
7. Remove the emergency brake lever from the rear shoe.
8. Lubricate the adjusting screws and the star wheel against the head of the adjusting screw.
9. Reverse Steps 1–7 to install the shoes.
10. Adjust the brakes.

WHEEL CYLINDER REMOVAL AND INSTALLATION

Remove the brake drum and brake shoes. Disconnect the brake line from the cylinder and remove the bolts which secure the cylinder to the backing plate. Remove the cylinder from the vehicle.

OVERHAUL

Overhaul is the same as given in the "Front Drum Brake" section.

PARKING BRAKE

CABLE ADJUSTMENT

Brake cable adjustment is performed at the handbrake lever in the passenger compart-

Parking brake lever attachment

ment on all except Type 2. There is a cable for each rear wheel and there are two adjusting nuts at the lever. On Type 2, adjust from below the vehicle.

To adjust the cable, loosen the locknut. Jack up the rear wheel to be adjusted so that it can be hand spun. Turn the adjusting nut until a very slight drag is felt as the wheel is spun. Then back off on the adjusting nut until the lever can be pulled up three notches on all but Type 2, six notches on Type 2.

CAUTION: *Never pull up on the handbrake lever with the cables disconnected.*

CABLE REMOVAL AND INSTALLATION

1. Disconnect the cables at the handbrake lever by removing the two nuts which secure

1. Pin   4. Shoe
2. Spring washer 5. Clip
3. Lever

Details of parking brake lever attachment to rear shoe

the cables to the lever. Pull the cables rearward to remove that end from the lever bracket.

2. Remove the brake drums and detach the cable end from the lever attached to the rear brake shoe.

3. Remove the brake cable bracket from the backing plate and remove the cable from the vehicle.

4. Reverse the above steps to install and adjust the cable.

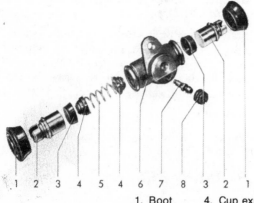

1. Boot   4. Cup expander   7. Bleeder valve
2. Piston   5. Spring   8. Dust cap
3. Cup   6. Housing   9. Circlip

Exploded view of rear wheel cylinder assemblies—Types 1, 3 and 4 (left) and Type 2 (right)

Brake Specifications
All measurements given are (in.) unless noted

Year	Model	Lug Nut Torque (ft. lb.)	Master Cyl- inder Bore	Brake Disc		Brake Drum			Minimum Lining Thickness	
				Min- imum Thick- ness	Maxi- mum Run- Out-	Dia- meter	Max Machine O/S	Max Wear Limit	Front	Rear
1970–77	Type 1 (Beetle)	87–94	0.750	—	—	9.059	9.10	9.114	0.100	0.100
1970–80	Type 1 (Super Beetle)	87–94	0.750	—	—	9.768 (fr) 9.059 (rr)	9.80 (fr) 9.10 (rr)	9.823 (fr) 9.114 (rr)	0.100 0.079	0.100 0.100
1970–74	Karmann Ghia	87–94	0.938	0.335	0.0008	9.059	9.10	9.114		
1970–81	Type 2 (Bus)	87–94	0.938	0.472 ①	0.0008	9.920	9.97	9.98	0.079	0.100
1970–73	Type 3	87–94	0.750	0.393	0.0008	9.768	9.80	9.82	0.079	0.100
1970–74	Type 4	87–94	0.750	0.393	0.0008	9.768	9.80	9.82	0.079	0.100

NOTE: *Minimum lining thickness is as recommended by the manufacturer. Due to variations in state inspection regulations, the minimum allowable thickness may be different than recommended by the manufacturer.*
① 0.433 in.-Vanagon
(fr)—Front
(rr)—rear
—Not Applicable

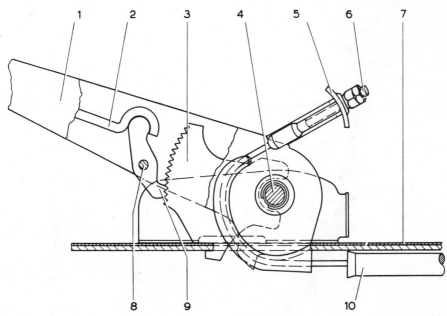

1. Hand brake lever
2. Pawl rod
3. Ratchet segment
4. Lever pin
5. Cable compensator
6. Brake cable
7. Frame
8. Pawl pin
9. Pawl
10. Cable guide tube

Parking brake hand lever and cable end assembly—Type 1 shown

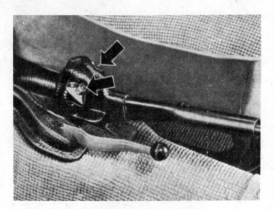

Parking brake cable adjusting nuts

Adjust both brake cables an equal amount—Type 2 parking brake adjustment

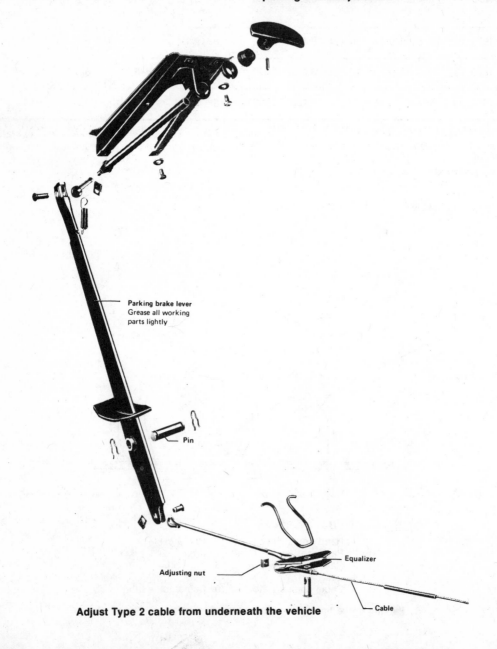

Parking brake lever
Grease all working
parts lightly

Pin

Equalizer

Adjusting nut

Cable

Adjust Type 2 cable from underneath the vehicle

Body

You can repair most minor auto body damage yourself. Minor damage usually falls into one of several categories: (1) small scratches and dings in the paint that can be repaired without the use of body filler, (2) deep scratches and dents that require body filler, but do not require pulling, or hammering metal back into shape and (3) rust-out repairs. The repair sequences illustrated in this chapter are typical of these types of repairs. If you want to get involved in more complicated repairs including pulling or hammering sheet metal back into shape, you will probably need more detailed instructions. Chilton's *Minor Auto Body Repair, 2nd Edition* is a comprehensive guide to repairing auto body damage yourself.

TOOLS AND SUPPLIES

The list of tools and equipment you may need to fix minor body damage ranges from very basic hand tools to a wide assortment of specialized body tools. Most minor scratches, dings and rust holes can be fixed using an electric drill, wire wheel or grinder attachment, half-round plastic file, sanding block, various grades of sandpaper (#36, which is coarse through #600, which is fine) in both wet and dry types, auto body plastic,

primer, touch-up paint, spreaders, newspaper and masking tape.

Most manufacturers of auto body repair products began supplying materials to professionals. Their knowledge of the best, most-used products has been translated into body repair kits for the do-it-yourselfer. Kits are available from a number of manufacturers and contain the necessary materials in the required amounts for the repair identified on the package.

Kits are available for a wide variety of uses, including:

- Rusted out metal
- All purpose kit for dents and holes
- Dents and deep scratches
- Fiberglass repair kit
- Epoxy kit for restyling.

Kits offer the advantage of buying what you need for the job. There is little waste and little chance of materials going bad from not being used. The same manufacturers also merchandise all of the individual products used—spreaders, dent pullers, fiberglass cloth, polyester resin, cream hardener, body filler, body files, sandpaper, sanding discs and holders, primer, spray paint, etc.

CAUTION: *Most of the products you will be using contain harmful chemicals, so be extremely careful. Always read the complete label before opening the containers. When* *you put them away for future use, be sure they are out of children's reach!*

Most auto body repair kits contain all the materials you need to do the job right in the kit. So, if you have a small rust spot or dent you want to fix, check the contents of the kit before you run out and buy any additional tools.

ALIGNING BODY PANELS

Doors

There are several methods of adjusting doors. Your vehicle will probably use one of those illustrated.

Whenever a door is removed and is to be reinstalled, you should matchmark the position of the hinges on the door pillars. The holes of the hinges and/or the hinge attaching points are usually oversize to permit alignment of doors. The striker plate is also moveable, through oversize holes, permitting up-and-down, in-and-out and fore-and-aft movement. Fore-and-aft movement is made by adding or subtracting shims from behind the striker and pillar post. The striker should be adjusted so that the door closes fully and remains closed, yet enters the lock freely.

DOOR HINGES

Don't try to cover up poor door adjustment with a striker plate adjustment. The gap on each side of the door should be equal and uniform and there should be no metal-to-metal contact as the door is opened or closed.

1. Determine which hinge bolts must be loosened to move the door in the desired direction.

2. Loosen the hinge bolt(s) just enough to allow the door to be moved with a padded pry bar.

3. Move the door a small amount and check the fit, after tightening the bolts. Be sure that there is no bind or interference with adjacent panels.

4. Repeat this until the door is properly positioned, and tighten all the bolts securely.

Hood, Trunk or Tailgate

As with doors, the outline of hinges should be scribed before removal. The hood and trunk can be aligned by loosening the hinge bolts in their slotted mounting holes and moving the hood or trunk lid as necessary.

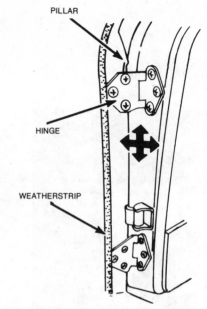

Door hinge adjustment

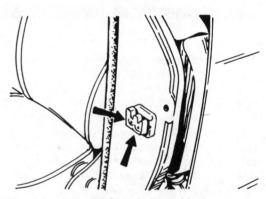

Move the door striker as indicated by arrows

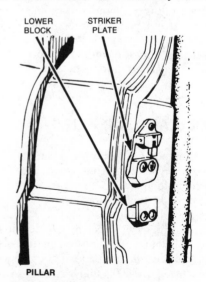

Striker plate and lower block

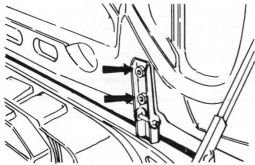

Loosen the hinge boots to permit fore-and-aft and horizontal adjustment

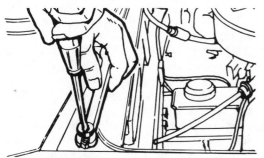

The hood is adjusted vertically by stop-screws at the front and/or rear

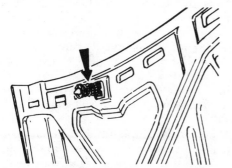

The hood pin can be adjusted for proper lock engagement

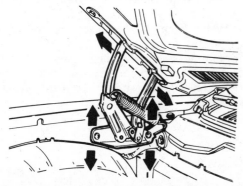

The height of the hood at the rear is adjusted by loosening the bolts that attach the hinge to the body and moving the hood up or down

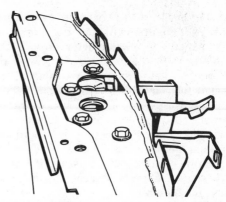

The base of the hood lock can also be repositioned slightly to give more positive lock engagement

The hood and trunk have adjustable catch locations to regulate lock engagement. Bumpers at the front and/or rear of the hood provide a vertical adjustment and the hood lockpin can be adjusted for proper engagement.

The tailgate on the station wagon can be adjusted by loosening the hinge bolts in their slotted mounting holes and moving the tailgate on its hinges. The latchplate and latch striker at the bottom of the tailgate opening can be adjusted to stop rattle. An adjustable bumper is located on each side.

RUST, UNDERCOATING, AND RUSTPROOFING

Rust

Rust is an electrochemical process. It works on ferrous metals (iron and steel) from the inside out due to exposure of unprotected surfaces to air and moisture. The possibility of rust exists practically nationwide—anywhere humidity, industrial pollution or chemical salts are present, rust can form. In coastal areas, the problem is high humidity and salt air; in snowy areas, the problem is chemical salt (de-icer) used to keep the roads clear, and in industrial areas, sulphur dioxide is present in the air from industrial pollution and is changed to sulphuric acid when it rains. The rusting process is accelerated by high temperatures, especially in snowy areas, when vehicles are driven over slushy roads and then left overnight in a heated garage.

Automotive styling also can be a contributor to rust formation. Spot welding of panels creates small pockets that trap moisture and form an environment for rust formation. Fortunately, auto manufacturers have been working hard to increase the corrosion protection of their products. Galvanized sheet metal enjoys much wider use, along with the increased use of plastic and various rust retardant coatings. Manufacturers are also designing out areas in the body where rust-forming moisture can collect.

To prevent rust, you must stop it before it gets started. On new vehicles, there are two ways to accomplish this.

First, the car or truck should be treated with a commercial rustproofing compound. There are many different brands of franchised rustproofers, but most processes involve spraying a waxy "self-healing" compound under the chassis, inside rocker panels, inside doors and fender liners and similar places where rust is likely to form. Prices for a quality rustproofing job range from $100–$250, depending on the area, the brand name and the size of the vehicle.

Ideally, the vehicle should be rustproofed as soon as possible following the purchase. The surfaces of the car or truck have begun to oxidize and deteriorate during shipping. In addition, the car may have sat on a dealer's lot or on a lot at the factory, and once the rust has progressed past the stage of light, powdery surface oxidation rustproofing is not likely to be worthwhile. Professional rustproofers feel that once rust has formed, rustproofing will simply seal in moisture already present. Most franchised rustproofing operations offer a 3–5 year warranty against rust-through, but will not support that warranty if the rustproofing is not applied within three months of the date of manufacture.

Undercoating should not be mistaken for rustproofing. Undercoating is a black, tar-like substance that is applied to the underside of a vehicle. Its basic function is to deaden noises that are transmitted from under the car. It simply cannot get into the crevices and seams where moisture tends to collect. In fact, it may clog up drainage holes and ventilation passages. Some undercoatings also tend to crack or peel with age and only create more moisture and corrosion attracting pockets.

The second thing you should do immediately after purchasing the car is apply a paint sealant. A sealant is a petroleum based product marketed under a wide variety of brand names. It has the same protective properties as a good wax, but bonds to the paint with a chemically inert layer that seals it from the air. If air can't get at the surface, oxidation cannot start.

The paint sealant kit consists of a base coat and a conditioning coat that should be applied every 6–8 months, depending on the manufacturer. The base coat must be applied before waxing, or the wax must first be removed.

Third, keep a garden hose handy for your car in winter. Use it a few times on nice days during the winter for underneath areas, and it will pay big dividends when spring arrives. Spraying under the fenders and other areas which even car washes don't reach will help remove road salt, dirt and other build-ups which help breed rust. Adjust the nozzle to a high-force spray. An old brush will help break up residue, permitting it to be washed away more easily.

It's a somewhat messy job, but worth it in the long run because rust often starts in those hidden areas.

At the same time, wash grime off the door sills and, more importantly, the under portions of the doors, plus the tailgate if you have a station wagon or truck. Applying a coat of wax to those areas at least once before and once during winter will help fend off rust.

When applying the wax to the under parts of the doors, you will note small drain holes. These holes often are plugged with undercoating or dirt. Make sure they are cleaned out to prevent water build-up inside the doors. A small punch or penknife will do the job.

Water from the high-pressure sprays in car washes sometimes can get into the housings for parking and taillights, so take a close look. If they contain water merely loosen the retaining screws and the water should run out.

Repairing Scratches and Small Dents

Step 1. This dent (arrow) is typical of a deep scratch or minor dent. If deep enough, the dent or scratch can be pulled out or hammered out from behind. In this case no straightening is necessary

Step 2. Using an 80-grit grinding disc on an electric drill grind the paint from the surrounding area down to bare metal. This will provide a rough surface for the body filler to grab

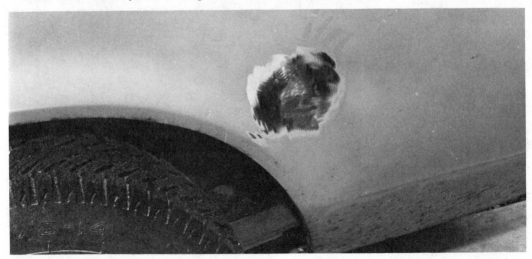

Step 3. The area should look like this when you're finished grinding

Step 4. Mix the body filler and cream hardener according to the directions

Step 5. Spread the body filler evenly over the entire area. Be sure to cover the area completely

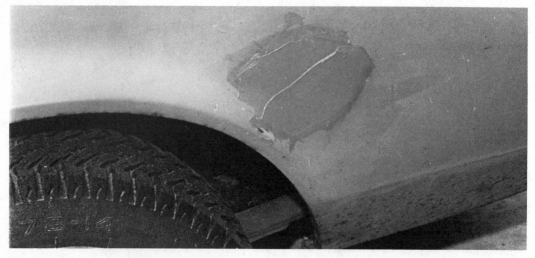

Step 6. Let the body filler dry until the surface can just be scratched with your fingernail

Step 7. Knock the high spots from the body filler with a body file

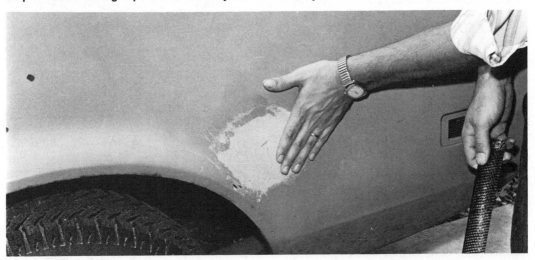

Step 8. Check frequently with the palm of your hand for high and low spots. If you wind up with low spots, you may have to apply another layer of filler

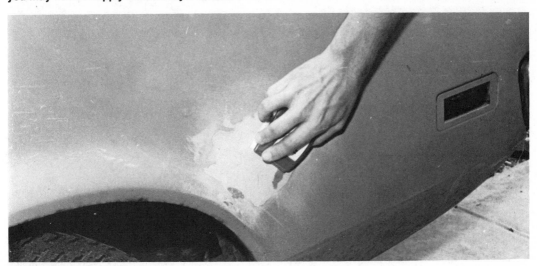

Step 9. Block sand the entire area with 320 grit paper

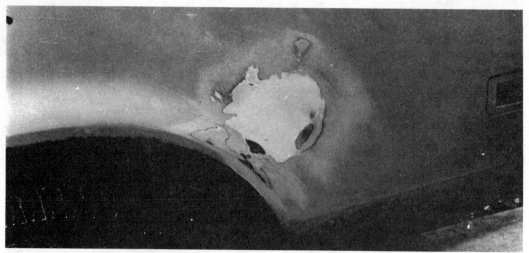

Step 10. When you're finished, the repair should look like this. Note the sand marks extending 2—3 inches out from the repaired area

Step 11. Prime the entire area with automotive primer

Step 12. The finished repair ready for the final paint coat. Note that the primer has covered the sanding marks (see Step 10). A repair of this size should be able to be spotpainted with good results

REPAIRING RUST HOLES

One thing you have to remember about rust: even if you grind away all the rusted metal in a panel, and repair the area with any of the kits available, *eventually* the rust will return. There are two reasons for this. One, rust is a chemical reaction that causes pressure under the repair from the inside out. That's how the blisters form. Two, the back side of the panel (and the repair) is wide open to moisture, and unpainted body filler acts like a sponge. That's why the best solution to rust problems is to remove the rusted panel and install a new one or have the rusted area cut out and a new piece of sheet metal welded in its place. The trouble with welding is the expense; sometimes it will cost more than the car or truck is worth.

One of the better solutions to do-it-yourself rust repair is the process using a fiberglass cloth repair kit (shown here). This will give a strong repair that resists cracking and moisture and is relatively easy to use. It can be used on large or small holes and also can be applied over contoured surfaces.

Step 1. Rust areas such as this are common and are easily fixed

Step 2. Grind away all traces of rust with a 24-grit grinding disc. Be sure to grind back 3—4 inches from the edge of the hole down to bare metal and be sure all traces of rust are removed

Step 3. Be sure all rust is removed from the edges of the metal. The edges must be ground back to un-rusted metal

Step 4. If you are going to use release film, cut a piece about 2″ larger than the area you have sanded. Place the film over the repair and mark the sanded area on the film. Avoid any unnecessary wrinkling of the film

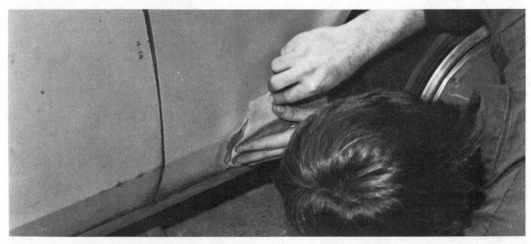

Step 5. Cut 2 pieces of fiberglass matte. One piece should be about 1″ smaller than the sanded area and the second piece should be 1″ smaller than the first. Use sharp scissors to avoid loose ends

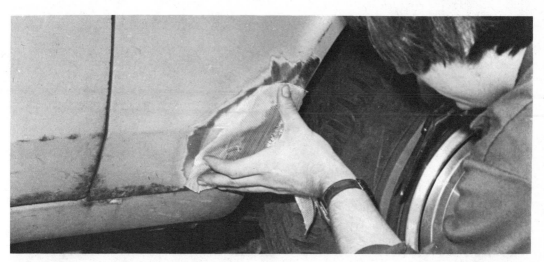

Step 6. Check the dimensions of the release film and cloth by holding them up to the repair area

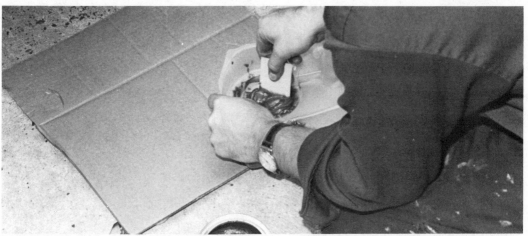

Step 7. Mix enough repair jelly and cream hardener in the mixing tray to saturate the fiberglass material or fill the repair area. Follow the directions on the container

Step 8. Lay the release sheet on a flat surface and spread an even layer of filler, large enough to cover the repair. Lay the smaller piece of fiberglass cloth in the center of the sheet and spread another layer of repair jelly over the fiberglass cloth. Repeat the operation for the larger piece of cloth. If the fiberglass cloth is not used, spread the repair jelly on the release film, concentrated in the middle of the repair

Step 9. Place the repair material over the repair area, with the release film facing outward

Step 10. Use a spreader and work from the center outward to smooth the material, following the body contours. Be sure to remove all air bubbles

Step 11. Wait until the repair has dried tack-free and peel off the release sheet. The ideal working temperature is 65—90° F. Cooler or warmer temperatures or high humidity may require additional curing time

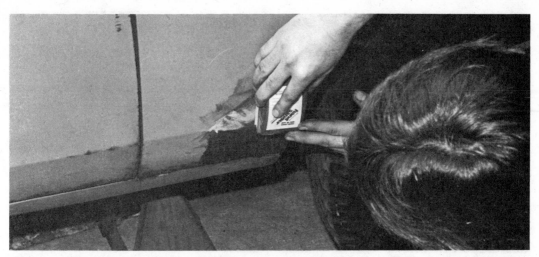

Step 12. Sand and feather-edge the entire area. The initial sanding can be done with a sanding disc on an electric drill if care is used. Finish the sanding with a block sander

Step 13. When the area is sanded smooth, mix some topcoat and hardener and apply it directly with a spreader. This will give a smooth finish and prevent the glass matte from showing through the paint

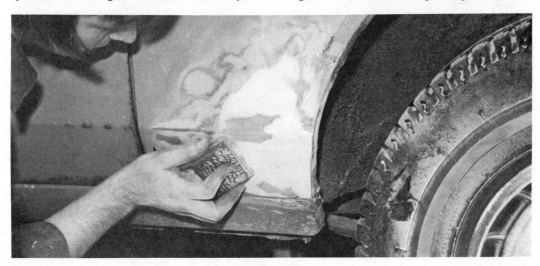

Step 14. Block sand the topcoat with finishing sandpaper

Step 15. To finish this repair, grind out the surface rust along the top edge of the rocker panel

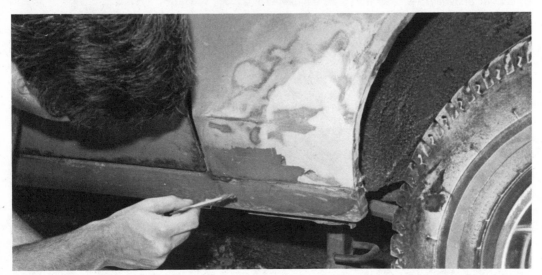

Step 16. Mix some more repair jelly and cream hardener and apply it directly over the surface

Step 17. When it dries tack-free, block sand the surface smooth

Step 18. If necessary, mask off adjacent panels and spray the entire repair with primer. You are now ready for a color coat

AUTO BODY CARE

There are hundreds—maybe thousands—of products on the market, all designed to protect or aid your car's finish in some manner. There are as many different products as there are ways to use them, but they all have one thing in common—the surface must be clean.

Washing

The primary ingredient for washing your car is water, preferably "soft" water. In many areas of the country, the local water supply is "hard" containing many minerals. The little rings or film that is left on your car's surface after it has dried is the result of "hard" water.

Since you usually can't change the local water supply, the next best thing is to dry the surface before it has a chance to dry itself.

Into the water you usually add soap. Don't use detergents or common, coarse soaps. Your car's paint never truly dries out, but is always evaporating residual oils into the air. Harsh detergents will remove these oils, causing the paint to dry faster than normal. Instead use warm water and a non-detergent soap made especially for waxed surfaces or a liquid soap made for waxed surfaces or a liquid soap made for washing dishes by hand.

Other products that can be used on painted surfaces include baking soda or plain soda water for stubborn dirt.

Wash the car completely, starting at the top, and rinse it completely clean. Abrasive grit should be loaded off under water pressure; scrubbing grit off will scratch the finish. The best washing tool is a sponge, cleaning mitt or soft towel. Whichever you choose, replace it often as each tends to absorb grease and dirt.

Other ways to get a better wash include:

• Don't wash your car in the sun or when the finish is hot.

• Use water pressure to remove caked-on dirt.

• Remove tree-sap and bird effluence immediately. Such substances will eat through wax, polish and paint.

One of the best implements to dry your car is a turkish towel or an old, soft bath towel. Anything with a deep nap will hold any dirt in suspension and not grind it into the paint.

Harder cloths will only grind the grit into the paint making more scratches. Always start drying at the top, followed by the hood and trunk and sides. You'll find there's always more dirt near the rocker panels and wheelwells which will wind up on the rest of the car if you dry these areas first.

Cleaners, Waxes and Polishes

Before going any farther you should know the function of various products.

Cleaners—remove the top layer of dead pigment or paint.

Rubbing or polishing compounds—used to remove stubborn dirt, get rid of minor scratches, smooth away imperfections and partially restore badly weathered paint.

Polishes—contain no abrasives or waxes; they shine the paint by adding oils to the paint.

Waxes—are a protective coating for the polish.

CLEANERS AND COMPOUNDS

Before you apply any wax, you'll have to remove oxidation, road film and other types of pollutants that washing alone will not remove.

The paint on your car never dries completely. There are always residual oils evaporating from the paint into the air. When enough oils are present in the paint, it has a healthy shine (gloss). When too many oils evaporate the paint takes on a whitish cast known as oxidation. The idea of polishing and waxing is to keep enough oil present in the painted surface to prevent oxidation; but when it occurs, the only recourse is to remove the top layer of "dead" paint, exposing the healthy paint underneath.

Products to remove oxidation and road film are sold under a variety of generic names—polishes, cleaner, rubbing compound, cleaner/polish, polish/cleaner, self-polishing wax, pre-wax cleaner, finish restorer and many more. Regardless of name there are two types of cleaners—abrasive cleaners (sometimes called polishing or rubbing compounds) that remove oxidation by grinding away the top layer of "dead" paint, or chemical cleaners that dissolve the "dead" pigment, allowing it to be wiped away.

Abrasive cleaners, by their nature, leave thousands of minute scratches in the finish, which must be polished out later. These should only be used in extreme cases, but are usually the only thing to use on badly oxidized paint finishes. Chemical cleaners are much milder but are not strong enough for severe cases of oxidation or weathered paint.

The most popular cleaners are liquid or paste abrasive polishing and rubbing compounds. Polishing compounds have a finer abrasive grit for medium duty work. Rubbing compounds are a coarser abrasive and for heavy duty work. Unless you are familiar with how to use compounds, be very careful. Excessive rubbing with any type of compound or cleaner can grind right through the paint to primer or bare metal. Follow the directions on the container—depending on type, the cleaner may or may not be OK for your paint. For example, some cleaners are not formulated for acrylic lacquer finishes.

When a small area needs compounding or heavy polishing, it's best to do the job by hand. Some people prefer a powered buffer for large areas. Avoid cutting through the paint along styling edges on the body. Small, hand operations where the compound is applied and rubbed using cloth folded into a thick ball allow you to work in straight lines along such edges.

To avoid cutting through on the edges when using a power buffer, try masking tape. Just cover the edge with tape while using power. Then finish the job by hand with the tape removed. Even then work carefully. The paint tends to be a lot thinner along the sharp ridges stamped into the panels.

Whether compounding by machine or by hand, only work on a small area and apply the compound sparingly. If the materials are spread too thin, or allowed to sit too long, they dry out. Once dry they lose the ability to deliver a smooth, clean finish. Also, dried out polish tends to cause the buffer to stick in one spot. This in turn can burn or cut through the finish.

WAXES AND POLISHES

Your car's finish can be protected in a number of ways. A cleaner/wax or polish/cleaner followed by wax or variations of each all provide good results. The two-step approach (polish followed by wax) is probably slightly better but consumes more time and effort. Properly fed with oils, your paint should never need cleaning, but despite the best polishing job, it won't last unless it's protected with wax. Without wax, polish must be renewed at least once a month to prevent oxidation. Years ago (some still swear by it today), the best wax was made from the Brazilian palm, the Carnuba, favored for its vegetable base and high melting point. However, modern synthetic waxes are harder, which means they protect against moisture better, and chemically inert silicone is used for a long lasting protection. The only problem with silicone wax is that it penetrates all layers of paint. To repaint or touch up a panel or car protected by silicone wax, you have to completely strip the finish to avoid "fish-eyes."

Under normal conditions, silicone waxes will last 4–6 months, but you have to be careful of wax build-up from too much waxing. Too thick a coat of wax is just as bad as no wax at all; it stops the paint from breathing.

Combination cleaners/waxes have become popular lately because they remove the old layer of wax plus light oxidation, while putting on a fresh coat of wax at the same time. Some cleaners/waxes contain abrasive cleaners which require caution, although many cleaner/waxes use a chemical cleaner.

Applying Wax or Polish

You may view polishing and waxing your car as a pleasant way to spend an afternoon, or as a boring chore, but it has to be done to keep the paint on your car. Caring for the paint doesn't require special tools, but you should follow a few rules.

1. Use a good quality wax.
2. Before applying any wax or polish, be sure the surface is completely clean. Just because the car looks clean, doesn't mean it's ready for polish or wax.
3. If the finish on your car is weathered, dull, or oxidized, it will probably have to be compounded to remove the old or oxidized paint. If the paint is simply dulled from lack of care, one of the non-abrasive cleaners known as polishing compounds will do the trick. If the paint is severely scratched or really dull, you'll probably have to use a rubbing compound to prepare the finish for waxing. If you're not sure which one to use, use the polishing compound, since you can easily ruin the finish by using too strong a compound.
4. Don't apply wax, polish or compound in direct sunlight, even if the directions on the can say you can. Most waxes will not cure properly in bright sunlight and you'll probably end up with a blotchy looking finish.
5. Don't rub the wax off too soon. The result will be a wet, dull looking finish. Let the wax dry thoroughly before buffing it off.
6. A constant debate among car enthusiasts is how wax should be applied. Some maintain pastes or liquids should be applied in a circular motion, but body shop experts have long thought that this approach results in barely detectable circular abrasions, especially on cars that are waxed frequently. They

advise rubbing in straight lines, especially if any kind of cleaner is involved.
7. If an applicator is not supplied with the wax, use a piece of soft cheesecloth or very soft lint-free material. The same applies to buffing the surface.

SPECIAL SURFACES

One-step combination cleaner and wax formulas shouldn't be used on many of the special surfaces which abound on cars. The one-step materials contain abrasives to achieve a clean surface under the wax top coat. The abrasives are so mild that you could clean a car every week for a couple of years without fear of rubbing through the paint. But this same level of abrasiveness might, through repeated use, damage decals used for special trim effects. This includes wide stripes, wood-grain trim and other appliques.

Painted plastics must be cleaned with care. If a cleaner is too aggressive it will cut through the paint and expose the primer. If bright trim such as polished aluminum or chrome is painted, cleaning must be performed with even greater care. If rubbing compound is being used, it will cut faster than polish.

Abrasive cleaners will dull an acrylic finish. The best way to clean these newer finishes is with a non-abrasive liquid polish. Only dirt and oxidation, not paint, will be removed.

Taking a few minutes to read the instructions on the can of polish or wax will help prevent making serious mistakes. Not all preparations will work on all surfaces. And some are intended for power application while others will only work when applied by hand.

Don't get the idea that just pouring on some polish and then hitting it with a buffer will suffice. Power equipment speeds the operation. But it also adds a measure of risk. It's very easy to damage the finish if you use the wrong methods or materials.

Caring for Chrome

Read the label on the container. Many products are formulated specifically for chrome, but others contain abrasives that will scratch the chrome finish. If it isn't recommended for chrome, don't use it.

Never use steel wool or kitchen soap pads to clean chrome. Be careful not to get chrome cleaner on paint or interior vinyl surfaces. If you do, get it off immediately.

Troubleshooting

This section is designed to aid in the quick, accurate diagnosis of automotive problems. While automotive repairs can be made by many people, accurate troubleshooting is a rare skill for the amateur and professional alike.

In its simplest state, troubleshooting is an exercise in logic. It is essential to realize that an automobile is really composed of a series of systems. Some of these systems are interrelated; others are not. Automobiles operate within a framework of logical rules and physical laws, and the key to troubleshooting is a good understanding of all the automotive systems.

This section breaks the car or truck down into its component systems, allowing the problem to be isolated. The charts and diagnostic road maps list the most common problems and the most probable causes of trouble. Obviously it would be impossible to list every possible problem that could happen along with every possible cause, but it will locate MOST problems and eliminate a lot of unnecessary guesswork. The systematic format will locate problems within a given system, but, because many automotive systems are interrelated, the solution to your particular problem may be found in a number of systems on the car or truck.

USING THE TROUBLESHOOTING CHARTS

This book contains all of the specific information that the average do-it-yourself mechanic needs to repair and maintain his or her car or truck. The troubleshooting charts are designed to be used in conjunction with the specific procedures and information in the text. For instance, troubleshooting a point-type ignition system is fairly standard for all models, but you may be directed to the text to find procedures for troubleshooting an individual type of electronic ignition. You will also have to refer to the specification charts throughout the book for specifications applicable to your car or truck.

TOOLS AND EQUIPMENT

The tools illustrated in Chapter 1 (plus two more diagnostic pieces) will be adequate to troubleshoot most problems. The two other tools needed are a voltmeter and an ohmmeter. These can be purchased separately or in combination, known as a VOM meter.

In the event that other tools are required, they will be noted in the procedures.

Troubleshooting Engine Problems

See Chapters 2, 3, 4 for more information and service procedures.

Index to Systems

System	To Test	Group
Battery	Engine need not be running	1
Starting system	Engine need not be running	2
Primary electrical system	Engine need not be running	3
Secondary electrical system	Engine need not be running	4
Fuel system	Engine need not be running	5
Engine compression	Engine need not be running	6
Engine vacuum	Engine must be running	7
Secondary electrical system	Engine must be running	8
Valve train	Engine must be running	9
Exhaust system	Engine must be running	10
Cooling system	Engine must be running	11
Engine lubrication	Engine must be running	12

Index to Problems

Problem: Symptom	Begin at Specific Diagnosis, Number ____
Engine Won't Start:	
Starter doesn't turn	1.1, 2.1
Starter turns, engine doesn't	2.1
Starter turns engine very slowly	1.1, 2.4
Starter turns engine normally	3.1, 4.1
Starter turns engine very quickly	6.1
Engine fires intermittently	4.1
Engine fires consistently	5.1, 6.1
Engine Runs Poorly:	
Hard starting	3.1, 4.1, 5.1, 8.1
Rough idle	4.1, 5.1, 8.1
Stalling	3.1, 4.1, 5.1, 8.1
Engine dies at high speeds	4.1, 5.1
Hesitation (on acceleration from standing stop)	5.1, 8.1
Poor pickup	4.1, 5.1, 8.1
Lack of power	3.1, 4.1, 5.1, 8.1
Backfire through the carburetor	4.1, 8.1, 9.1
Backfire through the exhaust	4.1, 8.1, 9.1
Blue exhaust gases	6.1, 7.1
Black exhaust gases	5.1
Running on (after the ignition is shut off)	3.1, 8.1
Susceptible to moisture	4.1
Engine misfires under load	4.1, 7.1, 8.4, 9.1
Engine misfires at speed	4.1, 8.4
Engine misfires at idle	3.1, 4.1, 5.1, 7.1, 8.4

Sample Section

Test and Procedure	Results and Indications	Proceed to
4.1—Check for spark: Hold each spark plug wire approximately ¼" from ground with gloves or a heavy, dry rag. Crank the engine and observe the spark.	→ If no spark is evident:	→4.2
	→ If spark is good in some cases:	→4.3
	→ If spark is good in all cases:	→4.6

Specific Diagnosis

This section is arranged so that following each test, instructions are given to proceed to another, until a problem is diagnosed.

Section 1—Battery

Test and Procedure	Results and Indications	Proceed to
1.1—Inspect the battery visually for case condition (corrosion, cracks) and water level.	If case is cracked, replace battery:	**1.4**
	If the case is intact, remove corrosion with a solution of baking soda and water (**CAUTION**: *do not get the solution into the battery*), and fill with water:	**1.2**

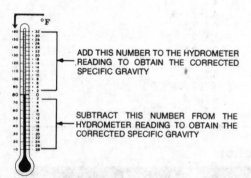

DIRT ON TOP OF BATTERY

CORROSION

PLUGGED VENT

LOOSE CABLE OR POSTS

CRACKS

LOW WATER LEVEL

Inspect the battery case

1.2—Check the battery cable connections: Insert a screwdriver between the battery post and the cable clamp. Turn the headlights on high beam, and observe them as the screwdriver is gently twisted to ensure good metal to metal contact.	If the lights brighten, remove and clean the clamp and post; coat the post with petroleum jelly, install and tighten the clamp:	**1.4**
	If no improvement is noted:	**1.3**

TESTING BATTERY
CABLE CONNECTIONS
USING A SCREWDRIVER

1.3—Test the state of charge of the battery using an individual cell tester or hydrometer.	If indicated, charge the battery. **NOTE:** *If no obvious reason exists for the low state of charge (i.e., battery age, prolonged storage), proceed to:*	**1.4**

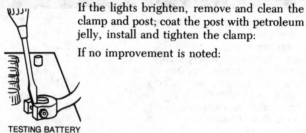

°F

ADD THIS NUMBER TO THE HYDROMETER READING TO OBTAIN THE CORRECTED SPECIFIC GRAVITY

SUBTRACT THIS NUMBER FROM THE HYDROMETER READING TO OBTAIN THE CORRECTED SPECIFIC GRAVITY

Specific Gravity (@ 80° F.)

Minimum	Battery Charge
1.260	100% Charged
1.230	75% Charged
1.200	50% Charged
1.170	25% Charged
1.140	Very Little Power Left
1.110	Completely Discharged

The effects of temperature on battery specific gravity (left) and amount of battery charge in relation to specific gravity (right)

1.4—Visually inspect battery cables for cracking, bad connection to ground, or bad connection to starter.	If necessary, tighten connections or replace the cables:	**2.1**

Section 2—Starting System
See Chapter 3 for service procedures

Test and Procedure	Results and Indications	Proceed to
Note: Tests in Group 2 are performed with coil high tension lead disconnected to prevent accidental starting.		
2.1—Test the starter motor and solenoid: Connect a jumper from the battery post of the solenoid (or relay) to the starter post of the solenoid (or relay).	If starter turns the engine normally:	2.2
	If the starter buzzes, or turns the engine very slowly:	2.4
	If no response, replace the solenoid (or relay).	3.1
	If the starter turns, but the engine doesn't, ensure that the flywheel ring gear is intact. If the gear is undamaged, replace the starter drive.	3.1
2.2—Determine whether ignition override switches are functioning properly (clutch start switch, neutral safety switch), by connecting a jumper across the switch(es), and turning the ignition switch to "start".	If starter operates, adjust or replace switch:	3.1
	If the starter doesn't operate:	2.3
2.3—Check the ignition switch "start" position: Connect a 12V test lamp or voltmeter between the starter post of the solenoid (or relay) and ground. Turn the ignition switch to the "start" position, and jiggle the key.	If the lamp doesn't light or the meter needle doesn't move when the switch is turned, check the ignition switch for loose connections, cracked insulation, or broken wires. Repair or replace as necessary:	3.1
	If the lamp flickers or needle moves when the key is jiggled, replace the ignition switch.	3.3

Checking the ignition switch "start" position

STARTER RELAY
(IF EQUIPPED)

Test and Procedure	Results and Indications	Proceed to
2.4—Remove and bench test the starter, according to specifications in the engine electrical section.	If the starter does not meet specifications, repair or replace as needed:	3.1
	If the starter is operating properly:	2.5
2.5—Determine whether the engine can turn freely: Remove the spark plugs, and check for water in the cylinders. Check for water on the dipstick, or oil in the radiator. Attempt to turn the engine using an 18″ flex drive and socket on the crankshaft pulley nut or bolt.	If the engine will turn freely only with the spark plugs out, and hydrostatic lock (water in the cylinders) is ruled out, check valve timing:	9.2
	If engine will not turn freely, and it is known that the clutch and transmission are free, the engine must be disassembled for further evaluation:	Chapter 3

Section 3—Primary Electrical System

Test and Procedure	Results and Indications	Proceed to
3.1—Check the ignition switch "on" position: Connect a jumper wire between the distributor side of the coil and ground, and a 12V test lamp between the switch side of the coil and ground. Remove the high tension lead from the coil. Turn the ignition switch on and jiggle the key.	If the lamp lights:	**3.2**
	If the lamp flickers when the key is jiggled, replace the ignition switch:	**3.3**
	If the lamp doesn't light, check for loose or open connections. If none are found, remove the ignition switch and check for continuity. If the switch is faulty, replace it:	**3.3**

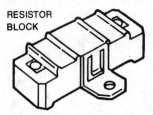

Checking the ignition switch "on" position

3.2—Check the ballast resistor or resistance wire for an open circuit, using an ohmmeter. See Chapter 3 for specific tests.	Replace the resistor or resistance wire if the resistance is zero. **NOTE:** *Some ignition systems have no ballast resistor.*	**3.3**

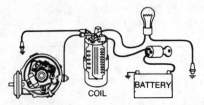

RESISTOR BLOCK

CALIBRATED RESISTANCE LEAD

Two types of resistors

3.3—On point-type ignition systems, visually inspect the breaker points for burning, pitting or excessive wear. Gray coloring of the point contact surfaces is normal. Rotate the crankshaft until the contact heel rests on a high point of the distributor cam and adjust the point gap to specifications. On electronic ignition models, remove the distributor cap and visually inspect the armature. Ensure that the armature pin is in place, and that the armature is on tight and rotates when the engine is cranked. Make sure there are no cracks, chips or rounded edges on the armature.	If the breaker points are intact, clean the contact surfaces with fine emery cloth, and adjust the point gap to specifications. If the points are worn, replace them. On electronic systems, replace any parts which appear defective. If condition persists:	**3.4**

Test and Procedure	Results and Indications	Proceed to
3.4—On point-type ignition systems, connect a dwell-meter between the distributor primary lead and ground. Crank the engine and observe the point dwell angle. On electronic ignition systems, conduct a stator (magnetic pickup assembly) test. See Chapter 3.	On point-type systems, adjust the dwell angle if necessary. **NOTE:** *Increasing the point gap decreases the dwell angle and vice-versa.*	**3.6**
	If the dwell meter shows little or no reading;	**3.5**
	On electronic ignition systems, if the stator is bad, replace the stator. If the stator is good, proceed to the other tests in Chapter 3.	

Dwell is a function of point gap

3.5—On the point-type ignition systems, check the condenser for short: connect an ohmeter across the condenser body and the pigtail lead.	If any reading other than infinite is noted, replace the condenser	**3.6**

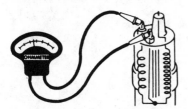

Checking the condenser for short

3.6—Test the coil primary resistance: On point-type ignition systems, connect an ohmmeter across the coil primary terminals, and read the resistance on the low scale. Note whether an external ballast resistor or resistance wire is used. On electronic ignition systems, test the coil primary resistance as in Chapter 3.	Point-type ignition coils utilizing ballast resistors or resistance wires should have approximately 1.0 ohms resistance. Coils with internal resistors should have approximately 4.0 ohms resistance. If values far from the above are noted, replace the coil.	**4.1**

Check the coil primary resistance

Section 4—Secondary Electrical System
See Chapters 2–3 for service procedures

Test and Procedure	Results and Indications	Proceed to
4.1—Check for spark: Hold each spark plug wire approximately ¼″ from ground with gloves or a heavy, dry rag. Crank the engine, and observe the spark.	If no spark is evident:	4.2
	If spark is good in some cylinders:	4.3
	If spark is good in all cylinders:	4.6

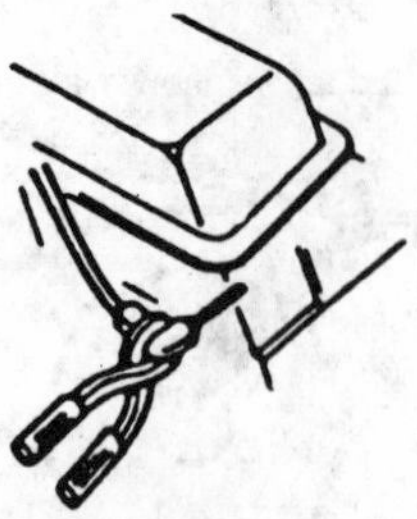

Check for spark at the plugs

Test and Procedure	Results and Indications	Proceed to
4.2—Check for spark at the coil high tension lead: Remove the coil high tension lead from the distributor and position it approximately ¼″ from ground. Crank the engine and observe spark. **CAUTION:** *This test should not be performed on engines equipped with electronic ignition.*	If the spark is good and consistent:	4.3
	If the spark is good but intermittent, test the primary electrical system starting at 3.3:	3.3
	If the spark is weak or non-existent, replace the coil high tension lead, clean and tighten all connections and retest. If no improvement is noted:	4.4
4.3—Visually inspect the distributor cap and rotor for burned or corroded contacts, cracks, carbon tracks, or moisture. Also check the fit of the rotor on the distributor shaft (where applicable).	If moisture is present, dry thoroughly, and retest per 4.1:	4.1
	If burned or excessively corroded contacts, cracks, or carbon tracks are noted, replace the defective part(s) and retest per 4.1:	4.1
	If the rotor and cap appear intact, or are only slightly corroded, clean the contacts thoroughly (including the cap towers and spark plug wire ends) and retest per 4.1:	
	If the spark is good in all cases:	4.6
	If the spark is poor in all cases:	4.5

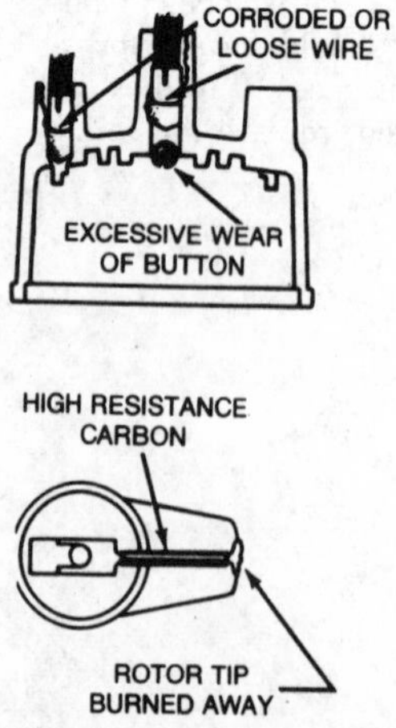

CORRODED OR LOOSE WIRE

EXCESSIVE WEAR OF BUTTON

HIGH RESISTANCE CARBON

ROTOR TIP BURNED AWAY

Inspect the distributor cap and rotor

Test and Procedure	Results and Indications	Proceed to
4.4—Check the coil secondary resistance: On point-type systems connect an ohmmeter across the distributor side of the coil and the coil tower. Read the resistance on the high scale of the ohmmeter. On electronic ignition systems, see Chapter 3 for specific tests.	The resistance of a satisfactory coil should be between 4,000 and 10,000 ohms. If resistance is considerably higher (i.e., 40,000 ohms) replace the coil and retest per 4.1. **NOTE:** *This does not apply to high performance coils.*	

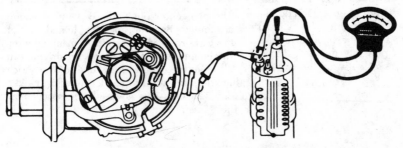

Testing the coil secondary resistance

4.5—Visually inspect the spark plug wires for cracking or brittleness. Ensure that no two wires are positioned so as to cause induction firing (adjacent and parallel). Remove each wire, one by one, and check resistance with an ohmmeter.	Replace any cracked or brittle wires. If any of the wires are defective, replace the entire set. Replace any wires with excessive resistance (over $8000\,\Omega$ per foot for suppression wire), and separate any wires that might cause induction firing.	**4.6**

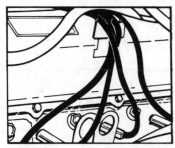
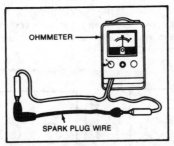
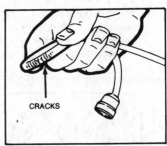

Misfiring can be the result of spark plug leads to adjacent, consecutively firing cylinders running parallel and too close together	**On point-type ignition systems, check the spark plug wires as shown. On electronic ignitions, do not remove the wire from the distributor cap terminal; instead, test through the cap**	**Spark plug wires can be checked visually by bending them in a loop over your finger. This will reveal any cracks, burned or broken insulation. Any wire with cracked insulation should be replaced**

4.6—Remove the spark plugs, noting the cylinders from which they were removed, and evaluate according to the color photos in the middle of this book.	See following.	**See following.**

Test and Procedure	Results and Indications	Proceed to
4.7—Examine the location of all the plugs.	The following diagrams illustrate some of the conditions that the location of plugs will reveal.	4.8

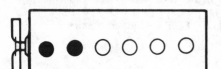

Two adjacent plugs are fouled in a 6-cylinder engine, 4-cylinder engine or either bank of a V-8. This is probably due to a blown head gasket between the two cylinders

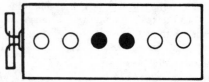

The two center plugs in a 6-cylinder engine are fouled. Raw fuel may be "boiled" out of the carburetor into the intake manifold after the engine is shut-off. Stop-start driving can also foul the center plugs, due to overly rich mixture. Proper float level, a new float needle and seat or use of an insulating spacer may help this problem

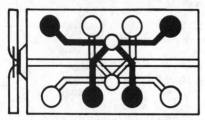

An unbalanced carburetor is indicated. Following the fuel flow on this particular design shows that the cylinders fed by the right-hand barrel are fouled from overly rich mixture, while the cylinders fed by the left-hand barrel are normal

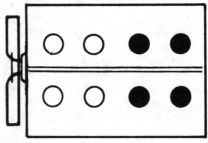

If the four rear plugs are overheated, a cooling system problem is suggested. A thorough cleaning of the cooling system may restore coolant circulation and cure the problem

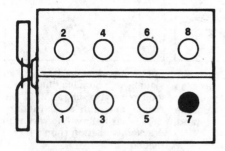

Finding one plug overheated may indicate an intake manifold leak near the affected cylinder. If the overheated plug is the second of two adjacent, consecutively firing plugs, it could be the result of ignition cross-firing. Separating the leads to these two plugs will eliminate cross-fire

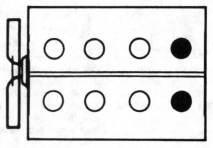

Occasionally, the two rear plugs in large, lightly used V-8's will become oil fouled. High oil consumption and smoky exhaust may also be noticed. It is probably due to plugged oil drain holes in the rear of the cylinder head, causing oil to be sucked in around the valve stems. This usually occurs in the rear cylinders first, because the engine slants that way

Test and Procedure	Results and Indications	Proceed to
4.8—Determine the static ignition timing. Using the crankshaft pulley timing marks as a guide, locate top dead center on the compression stroke of the number one cylinder.	The rotor should be pointing toward the No. 1 tower in the distributor cap, and, on electronic ignitions, the armature spoke for that cylinder should be lined up with the stator.	**4.8**
4.9—Check coil polarity: Connect a voltmeter negative lead to the coil high tension lead, and the positive lead to ground (**NOTE:** *Reverse the hook-up for positive ground systems*). Crank the engine momentarily. **Checking coil polarity**	If the voltmeter reads up-scale, the polarity is correct: If the voltmeter reads down-scale, reverse the coil polarity (switch the primary leads):	**5.1** **5.1**

Section 5—Fuel System
See Chapter 4 for service procedures

Test and Procedure	Results and Indications	Proceed to
5.1—Determine that the air filter is functioning efficiently: Hold paper elements up to a strong light, and attempt to see light through the filter.	Clean permanent air filters in solvent (or manufacturer's recommendation), and allow to dry. Replace paper elements through which light cannot be seen:	**5.2**
5.2—Determine whether a flooding condition exists: Flooding is identified by a strong gasoline odor, and excessive gasoline present in the throttle bore(s) of the carburetor.	If flooding is not evident: If flooding is evident, permit the gasoline to dry for a few moments and restart. If flooding doesn't recur: If flooding is persistent:	**5.3** **5.7** **5.5**

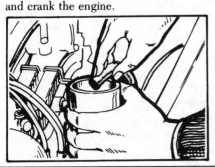

If the engine floods repeatedly, check the choke butterfly flap

5.3—Check that fuel is reaching the carburetor: Detach the fuel line at the carburetor inlet. Hold the end of the line in a cup (not styrofoam), and crank the engine.	If fuel flows smoothly: If fuel doesn't flow (**NOTE:** *Make sure that there is fuel in the tank*), or flows erratically:	**5.7** **5.4**

Check the fuel pump by disconnecting the output line (fuel pump-to-carburetor) at the carburetor and operating the starter briefly

Test and Procedure	Results and Indications	Proceed to
5.4—Test the fuel pump: Disconnect all fuel lines from the fuel pump. Hold a finger over the input fitting, crank the engine (with electric pump, turn the ignition or pump on); and feel for suction.	If suction is evident, blow out the fuel line to the tank with low pressure compressed air until bubbling is heard from the fuel filler neck. Also blow out the carburetor fuel line (both ends disconnected):	5.7
	If no suction is evident, replace or repair the fuel pump: **NOTE:** *Repeated oil fouling of the spark plugs, or a no-start condition, could be the result of a ruptured vacuum booster pump diaphragm, through which oil or gasoline is being drawn into the intake manifold (where applicable).*	5.7
5.5—Occasionally, small specks of dirt will clog the small jets and orifices in the carburetor. With the engine cold, hold a flat piece of wood or similar material over the carburetor, where possible, and crank the engine.	If the engine starts, but runs roughly the engine is probably not run enough. If the engine won't start:	5.9
5.6—Check the needle and seat: Tap the carburetor in the area of the needle and seat.	If flooding stops, a gasoline additive (e.g., Gumout) will often cure the problem:	5.7
	If flooding continues, check the fuel pump for excessive pressure at the carburetor (according to specifications). If the pressure is normal, the needle and seat must be removed and checked, and/or the float level adjusted:	5.7
5.7—Test the accelerator pump by looking into the throttle bores while operating the throttle.	If the accelerator pump appears to be operating normally:	5.8
	If the accelerator pump is not operating, the pump must be reconditioned. Where possible, service the pump with the carburetor(s) installed on the engine. If necessary, remove the carburetor. Prior to removal:	5.8
5.8—Determine whether the carburetor main fuel system is functioning: Spray a commercial starting fluid into the carburetor while attempting to start the engine.	If the engine starts, runs for a few seconds, and dies:	5.9
	If the engine doesn't start:	6.1

Check for gas at the carburetor by looking down the carburetor throat while someone moves the accelerator

Test and Procedure	Results and Indications	Proceed to
5.9—Uncommon fuel system malfunctions: See below:	If the problem is solved: If the problem remains, remove and recondition the carburetor.	**6.1**

Condition	Indication	Test	Prevailing Weather Conditions	Remedy
Vapor lock	Engine will not restart shortly after running.	Cool the components of the fuel system until the engine starts. Vapor lock can be cured faster by draping a wet cloth over a mechanical fuel pump.	Hot to very hot	Ensure that the exhaust manifold heat control valve is operating. Check with the vehicle manufacturer for the recommended solution to vapor lock on the model in question.
Carburetor icing	Engine will not idle, stalls at low speeds.	Visually inspect the throttle plate area of the throttle bores for frost.	High humidity, 32–40° F.	Ensure that the exhaust manifold heat control valve is operating, and that the intake manifold heat riser is not blocked.
Water in the fuel	Engine sputters and stalls; may not start.	Pump a small amount of fuel into a glass jar. Allow to stand, and inspect for droplets or a layer of water.	High humidity, extreme temperature changes.	For droplets, use one or two cans of commercial gas line anti-freeze. For a layer of water, the tank must be drained, and the fuel lines blown out with compressed air.

Section 6—Engine Compression
See Chapter 3 for service procedures

Test and Procedure	Results and Indications	Proceed to
6.1—Test engine compression: Remove all spark plugs. Block the throttle wide open. Insert a compression gauge into a spark plug port, crank the engine to obtain the maximum reading, and record.	If compression is within limits on all cylinders: If gauge reading is extremely low on all cylinders: If gauge reading is low on one or two cylinders: (If gauge readings are identical and low on two or more adjacent cylinders, the head gasket must be replaced.)	**7.1** **6.2** **6.2**

Checking compression

Test and Procedure	Results and Indications	Proceed to
6.2—Test engine compression (wet): Squirt approximately 30 cc. of engine oil into each cylinder, and retest per 6.1.	If the readings improve, worn or cracked rings or broken pistons are indicated: If the readings do not improve, burned or excessively carboned valves or a jumped timing chain are indicated: **NOTE:** *A jumped timing chain is often indicated by difficult cranking.*	**See Chapter 3** **7.1**

Section 7—Engine Vacuum
See Chapter 3 for service procedures

Test and Procedure	Results and Indications	Proceed to
7.1—Attach a vacuum gauge to the intake manifold beyond the throttle plate. Start the engine, and observe the action of the needle over the range of engine speeds.	See below.	**See below**

INDICATION: normal engine in good condition

Proceed to: 8.1

Normal engine
Gauge reading: steady, from 17–22 in./Hg.

INDICATION: sticking valves or ignition miss

Proceed to: 9.1, 8.3

Sticking valves
Gauge reading: intermittent fluctuation at idle

INDICATION: late ignition or valve timing, low compression, stuck throttle valve, leaking carburetor or manifold gasket

Proceed to: 6.1

Incorrect valve timing
Gauge reading: low (10–15 in./Hg) but steady

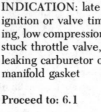

INDICATION: improper carburetor adjustment or minor intake leak.

Proceed to: 7.2

Carburetor requires adjustment
Gauge reading: drifting needle

INDICATION: ignition miss, blown cylinder head gasket, leaking valve or weak valve spring

Proceed to: 8.3, 6.1

Blown head gasket
Gauge reading: needle fluctuates as engine speed increases

INDICATION: burnt valve or faulty valve clearance. Needle will fall when defective valve operates

Proceed to: 9.1

Burnt or leaking valves
Gauge reading: steady needle, but drops regularly

INDICATION: choked muffler, excessive back pressure in system

Proceed to: 10.1

Clogged exhaust system
Gauge reading: gradual drop in reading at idle

INDICATION: worn valve guides

Proceed to: 9.1

Worn valve guides
Gauge reading: needle vibrates excessively at idle, but steadies as engine speed increases

White pointer = steady gauge hand   Black pointer = fluctuating gauge hand

Test and Procedure	Results and Indications	Proceed to
7.2—Attach a vacuum gauge per 7.1, and test for an intake manifold leak. Squirt a small amount of oil around the intake manifold gaskets, carburetor gaskets, plugs and fittings. Observe the action of the vacuum gauge.	If the reading improves, replace the indicated gasket, or seal the indicated fitting or plug: If the reading remains low:	**8.1** **7.3**
7.3—Test all vacuum hoses and accessories for leaks as described in 7.2. Also check the carburetor body (dashpots, automatic choke mechanism, throttle shafts) for leaks in the same manner.	If the reading improves, service or replace the offending part(s): If the reading remains low:	**8.1** **6.1**

Section 8—Secondary Electrical System
See Chapter 2 for service procedures

Test and Procedure	Results and Indications	Proceed to
8.1—Remove the distributor cap and check to make sure that the rotor turns when the engine is cranked. Visually inspect the distributor components.	Clean, tighten or replace any components which appear defective.	**8.2**
8.2—Connect a timing light (per manufacturer's recommendation) and check the dynamic ignition timing. Disconnect and plug the vacuum hose(s) to the distributor if specified, start the engine, and observe the timing marks at the specified engine speed.	If the timing is not correct, adjust to specifications by rotating the distributor in the engine: (Advance timing by rotating distributor opposite normal direction of rotor rotation, retard timing by rotating distributor in same direction as rotor rotation.)	**8.3**
8.3—Check the operation of the distributor advance mechanism(s): To test the mechanical advance, disconnect the vacuum lines from the distributor advance unit and observe the timing marks with a timing light as the engine speed is increased from idle. If the mark moves smoothly, without hesitation, it may be assumed that the mechanical advance is functioning properly. To test vacuum advance and/or retard systems, alternately crimp and release the vacuum line, and observe the timing mark for movement. If movement is noted, the system is operating.	If the systems are functioning: If the systems are not functioning, remove the distributor, and test on a distributor tester:	**8.4** **8.4**
8.4—Locate an ignition miss: With the engine running, remove each spark plug wire, one at a time, until one is found that doesn't cause the engine to roughen and slow down.	When the missing cylinder is identified:	**4.1**

Section 9—Valve Train
See Chapter 3 for service procedures

Test and Procedure	Results and Indications	Proceed to
9.1—Evaluate the valve train: Remove the valve cover, and ensure that the valves are adjusted to specifications. A mechanic's stethoscope may be used to aid in the diagnosis of the valve train. By pushing the probe on or near push rods or rockers, valve noise often can be isolated. A timing light also may be used to diagnose valve problems. Connect the light according to manufacturer's recommendations, and start the engine. Vary the firing moment of the light by increasing the engine speed (and therefore the ignition advance), and moving the trigger from cylinder to cylinder. Observe the movement of each valve.	Sticking valves or erratic valve train motion can be observed with the timing light. The cylinder head must be disassembled for repairs.	**See Chapter 3**
9.2—Check the valve timing: Locate top dead center of the No. 1 piston, and install a degree wheel or tape on the crankshaft pulley or damper with zero corresponding to an index mark on the engine. Rotate the crankshaft in its direction of rotation, and observe the opening of the No. 1 cylinder intake valve. The opening should correspond with the correct mark on the degree wheel according to specifications.	If the timing is not correct, the timing cover must be removed for further investigation.	**See Chapter 3**

Section 10—Exhaust System

Test and Procedure	Results and Indications	Proceed to
10.1—Determine whether the exhaust manifold heat control valve is operating: Operate the valve by hand to determine whether it is free to move. If the valve is free, run the engine to operating temperature and observe the action of the valve, to ensure that it is opening.	If the valve sticks, spray it with a suitable solvent, open and close the valve to free it, and retest.	
	If the valve functions properly:	**10.2**
	If the valve does not free, or does not operate, replace the valve:	**10.2**
10.2—Ensure that there are no exhaust restrictions: Visually inspect the exhaust system for kinks, dents, or crushing. Also note that gases are flowing freely from the tailpipe at all engine speeds, indicating no restriction in the muffler or resonator.	Replace any damaged portion of the system:	**11.1**

Section 11—Cooling System
See Chapter 3 for service procedures

Test and Procedure	Results and Indications	Proceed to
11.1—Visually inspect the fan belt for glazing, cracks, and fraying, and replace if necessary. Tighten the belt so that the longest span has approximately ½″ play at its midpoint under thumb pressure (see Chapter 1).	Replace or tighten the fan belt as necessary:	**11.2**

Checking belt tension

Test and Procedure	Results and Indications	Proceed to
11.2—Check the fluid level of the cooling system.	If full or slightly low, fill as necessary:	**11.5**
	If extremely low:	**11.3**
11.3—Visually inspect the external portions of the cooling system (radiator, radiator hoses, thermostat elbow, water pump seals, heater hoses, etc.) for leaks. If none are found, pressurize the cooling system to 14–15 psi.	If cooling system holds the pressure:	**11.5**
	If cooling system loses pressure rapidly, reinspect external parts of the system for leaks under pressure. If none are found, check dipstick for coolant in crankcase. If no coolant is present, but pressure loss continues:	**11.4**
	If coolant is evident in crankcase, remove cylinder head(s), and check gasket(s). If gaskets are intact, block and cylinder head(s) should be checked for cracks or holes.	
	If the gasket(s) is blown, replace, and purge the crankcase of coolant:	**12.6**
	NOTE: *Occasionally, due to atmospheric and driving conditions, condensation of water can occur in the crankcase. This causes the oil to appear milky white. To remedy, run the engine until hot, and change the oil and oil filter.*	
11.4—Check for combustion leaks into the cooling system: Pressurize the cooling system as above. Start the engine, and observe the pressure gauge. If the needle fluctuates, remove each spark plug wire, one at a time, noting which cylinder(s) reduce or eliminate the fluctuation.	Cylinders which reduce or eliminate the fluctuation, when the spark plug wire is removed, are leaking into the cooling system. Replace the head gasket on the affected cylinder bank(s).	

Pressurizing the cooling system

Test and Procedure	Results and Indications	Proceed to
11.5—Check the radiator pressure cap: Attach a radiator pressure tester to the radiator cap (wet the seal prior to installation). Quickly pump up the pressure, noting the point at which the cap releases.	If the cap releases within ± 1 psi of the specified rating, it is operating properly:	**11.6**
	If the cap releases at more than ± 1 psi of the specified rating, it should be replaced:	**11.6**

Checking radiator pressure cap

Test and Procedure	Results and Indications	Proceed to
11.6—Test the thermostat: Start the engine cold, remove the radiator cap, and insert a thermometer into the radiator. Allow the engine to idle. After a short while, there will be a sudden, rapid increase in coolant temperature. The temperature at which this sharp rise stops is the thermostat opening temperature.	If the thermostat opens at or about the specified temperature:	**11.7**
	If the temperature doesn't increase: (If the temperature increases slowly and gradually, replace the thermostat.)	**11.7**
11.7—Check the water pump: Remove the thermostat elbow and the thermostat, disconnect the coil high tension lead (to prevent starting), and crank the engine momentarily.	If coolant flows, replace the thermostat and retest per 11.6:	**11.6**
	If coolant doesn't flow, reverse flush the cooling system to alleviate any blockage that might exist. If system is not blocked, and coolant will not flow, replace the water pump.	

Section 12—Lubrication
See Chapter 3 for service procedures

Test and Procedure	Results and Indications	Proceed to
12.1—Check the oil pressure gauge or warning light: If the gauge shows low pressure, or the light is on for no obvious reason, remove the oil pressure sender. Install an accurate oil pressure gauge and run the engine momentarily.	If oil pressure builds normally, run engine for a few moments to determine that it is functioning normally, and replace the sender.	—
	If the pressure remains low:	**12.2**
	If the pressure surges:	**12.3**
	If the oil pressure is zero:	**12.3**
12.2—Visually inspect the oil: If the oil is watery or very thin, milky, or foamy, replace the oil and oil filter.	If the oil is normal:	**12.3**
	If after replacing oil the pressure remains low:	**12.3**
	If after replacing oil the pressure becomes normal:	—

Test and Procedure	Results and Indications	Proceed to
12.3—Inspect the oil pressure relief valve and spring, to ensure that it is not sticking or stuck. Remove and thoroughly clean the valve, spring, and the valve body.	If the oil pressure improves: If no improvement is noted:	— **12.4**
12.4—Check to ensure that the oil pump is not cavitating (sucking air instead of oil): See that the crankcase is neither over nor underfull, and that the pickup in the sump is in the proper position and free from sludge.	Fill or drain the crankcase to the proper capacity, and clean the pickup screen in solvent if necessary. If no improvement is noted:	**12.5**
12.5—Inspect the oil pump drive and the oil pump:	If the pump drive or the oil pump appear to be defective, service as necessary and retest per 12.1: If the pump drive and pump appear to be operating normally, the engine should be disassembled to determine where blockage exists:	**12.1** **See Chapter 3**
12.6—Purge the engine of ethylene glycol coolant: Completely drain the crankcase and the oil filter. Obtain a commercial butyl cellosolve base solvent, designated for this purpose, and follow the instructions precisely. Following this, install a new oil filter and refill the crankcase with the proper weight oil. The next oil and filter change should follow shortly thereafter (1000 miles).		

TROUBLESHOOTING EMISSION CONTROL SYSTEMS

See Chapter 4 for procedures applicable to individual emission control systems used on specific combinations of engine/transmission/model.

TROUBLESHOOTING THE CARBURETOR

See Chapter 4 for service procedures

Carburetor problems cannot be effectively isolated unless all other engine systems (particularly ignition and emission) are functioning properly and the engine is properly tuned.

Condition	Possible Cause
Engine cranks, but does not start	1. Improper starting procedure 2. No fuel in tank 3. Clogged fuel line or filter 4. Defective fuel pump 5. Choke valve not closing properly 6. Engine flooded 7. Choke valve not unloading 8. Throttle linkage not making full travel 9. Stuck needle or float 10. Leaking float needle or seat 11. Improper float adjustment
Engine stalls	1. Improperly adjusted idle speed or mixture **Engine hot** 2. Improperly adjusted dashpot 3. Defective or improperly adjusted solenoid 4. Incorrect fuel level in fuel bowl 5. Fuel pump pressure too high 6. Leaking float needle seat 7. Secondary throttle valve stuck open 8. Air or fuel leaks 9. Idle air bleeds plugged or missing 10. Idle passages plugged **Engine Cold** 11. Incorrectly adjusted choke 12. Improperly adjusted fast idle speed 13. Air leaks 14. Plugged idle or idle air passages 15. Stuck choke valve or binding linkage 16. Stuck secondary throttle valves 17. Engine flooding—high fuel level 18. Leaking or misaligned float
Engine hesitates on acceleration	1. Clogged fuel filter 2. Leaking fuel pump diaphragm 3. Low fuel pump pressure 4. Secondary throttle valves stuck, bent or misadjusted 5. Sticking or binding air valve 6. Defective accelerator pump 7. Vacuum leaks 8. Clogged air filter 9. Incorrect choke adjustment (engine cold)
Engine feels sluggish or flat on acceleration	1. Improperly adjusted idle speed or mixture 2. Clogged fuel filter 3. Defective accelerator pump 4. Dirty, plugged or incorrect main metering jets 5. Bent or sticking main metering rods 6. Sticking throttle valves 7. Stuck heat riser 8. Binding or stuck air valve 9. Dirty, plugged or incorrect secondary jets 10. Bent or sticking secondary metering rods. 11. Throttle body or manifold heat passages plugged 12. Improperly adjusted choke or choke vacuum break.
Carburetor floods	1. Defective fuel pump. Pressure too high. 2. Stuck choke valve 3. Dirty, worn or damaged float or needle valve/seat 4. Incorrect float/fuel level 5. Leaking float bowl

Condition	Possible Cause
Engine idles roughly and stalls	1. Incorrect idle speed 2. Clogged fuel filter 3. Dirt in fuel system or carburetor 4. Loose carburetor screws or attaching bolts 5. Broken carburetor gaskets 6. Air leaks 7. Dirty carburetor 8. Worn idle mixture needles 9. Throttle valves stuck open 10. Incorrectly adjusted float or fuel level 11. Clogged air filter
Engine runs unevenly or surges	1. Defective fuel pump 2. Dirty or clogged fuel filter 3. Plugged, loose or incorrect main metering jets or rods 4. Air leaks 5. Bent or sticking main metering rods 6. Stuck power piston 7. Incorrect float adjustment 8. Incorrect idle speed or mixture 9. Dirty or plugged idle system passages 10. Hard, brittle or broken gaskets 11. Loose attaching or mounting screws 12. Stuck or misaligned secondary throttle valves
Poor fuel economy	1. Poor driving habits 2. Stuck choke valve 3. Binding choke linkage 4. Stuck heat riser 5. Incorrect idle mixture 6. Defective accelerator pump 7. Air leaks 8. Plugged, loose or incorrect main metering jets 9. Improperly adjusted float or fuel level 10. Bent, misaligned or fuel-clogged float 11. Leaking float needle seat 12. Fuel leak 13. Accelerator pump discharge ball not seating properly 14. Incorrect main jets
Engine lacks high speed performance or power	1. Incorrect throttle linkage adjustment 2. Stuck or binding power piston 3. Defective accelerator pump 4. Air leaks 5. Incorrect float setting or fuel level 6. Dirty, plugged, worn or incorrect main metering jets or rods 7. Binding or sticking air valve 8. Brittle or cracked gaskets 9. Bent, incorrect or improperly adjusted secondary metering rods 10. Clogged fuel filter 11. Clogged air filter 12. Defective fuel pump

TROUBLESHOOTING FUEL INJECTION PROBLEMS

Each fuel injection system has its own unique components and test procedures, for which it is impossible to generalize. Refer to Chapter 4 of this Repair & Tune-Up Guide for specific test and repair procedures, if the vehicle is equipped with fuel injection.

TROUBLESHOOTING ELECTRICAL PROBLEMS

See Chapter 5 for service procedures

For any electrical system to operate, it must make a complete circuit. This simply means that the power flow from the battery must make a complete circle. When an electrical component is operating, power flows from the battery to the component, passes through the component causing it to perform its function (lighting a light bulb), and then returns to the battery through the ground of the circuit. This ground is usually (but not always) the metal part of the car or truck on which the electrical component is mounted.

Perhaps the easiest way to visualize this is to think of connecting a light bulb with two wires attached to it to the battery. If one of the two wires attached to the light bulb were attached to the negative post of the battery and the other were attached to the positive post of the battery, you would have a complete circuit. Current from the battery would flow to the light bulb, causing it to light, and return to the negative post of the battery.

The normal automotive circuit differs from this simple example in two ways. First, instead of having a return wire from the bulb to the battery, the light bulb returns the current to the battery through the chassis of the vehicle. Since the negative battery cable is attached to the chassis and the chassis is made of electrically conductive metal, the chassis of the vehicle can serve as a ground wire to complete the circuit. Secondly, most automotive circuits contain switches to turn components on and off as required.

Every complete circuit from a power source must include a component which is using the power from the power source. If you were to disconnect the light bulb from the wires and touch the two wires together (don't do this) the power supply wire to the component would be grounded before the normal ground connection for the circuit.

Because grounding a wire from a power source makes a complete circuit—less the required component to use the power—this phenomenon is called a short circuit. Common causes are: broken insulation (exposing the metal wire to a metal part of the car or truck), or a shorted switch.

Some electrical components which require a large amount of current to operate also have a relay in their circuit. Since these circuits carry a large amount of current, the thickness of the wire in the circuit (gauge size) is also greater. If this large wire were connected from the component to the control switch on the instrument panel, and then back to the component, a voltage drop would occur in the circuit. To prevent this potential drop in voltage, an electromagnetic switch (relay) is used. The large wires in the circuit are connected from the battery to one side of the relay, and from the opposite side of the relay to the component. The relay is normally open, preventing current from passing through the circuit. An additional, smaller, wire is connected from the relay to the control switch for the circuit. When the control switch is turned on, it grounds the smaller wire from the relay and completes the circuit. This closes the relay and allows current to flow from the battery to the component. The horn, headlight, and starter circuits are three which use relays.

It is possible for larger surges of current to pass through the electrical system of your car or truck. If this surge of current were to reach an electrical component, it could burn it out. To prevent this, fuses, circuit breakers or fusible links are connected into the current supply wires of most of the major electrical systems. When an electrical current of excessive power passes through the component's fuse, the fuse blows out and breaks the circuit, saving the component from destruction.

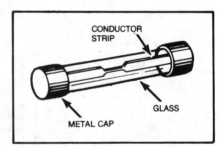

Typical automotive fuse

A circuit breaker is basically a self-repairing fuse. The circuit breaker opens the circuit the same way a fuse does. However, when either the short is removed from the circuit or the surge subsides, the circuit breaker resets itself and does not have to be replaced as a fuse does.

A fuse link is a wire that acts as a fuse. It is normally connected between the starter relay and the main wiring harness. This connection is usually under the hood. The fuse link (if installed) protects all the

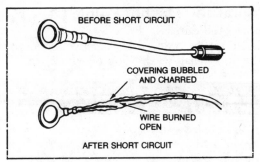

BEFORE SHORT CIRCUIT

COVERING BUBBLED AND CHARRED

WIRE BURNED OPEN

AFTER SHORT CIRCUIT

Most fusible links show a charred, melted insulation when they burn out

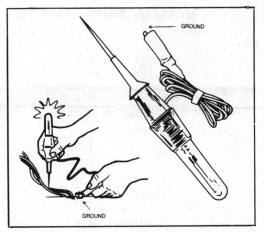

GROUND

GROUND

The test light will show the presence of current when touched to a hot wire and grounded at the other end

chassis electrical components, and is the probable cause of trouble when none of the electrical components function, unless the battery is disconnected or dead.

Electrical problems generally fall into one of three areas:

1. The component that is not functioning is not receiving current.

2. The component itself is not functioning.

3. The component is not properly grounded.

The electrical system can be checked with a test light and a jumper wire. A test light is a device that looks like a pointed screwdriver with a wire attached to it and has a light bulb in its handle. A jumper wire is a piece of insulated wire with an alligator clip attached to each end.

If a component is not working, you must follow a systematic plan to determine which of the three causes is the villain.

1. Turn on the switch that controls the inoperable component.

2. Disconnect the power supply wire from the component.

3. Attach the ground wire on the test light to a good metal ground.

4. Touch the probe end of the test light to the end of the power supply wire that was disconnected from the component. If the component is receiving current, the test light will go on.

NOTE: *Some components work only when the ignition switch is turned on.*

If the test light does not go on, then the problem is in the circuit between the battery and the component. This includes all the switches, fuses, and relays in the system. Follow the wire that runs back to the battery. The problem is an open circuit between the

battery and the component. If the fuse is blown and, when replaced, immediately blows again, there is a short circuit in the system which must be located and repaired. If there is a switch in the system, bypass it with a jumper wire. This is done by connecting one end of the jumper wire to the power supply wire into the switch and the other end of the jumper wire to the wire coming out of the switch. If the test light lights with the jumper wire installed, the switch or whatever was bypassed is defective.

NOTE: *Never substitute the jumper wire for the component, since it is required to use the power from the power source.*

5. If the bulb in the test light goes on, then the current is getting to the component that is not working. This eliminates the first of the three possible causes. Connect the power supply wire and connect a jumper wire from the component to a good metal ground. Do this with the switch which controls the component turned on, and also the ignition switch turned on if it is required for the component to work. If the component works with the jumper wire installed, then it has a bad ground. This is usually caused by the metal area on which the component mounts to the chassis being coated with some type of foreign matter.

6. If neither test located the source of the trouble, then the component itself is defective. Remember that for any electrical system to work, all connections must be clean and tight.

Troubleshooting Basic Turn Signal and Flasher Problems
See Chapter 5 for service procedures

Most problems in the turn signals or flasher system can be reduced to defective flashers or bulbs, which are easily replaced. Occasionally, the turn signal switch will prove defective.

F = Front   R = Rear   ● = Lights off   ○ = Lights on

Condition		Possible Cause
Turn signals light, but do not flash	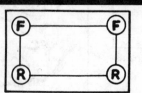	Defective flasher
No turn signals light on either side	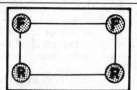	Blown fuse. Replace if defective. Defective flasher. Check by substitution. Open circuit, short circuit or poor ground.
Both turn signals on one side don't work	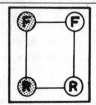	Bad bulbs. Bad ground in both (or either) housings.
One turn signal light on one side doesn't work	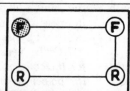	Defective bulb. Corrosion in socket. Clean contacts. Poor ground at socket.
Turn signal flashes too fast or too slowly	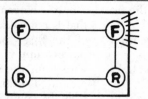	Check any bulb on the side flashing too fast. A heavy-duty bulb is probably installed in place of a regular bulb. Check the bulb flashing too slowly. A standard bulb was probably installed in place of a heavy-duty bulb. Loose connections or corrosion at the bulb socket.
Indicator lights don't work in either direction		Check if the turn signals are working. Check the dash indicator lights. Check the flasher by substitution.
One indicator light doesn't light		On systems with one dash indicator: See if the lights work on the same side. Often the filaments have been reversed in systems combining stoplights with taillights and turn signals. Check the flasher by substitution. On systems with two indicators: Check the bulbs on the same side. Check the indicator light bulb. Check the flasher by substitution.

Troubleshooting Lighting Problems
See Chapter 5 for service procedures

Condition	Possible Cause
One or more lights don't work, but others do	1. Defective bulb(s) 2. Blown fuse(s) 3. Dirty fuse clips or light sockets 4. Poor ground circuit
Lights burn out quickly	1. Incorrect voltage regulator setting or defective regulator 2. Poor battery/alternator connections
Lights go dim	1. Low/discharged battery 2. Alternator not charging 3. Corroded sockets or connections 4. Low voltage output
Lights flicker	1. Loose connection 2. Poor ground. (Run ground wire from light housing to frame) 3. Circuit breaker operating (short circuit)
Lights "flare"—Some flare is normal on acceleration—If excessive, see "Lights Burn Out Quickly"	High voltage setting
Lights glare—approaching drivers are blinded	1. Lights adjusted too high 2. Rear springs or shocks sagging 3. Rear tires soft

Troubleshooting Dash Gauge Problems
Most problems can be traced to a defective sending unit or faulty wiring. Occasionally, the gauge itself is at fault. See Chapter 5 for service procedures.

Condition	Possible Cause
COOLANT TEMPERATURE GAUGE	
Gauge reads erratically or not at all	1. Loose or dirty connections 2. Defective sending unit. 3. Defective gauge. To test a bi-metal gauge, remove the wire from the sending unit. Ground the wire for an instant. If the gauge registers, replace the sending unit. To test a magnetic gauge, disconnect the wire at the sending unit. With ignition ON gauge should register COLD. Ground the wire; gauge should register HOT.
AMMETER GAUGE—TURN HEADLIGHTS ON (DO NOT START ENGINE). NOTE REACTION	
Ammeter shows charge Ammeter shows discharge Ammeter does not move	1. Connections reversed on gauge 2. Ammeter is OK 3. Loose connections or faulty wiring 4. Defective gauge

Condition	Possible Cause

OIL PRESSURE GAUGE

Gauge does not register or is inaccurate	1. On mechanical gauge, Bourdon tube may be bent or kinked. 2. Low oil pressure. Remove sending unit. Idle the engine briefly. If no oil flows from sending unit hole, problem is in engine. 3. Defective gauge. Remove the wire from the sending unit and ground it for an instant with the ignition ON. A good gauge will go to the top of the scale. 4. Defective wiring. Check the wiring to the gauge. If it's OK and the gauge doesn't register when grounded, replace the gauge. 5. Defective sending unit.

ALL GAUGES

All gauges do not operate All gauges read low or erratically All gauges pegged	1. Blown fuse 2. Defective instrument regulator 3. Defective or dirty instrument voltage regulator 4. Loss of ground between instrument voltage regulator and frame 5. Defective instrument regulator

WARNING LIGHTS

Light(s) do not come on when ignition is ON, but engine is not started Light comes on with engine running	1. Defective bulb 2. Defective wire 3. Defective sending unit. Disconnect the wire from the sending unit and ground it. Replace the sending unit if the light comes on with the ignition ON. 4. Problem in individual system 5. Defective sending unit

Troubleshooting Clutch Problems

It is false economy to replace individual clutch components. The pressure plate, clutch plate and throwout bearing should be replaced as a set, and the flywheel face inspected, whenever the clutch is overhauled. See Chapter 6 for service procedures.

Condition	Possible Cause
Clutch chatter	1. Grease on driven plate (disc) facing 2. Binding clutch linkage or cable 3. Loose, damaged facings on driven plate (disc) 4. Engine mounts loose 5. Incorrect height adjustment of pressure plate release levers 6. Clutch housing or housing to transmission adapter misalignment 7. Loose driven plate hub
Clutch grabbing	1. Oil, grease on driven plate (disc) facing 2. Broken pressure plate 3. Warped or binding driven plate. Driven plate binding on clutch shaft
Clutch slips	1. Lack of lubrication in clutch linkage or cable (linkage or cable binds, causes incomplete engagement) 2. Incorrect pedal, or linkage adjustment 3. Broken pressure plate springs 4. Weak pressure plate springs 5. Grease on driven plate facings (disc)

Troubleshooting Clutch Problems (cont.)

Condition	Possible Cause
Incomplete clutch release	1. Incorrect pedal or linkage adjustment or linkage or cable binding 2. Incorrect height adjustment on pressure plate release levers 3. Loose, broken facings on driven plate (disc) 4. Bent, dished, warped driven plate caused by overheating
Grinding, whirring grating noise when pedal is depressed	1. Worn or defective throwout bearing 2. Starter drive teeth contacting flywheel ring gear teeth. Look for milled or polished teeth on ring gear.
Squeal, howl, trumpeting noise when pedal is being released (occurs during first inch to inch and one-half of pedal travel)	Pilot bushing worn or lack of lubricant. If bushing appears OK, polish bushing with emery cloth, soak lube wick in oil, lube bushing with oil, apply film of chassis grease to clutch shaft pilot hub, reassemble. NOTE: Bushing wear may be due to misalignment of clutch housing or housing to transmission adapter
Vibration or clutch pedal pulsation with clutch disengaged (pedal fully depressed)	1. Worn or defective engine transmission mounts 2. Flywheel run out. (Flywheel run out at face not to exceed 0.005") 3. Damaged or defective clutch components

Troubleshooting Manual Transmission Problems
See Chapter 6 for service procedures

Condition	Possible Cause
Transmission jumps out of gear	1. Misalignment of transmission case or clutch housing. 2. Worn pilot bearing in crankshaft. 3. Bent transmission shaft. 4. Worn high speed sliding gear. 5. Worn teeth or end-play in clutch shaft. 6. Insufficient spring tension on shifter rail plunger. 7. Bent or loose shifter fork. 8. Gears not engaging completely. 9. Loose or worn bearings on clutch shaft or mainshaft. 10. Worn gear teeth. 11. Worn or damaged detent balls.
Transmission sticks in gear	1. Clutch not releasing fully. 2. Burred or battered teeth on clutch shaft, or sliding sleeve. 3. Burred or battered transmission mainshaft. 4. Frozen synchronizing clutch. 5. Stuck shifter rail plunger. 6. Gearshift lever twisting and binding shifter rail. 7. Battered teeth on high speed sliding gear or on sleeve. 8. Improper lubrication, or lack of lubrication. 9. Corroded transmission parts. 10. Defective mainshaft pilot bearing. 11. Locked gear bearings will give same effect as stuck in gear.
Transmission gears will not synchronize	1. Binding pilot bearing on mainshaft, will synchronize in high gear only. 2. Clutch not releasing fully. 3. Detent spring weak or broken. 4. Weak or broken springs under balls in sliding gear sleeve. 5. Binding bearing on clutch shaft, or binding countershaft. 6. Binding pilot bearing in crankshaft. 7. Badly worn gear teeth. 8. Improper lubrication. 9. Constant mesh gear not turning freely on transmission mainshaft. Will synchronize in that gear only.

Condition	Possible Cause
Gears spinning when shifting into gear from neutral	1. Clutch not releasing fully. 2. In some cases an extremely light lubricant in transmission will cause gears to continue to spin for a short time after clutch is released. 3. Binding pilot bearing in crankshaft.
Transmission noisy in all gears	1. Insufficient lubricant, or improper lubricant. 2. Worn countergear bearings. 3. Worn or damaged main drive gear or countergear. 4. Damaged main drive gear or mainshaft bearings. 5. Worn or damaged countergear anti-lash plate.
Transmission noisy in neutral only	1. Damaged main drive gear bearing. 2. Damaged or loose mainshaft pilot bearing. 3. Worn or damaged countergear anti-lash plate. 4. Worn countergear bearings.
Transmission noisy in one gear only	1. Damaged or worn constant mesh gears. 2. Worn or damaged countergear bearings. 3. Damaged or worn synchronizer.
Transmission noisy in reverse only	1. Worn or damaged reverse idler gear or idler bushing. 2. Worn or damaged mainshaft reverse gear. 3. Worn or damaged reverse countergear. 4. Damaged shift mechanism.

TROUBLESHOOTING AUTOMATIC TRANSMISSION PROBLEMS

Keeping alert to changes in the operating characteristics of the transmission (changing shift points, noises, etc.) can prevent small problems from becoming large ones. If the problem cannot be traced to loose bolts, fluid level, misadjusted linkage, clogged filters or similar problems, you should probably seek professional service.

Transmission Fluid Indications

The appearance and odor of the transmission fluid can give valuable clues to the overall condition of the transmission. Always note the appearance of the fluid when you check the fluid level or change the fluid. Rub a small amount of fluid between your fingers to feel for grit and smell the fluid on the dipstick.

If the fluid appears:	It indicates:
Clear and red colored	Normal operation
Discolored (extremely dark red or brownish) or smells burned	Band or clutch pack failure, usually caused by an overheated transmission. Hauling very heavy loads with insufficient power or failure to change the fluid often result in overheating. Do not confuse this appearance with newer fluids that have a darker red color and a strong odor (though not a burned odor).
Foamy or aerated (light in color and full of bubbles)	1. The level is too high (gear train is churning oil) 2. An internal air leak (air is mixing with the fluid). Have the transmission checked professionally.
Solid residue in the fluid	Defective bands, clutch pack or bearings. Bits of band material or metal abrasives are clinging to the dipstick. Have the transmission checked professionally.
Varnish coating on the dipstick	The transmission fluid is overheating

TROUBLESHOOTING DRIVE AXLE PROBLEMS

First, determine when the noise is most noticeable.

Drive Noise: Produced under vehicle acceleration.

Coast Noise: Produced while coasting with a closed throttle.

Float Noise: Occurs while maintaining constant speed (just enough to keep speed constant) on a level road.

External Noise Elimination

It is advisable to make a thorough road test to determine whether the noise originates in the rear axle or whether it originates from the tires, engine, transmission, wheel bearings or road surface. Noise originating from other places cannot be corrected by servicing the rear axle.

ROAD NOISE

Brick or rough surfaced concrete roads produce noises that seem to come from the rear axle. Road noise is usually identical in Drive or Coast and driving on a different type of road will tell whether the road is the problem.

TIRE NOISE

Tire noise can be mistaken as rear axle noise, even though the tires on the front are at fault. Snow tread and mud tread tires or tires worn unevenly will frequently cause vibrations which seem to originate elsewhere; *temporarily, and for test purposes only*, inflate the tires to 40–50 lbs. This will significantly alter the noise produced by the tires,

but will not alter noise from the rear axle. Noises from the rear axle will normally cease at speeds below 30 mph on coast, while tire noise will continue at lower tone as speed is decreased. The rear axle noise will usually change from drive conditions to coast conditions, while tire noise will not. Do not forget to lower the tire pressure to normal after the test is complete.

ENGINE/TRANSMISSION NOISE

Determine at what speed the noise is most pronounced, then stop in a quiet place. With the transmission in Neutral, run the engine through speeds corresponding to road speeds where the noise was noticed. Noises produced with the vehicle standing still are coming from the engine or transmission.

FRONT WHEEL BEARINGS

Front wheel bearing noises, sometimes confused with rear axle noises, will not change when comparing drive and coast conditions. While holding the speed steady, lightly apply the footbrake. This will often cause wheel bearing noise to lessen, as some of the weight is taken off the bearing. Front wheel bearings are easily checked by jacking up the wheels and spinning the wheels. Shaking the wheels will also determine if the wheel bearings are excessively loose.

REAR AXLE NOISES

Eliminating other possible sources can narrow the cause to the rear axle, which normally produces noise from worn gears or bearings. Gear noises tend to peak in a narrow speed range, while bearing noises will usually vary in pitch with engine speeds.

Noise Diagnosis

The Noise Is:	Most Probably Produced By:
1. Identical under Drive or Coast	Road surface, tires or front wheel bearings
2. Different depending on road surface	Road surface or tires
3. Lower as speed is lowered	Tires
4. Similar when standing or moving	Engine or transmission
5. A vibration	Unbalanced tires, rear wheel bearing, unbalanced driveshaft or worn U-joint
6. A knock or click about every two tire revolutions	Rear wheel bearing
7. Most pronounced on turns	Damaged differential gears
8. A steady low-pitched whirring or scraping, starting at low speeds	Damaged or worn pinion bearing
9. A chattering vibration on turns	Wrong differential lubricant or worn clutch plates (limited slip rear axle)
10. Noticed only in Drive, Coast or Float conditions	Worn ring gear and/or pinion gear

Troubleshooting Steering & Suspension Problems

Condition	Possible Cause
Hard steering (wheel is hard to turn)	1. Improper tire pressure 2. Loose or glazed pump drive belt 3. Low or incorrect fluid 4. Loose, bent or poorly lubricated front end parts 5. Improper front end alignment (excessive caster) 6. Bind in steering column or linkage 7. Kinked hydraulic hose 8. Air in hydraulic system 9. Low pump output or leaks in system 10. Obstruction in lines 11. Pump valves sticking or out of adjustment 12. Incorrect wheel alignment
Loose steering (too much play in steering wheel)	1. Loose wheel bearings 2. Faulty shocks 3. Worn linkage or suspension components 4. Loose steering gear mounting or linkage points 5. Steering mechanism worn or improperly adjusted 6. Valve spool improperly adjusted 7. Worn ball joints, tie-rod ends, etc.
Veers or wanders (pulls to one side with hands off steering wheel)	1. Improper tire pressure 2. Improper front end alignment 3. Dragging or improperly adjusted brakes 4. Bent frame 5. Improper rear end alignment 6. Faulty shocks or springs 7. Loose or bent front end components 8. Play in Pitman arm 9. Steering gear mountings loose 10. Loose wheel bearings 11. Binding Pitman arm 12. Spool valve sticking or improperly adjusted 13. Worn ball joints
Wheel oscillation or vibration transmitted through steering wheel	1. Low or uneven tire pressure 2. Loose wheel bearings 3. Improper front end alignment 4. Bent spindle 5. Worn, bent or broken front end components 6. Tires out of round or out of balance 7. Excessive lateral runout in disc brake rotor 8. Loose or bent shock absorber or strut
Noises (see also "Troubleshooting Drive Axle Problems")	1. Loose belts 2. Low fluid, air in system 3. Foreign matter in system 4. Improper lubrication 5. Interference or chafing in linkage 6. Steering gear mountings loose 7. Incorrect adjustment or wear in gear box 8. Faulty valves or wear in pump 9. Kinked hydraulic lines 10. Worn wheel bearings
Poor return of steering	1. Over-inflated tires 2. Improperly aligned front end (excessive caster) 3. Binding in steering column 4. No lubrication in front end 5. Steering gear adjusted too tight
Uneven tire wear (see "How To Read Tire Wear")	1. Incorrect tire pressure 2. Improperly aligned front end 3. Tires out-of-balance 4. Bent or worn suspension parts

HOW TO READ TIRE WEAR

The way your tires wear is a good indicator of other parts of the suspension. Abnormal wear patterns are often caused by the need for simple tire maintenance, or for front end alignment.

Excessive wear at the center of the tread indicates that the air pressure in the tire is consistently too high. The tire is riding on the center of the tread and wearing it prematurely. Occasionally, this wear pattern can result from outrageously wide tires on narrow rims. The cure for this is to replace either the tires or the wheels.

This type of wear usually results from consistent under-inflation. When a tire is under-inflated, there is too much contact with the road by the outer treads, which wear prematurely. When this type of wear occurs, and the tire pressure is known to be consistently correct, a bent or worn steering component or the need for wheel alignment could be indicated.

Feathering is a condition when the edge of each tread rib develops a slightly rounded edge on one side and a sharp edge on the other. By running your hand over the tire, you can usually feel the sharper edges before you'll be able to see them. The most common causes of feathering are incorrect toe-in setting or deteriorated bushings in the front suspension.

When an inner or outer rib wears faster than the rest of the tire, the need for wheel alignment is indicated. There is excessive camber in the front suspension, causing the wheel to lean too much putting excessive load on one side of the tire. Misalignment could also be due to sagging springs, worn ball joints, or worn control arm bushings. Be sure the vehicle is loaded the way it's normally driven when you have the wheels aligned.

Cups or scalloped dips appearing around the edge of the tread almost always indicate worn (sometimes bent) suspension parts. Adjustment of wheel alignment alone will seldom cure the problem. Any worn component that connects the wheel to the suspension can cause this type of wear. Occasionally, wheels that are out of balance will wear like this, but wheel imbalance usually shows up as bald spots between the outside edges and center of the tread.

Second-rib wear is usually found only in radial tires, and appears where the steel belts end in relation to the tread. It can be kept to a minimum by paying careful attention to tire pressure and frequently rotating the tires. This is often considered normal wear but excessive amounts indicate that the tires are too wide for the wheels.

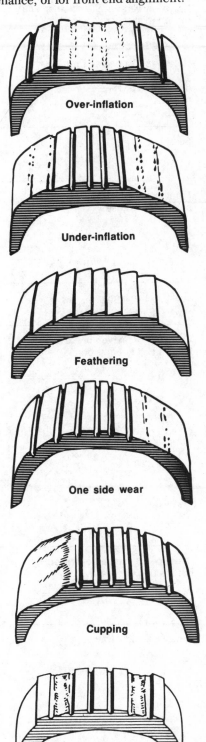

Over-inflation

Under-inflation

Feathering

One side wear

Cupping

Second-rib wear

Troubleshooting Disc Brake Problems

Condition	Possible Cause
Noise—groan—brake noise emanating when slowly releasing brakes (creep-groan)	Not detrimental to function of disc brakes—no corrective action required. (This noise may be eliminated by slightly increasing or decreasing brake pedal efforts.)
Rattle—brake noise or rattle emanating at low speeds on rough roads, (front wheels only).	1. Shoe anti-rattle spring missing or not properly positioned. 2. Excessive clearance between shoe and caliper. 3. Soft or broken caliper seals. 4. Deformed or misaligned disc. 5. Loose caliper.
Scraping	1. Mounting bolts too long. 2. Loose wheel bearings. 3. Bent, loose, or misaligned splash shield.
Front brakes heat up during driving and fail to release	1. Operator riding brake pedal. 2. Stop light switch improperly adjusted. 3. Sticking pedal linkage. 4. Frozen or seized piston. 5. Residual pressure valve in master cylinder. 6. Power brake malfunction. 7. Proportioning valve malfunction.
Leaky brake caliper	1. Damaged or worn caliper piston seal. 2. Scores or corrosion on surface of cylinder bore.
Grabbing or uneven brake action—Brakes pull to one side	1. Causes listed under "Brakes Pull". 2. Power brake malfunction. 3. Low fluid level in master cylinder. 4. Air in hydraulic system. 5. Brake fluid, oil or grease on linings. 6. Unmatched linings. 7. Distorted brake pads. 8. Frozen or seized pistons. 9. Incorrect tire pressure. 10. Front end out of alignment. 11. Broken rear spring. 12. Brake caliper pistons sticking. 13. Restricted hose or line. 14. Caliper not in proper alignment to braking disc. 15. Stuck or malfunctioning metering valve. 16. Soft or broken caliper seals. 17. Loose caliper.
Brake pedal can be depressed without braking effect	1. Air in hydraulic system or improper bleeding procedure. 2. Leak past primary cup in master cylinder. 3. Leak in system. 4. Rear brakes out of adjustment. 5. Bleeder screw open.
Excessive pedal travel	1. Air, leak, or insufficient fluid in system or caliper. 2. Warped or excessively tapered shoe and lining assembly. 3. Excessive disc runout. 4. Rear brake adjustment required. 5. Loose wheel bearing adjustment. 6. Damaged caliper piston seal. 7. Improper brake fluid (boil). 8. Power brake malfunction. 9. Weak or soft hoses.

Troubleshooting Disc Brake Problems (cont.)

Condition	Possible Cause
Brake roughness or chatter (pedal pumping)	1. Excessive thickness variation of braking disc. 2. Excessive lateral runout of braking disc. 3. Rear brake drums out-of-round. 4. Excessive front bearing clearance.
Excessive pedal effort	1. Brake fluid, oil or grease on linings. 2. Incorrect lining. 3. Frozen or seized pistons. 4. Power brake malfunction. 5. Kinked or collapsed hose or line. 6. Stuck metering valve. 7. Scored caliper or master cylinder bore. 8. Seized caliper pistons.
Brake pedal fades (pedal travel increases with foot on brake)	1. Rough master cylinder or caliper bore. 2. Loose or broken hydraulic lines/connections. 3. Air in hydraulic system. 4. Fluid level low. 5. Weak or soft hoses. 6. Inferior quality brake shoes or fluid. 7. Worn master cylinder piston cups or seals.

Troubleshooting Drum Brakes

Condition	Possible Cause
Pedal goes to floor	1. Fluid low in reservoir. 2. Air in hydraulic system. 3. Improperly adjusted brake. 4. Leaking wheel cylinders. 5. Loose or broken brake lines. 6. Leaking or worn master cylinder. 7. Excessively worn brake lining.
Spongy brake pedal	1. Air in hydraulic system. 2. Improper brake fluid (low boiling point). 3. Excessively worn or cracked brake drums. 4. Broken pedal pivot bushing.
Brakes pulling	1. Contaminated lining. 2. Front end out of alignment. 3. Incorrect brake adjustment. 4. Unmatched brake lining. 5. Brake drums out of round. 6. Brake shoes distorted. 7. Restricted brake hose or line. 8. Broken rear spring. 9. Worn brake linings. 10. Uneven lining wear. 11. Glazed brake lining. 12. Excessive brake lining dust. 13. Heat spotted brake drums. 14. Weak brake return springs. 15. Faulty automatic adjusters. 16. Low or incorrect tire pressure.

Condition	Possible Cause
Squealing brakes	1. Glazed brake lining. 2. Saturated brake lining. 3. Weak or broken brake shoe retaining spring. 4. Broken or weak brake shoe return spring. 5. Incorrect brake lining. 6. Distorted brake shoes. 7. Bent support plate. 8. Dust in brakes or scored brake drums. 9. Linings worn below limit. 10. Uneven brake lining wear. 11. Heat spotted brake drums.
Chirping brakes	1. Out of round drum or eccentric axle flange pilot.
Dragging brakes	1. Incorrect wheel or parking brake adjustment. 2. Parking brakes engaged or improperly adjusted. 3. Weak or broken brake shoe return spring. 4. Brake pedal binding. 5. Master cylinder cup sticking. 6. Obstructed master cylinder relief port. 7. Saturated brake lining. 8. Bent or out of round brake drum. 9. Contaminated or improper brake fluid. 10. Sticking wheel cylinder pistons. 11. Driver riding brake pedal. 12. Defective proportioning valve. 13. Insufficient brake shoe lubricant.
Hard pedal	1. Brake booster inoperative. 2. Incorrect brake lining. 3. Restricted brake line or hose. 4. Frozen brake pedal linkage. 5. Stuck wheel cylinder. 6. Binding pedal linkage. 7. Faulty proportioning valve.
Wheel locks	1. Contaminated brake lining. 2. Loose or torn brake lining. 3. Wheel cylinder cups sticking. 4. Incorrect wheel bearing adjustment. 5. Faulty proportioning valve.
Brakes fade (high speed)	1. Incorrect lining. 2. Overheated brake drums. 3. Incorrect brake fluid (low boiling temperature). 4. Saturated brake lining. 5. Leak in hydraulic system. 6. Faulty automatic adjusters.
Pedal pulsates	1. Bent or out of round brake drum.
Brake chatter and shoe knock	1. Out of round brake drum. 2. Loose support plate. 3. Bent support plate. 4. Distorted brake shoes. 5. Machine grooves in contact face of brake drum (Shoe Knock). 6. Contaminated brake lining. 7. Missing or loose components. 8. Incorrect lining material. 9. Out-of-round brake drums. 10. Heat spotted or scored brake drums. 11. Out-of-balance wheels.

Troubleshooting Drum Brakes (cont.)

Condition	Possible Cause
Brakes do not self adjust	1. Adjuster screw frozen in thread. 2. Adjuster screw corroded at thrust washer. 3. Adjuster lever does not engage star wheel. 4. Adjuster installed on wrong wheel.
Brake light glows	1. Leak in the hydraulic system. 2. Air in the system. 3. Improperly adjusted master cylinder pushrod. 4. Uneven lining wear. 5. Failure to center combination valve or proportioning valve.

Appendix

General Conversion Table

Multiply by	To convert	To	
2.54	Inches	Centimeters	.3937
30.48	Feet	Centimeters	.0328
.914	Yards	Meters	1.094
1.609	Miles	Kilometers	.621
6.45	Square inches	Square cm.	.155
.836	Square yards	Square meters	1.196
16.39	Cubic inches	Cubic cm.	.061
28.3	Cubic feet	Liters	.0353
.4536	Pounds	Kilograms	2.2045
3.785	Gallons	Liters	.264
.068	Lbs./sq. in. (psi)	Atmospheres	14.7
.138	Foot pounds	Kg. m.	7.23
1.014	H.P. (DIN)	H.P. (SAE)	.9861
—	To obtain	From	Multiply by

Note: 1 cm. equals 10 mm.; 1 mm. equals .0394".

Conversion—Common Fractions to Decimals and Millimeters

Common Fractions	Decimal Fractions	Millimeters (approx.)	Common Fractions	Decimal Fractions	Millimeters (approx.)	Common Fractions	Decimal Fractions	Millimeters (approx.)
1/128	.008	0.20	11/32	.344	8.73	43/64	.672	17.07
1/64	.016	0.40	23/64	.359	9.13	11/16	.688	17.46
1/32	.031	0.79	3/8	.375	9.53	45/64	.703	17.86
3/64	.047	1.19	25/64	.391	9.92	23/32	.719	18.26
1/16	.063	1.59	13/32	.406	10.32	47/64	.734	18.65
5/64	.078	1.98	27/64	.422	10.72	3/4	.750	19.05
3/32	.094	2.38	7/16	.438	11.11	49/64	.766	19.45
7/64	.109	2.78	29/64	.453	11.51	25/32	.781	19.84
1/8	.125	3.18	15/32	.469	11.91	51/64	.797	20.24
9/64	.141	3.57	31/64	.484	12.30	13/16	.813	20.64
5/32	.156	3.97	1/2	.500	12.70	53/64	.828	21.03
11/64	.172	4.37	33/64	.516	13.10	27/32	.844	21.43
3/16	.188	4.76	17/32	.531	13.49	55/64	.859	21.83
13/64	.203	5.16	35/64	.547	13.89	7/8	.875	22.23
7/32	.219	5.56	9/16	.563	14.29	57/64	.891	22.62
15/64	.234	5.95	37/64	.578	14.68	29/32	.906	23.02
1/4	.250	6.35	19/32	.594	15.08	59/64	.922	23.42
17/64	.266	6.75	39/64	.609	15.48	15/16	.938	23.81
9/32	.281	7.14	5/8	.625	15.88	61/64	.953	24.21
19/64	.297	7.54	41/64	.641	16.27	31/32	.969	24.61
5/16	.313	7.94	21/32	.656	16.67	63/64	.984	25.00
21/64	.328	8.33						

Conversion—Millimeters to Decimal Inches

mm	inches	mm	inches	mm	inches	mm	inches	mm	inches
1	.039 370	31	1.220 470	61	2.401 570	91	3.582 670	210	8.267 700
2	.078 740	32	1.259 840	62	2.440 940	92	3.622 040	220	8.661 400
3	.118 110	33	1.299 210	63	2.480 310	93	3.661 410	230	9.055 100
4	.157 480	34	1.338 580	64	2.519 680	94	3.700 780	240	9.448 800
5	.196 850	35	1.377 949	65	2.559 050	95	3.740 150	250	9.842 500
6	.236 220	36	1.417 319	66	2.598 420	96	3.779 520	260	10.236 200
7	.275 590	37	1.456 689	67	2.637 790	97	3.818 890	270	10.629 900
8	.314 960	38	1.496 050	68	2.677 160	98	3.858 260	280	11.032 600
9	.354 330	39	1.535 430	69	2.716 530	99	3.897 630	290	11.417 300
10	.393 700	40	1.574 800	70	2.755 900	100	3.937 000	300	11.811 000
11	.433 070	41	1.614 170	71	2.795 270	105	4.133 848	310	12.204 700
12	.472 440	42	1.653 540	72	2.834 640	110	4.330 700	320	12.598 400
13	.511 810	43	1.692 910	73	2.874 010	115	4.527 550	330	12.992 100
14	.551 180	44	1.732 280	74	2.913 380	120	4.724 400	340	13.385 800
15	.590 550	45	1.771 650	75	2.952 750	125	4.921 250	350	13.779 500
16	.629 920	46	1.811 020	76	2.992 120	130	5.118 100	360	14.173 200
17	.669 290	47	1.850 390	77	3.031 490	135	5.314 950	370	14.566 900
18	.708 660	48	1.889 760	78	3.070 860	140	5.511 800	380	14.960 600
19	.748 030	49	1.929 130	79	3.110 230	145	5.708 650	390	15.354 300
20	.787 400	50	1.968 500	80	3.149 600	150	5.905 500	400	15.748 000
21	.826 770	51	2.007 870	81	3.188 970	155	6.102 350	500	19.685 000
22	.866 140	52	2.047 240	82	3.228 340	160	6.299 200	600	23.622 000
23	.905 510	53	2.086 610	83	3.267 710	165	6.496 050	700	27.559 000
24	.944 880	54	2.125 980	84	3.307 080	170	6.692 900	800	31.496 000
25	.984 250	55	2.165 350	85	3.346 450	175	6.889 750	900	35.433 000
26	1.023 620	56	2.204 720	86	3.385 820	180	7.086 600	1000	39.370 000
27	1.062 990	57	2.244 090	87	3.425 190	185	7.283 450	2000	78.740 000
28	1.102 360	58	2.283 460	88	3.464 560	190	7.480 300	3000	118.110 000
29	1.141 730	59	2.322 830	89	3.503 903	195	7.677 150	4000	157.480 000
30	1.181 100	60	2.362 200	90	3.543 300	200	7.874 000	5000	196.850 000

To change decimal millimeters to decimal inches, position the decimal point where desired on either side of the millimeter measurement shown and reset the inches decimal by the same number of digits in the same direction. For example, to convert 0.001 mm to decimal inches, reset the decimal behind the 1 mm (shown on the chart) to 0.001; change the decimal inch equivalent (0.039″ shown) to 0.000039″.

Tap Drill Sizes

Screw & Tap Size	National Fine or S.A.E. Threads Per Inch	Use Drill Number
No. 5	44	37
No. 6	40	33
No. 8	36	29
No. 10	32	21
No. 12	28	15
1/4	28	3
5/16	24	1
3/8	24	Q
7/16	20	W
1/2	20	29/64
9/16	18	33/64
5/8	18	37/64
3/4	16	11/16
7/8	14	13/16
1 1/8	12	1 3/64
1 1/4	12	1 11/64
1 1/2	12	1 27/64

Tap Drill Sizes

Screw & Tap Size	National Coarse or U.S.S. Threads Per Inch	Use Drill Number
No. 5	40	39
No. 6	32	36
No. 8	32	29
No. 10	24	25
No. 12	24	17
1/4	20	8
5/16	18	F
3/8	16	5/16
7/16	14	U
1/2	13	27/64
9/16	12	31/64
5/8	11	17/32
3/4	10	21/32
7/8	9	49/64
1	8	7/8
1 1/8	7	63/64
1 1/4	7	1 7/64
1 1/2	6	1 11/32

Decimal Equivalent Size of the Number Drills

Drill No.	Decimal Equivalent	Drill No.	Decimal Equivalent	Drill No.	Decimal Equivalent
80	.0135	53	.0595	26	.1470
79	.0145	52	.0635	25	.1495
78	.0160	51	.0670	24	.1520
77	.0180	50	.0700	23	.1540
76	.0200	49	.0730	22	.1570
75	.0210	48	.0760	21	.1590
74	.0225	47	.0785	20	.1610
73	.0240	46	.0810	19	.1660
72	.0250	45	.0820	18	.1695
71	.0260	44	.0860	17	.1730
70	.0280	43	.0890	16	.1770
69	.0292	42	.0935	15	.1800
68	.0310	41	.0960	14	.1820
67	.0320	40	.0980	13	.1850
66	.0330	39	.0995	12	.1890
65	.0350	38	.1015	11	.1910
64	.0360	37	.1040	10	.1935
63	.0370	36	.1065	9	.1960
62	.0380	35	.1100	8	.1990
61	.0390	34	.1110	7	.2010
60	.0400	33	.1130	6	.2040
59	.0410	32	.1160	5	.2055
58	.0420	31	.1200	4	.2090
57	.0430	30	.1285	3	.2130
56	.0465	29	.1360	2	.2210
55	.0520	28	.1405	1	.2280
54	.0550	27	.1440		

Decimal Equivalent Size of the Letter Drills

Letter Drill	Decimal Equivalent	Letter Drill	Decimal Equivalent	Letter Drill	Decimal Equivalent
A	.234	J	.277	S	.348
B	.238	K	.281	T	.358
C	.242	L	.290	U	.368
D	.246	M	.295	V	.377
E	.250	N	.302	W	.386
F	.257	O	.316	X	.397
G	.261	P	.323	Y	.404
H	.266	Q	.332	Z	.413
I	.272	R	.339		

Anti-Freeze Chart

Temperatures Shown in Degrees Fahrenheit +32 is Freezing

Cooling System Capacity Quarts	Quarts of ETHYLENE GLYCOL Needed for Protection to Temperatures Shown Below													
	1	2	3	4	5	6	7	8	9	10	11	12	13	14
10	+24°	+16°	+ 4°	−12°	−34°	−62°								
11	+25	+18	+ 8	− 6	−23	−47			For capacities over 30 quarts di-					
12	+26	+19	+10	0	−15	−34	−57°		vide true capacity by 3. Find quarts					
13	+27	+21	+13	+ 3	− 9	−25	−45		Anti-Freeze for the ⅓ and multiply					
14			+15	+ 6	− 5	−18	−34		by 3 for quarts to add.					
15			+16	+ 8	0	−12	−26							
16			+17	+10	+ 2	− 8	−19	−34	−52°					
17			+18	+12	+ 5	− 4	−14	−27	−42					
18			+19	+14	+ 7	0	−10	−21	−34	−50°				
19			+20	+15	+ 9	+ 2	− 7	−16	−28	−42				
20				+16	+10	+ 4	− 3	−12	−22	−34	−48°			
21				+17	+12	+ 6	0	− 9	−17	−28	−41			
22				+18	+13	+ 8	+ 2	− 6	−14	−23	−34	−47°		
23				+19	+14	+ 9	+ 4	− 3	−10	−19	−29	−40		
24				+19	+15	+10	+ 5	0	− 8	−15	−23	−34	−46°	
25				+20	+16	+12	+ 7	+ 1	− 5	−12	−20	−29	−40	−50°
26					+17	+13	+ 8	+ 3	− 3	− 9	−16	−25	−34	−44
27					+18	+14	+ 9	+ 5	− 1	− 7	−13	−21	−29	−39
28					+18	+15	+10	+ 6	+ 1	− 5	−11	−18	−25	−34
29					+19	+16	+12	+ 7	+ 2	− 3	− 8	−15	−22	−29
30					+20	+17	+13	+ 8	+ 4	− 1	− 6	−12	−18	−25

For capacities under 10 quarts multiply true capacity by 3. Find quarts Anti-Freeze for the tripled volume and divide by 3 for quarts to add.

To Increase the Freezing Protection of Anti-Freeze Solutions Already Installed

Cooling System Capacity Quarts	Number of Quarts of ETHYLENE GLYCOL Anti-Freeze Required to Increase Protection													
	From +20° F. to					From +10° F. to					From 0° F. to			
	0°	−10°	−20°	−30°	−40°	0°	−10°	−20°	−30°	−40°	−10°	−20°	−30°	−40°
10	1¾	2¼	3	3½	3¾	¾	1½	2¼	2¾	3¼	¾	1½	2	2½
12	2	2¾	3½	4	4½	1	1¾	2½	3¼	3¾	1	1¾	2½	3¼
14	2¼	3¼	4	4¾	5½	1¼	2	3	3¾	4½	1	2	3	3½
16	2½	3½	4½	5¼	6	1¼	2½	3½	4¼	5¼	1¼	2¼	3¼	4
18	3	4	5	6	7	1½	2¾	4	5	5¾	1½	2½	3¾	4¾
20	3¼	4½	5¾	6¾	7½	1¾	3	4¼	5½	6½	1½	2¾	4¼	5¼
22	3½	5	6¼	7¼	8¼	1¾	3¼	4¾	6	7¼	1¾	3¼	4½	5½
24	4	5½	7	8	9	2	3½	5	6½	7½	1¾	3½	5	6
26	4¼	6	7½	8¾	10	2	4	5½	7	8¼	2	3¾	5½	6¾
28	4½	6¼	8	9½	10½	2¼	4¼	6	7½	9	2	4	5¾	7¼
30	5	6¾	8½	10	11½	2½	4½	6½	8	9½	2¼	4¼	6¼	7¾

Test radiator solution with proper hydrometer. Determine from the table the number of quarts of solution to be drawn off from a full cooling system and replace with undiluted anti-freeze, to give the desired increased protection. For example, to increase protection of a 22-quart cooling system containing Ethylene Glycol (permanent type) anti-freeze, from +20° F. to −20° F. will require the replacement of 6¼ quarts of solution with undiluted anti-freeze.

Index